Power, Trust, and Meaning

POWER, TRUST, AND MEANING

Essays in Sociological Theory and Analysis

S. N. Eisenstadt

THE UNIVERSITY OF CHICAGO PRESS
Chicago & London

S. N. Eisenstadt is the Rose Isaacs Professor Emeritus of Sociology
at the Hebrew University of Jerusalem. He is the editor of
Max Weber on Charisma (1968) and *Martin Buber on Intersubjectivity
and Cultural Creativity* (1992), both published by
the University of Chicago Press.

The University of Chicago Press, Chicago 60637
The University of Chicago Press, Ltd., London
©1995 by The University of Chicago
All rights reserved. Published 1995
Printed in the United States of America
04 03 02 01 00 99 98 97 96 95   1 2 3 4 5
ISBN: 0-226-19555-4 (cloth)
0-226-19556-2 (paper)

Library of Congress Cataloging-in-Publication Data

Eisenstadt, S. N. (Shmuel Noah), 1923–
    Power, trust, and meaning: essays in sociological theory
and analysis / S. N. Eisenstadt.
        p.   cm.
    Includes bibliographical references (p.   ) and index.
    1. Sociology—Philosophy.   I. Title.
HM24.E36   1995
301'.01—dc20   94-38879
                                                    CIP

To the memory of Edward Shils

CONTENTS

ACKNOWLEDGMENTS

I WOULD LIKE TO THANK all the people and institutions that have helped me prepare this collection of essays. First of all, I would like to thank Doug Mitchell at the University of Chicago Press for his continual encouragement and support. The introduction and chapter 13, written especially for this collection, were prepared with the assistance of Helena Flusfeder and Esther Rosenfeld in Jerusalem, and Claude Grangier in Chicago. The other chapters were collected by my secretary, Batia Slonim, also in Jerusalem. The ultimate versions of these chapters were typed by Aso Lundberg at the Swedish Collegium of Advanced Study in Uppsala during my stay there as a Fellow in April-June 1994. In the spring quarters of 1989, 1990, 1991, and 1992, Professors J. S. Coleman and E. Shils and myself (joined by Professor J. Elster in 1991 and Professor D. Laitin in 1992) undertook seminars on the foundations of sociological theory at the University of Chicago. The discussions at these seminars have been very important for me in the formulation of chapter 13 of this collection. I would also like to thank Columbia University Press, Cambridge University Press, the University of California Press, the University of Chicago Press, the American Sociological Association, *International Sociology*, *Daedalus*, and Macmillan College Publishing Company for permission to reprint the various articles collected here, and Luis Roniger for his approval of my reprinting here, as chapter 9, an article he coauthored.

Introduction

Social Structure, Culture, Agency, and Change

I

THE ARTICLES COLLECTED HERE cover a period of more than forty years and share an exploration of the relations between social structure, culture, and social change within the framework of sociological theory. In the background looms the more general, principled problem of human creativity, especially as it relates to the social arena, the construction of different social formations—ranging from the so-called micro situations to the more formalized macro institutional formations.

The problem of such creativity, and the closely connected problem of the potential range of human freedom in social contexts, have recently reemerged in theoretical discussions in the social sciences as the problem of human agency in relation to social structure. This problem was, of course, already central in classical sociological theory. One of the most succinct formulations of it can be found in Marx's famous statement in The Eighteenth Brumaire of Louis Napoleon, "Men make their own history, but they do not make it as they please; they do not make it under circumstances chosen by themselves, but under circumstances directly encountered, given, and transmitted from the past." Similarly, Weber's continual concern with charisma is, of course, tantamount to this problem.

My own interest in this problem was greatly influenced by my studies with Martin Buber, whose major sociological concern was to identify those situations wherein there exist the greatest chances for human creativity in the social and cultural realm.[1] It was also greatly influenced by the comparative approach to which—in two of its major guises, the Weberian one and that of compara-

1. See S. N. Eisenstadt's introduction to *Martin Buber on Intersubjectivity and Cultural Identity* (Chicago: University of Chicago Press, 1992), 1–22.

tive institutional analysis as it developed above all in British sociology and social anthropology—I was fortunate to be exposed during my graduate and postgraduate studies. I was exposed to the Weberian approach first through Buber's teaching and later at the London School of Economics, especially in the seminars of Edward Shils. It was also during my postdoctoral studies at the London School of Economics that I came face to face with the great tradition of comparative studies represented by Morris Ginsberg and T. H. Marshall and by the then leading group of British anthropologists—Raymond Firth, E. E. Evans Pritchard, M. Fortes, Edmund Leach, Audrey Richards, Max Gluckman, and their students.

It is thus not very surprising that I approached—as the essays collected here attest to—some of the major problems of sociological theory, as well as the more general problem of human creativity in the social and cultural realm, mostly through comparative studies.

II

My first research was only tangentially comparative—but it dealt with some central aspects of social change. This was the research on the absorption of new immigrants in Israel, undertaken between 1949 and 1950, published in Hebrew in 1951, and then in a broader version in English in 1953.[2] I have included here two of the various articles published in connection with this research program, which refer to some central theoretical problems that I analyzed in a more systematic way in later research.

The first, "The Place of Elites and Primary Groups in the Process of Absorption of New Immigrants," addressed the problems of construction of trust and solidarity and their importance in processes of change. More specifically, this article—as do several others which reported on this research[3]—emphasizes the fact that those groups which evince a high level of internal solidarity and trust are best able to adjust or adapt themselves in situations of change. This conclusion was based on the work on primary groups developed during that period by Edward Shils. Basing my approach on this work, I not only analyzed the internal cohesiveness of different immigrant groups but also emphasized the importance of different elites in building such cohesiveness and solidarity, especially their role in connecting the solidarity of small groups with that of broader organizational, institutional, even macrosocietal, frameworks. In this connection, another analytical point was made, namely the importance of various influentials and elites in constructing the reference orientations

---

2. S. N. Eisenstadt, *The Absorption of Immigrants* (Glencoe, Ill.: The Free Press, 1953).

3. S. N. Eisenstadt, "Communication Processes among Immigrants in Israel," *Public Opinion Quarterly* 16 (1952):42–58; idem, "The Process of Absorption of New Immigrants in Israel," *Human Relations* 5 (1952):223–45; idem, Institutionalization of Immigrant Behavior, ibid., 373–95.

and reference groups of members of different social sectors—concepts which were developed and applied in research in that period by R. K. Merton[4] and P. Lazarsfeld[5] as well as by the social psychologist Muzafer Sherif[6] and, somewhat later on, by T. Shibutani and H. Hyman[7] and their students. Finally, I pointed out the importance of such orientations in structuring patterns of behavior and modes of integration in different social settings. These points are presented in "Reference Groups and Social Integration," included here as chapter 2.

These problems of transference and transformation of trust from family and kinship groups to broader societal settings, and the general importance of such transference in the constitution of social order were subsequently explored more systematically in several research projects.

These problems constituted the central problem of my first broad systematic comparative work, *From Generation to Generation*.[8] In that work, which analyzed the different types of age and youth groups in different societies, I showed that such groups tend to arise especially in societies in which there is a basic discontinuity between the particularistic and ascriptive principles regulating behavior within family and kinship groups on the one hand and, on the other, those usually universalistic principles and those of achievement which regulate the broader sectors or institutional formations. In such societies, whether primitive, tribal, archaic, historical, or modern, there tend to arise age and youth groups.

Within such groups, attempts are made to transfer the solidarity and trust of the family and kinship group to broader sectors of society with more universalistic and achievement orientations. This is done by connecting the achievement-oriented activities which are embedded in relatively particularistic settings of these groups. In those cases in which such attempts are borne by elites and influentials who are weak or ineffective, or when a rupture occurs between the influentials or leaders of such groups and those of wider sectors of society, there tend to develop strong tendencies to nonconformist (deviant and/or innovative) activities within such groups.[9] I have extended this analysis in a series

---

4. R. K. Merton, *Continuities in Social Research* (Glencoe, Ill.: The Free Press, 1950); idem, *Mass Persuasion* (New York: Columbia University Press, 1982).

5. P. F. Lazarsfeld, *The People's Choice* (New York: Columbia University Press, 1982); idem, *The Varied Sociology of Paul F. Lazarsfeld* (New York: Columbia University Press, 1982).

6. M. Sherif, *Groups in Harmony and Tension* (New York: Harper, 1953); idem, *Intergroup Relations and Leadership* (New York: J. Wiley, 1962); idem, *Social Interaction Process and Products* (Chicago: Aldine, 1967).

7. H. H. Hyman, ed., *Readings in Reference Group Theory and Research* (New York: The Free Press, 1968).

8. See S. N. Eisenstadt, *From Generation to Generation* (Glencoe, Ill.: The Free Press, 1956).

9. "Delinquent Group-Formation Among Immigrant Youth," *British Journal of Delinquency* 2 (1951):34–45.

of later papers, one of which, *The Archetypal Patterns of Youth*, is included here as chapter 3.

The problems of trust and solidarity and their flow between different sectors of a society and their interweaving with the institutional foundations have also been discussed in analyses of ritual kinship,[10] of friendship,[11] and especially in studies of patron-client relations, which I undertook later in the early eighties with Luis Roniger.

III

Both in the studies of immigrants as well as of different age groups and youth movements (and in the study of ritual kinship and ritual friendship which preceded that of patron-client relationships), the various theoretical and analytical problems referred to above provided essential frameworks for comparative analysis, but these problems were not taken up directly. It was in the analysis presented in *The Political Systems of Empires*[12] and its offshoots that I first addressed major problems of sociological analysis.

These theoretical and analytical problems were discussed mostly in the framework of the then prevalent structural-functional approach, and they are presented in this collection in two articles: "Institutionalization and Change" (chapter 4) and "Social Change, Differentiation, and Evolution" (chapter 5).

While the overall vision of *Political Systems* was rooted in my comparative interests, its theoretical framework was also basically a structural-functional one. The argument focused on an analysis of the basic systemic characters of these regimes, and on an examination of the most important social processes or mechanisms which developed in them. I especially emphasized the various policies undertaken by rulers aiming to maintain the respective systemic boundaries of their regimes. A central part of the argument of *Political Systems* is an analysis of various organizations including bureaucracies which developed within these empires, mostly through the efforts of rulers who wished to implement policies designed to maintain the basic institutional contours and characteristics of their empires.

However, the analysis presented in *Political Systems* in many ways went beyond what were the prevalent thrusts of structural-functionalism at the time because it did not accept the natural givenness of any social system—in this

10. "Ritualized Personal Relations—Blood Brotherhood, Best Friends, Compadre, etc.: Some Comparative Hypotheses and Suggestions," *Man* 55 (1956): 90–95.

11. "Friendship and the Structure of Trust and Solidarity in Society" in *The Compact: Selected Dimensions of Friendship*, ed. E. Leyton, Newfoundland Social and Economic Papers No. 3. (Newfoundland: Memorial Society of Newfoundland, Institute of Social and Economic Research, 1974), 138–45.

12. S. N. Eisenstadt, *The Political System of Empires* (New York: The Free Press, 1963).

case of these empires—and it emphasized the central role of institutional entrepreneurs in the construction of such systems. This analysis also went beyond
the assumptions of structural-functional analysis by its emphasis on the internal
contradictions which develop in any such system (a theme which is the focus
of chapter 4, "Institutionalization and Change"), on the processes of change
that take place in it, and on the importance of internal and external forces in
giving rise to such changes in—and possibly demises of—such systems. It also
went beyond these assumptions—even if just implicitly—by recognizing the
autonomy of cultural visions and, in turn, their impact on the promulgation of
various goals by both rulers and other groups and on the specific dynamics of
the respective empires.[13]

Thus, to describe it in greater detail, the analysis presented in *Political Systems* first emphasized that the institutionalization of such systems was not assured by some overall trend to greater structural differentiation—a trend very
strongly emphasized in structural-functional analysis and in the early studies
of modernization which were closely connected with that approach. Instead,
such institutionalization was contingent upon several historical conditions;
first, on the coming together of certain levels of structural differentiation,
which gives rise to the development of free resources, i.e., of resources not
embedded in any fixed, especially ascriptive settings; and secondly, on the
emergence of political entrepreneurs, or elites—the would-be rulers with the
vision and ability to create new political entities. Such combinations developed
in some societies—societies within which the empires in question developed—and not in others.

Thus, this analysis strongly emphasized the importance of a special type
of social actor—in this case, the political entrepreneurs, the would-be rulers—
and at least implicitly assumed that the emergence of such actors was not automatically assured by the existence of specific levels of structural differentiation.
It also assumed, on the other hand, that they may also emerge in seemingly
inappropriate levels of differentiation.

Secondly, the central focus of the book was the analysis of the *internal*
contradictions inherent in the very constitution and continuity or "reproduction" of these empires. This theme is also the focus of chapter 4, "Institutionalization and Change."

The most important contradictions were those between the rulers' interests in generating free resources and their attempts to control them; between
the rulers' goals and the possibility that such goals might exhaust resources,
thus strengthening various traditional groups; and between the rulers' wish to
free themselves of the dependence on these groups and their own traditional

---

13. See in greater detail S. N. Eisenstadt's introduction to the Transaction edition of *The Political System of Empires* (New Brunswick, NJ: Transaction Publications, 1992).

legitimation that put severe limitations on their more differentiated, autonomous activities. A central aspect of *Political Systems* was the examination of the ways in which such contradictions generated struggle, change, and the eventual demise—or transformation—of these systems.

Accordingly, thirdly, I analyzed how the interaction between external and internal forces is of crucial importance in activating the contradictions inherent in and shaping the dynamics of these systems, especially the specific conditions under which the empires broke down.

Fourthly, a central aspect of *Political Systems* was the emphasis on how different cultural orientations and goals as promulgated in the various empires influenced their respective dynamics, above all through the ruling coalitions within them; for instance, the very strong emphasis on cultural goals in China, as against the stronger one on military projects in the Roman and Byzantine empires. The emphasis on these goals and their impact on the dynamics on different empires did at least imply the importance of cultural traditions.

As can be seen in chapter 5, "Social Change, Differentiation, and Evolution," *Political Systems* also went beyond the evolutionary assumptions which were most prominent in many studies connected with the structural-functional school, especially in the early studies of modernization which developed in the late forties and early fifties. The first criticism held that not all massive social change necessarily leads to differentiation. The second, and more important, maintained that institutional developments that take place at seemingly similar "stages" of differentiation may nevertheless lead in different directions. In other words, the institutional responses to the problems arising out of growing structural differentiation—the patterns of integration—that emerge in different societies at seemingly similar stages of differentiation may vary considerably across societies.

Here again I stressed the central role of various entrepreneurs, elites and their coalition, the visions they bore and the goals they promulgated, in the crystallization and reproduction of different types of institutional formations.

In all these ways, the analysis in *Political Systems* went beyond the basic assumptions of the structural-functional school. But this analysis did not go far enough in examining the processes through which the systemic boundaries and institutional formations of these empires were constructed and reconstructed; it did not elaborate on the implications of the ways in which continuous interweaving of cultural forces, power dimensions, and material resources through the activities of various social actors shape institutional formations and dynamics. In particular, the articulation of the boundaries of collectivities, the regulation of power, the construction of meaning, and those activities that are centered around the construction of trust were not systematically examined.

IV

To the extent that *Political Systems* went beyond the premises of the structural-functional model, it evinced, at least implicitly, a close affinity with some of the strong criticisms directed at this model by different "schools" or "approaches" which gathered momentum from the early sixties on.

The most important of these "schools" or "approaches" in this period were the conflict model espoused by Ralf Dahrendorf[14] and later on by R. Collins;[15] the exchange model as developed by George C. Homans[16] and somewhat later by Peter Blau;[17] and the symbolic structuralist model of Claude Lévi-Strauss.[18] Other older models were reaffirmed or elaborated further; these included the symbolic-interactionist one and later the ethnomethodology and Marxist ones—or rather the great variety of different Marxist and neo-Marxist approaches.

The common denominator of all these approaches was that instead of taking any concrete institutional formation or setting as given and as the starting point of social order and sociological analysis, the very construction of such settings became a central problem of sociological analysis.[19] In fact, all these approaches shared an unwillingness to accept the "natural" givenness of any single institutional setting in terms of the systemic needs of the social system to which it belonged. Any given setting—be it the formal structure of a factory or hospital, the division of labor in a family, the definition of deviance, the different classifications of people, the place of ritual, or the patterns of behavior that developed in a given social setting—were no longer primarily exam-

14. R. Dahrendorf, "Out of Utopia: Toward a Reorientation of Sociological Analysis," *American Journal of Sociology* 64 (1958):115–27; idem, *Class and Class Conflict in Industrial Society* (Stanford: Stanford University Press, 1959).

15. R. Collins, "A Comparative Approach to Political Sociology" in *State and Society*, ed. Reinhard Bendix (Boston: Little, Brown and Company, 1968), 42–67; idem, *Conflict Sociology: Toward an Explanatory Science* (New York: Academic Press, 1975).

16. G. C. Homans, *Social Behavior: Its Elementary Forms* (New York: Harcourt, Brace & World, 1961).

17. P. Blau, "Justice in Social Exchange," *Sociological Inquiry* (1964): 193–206; idem, *Exchange and Power in Social Life* (New York: John Wiley & Sons, 1964).

18. C. Lévi-Strauss, "Introduction à l'oeuvre de Marcel Mauss" in *Sociologie et Anthropologie*, ed. M. Mauss (Paris: Presses Universitaires de France, 1950), ix-lii; idem, *Structural Anthropology* (New York: Basic Books, 1963, 1982); idem, *The Savage Mind* (London: Weidenfeld and Nicolson, 1966); idem, *Totemism* (Boston: Beacon Press, 1967); idem, *Mythologiques: du Miel aux Centres* (Paris: Librairie Plon, 1967); idem, *Mythologiques: L'origine des manieres de table* (Paris: Plon, 1968); idem, *The Raw and the Cooked, Volume 1: Mythologiques* (New York: Harper and Row, 1969); idem, *Mythologiques: L'homme nu* (Paris: Librairie Plon, 1971).

19. On these controversies and criticisms see S. N. Eisenstadt and M. Curelaru, *The Form of Sociology: Paradigms and Crises* (New York: John Wiley & Co., 1976) and "Some Reflections on the 'Crisis' in Sociology, *Sociologische Gids* 73, 255–69.

ined in terms of their contributions to the maintenance of any given group or society. Instead, the very setting up of such institutional arrangements was problematized; i.e., it was transposed from a given into a problem-to-be-explained, and the question was now asked what the forces were, beyond the major organizational needs of any social setting, that could explain these institutional arrangements.

Such explanations crystallized in these approaches around two analytical poles—that of "negotiated order" vs. that of "deep structure"—and cutting across these two poles was the emphasis on "culture," or the symbolic dimension of human interactions, as against the emphasis on "material" or power dimensions.

The emphasis on negotiated order was to be found in the exchange and conflict models as well as among the symbolic-interactionist ones. This emphasis stressed that any such institutional order develops, is maintained, and changes through a process of continuous interaction, negotiation, and struggle among those who participate in it. This approach stressed that any institutional arrangement has to be explained in terms of power relations and negotiations, power struggles and conflicts, with the symbolic-interactionist approach emphasizing the "symbolic" dimension more than the others.

In some of these approaches, especially among the symbolic-interactionists and in a different vein among the ethnomethodologists, it was also very strongly emphasized that such activities generated processes of the classification of persons and situations.[20]

Concomitantly, a strong emphasis was placed on the autonomy of any subsetting, subgroup, or system—and perhaps above all of individuals—that could find expression in the definitions of goals that differed from those of the broader organizational or institutional setting and of the groups dominant in it. Emphasis was also put on the "environments" within which the social setting operates, and, above all, on the international system for the analysis of "total" societies or macrosocietal orders.

The second, seemingly contradictory approach is to be found among the structuralists á la Lévi-Strauss and among some, especially French, Marxists.[21]

20. The emphasis of such labeling and classification of the concomitant structuring of ways of life in historical settings and in the crystallization of different civilizations was expounded earlier in Norbert Elias's *Process der Zivilisation*, which was published in Switzerland in 1939 on the eve of the Second World War and forgotten until the late sixties or early seventies, when Elias's work re-emerged at the center of sociological discourse. See N. Elias, *Process of Civilizations* (New York: Vixen Books, 1982).

21. See, for instance, M. Godelier, *Horizons, Trajets Marxistes en Anthropologie* (Paris: Maspero, 1973); L. Goldmann, *Sciences Humaines et Philosophie* (Paris: Editions Gallimard, 1964); idem, *Structures Mentales et Creation Culturelle* (Paris: Edition Anthropos, 1970); H. Lefebvre, *Everyday Life in the Modern World* (London: Allen Lane); L. Sebag, *Structuralisme et Marxisme* (Paris: Petite Bibliotheque Payot, 1964); *Sur le Mode de Production Asiatique*, with a preface by R. Garaudy (Paris: Editions Sociales,

That approach explained the nature of any given institutional order—and especially its dynamics—in terms of some principles of "deep" or "hidden" structure akin to those which provide the deep structure of language, according to linguists such as Chomsky.

In attempting to identify the principles of this framework, the structuralists stressed the importance of the symbolic dimensions of human activity and some inherent rules of the human mind, while the Marxists stressed above all the rules of production and reproduction of different social formations and the relations or contradictions between modes and relations of production as carried out by different classes.

These controversies were in many ways the forerunners of the more radical ones which developed, as we shall see, from about the seventies on and which raised the problems of the relations between agency and structure, and between culture and social structure.

Although these controversies did not deal directly with the problems of creativity in the social realm, the problem was, to some extent at least, implicit in them, in the stress on the autonomy of culture and of individuals, on going beyond the "oversocialized conception of man."[22]

V

Around this period—the late sixties and early seventies—I started to pursue some of the major theoretical problems which were raised in these controversies in two directions or lines of analysis which gradually converged. Naturally, I based my work on the implications of the analysis in *Political Systems*. The first line was the analysis of some of the processes through which institutional patterns are formed; the second line was the analysis of those dimensions of social order which go beyond the constitution of social division of labor. When these two lines of analysis converged, they facilitated a reappraisal of the process of reconstitution of social order, social change, and dynamics.

I addressed these problems, especially the central problem of the relation between the actions of individuals and social structure, in "Societal Goals, Systemic Needs, Social Interaction, and Individual Behavior" originally included in a book devoted to the confrontation of the sociologies of Talcott Parsons and George C. Homans[23] (reprinted here as chapter 6 and as the first chapter

1969); F. Tokei *Sur le Mode de Production Asiatique* (Budapest: Academiae Scientiarum Hungaricae, 1966).

22. D. Wrong, "The Oversocialized Conception of Man in Modern Sociology," in *Skeptical Sociology* (New York: Columbia University Press, 1975), 31–46, postscript 47–54.

23. H. Turk and R. L. Simpson, ed., *Institutions and Social Exchange: The Sociologies of Talcott Parsons and George C. Homans* (Indianapolis and New York: Bobbs Merrill Co., 1971).

in *Essays in Comparative Institutions*).[24] In this chapter I focused on what in later parlance was called the problem of agency vs. structure.

The starting point of these analyses was a concept which was central to the controversies of that period—namely, that of exchange. The exchange model constituted one of the major critics of the structural-functional approach. It stressed very strongly—in a way which would be later taken up by various "rational choice" models or approaches—that social behavior cannot be explained in terms of norms or roles but rather in terms of interaction between social actors, especially individuals, acting rationally in terms of some combination of utilitarian considerations and a punishment-reward system in pursuance of their goals.

It attempted to explain not only patterns of individual behavior but also of the formation of institutions—a line which was to be followed later on, in the seventies and eighties, in a much more diversified and sophisticated way by the various rational choice approaches.

However, already at this stage of discussion some very important caveats to the assumptions of the exchange model, which it basically shared with the later rational-choice mode, were identified. One was the recognition of goals, preferences, and considerations beyond the utilitarian ones. Homans already had to recognize—in order to explain concrete patterns of exchange behavior—the importance of "forces" exogenous to such process of exchange, including the concepts of distributive justice prevalent in any social setting. Such recognition by Homans—and other promulgators of the exchange model such as Peter Blau,[25] and somewhat later in a much more diversified way James Coleman[26]—pointed to a more general problem, namely, the necessity first of identifying and analyzing the goals which are pursued in human interaction and exchange and of the preferences among such goals; of the criteria according to which such interaction and exchange, and the institutional settings within which it takes place; and the different modes in which exchange may be regulated in different arenas of social Life. In my work from the mid-sixties on, I have addressed all these problems, indicating that they all indicate the limitations of the "simple", "direct" exchange modes.

In chapter 6, "Societal Goals, Systemic Needs, Social Interaction, and In-

24. S. N. Eisenstadt, "The Study of the Process of Institutionalization: Institutional Change and Comparative Institutions," in *Essays in Comparative Institutions* (New York: John Wiley & Sons, 1965), 1–68.

25. P. Blau, "Justice in Social Exchange," *Sociological Inquiry* (1964):193–206; idem, *Exchange and Power in Social Life* (New York: John Wiley & Sons, 1964).

26. J. S. Coleman, "Foundations for a Theory of Collective Decisions," *American Journal of Sociology* 71 (1966):615–27; idem, "Individual Interests and Collective Action," *Papers on Non-Market Decision Making* (1966):49–62; idem, "Political Money," *The American Political Science Review* 64/4 (1970):1074–87. These and other papers of Coleman were collected in *J. S. Coleman—Individual Interests and Collective Action: Selected Essays* (Cambridge: Cambridge University Press, 1986). Later on

dividual Behavior," I discussed first the importance of individuals' different goals, not only the utilitarian ones assumed by exchange models but also other ones, especially the search for a good social order. Moreover, I indicated that goals and preferences are themselves socially constituted through what I called simulation of desiderata and that a crucial aspect of any exchange process is the creation of artificial scarcities which influence the starting positions of different individuals in the process of exchange and the institutional frameworks of such exchange.

Secondly, I also started to explore systematically the limitations on "pure" exchange which are inherent in the constitution of social life and to analyze the institutional frameworks within which exchange takes place. In this context E. O. Schild and myself, in a series of unpublished papers, explored and analyzed the inherent features of the media of exchange—money, power, and prestige—and the ways in which such features also structure such limitations on simple exchange, especially the access to exchange and to positions of differential power in such exchange.

In this context, we have reformulated the concept of prestige. Instead of looking at prestige as an interpersonal expression of deference, it was reformulated as one of the major dimensions of social action—a major generalized medium of exchange (albeit of a very distinct type) which effects control of access to different collectivities and centers and the concomitant constitution of boundaries of such collectivities.

Above all this view emphasized that prestige is not only a desideratum but also a medium of institutional interaction and exchange. It can also serve as a medium of exchange, as a basis for getting other commodities such as money or power or services. Here prestige becomes in some respects not entirely dissimilar from money or power. It is indeed the various attempts to link, in some indirect way, the ownership of other resources with the attainment of prestige that constitutes the major structural implications of prestige as a medium of exchange in society, and such attempts also constitute a core component of stratification. The core of this component is a very distinct structural mechanism among the various mechanisms which attempt to link prestige structurally, in the sense defined above, with other positions and resources.

The most important aspect of these mechanisms, from the point of view of stratification analysis—analyzed in detail in the article on "Prestige, Participation, and Strata Formation," the first, more analytical part of which is included here as chapter 10—is the institutionalization of the upholding of the different styles of life and of various ascriptive limitations on institutional interaction, exchange, and access to positions and on participation in exchange.

---

his basic approach was presented in a fully elaborated and systematic way in *Foundations of Sociological Theory* (Cambridge: Harvard University Press, 1990).

In the most general terms such ascriptive restrictions on access mean that entry into a position is contingent not only upon satisfying requirements which can be attained in open interaction and exchange, but that in addition or in place of such requirements the candidate must belong to a certain social category or be an incumbent of certain other positions.

Thus, this analysis has indicated at least one institutional arena in which exchange is regulated in a distinct mode, quite different from "routine," direct exchange.

It is the various structural derivatives of prestige analyzed above that constitute some of the most important mechanisms through which the major aspects of stratification—the differential evaluation of positions, the uses of the rewards received for the regulation of access to positions and for symbolic consumption which denotes the upholding of certain styles of life—become interconnected, albeit in different degrees and in different societies, and become the starting points of the process of strata formation.[27]

Different modes of social hierarchies were shown to be closely related to the different goals or orientations of centers, thus bringing in from yet another point of view the importance of the cultural dimension in the processes of institutional formations and change.

VI

The problem of limitations on "simple" routine exchange, which are inherent in any continual setting of social interaction, brought me, following the earlier analysis of Homans and Schneider,[28] to a reexamination, detailed in chapter 6, of the relations of the Homans-Blau concept of exchange with that of generalized exchange as developed by Lévi-Strauss in the late forties.[29] I continued this line of thought later in "Symbolic Structures and Social Dynamics" included in this collection as chapter 7.

Generalized exchange, which is often expressed in various "symbolic" patterns of behavior such as gifts, is manifest within such formations in contrast to direct exchange, which presumably takes place in situations approximating pure market and/or barter models, in the affirmation of those aspects of social

---

27. S. N. Eisenstadt, "Prestige, Participation, and Strata Formation," in *Social Stratification*, ed. J. A. Jackson, (Cambridge: Cambridge University Press, 1968), the first part of which is included here as chapter 10; and S. N. Eisenstadt, *Social Differentiation and Stratification* (Glenview: Scott Foresman, 1971).

28. G. C. Homans and D. M. Schneider, *Marriage, Authority, and Final Cause* (New York: The Free Press, 1955).

29. C. Lévi-Strauss, *Elementary Forms of Kinship*, ed. R. Needham (Boston: Beacon Press, 1969); G. C. Homans and D. M. Schneider, *Marriage, Authority, and Final Cause.*

interaction which go beyond such models. A central aspect of such generalized exchange is the construction of long-range trust and of legitimation which assures the long-range predictability of social interaction and, concomitantly, the continuity of the frameworks within which the routine, "market" type of exchange takes place.

This article is in a sense a complementary, almost mirror image of "Societal Goals." In "Societal Goals" I focused on the analysis of those aspects of institutional formations which cannot be understood in terms of one central type of negotiated order—of "routine exchange"—while in "Symbolic Structures" I have analyzed some of the social processes through which such institutional frameworks are instituted.

Such formation of the institutional contours of any society is effected through the regulation of the allocation resources, the central focus of which is the constitution, in any system of social interaction, of the basic ground rules of social interaction. According to Buchler and Nutini's definition, "The ground rules . . . structure the basic frameworks within which decision-making in different areas of social life is possible and, second (albeit here already in different degrees in different societies or parts thereof) some of the broad criteria that guide choices among the options which such frameworks allow."[30]

Although such frameworks develop in all societies, they differ in their concrete specifications. Such differences are greatly influenced by the cultural orientations, visions, and basic premises prevalent in different societies. But contrary to the structuralists' view, generalized exchange is not rooted in some deep, universal structure which, possibly through some processes of emanation, shapes institutional formations. In "Symbolic Structures" I attempted to show how such formations may indeed be closely related to generic cultural orientations. But I have also shown that not only do such orientations vary between different societies and that the very constitution of such ground rules—which epitomize the processes of generalized exchange—takes place not through some emanation of the basic codes of the human mind but through social processes and struggles in which power, material, and cultural orientations are closely interwoven. At the same time, such struggles differ from the "routine" struggles.

The discussion about the two different types of exchange bore within itself not only the seeds of a constructive confrontation of the structuralist approaches (which emphasize "deep structure") with those which emphasized negotiated order but also reopened the problem of the relations between culture and social structure. It was the concept of ground rules which provided a

---

30. I. R. Buechler and H. G. Nutini, ed., *Game Theory in the Behavioral Sciences* (Pittsburgh: University of Pittsburgh Press, 1969), 8.

meeting point between specific and general exchange—between the approaches emphasizing deep structure and those which emphasize negotiated order.

VII

At that stage of my work I had not yet systematically analyzed—with the partial exception of the analysis of prestige, participation, and center-formation—the social processes through which such ground rules are institutionalized, the actors who are the bearers of such processes, or the ways in which they shape the concrete institutional formations of different societies. I had also only tangentially touched on the specification of the major ground rules of social interaction.

The analysis of friendship and patron-client relations which Luis Roniger and I undertook in the early eighties[31] was a first step in the direction of a systematic analysis of such processes and of a comparative exploration of the relations between generalized and specific or routine exchange. It built on the earlier research on strata formation but went beyond it.

It also connected systematically the analysis of general exchange with that of constitution of trust and solidarity and their flow between different sectors of society. In these researches we again analyzed, albeit in a broader theoretical and comparative setting, how the different patterns of trust in both micro and macro settings were related systematically to different patterns of institutional formations, especially to the prevalence of different types of patron-client relationships. Here, a major distinction was made between those societies whose "clientelistic" relations constitute a central core of the institutional structure—are characterized by a low level of trust within their different sectors—and those societies in which they constitute a sort of addendum to other, more universalistic, principles—characterized by a higher degree of trust. It was shown that each of these institutional patterns entails a different mode of inter-

---

31. S. N. Eisenstadt and L. Roniger, *Patrons, Clients, and Friends* (Cambridge: Cambridge University Press, 1984). See also, for other formulations, L. Roniger, "Patron-Client Relations as a Model of Structuring Social Exchange," *Comparative Studies in Society and History* 22, 42–77 will be brought into this collection. R. Lemarchand, ed., *Political Clientelism, Patronage and Development* (Beverly Hills: Sage Publications); S. N. Eisenstadt and L. Roniger, "The Study of Patron-Client Relations" and "Recent Developments in Sociological Theory"; S. N. Eisenstadt and L. Roniger, "Cultural and Structural Continuities in Situations of Change and Development: Persistence and Transformation of Patron-Client Relations," in *Die post-tradionelle Welt der Bauern/Le Monde post-traditional du paysan*, ed. R. Hettlage, a special issue of *Schweizerische Zeitschrift für Soziologie/Revue suisse de Sociologie* 8, 29–52. L. Roniger has continued the analysis of trust in numerous publications, among them "Public Trust and the Consolidation of Latin American Democracies" in *Latin America to the Year 2000*, ed. A. R. M. Ritter, M. A. Cameron, and D. H. Pollock (New York: Praeger, 1992) and *La Fiducia Nelle Societa Moderne—Un Approccio* (Messina: Rubbettino, 1992).

weaving of generalized and specific exchange. In those societies where the "clientilistic" pattern is predominant, a continual blurring takes place between the two types of exchange, while in the others, distinct institutional settings develop (such as the age groups which we have analyzed above) which both separate between these types of exchange as well as create interlinking institutions which are not embedded in either type of exchange.

In this research, we also systematically explored the relation between such institutional patterns and cultural orientations and identified the social actors who play a central role in effecting such patterns. Thus, we have shown that the development of the "clientilistic" pattern is very closely related to the prevalence in their societies or sectors of distinct cosmological conceptions, namely those conceptions in which the tension between the transcendental and mundane worlds is relatively low, usually combined with a strong otherworldly orientation. Secondly, we showed how such conceptions are borne by elites embedded in particularistic settings who usually serve as the apex of the patron-client hierarchies and how these conceptions and elites are related to the structure of trust in these societies.

VIII

The analysis of the relations between generalized and specific exchange and of the structure of elites and cultural orientations, ontological premises, and cosmological visions that was undertaken in *Patrons, Clients and Friends* in turn brought the analysis of institutional formations to the point where the dimensions of social order which go beyond the social division of labor could be systematically explored.

This analysis developed first in the late sixties through the reexamination of two central concepts: charisma and center. Charisma has constituted, of course, a central concept in sociological analysis since Weber. It was the way in which Edward Shils reinterpreted and combined this term with the concept of center—which he had coined—that provided the starting point of the line of analysis which I undertook in that period.[32]

I first examined the analytical dimensions of the concept of center and center-periphery relations and applied them in comparative analysis in the introduction to the 1969 paperback edition of the *Political Systems*. This analysis emphasized the importance of center and center-periphery relations as a distinct analytical dimension of the institutional format of centralized empires— in principle, of any society. It emphasized that this dimension is not subsumed under the scope of structural differentiation of the social division of labor.

32. E. Shils, "Center and Periphery" and "Charisma: Order and Status" in *Center and Periphery* (Chicago: University of Chicago Press, 1975), 3–17, 256–76.

In this analysis, the center or centers of a society were conceived as dealing not only with the organizational aspects of the social division of labor but were also seen as primarily dealing with the connection of these aspects of the social division of labor to the charismatic dimensions of social order. That is to say, the centers of society were connected to the attempts to relate the mundane realities of social life, of institutional formations to what is conceived by humans as the source of existence, of life, and its predicaments.

I had addressed myself earlier to some of the more general principled problems of the nature of the processes through which the charismatic dimensions of human action become interwoven with processes of institution building or with the crystallization of institutional formations in the article on "Charisma and Institution Building." In this article, included here as chapter 8, I gave several indicators about the nature of the major actors, who are bearers of such charismatic visions, and of the loci in which, and the processes through which, such visions are implemented.

One of the central insights of "Charisma and Institution Building," following the earlier "Institutionalization and Change," is that change (and conflict) is not exogenous to the construction of social formations but constitutes an inherent component thereof. In "Charisma and Institution Building" this inherence of change in the process of institution formations, in the very construction of social life, was attributed not only to the inherent systemic contradictions and conflicts it entails but also to the very nature of the charismatic dimension of human action. It was suggested that the central characteristic of this dimension—the attempt to come close to the very essence of human endeavor, to the essence of being, i.e., to come close to the cosmological visions and conceptions of social order—entails by its very nature both constructive and destructive elements or components.

Parallel to the analysis of charisma and institution building, I have also explored in greater detail the nature or contents of the ground rules of social interaction. It became clear to me that they are related to those dimensions of social order which have been identified by the founding fathers of sociology as going beyond the social division of labor—namely, in addition to the construction of trust and solidarity, the regulation of power and the legitimation of major patterns of social interaction.

In later formulations (most fully presented in the concluding chapter of this collection, "Action, Resources, Structure, and Meaning") I showed that it is the promulgation and concretization of these ground rules that constitute the major foci of the institutionalization of the charismatic dimensions of social relations and of social order, of the relation between charisma and institution building, thus bringing together the major threads of the analyses which I had developed throughout this period.

IX

These analyses of the relations between charisma and institution building and of the constitution of the ground rules of social interaction went beyond the stage of controversy prevalent in the social sciences in the sixties and even beyond the declarations about the crisis of sociology which abounded in the seventies[33] and touched on the more radical controversies which arose during the middle seventies.

These controversies focused on the nongivenness of any institutional formations and on the necessity of explaining the processes through which such formations are crystallized and changed. More radical was their very powerful rejection of the assumption (only implicit in the earlier controversies)—which could be attributed to the structural-functional approach—that it is the organization of social division of labor in systemic patterns that constitutes the central focus of the constitution of social order. Social division of labor organized in systemic frameworks was no longer seen as being at the core of the constitution of social orders. Such a core was searched for in "culture," in some social structural entities such as the state, or in individuals' behavior.

This radical rejection led also to the reconsideration of the epistemological and ontological standing of the major concepts of sociological analysis—especially of those of culture, social structure, and individuals—and of the relations between them. These controversies, briefly discussed in "Culture and Social Structure Revisited," entailed far-reaching shifts in the basic concepts of social science analysis that include culture as well as religion and social structure. These concepts became increasingly conceptualized as distinct and "real" ontological entities and not (as in earlier periods of sociological and anthropological analysis) as analytical constructs referring to different aspects or dimensions of human action and social interaction, constitutive of each other and of patterns of social interaction. Concomitantly, a shift of emphasis developed with respect to several dimensions of culture and social structure—especially a shift away from the structural-functional school's emphasis on values and norms.

33. At the time, I examined these controversies from the point of view of the development of sociology as a scholarly endeavor in the sociological tradition. I wanted to especially understand here why it is that in sociology a strong tendency developed towards a combination of scholarly discourses with ideological sectarianism and with "crises." I have addressed this last problem in a book coauthored with Miriam Curelaru, *The Form of Sociology: Paradigms and Crises*, referred to above; in "Some Reflections on the 'Crisis' in Sociology," *Sociologische Gids* 73, 255–69; in "The Sociological Tradition: Origins, Boundaries, Patterns of Innovation, and Crises" in *Culture and Its Creators: Essays in Honor of Edward Shils*, ed. J. Ben-David and T. N. Clark (Chicago: University of Chicago Press, 1977), 43–72. See also "Autonomy of Sociology and Its Emancipatory Dimensions," *Transactions of the New York Academy of Sciences* series 2/39, 28–31.

One view of this shift—explicit among the structuralists and implicit to some degree at least among some of the ethnomethodologists—regarded culture as containing the programmatic code of human behavior, and espoused (to use Geertz's felicitous if ironic expression) the view of man as cerebral savage.

According to this view, culture is fully structured or programmed based on clear principles embedded in the nature of the human mind, which, through a series of codes, regulate human behavior. In contrast, the symbolic anthropologists such as Clifford Geertz,[34] Victor Turner,[35] and David M. Schneider[36] shifted away from values and norms to a conception of culture as a set of expressive symbols of ethos, a "worldview" constructed through active human interaction.

Parallel shifts in the concept of social structure have also evolved since the mid-sixties. The concept has become reified in new definitions of social structure and institutions, especially the "State," as "real" and "autonomous" agents or actors.[37]

A parallel—if somewhat paradoxical—trend developed with respect to the conception of the individual, especially in various rational choice approaches which have become prominent in contemporary theoretical discourse in the social sciences. Building on the foundations of the earlier exchange theory, these approaches depicted the individual as a totally independent, autonomous, ontologically distinct entity or monad. In these approaches, social structure and culture were viewed as networks or organizations arising from the aggregation of individual interactions, with almost no autonomous characteristics except for some emergent qualities often described as "primitive effects."[38]

X

These shifts, and the researches connected with them, sharpened the problem of the place of culture in the construction of social order and of the relations

34. See, for instance, C. Geertz, "Religion as a Cultural System," "Ritual and Social Change: A Javanese Example," and "Deep Play: Notes on the Balinese Cockfight," in *The Interpretation of Cultures* (New York: Basic Books, 1973), 142–70, 87–126, 412–55.

35. V. W. Turner, *Fields and Metaphors* (Ithaca: Cornell University Press, 1974); idem, *The Forest of Symbols* (Ithaca: Cornell University Press, 1967); idem, *The Drums of Affliction* (Oxford: Clarendon Press, 1968).

36. D. M. Schneider, *Class Differences and Sex Roles in American Kinship and Family Structure* (Englewood Cliffs: Prentice Hall, 1973); idem, *American Kinship* (Chicago: University of Chicago Press, 1980); idem, *Symbolic Anthropology* (New York: Columbia University Press, 1977).

37. T. Skocpol, *States of Social Revolutions: A Comparative Analysis of France, Russia, and China* (Cambridge: Cambridge University Press, 1979); P. B. Evans, R. Dietrich, and T. Skocpol, ed., *Bringing the State Back In* (Cambridge: Cambridge University Press, 1985).

38. L. A. Hirshfeld, S. Atran, and A. A. Yengoyan, "Theories of Knowledge and Culture," *Social Science Information* 21 (1982):161–98.

between culture and social structure. These shifts continuously oscillated between seeing the relationship between "culture" and social structure in any given society as either static and homogenous—or as entirely open, almost endlessly malleable, and continuously changing.

The first view, typical of some structuralists and extreme Marxists, depicts cultural orientations or rules as relatively uniform and homogenous within society and as relatively static throughout the major period of the histories of the societies or civilizations in which they are institutionalized. This is true in both cases, whether they are, as among the structuralists, reflections of some basic rules of the human mind, or, as among the Marxists, reflections of some "deep" social forces. Such a picture leaves little room (beyond the initial institutionalization of the different cultural visions) for reconstruction and change in the relations between culture and social structure, nor does it explain the development of strategies of choice, maximization, and possible innovation as they are depicted in individualistic approaches.

In the second view, culture is seen as an aggregate result of patterns of behavior, of structure, or of power, or, as Ann Swidler put it, "as a tool-kit of different strategies of action which can be activated in different situations, according to the 'material' and 'ideal' interests of different social actors,"[39] and apparently entirely without any specific contours of its own.

These shifts in the definition and status of both culture and social structure were accompanied by a preference for exclusively deterministic, reductionist, "idealist," or "materialist" interpretations of social action and cultural creativity. This tendency to the reification of major concepts of social analysis became closely interwoven with an ontological reduction of all social behavior to some of them, especially to power such as in the work of Michel Foucault, which gained great popularity in that period. These shifts were also connected with a growing dissociation between the studies of culture and those of social structure.

XI

One of the rather paradoxical outcomes of these shifts in the ontological standing of the basic concepts of sociological analysis and of the oscillation in views about the relative importance of culture and social structure was the almost total initial neglect of the analysis of the construction of the division of labor and of rules and norms, rates, and institutions. All these aspects of social life were either taken for granted, simply ignored, or seen as derived from culture, "social structure," or individuals, conceived as distinct ontological entities.

39. A. Swidler, "Culture in Action: Symbols and Strategies," *American Sociological Review* 51 (1986):273–86.

In a sense what took place here was that the "baby"—division of labor, rules, norms, and institutions—was thrown out with the "bathwater" of the closed structural-functional analysis.

It is only recently that attempts have been made to explain the emergence of norms and institutions[40]—at least from the individualist, rational choice point of view. These attempts have highlighted the importance of the processes through which institutional formations crystallize and have made interesting contributions to the analysis of such processes. But at the same time they have clearly indicated the limits of the applicability of the rational choice approach, based on the conceptions of the optimization of utilities, in explaining norms and institutions—and even peoples'—preferences. In general, these various researches have provided very interesting indications about the ways in which people behave within given sets of rules, but not of the processes through which such rules, especially the ground rules of social interaction, are set up.

Interestingly enough, there have been attempts to explain some especially cooperative rules of the game in terms of evolutionary (biological) adaptation. Whatever the ultimate verdict about these explanations, they were already made in terms of behavior—and possibly actors—which differ greatly from that presumed by the natural choice approach.[41]

Similarly, the culturalist approaches—those which emphasized social-structural entities like the state, while often stressing the importance of rules or conceptions—did not analyze the processes through which such entities and the rules they promulgate are constituted beyond the pursual by different actors of their direct interests.

XII

Thus, all these controversies and researches have highlighted the necessity to reexamine and reanalyze the processes through which social formations are

40. J. S. Coleman, *Foundations of Social Theory* (Cambridge: Harvard University Press, 1990); M. Hechter, K.-D. Opp, and R. Wippler, ed., *Social Institutions: Their Emergence, Maintenance, and Effects* (New York: Aldine de Gruyter, 1990); K. S. Cook and M. Levi, ed., *The Limits of Rationality* (Chicago: University of Chicago Press, 1990); K. S. Cook, ed., *Social Exchange Theory* (Newbury Park: Sage Publications, 1987); J. J. Mansbridge, ed., *Beyond Self-Interest* (Chicago: University of Chicago Press, 1990).

41. See, from among many other views, R. Axelrod and D. Dlon, "The Further Evolution of Cooperation," *Science* 242 (1988):1385–88; and K. Sigmund, "On Prisoners and Cells," *Nature* 359 (1992):774. N. J. Smelser, "The Rational Choice Perspective: A Theoretical Assessment," *Rationality and Society* 4, 381–410; J. Hirschliefer, "Evolutionary Models in Economics and Law: Cooperation versus Conflict Strategies," *Research In Law & Economics* 4, 1–60; idem, "On the Emotions as Guarantors of Threats and Promises," in *The Latest on the Best: Essays on Evolution and Optimality*, ed. John Dupre (Cambridge: MIT Press, 1987); C. Martinez, J. Carlos, and J. Hirschliefer, "The Limited

crystallized. This necessity was to a very large extent epitomized, from the seventies on, in Anthony Giddens' development of the theory of structuration,[42] as well as in the works of Pierre Bourdieu[43] and Alain Touraine.[44]

The very term "structuration" was coined by Giddens in contrast to the older (especially structural-functional) emphasis on structure and constituted a salutary correction to what was conceived among large parts of the sociological community as reified conceptions of social structure. Throughout his analyses, Giddens stressed that structure is continually created by human factors and that it both enables and constrains human action. Throughout his numerous works Giddens also dealt with many of the other theoretical problems which arose in this period and provided many insights, especially with respect to the relation of the process of structuration to culture and human agency, and in their embedding in specific temporal and spatial frameworks. But throughout most of these analyses he did not distinguish sharply enough between different levels of structuration, especially between the structuration of activities which are *within* given institutional frameworks, those through which such frameworks are constructed, and between levels or types of systemic tendencies in different levels and patterns of social interaction.

Bourdieu's emphasis on "situs" or "habitus" as the major unit of reflexive social action and on social action as reflexive praxis has—as well as his development of such concepts as social capital and "distinction"—also strongly emphasized the dynamic aspects of structuration of social action and situations, and the continual interweaving and confrontation between subjective meaning and objective structure. Both he and Giddens have very strongly emphasized the dynamic interrelation between such structuration and culture and power. Yet with the possible exception of his earlier book on the theory of praxis[45] (his many insights about, and explorations of, the different rich nuances through which aspects of culture and social processes are interwoven notwithstanding—as, for instance, the different processes through which "distinctions"

of Reciprocity: Solution Concepts and Reactive Strategies in Evolutionary Equilibrium Models," *Rationality and Society* 3, 35–64.

42. A. Giddens, *Central Problems in Social Theory* (Cambridge: Cambridge University Press, 1979); idem, *The Constitution and Society: Outline of the Theory of Structuration* (Oxford: Polity Press, 1984); idem, *Studies in Social and Political Theory* (1977). For a general approach of Giddens, see, for instance, J. Cohen, *Structural Theory: A. Giddens, and the Constitution of Social Life* (London: Macmillan, 1989).

43. P. Bourdieu, *Outline of a Theory of Practice* (Cambridge: Cambridge University Press, 1977); idem, *Distinction* (Cambridge: Harvard University Press, 1984); idem, *The Logic of Practice* (1990); idem, *The Love of Art* (Stanford: Stanford University Press, 1990).

44. A. Touraine, *The Post-Industrial Society* (1971); idem, *Production de la Societe* (Paris: Editions du Seuil, 1973); idem, *Return of the Actor* (Minneapolis: University of Minnesota Press, 1988).

45. P. Bourdieu, *Outline of a Theory of Practice* (Cambridge: Cambridge University Press, 1977).

are constituted in social life) his work sometimes gives a rather strong reductionist impression, reducing cultural creativity to its social and, above all, its class basis.[46]

Alain Touraine has in many works emphasized the importance of social movements in the constitution and transformation of societies. Many of his concrete analyses, be they of social movements in Latin America, of the student movement in Europe, or of Solidarity in Poland, provide fascinating accounts and analyses of these movements and of their impact.[47] They do not, however, substantiate his claim that they prove, or even illustrate, the necessity to discard the concepts of society or the like, though they do point out the necessity to reexamine the process through which "societies" are constructed and to conceptualize that construction in a more diversified way than was prevalent in the fifties and sixties in much sociological literature.

Within many of these approaches also developed a very reductionist orientation to the evaluation of power. They have correctly pointed out that the concern with power as domination was rather weak in most of the dominant approaches of the sixties, especially in the structural-functional ones. They have also pointed out that the relation between culture, values, consensus, and power was underemphasized in large parts of the literature of the sixties and they have set out the correct the situation, often referring, as we have mentioned already above, to the works of Foucault. But however rich their concrete analyses of different cults they tended toward a highly reductionist approach in which "culture" was often seen as epiphenonemal to power. They tended to neglect the fact or the problem that the crystallization of any "intellectual" hegemony (to use Gramsci's terminology) does not only create domination but also empowers broader sectors of a society; that such empowerment is to no small extent given in the limitation which legitimation puts on the power holders and on the expectations from them; on the tendency for protest and heterodoxy is that to develop and challenge such legitimation; and that the concrete forms of such legitimation and challenges to it are influenced not only by the concrete power relations between different groups in a society but also by the contents of the respective cultural orientations, premises, and patterns of legitimation that develop in different societies.

XIII

These different approaches, with their emphases on the shifts in the ontological definition of the major concepts of social science analysis, became con-

46. For recent critical evaluations of Bourdieu, see J. C. Alexander, *The Reality of Reduction: The Fabled Synthesis of Pierre Bourdieu* (forthcoming); C. Calhoun, E. LiPuma, and M. Postone, ed., *Bourdieu: Critical Perspectives* (Chicago: The University of Chicago Press, 1993); R. Jenkins, *Pierre Bourdieu* (London: Routledge, 1992).

47. A. Touraine, *The Post-Industrial Society* (1971); idem, *Production de la Societe* (Paris: Editions du Seuil, 1973); idem, *Return of the Actor* (Minneapolis: University of Minnesota Press, 1988).

nected with very rich research programs. Among these programs were macrosociological analyses which had been rather neglected from the mid-sixties on and which reemerged in the early eighties—thus bringing macrosociological studies and theoretical analysis back together.

In the early eighties, I analyzed the problem of the relations between macrosociological analysis and sociological theory.[48] In 1987, I published a long review of the new macrosociological analyses which had come out in the eighties and which focused on the classical problem of the origins of the West. In this review article, I highlighted the problems raised by these researches from the point of view of sociological theory, especially how they call for a reconceptualization of culture and social structure, for a reexamination of the relations between agency, culture, and social structure between culture and power, and above all, for the identification of the processes and actors through which such relations are interwoven in shaping the crystallization, reproduction, and change of social formations.[49]

XIV

These theoretical problems have become closely interwoven with shifts in my own work, especially with that from comparative institutional to comparative civilizational analysis in which I frontally analyzed the process through which relations are interwoven in shaping the crystallization, reproduction, and change of social formations. In this way, I also attempted to redefine the relations between agency, culture, and social structure.

The kernels of such analysis could be found in *Prestige, Stratification and Center Formation* and in *Patrons, Clients and Friends*. But it was only in a series of comparative civilizational analyses—especially in the early researches on Axial Age civilizations—that I was able to take up these problems systematically.

One of the first foci of this analysis was a more detailed look at different types of centers and processes of center formation, the beginnings of which were already presented in the analysis of strata formation and patron-client relations.

The analysis of different types of centers, the first steps of which were undertaken in the introduction to the paperback edition of *Political Systems*, was developed further in the introductions to the various sectors of the reader *Politi-*

---

48. S. N. Eisenstadt, "Neue Trends in der Makro-Soziologie," in *Soziologie in weltburgerlicher Absicht*, ed. H. von Alemann and H. P. Thurn (Opladen: Westdeutscher Verlag); S. N. Eisenstadt and M. Curelaru, "Macro-Sociology-Theory, Analysis, and Comparative Studies," *Current Sociology* 25, 1–112; S. N. Eisenstadt, "Macro-societal Analysis: Background, Development, and Indications" in *Beyond Progress and Development*, ed. J. Berting and W. Blockmans (Avebury, 1987), 10–25.

49. S. N. Eisenstadt, "Macrosociology and Sociological Theory: Some New Dimensions," *Contemporary Sociology* 16 (1987):602–9.

cal Sociology,[50] which I edited. Here, the distinctive characteristics of centers and center-periphery relations are described in different types of regimes, tribal societies, city-states, patrimonial regimes, and the like. The differences between the respective centers of such regimes are analyzed in terms of their structural and symbolic autonomy, their distinctiveness, their types of activities, their relationship to the periphery, and their capacity for change.

The insights presented in these introductions were taken up much more systematically in the study of the origins of the state with special reference to Africa, which Michel Abitbol, Naomi Chazan, and myself undertook[51] in the framework of the program on Comparative Civilizations in the Department of Anthropology together with the Truman Research Institute of the Hebrew University of Jerusalem.[52]

In these studies, we attempted systematically to examine the relations between the social division of labor and structural differentiation on the one hand, and the other dimensions of social order on the other, especially the construction of trust, the solidarity of different collectivities, the regulation of power and meaning, and legitimation. We analyzed the cultural dimension of social order as it is interwoven into social structures, the roles of different types of social actors, especially the coalition of elites, and influential processes of conflict and change.

We emphasized that these various components of centers and elite functions—the regulation of power, the constitution of trust and of legitimation—do not always go together; that each component may be articulated within different centers to different degrees, giving rise to different modes of control by the ruling elites.

These components may come together in different centers in various combinations, and the relative importance of each component may vary in different centers. These differences, in turn, are closely related to the nature of the elite coalitions that predominate in a given center and society and to the cultural orientations they articulate. As a result, different centers and societies exhibit diverse structures and dynamics.

XV

The classification of different types of centers constituted only the first step in our analysis. Next, we attempted to identify the processes through which cen-

50. S. N. Eisenstadt, ed., *Political Sociology* (New York: Basic Books, 1970).

51. S. N. Eisenstadt, M. Abitbol, and N. Chazan, ed., *The Early State in African Perspective: Culture, Power, and Division of Labor* (Leiden: E. J. Brill, 1987), 1–27, 168–200.

52. S. N. Eisenstadt, *A Sociological Approach to Comparative Civilizations: The Development and Directions of a Research Program* (Jerusalem: The Harry S. Truman Research Institute for the Advancement of Peace, The Hebrew University of Jerusalem, 1986).

ters are constituted; the relation of such centers to cultural orientations on the one hand and to ecological and economic conditions on the other. Of central importance was the distinction between congruent and noncongruent societies, i.e., between those societies in which different elite functions and different components of centers are embedded within various ascriptive settings and those in which elite functions are dissociated from such settings.

All these analyses showed that different constellations of center types and activities are closely related to both the patterns of elite coalitions predominating in the centers and to the characteristics of their major elites. The main distinction here is the degree to which the elites are autonomous— i.e., constituted according to autonomous criteria and in distinct settings— as opposed to being embedded in various ascriptive units or acting as representatives of such units in society. It is the extent and direction of the autonomy of elites and influentials that was shown to constitute one of the most important tools for the analysis of the institutional dynamics of different societies.

At the same time, the elites' relative autonomy is closely related to different civilizational visions and cultural programs and to the premises of the cultural and social order promulgated by them, and are often challenged by different groups and counterelites. Of special importance here is the distinction between perceptions of low as against high degrees of tension or of a chasm in between the transcendental and the mundane, and between direct or mediated access to the sacred. There is an elective affinity between these visions and the degree of autonomy of elites, between embedded as opposed to autonomous elites. In most congruent societies, the prevalent cultural orientations are characterized by a very low degree of tension between the transcendental and the mundane, whereas in most noncongruent societies, the prevalent perception is of a very high degree of such tension. In these latter societies, the separation of the center from the organization of tasks in the social division of labor has led to the differentiation of elite functions and the consequent development of variously institutionalized charismatic visions. This differentiation and development constituted the nuclei of a variety of center activities. The range of possible coalitions that could develop in these circumstances was great.

XVI

Further analyses of the distinctions between congruent and noncongruent societies and the relations between the construction of the social division of labor, the regulation of power, the construction of trust (solidarity) and of meaning, and their impact on institutional and cultural dynamics, were undertaken in the study of so-called Axial civilizations which constituted one of the center-pieces of the research program on comparative civilizations.[53]

The Axial Age civilizations provide an unusually instructive arena for the examination of both the difference between structural differentiation and the differentiation of elite activities—as well as of the variety of possible elite coalitions bearing different cultural visions or orientations. They facilitate an analysis of the impact of these elite coalitions and countercoalitions on the institutional structure of their respective societies, on the *modes* of structural differentiation, and on the dynamics of these societies. Above all, the analysis of the Axial civilizations provides an arena for a most fruitful analysis of the relations between cultural, civilizational visions and institutional formations and for an analysis of the interweaving of cultural and structural social dimensions in the construction of such formations.

From our analytical perspective, the most central aspect of the Axial Age civilizations was that they exhibited, even if in different ways, the basic characteristics of noncongruent societies: they were characterized by a sharp distinction between the social division of labor and the functions which articulate the charismatic dimensions of the constitution of social order which are beyond the organization of the social division of labor. These latter functions were to a very large extent borne by various autonomous cultural elites and intellectuals which emerged as a distinct type of social actors within all Axial civilizations.

XVII

The emphasis on distinct, autonomous cultural actors—and on the articulators or promulgators of the solidarity of different social collectivities—brings us to a major aspect of civilizational dynamics of the Axial civilizations: processes of change within them.

The main point here involves the close relations between autonomous cultural elites and intellectuals and new types of social movements, especially different sects and heterodoxies, that upheld different conceptions of the resolution of the tension between the transcendental and the mundane order, as well as different sociological visions and the proper way to institutionalize such visions that also constituted the most active element in the protest movements.

The transformation of these alternative conceptions into heterodoxies was effected, of course, by their confrontation with some institutionalized orthodoxy, and it was from then on that the continuous confrontation between orthodoxy on the one hand, and schism and heterodoxy on the other, and with

---

53. See S. N. Eisenstadt, ed., *The Origins and Diversity of Axial Civilizations* (Albany: State University of New York Press, 1986); idem, *Kulturen der Achsenzeit*, 2 *Teil* 3 vols. (Frankfurt: Suhrkamp Verlag, 1991); idem, *Civilta Comparate* (Napoli: Liguori Editore, 1990).

it also the development of strong and potentially widespread antinomian tendencies, became a crucial component in the history of mankind.[54]

Because of this, the possibility of structural and ideological linkages between different movements of protest and foci of political conflict emerged in these civilizations. Thus, a new type of civilizational dynamic developed. These new dynamics of civilization transformed group conflicts into political class and ideological conflicts, cult conflicts into struggles between the orthodoxies and the heterodoxies. Conflicts between tribes and societies became missionary crusades for the transformation of civilizations. The zeal for reorganization, informed by each society's transcendental vision, made the whole world at least potentially subject to cultural-political reconstruction, and in all these new developments the different sectarian movements and movements of heterodoxy played a central role for the reasons outlined above. The place of such heterodoxies in the dynamics of Axial civilizations bears on a more general point of the central place of intellectuals in the construction of societal centers.[55]

XVIII

One of the most interesting subjects of comparative analysis—an unusual combination of a very high level of structural differentiation together with a low level of distinction between social division of labor and elite functions, that is, with a low degree of autonomy of the major elites—is Japan.

In terms of comparative analysis, the uniqueness of Japanese civilization lies in the fact that it did not experience an Axial Age transformation leading to a strong conception of a very wide chasm between the transcendental and the mundane order, yet it did exhibit some of the structural characteristics as well as a very high level of philosophical, literary, and ideological discourse, and self-reflexivity that can be found in Axial Age civilizations.[56]

Thus there developed a rather unusual combination of similarity of many institutional aspects of Japan with those of western Europe together with some

54. S. N. Eisenstadt, "Heterodoxies, Sectarianism, and Dynamics of Civilizations," *Diogenes* 120 (1982):5–26; idem, "Transcendental Visions, Other Worldliness, and its Transformations: Some More Comments on L. Dumont" *Religion* 13 (1983):1–17.

55. See S. N. Eisenstadt, "Heterodoxies, Sectarianism, and Dynamics of Civilizations"; and S. N. Eisenstadt and R. Graubard, ed., *Intellectuals and Tradition* (New York: Humanities Press, 1973); idem, "Transcendental Vision, Center Formations, and the Role of Intellectuals" in *Center: Ideas and Institutions*, ed. L. Greenfeld and M. Martin (Chicago, University of Chicago Press, 1988), 96–109.

56. S. N. Eisenstadt, "Cultural Premises and the Limits of Convergence in Modern Societies: An Examination of Some Aspects of Japanese Society," *Diogenes* 147 (1987):125–46; idem, "Civilizational Frameworks, Historical Experiences, and Cultural Programmes of Modernity: The Structuring of Protest in Modern Societies," in *Development and Modernity: Perspectives on Western Theories on Modernisation*, ed. L. Gule and O. Storebo (Bergen: Ariadne, 1993), 11–37.

very distinct characteristics. This can be identified not only in the contemporary era, when Japan became incorporated in their modern world system, but also in earlier periods of history when almost no contact existed between the two. Japan shared with western Europe many characteristics of major institutional arenas and processes: patterns of family structure and kinship organization; feudalism and the development of the absolutist state; a relatively high degree of urban development and organization; the development of many peasant rebellions, especially in the medieval and Tokugawa periods; the great modern transformation attendant on the Meiji restoration giving rise to the establishment of a modern state; far-reaching social and economic modernization and numerous related crises; and finally, the crystallization of a democratic-capitalist regime after the Second World War. Moreover, Japan shared with Europe not only the existence of such arenas but also the historical sequence of their development.

At the same time some very far-reaching differences from Europe can be identified. As Marc Bloch pointed out long ago, in Japanese feudalism there never developed full-fledged contractual relations between vassal and lord; Japanese vassals could have only one lord; fully autonomous Assemblies of Estates were weak, if they existed at all; and Japanese feudalism was much more centralized than European, with distinct foci of such centralization—Emperor and Shogun (or the Bakafu)—the former being, unlike in Europe, outside the feudal nexus.

Within Japanese peasant rebellions there never developed very strong utopian (as distinct from millenarist) orientations, a strong class consciousness, or strong linkages with heterodox intellectual elites and with rebellious samurai groups.

Similarly, the strong semiautonomous and independent castle towns of the pre-Tokugawa period and early Tokugawa period never evolved the conceptions and institutionalization of corporate urban autonomy that constituted the major characteristic of western European cities.

The common denominator of all these differences in the arenas that were structurally similar to those of western Europe was that they were not defined in terms that differentiated them sharply from one another. Instead, they were defined in some common primordial, sacral, or "natural" terms as embedded in the overall societal contexts.

Accordingly, the historical dynamics in Japan developed some very distinct characteristics. Of special interest to our discussion is the weakness, in comparative terms, of the institutional changes. Changes in structural differentiation or in regimes were not connected as on the Axial civilization with ideological changes couched in transcendental, universalistic terms. Rather they were aborted, as it were, within the framework of the continuously expanding immanentist and primordial conceptions. Significantly, Japan was able even to transform the major premises of Confucianism and Buddhism.

These definitions of the major institutional arenas were very closely related to the specific, strongly immanentist, and particularistic ontological conceptions and conceptions of social order that have been prevalent in Japan throughout its history. On the institutional level, this transformation was manifest in the absence, in Japan, of an autonomous stratum of literati and the examination system (so important in China, Korea, and Vietnam) and strong traditions of hereditary transmission of leadership roles which were embedded in family settings.

In parallel some of the major premises or concepts of Confucianism and Buddhism were transformed in Japan. Here we can note the transformation of transcendental orientations that stressed the chasm between the transcendental and mundane order into a more immanentist direction. Such transformation had far-reaching impact on some of the basic premises and concepts of the social order such as the Mandate of Heaven, with its implication for the conception of authority and the accountability of rulers as well as conceptions of community. Unlike China, where in principle the emperor, even if a sacral figure, was "under" the Mandate of Heaven, in Japan he was sacred and seen as the embodiment of the sun and could not be held accountable to anyone. Only the Shoguns and other officials—in ways not clearly specified and only in periods of crises, for instance, at the end of the Tokugawa regime—could be held accountable.

The strong universalistic orientations inherent in Buddhism, and more lately in Confucianism, were subdued and "nativized" in Japan. When Japan was defined as a divine nation, this meant a nation protected by the gods, being a chosen people in some sense, but not a nation carrying God's universal mission.

The specific institutional and cultural dynamics that developed in Japan were closely related to the fact that there did not develop strong autonomous elites, i.e., that the major elite functions were embedded in ascriptive settings.

The common characteristic of these elites and their major coalitions was their embedment in groups and settings (contexts) that were mainly defined in primordial, ascriptive, sacral, and often hierarical terms, and much less in terms of specialized functions or of universalistic criteria of social attributes.

Linked to these characteristics of the coalitions and countercoalitions prevalent in Japanese society was the relative weakness of autonomous cultural elites. True, many cultural actors—priests, monks, scholars, and the like—participated in such coalitions. But with very few exceptions, their participation was based on primordial and social attributes and on criteria of achievement and social obligations according to which these coalitions were structured and not on any distinct, autonomous criteria rooted in or related to the arenas of cultural specialization in which they were active. These arenas—cultural, religious, or literary—were themselves ultimately defined in primordial-sacral terms, notwithstanding the fact that many specialized activities developed within them.

These combinations of cultural and social dimensions as effected by coalitions of elites and counterelites shaped the distinctive characteristics of the Japanese historical experience.

XIX

The analysis of the interweaving of cultural and social structural dimensions, of human interaction and social order, was applied not only to the study of the overall, macrosociological dynamics of the Axial civilizations but also to that of specific institutional arenas within these civilizations.

Such analysis had already been undertaken in the comparative analysis of patron-client relations, in which it was first shown how the development of such relations is closely related to the prevalence—in different societies or sectors thereof—of distinct cosmological visions borne by highly embedded elites who usually serve as the apex of the patron-client hierarchies and how these conceptions and elites are related to the structure of trust in these societies.

Later on such analysis was undertaken systematically and in much greater detail in other studies. Thus, for instance, in a comparative study of cities and urban hierarchies of the major historical civilizations,[57] it was shown that major dimensions of urban structure cannot be explained purely in terms of ecological or economic conditions or in terms of structural differentiation. In addition to these factors, cosmological visions and conceptions of social order promulgated by the elites of the respective societies are of great importance. The importance of these latter factors can be seen in the impact of the Confucian cosmology promulgated by the Chinese literati in shaping the urban structure of Beijing, or of the Muslim conceptions of social order that have changed the construction of the urban space of Istanbul in comparison with that of Constantinople—both capitals of great agrarian bureaucratic empires with great similarities in their respective social structures and in their geopolitical location.

At the same time, I undertook an analysis of the different heterodoxies and their impact on the dynamics of their respective civilizations in a series of researches that started with a reexamination of Weber's Protestant ethic thesis

----

57. S. N. Eisenstadt and A. Shachar, *Society, Culture, and Urbanization* (Newbury Park: Sage Publications, 1987).

and continued in a series of preliminary analyses of some of the major civiliza-tions—Jewish, early Christian, Indian, Buddhist, Chinese, and Islamic.[58] These numerous researches were published in many papers and reports and I have included one, "Cultural and Social Structure Revisited," in this volume. It will serve as a good illustration of the basic analytical and comparative thrust of these researches.

Throughout these researches, I have also pointed to the ways in which the various Axial visions are institutionalized and their dynamics greatly influenced both by the technologies that develop within their respective societies as well as by the political-ecological conditions in which they develop. In the study of urban structure, I have shown how cultural orientations and social process shape (urban) spaces. A comparison between the Byzantine Empire and Euro-pean Christianity as well as between Hindu civilization and the more compact Buddhist polities has indicated the impact of political-ecological comparisons as opposed to the decentralization of formations and the dynamics of civiliza-tion. I have further analyzed the problem of the impact of political-ecological formations on institutional dynamics in a series of analyses of the different aspects of small states.[59]

All these constitute, however, only the first steps in a more systematic analysis of the relations between ecological patterns and institutional dynam-ics—a rather neglected problem, with the possible exception of the works of Hans Gehser,[60] Randall Collins,[61] Peter Katzenstein,[62] and a few others[63] in sociological analysis.

58. S. N. Eisenstadt, "Die Paradoxie von Zivilisationen mit ausserweltlichen Orientierungen" in *Max Webers Studie über Hinduismus und Buddhismus*, ed. W. Schluchter (Frankfurt: Suhrkamp Verlag, 1984); idem, "Webers Analyse des Islams und die Gestalt der Islamischen Zivilization" in *Max Webers Sicht des Islams*, ed. W. Schluchter (Frankfurt: Suhrkamp Verlag, 1987), 342–59; idem, "Max Webers Überlegungen zum Westlichen Christentums," in *Max Webers Sicht des Okzidentalen Chris-tentums*, ed. W. Schluchter (Frankfurt: Suhrkamp Taschenbuch Wissenschaft, 1988), 554–85; idem, Max Webers Sicht des frühen Christentums und die Entstehung der Westlichen Zivilisation," in *Max Webers Sicht des Antiken Christentums*, ed. W. Schluchter (Frankfurt: Suhrkamp Taschenbuch Wis-senschaft, 1985).

59. S. N. Eisenstadt, "Sociological Characteristics and Problems of Small States: A Research Note," *Jerusalem Journal of International Relations* 2, 35–50 and in German *Schweizerische Zeitschrift für Soziologie* 3 (1977): 41–49; idem, "Reflections on Center-Periphery Relations and Small European States" in *Small States in Comparative Perspective* (Oslo, 1985), 41–49.

60. H. Gehser, "Kleine Sozialsysteme: Strukturmerkmale und Leistungskapazitaten," *Koelner Zeitschrift für Soziologie und Sozialpsychologie* 32 (1980):205–39; H. Gehser, "Kleine Sozialsysteme: ein soziologisches Erklärungsmodell der Konkordanzdemokratie?" in *Politischer Wandel in konkordanz-demodratischen Systemen*, ed. H. Michalsky (Vaduz: Liechtenstein Plitische Schriften, 1991), 93–121.

61. R. Collins, *Weberian Sociological Theory* (Cambridge: Cambridge University Press, 1986), chapters 6, 7, 8f.

62. P. Katzenstein, *Small States in World Markets* (Ithaca: Cornell University Press, 1985).

63. A. Skuhra, "Industrialized Small States: Some Comparative Considerations," in *Small States in Europe and Dependence*, ed. O. Holl (Luxemburg: Austrian Institute for International Affairs, 1983),

XX

These analyses have far-reaching consequences for the analysis not only of institutional formations and dynamics but also of "culture" and of knowledge, or of religion. In a collective volume on the research program on comparative civilizations[64] we have explored the relations between cultural creativity and social process. In the introduction to that volume and in a paper on the sociology of knowledge[65] we explore the implications of this theoretical approach to the analysis of the sociology of knowledge—and by implication also to the sociology of religion or to any other types of cultural creativity. It indicates a way out of the impasse that the older classical Mannheimian and Marxist approaches find themselves in with their distinctions between *Realfaktoren* and *Idealfaktoren* and with their implicit or explicit assumption that culture is somehow epiphenomenal in the construction of social order. All these works—like those of Durkheim—failed to provide systematic, not merely illustrative, ad hoc indications of the nature of the social and cognitive mechanisms through which such symbols are generated and through which the connections between the systems of symbolic configurations and the institutional arrangements of a society are effected. In general, neither Mannheim nor the French school analyzed the ways in which the influence of "real factors" on different types of knowledge was effected. The classical sociology of knowledge compounded its difficulties by allowing itself, intermittently or marginally, to extend its unrealistic conception of "real factors" and "ideal factors" into epistemology.

Our approach, in fact, makes it possible to go beyond this impasse. This approach to the sociology of knowledge begins with the recognition of man as a symbol-constructing, cognitively oriented, reflexive, and self-reflective being who seeks to construct different symbolic configurations aimed at understanding the world or parts of it. It is through the formation of such symbolic configurations that man discovers and interprets his environment, his own organism, and the symbolic configurations themselves. Orientations to empirical reality constitute a very important—albeit only one—component in the construction of these symbolic configurations, and empirical reality itself is defined in different ways in different civilizations. These properties of human beings

69–82; A. Waschkuhn, ed., *Kleinstaat: Drundsatzliche und aktuelle Probleme* (Vaduz: Verlag der Liechtensteinischen Akademischen Gesellschaft, 1993).

64. S. N. Eisenstadt and I. F. Silber, ed., "Cultural Traditions and Worlds of Knowledge: Explorations in the Sociology of Knowledge," in *Knowledge and Society: Studies in the Sociology of Culture Past and Present* by S. N. Eisenstadt and I. F. Silber (Greenwich, CT: JAI Press, Inc., 1988).

65. "The Classical Sociology of Knowledge and Beyond," *Minerva* 25, 1–2 (1987):77–91.

are inherent components of the constitution of society; they are not merely the reflections or products of instrumental or adaptive needs of the organism or even of "social-integrative needs."

I have started to develop a similar approach to the study of religions in an article[66] in which I analyze the symbolic configurations which constitute the basic premises of social interaction—the basic cosmological conceptions and conceptions of social order—and are constitutive of the foundation of institutional orders and dynamics. These premises, as promulgated and institutionalized by different social actors, greatly influence different patterns of cultural creativity, of knowledge, religious beliefs, or aesthetic creation.[67] The concrete patterns of such creativity are shaped by the interaction between the inherent symbolic qualities of the basic cosmological premises and premises of social order and the institutional locations of their bearers. Such patterns of cultural creativity provide yet another manifestation of the continuous interweaving—in any pattern of social interaction—of the "cultural" and "social structural" components.

XXI

The various macrosociological and comparative institutional analyses in which I was engaged over the last twenty years have also facilitated the reexamination—in close connection with the reappraisal of basic issues of sociological theory—of some central aspects of historical processes, especially of the relations between cultural visions, institutional patterns, and "agency and historical contingency."

Such reexamination can be illustrated by the analysis of revolutions and in the reappraisal of the visions of modernity and modernization. The analysis of revolutions started with a critical review of the numerous studies of the "causes" of revolutions which strongly emphasized various structural and psychological factors. This review indicated that such causes may explain the breakdown of regimes but not the nature of the outcome of such breakdowns—that is, whether it will be a revolutionary one or not.[68]

66. S. N. Eisenstadt, "The Expansion of Religions: Some Comparative Observations on Different Modes," in *Comparative Social Research: Religions Institutions* Vol. 12, ed. C. Calhoun (1991):45–73; S. N. Eisenstadt and I. F. Silber, *Knowledge and Society;* S. N. Eisenstadt, "Explorations in the Sociology of Knowledge: The Soteriological Axis in the Construction of Domains of Knowledge," in S. N. Eisenstadt and I. F. Silber, *Knowledge and Society,* 1–71.

67. Ibid; ibid.

68. S. N. Eisenstadt, *Revolution and the Transformation of Societies* (New York: The Free Press, 1978). For a later formulation, see S. N. Eisenstadt, "The Social Framework and Conditions of Revolution," *Research on Social Movements, Conflicts, and Change* 1, 85–104; idem, "Frameworks of the Great Revolutions: Culture, Social Structure, History, and Human Agency," *International Social Science Journal* 33 (1992):385–401.

Since revolutions are, by definition, concomitant with the breakdown of regimes, the various causes or conditions of the breakdown of regimes—the various constellations of interelite and interclass struggles, the development of new social groups and economic forces which are blocked from access to power, the weakening of regimes through such struggles, through economic turbulence, and through the impact of international forces—constitute the necessary conditions for the development of revolutions.

But it is only insofar as these processes take place in specific historical circumstances, and within the frameworks of specific civilizational premises, political regimes, and specific types of political economy, that they may trigger revolutionary processes and outcomes.

The specific historical circumstances are those of early modernity, when the autocratic modernizing regimes face the contradictions inherent in their own legitimation and in their policies and confront the development of new economic strata and new "modern" ideologies.

The civilizational frameworks are those of "this-worldly" or combined this- and otherworldly Axial civilizations and political regimes—either imperial or feudal imperial ones. When, for various historical reasons, such regimes do not develop in these civilizational frameworks, the processes of change tend to be deflected from the revolutionary route.

The concrete outcome, however, of these processes depends greatly on the balance of power between the revolutionary and counterrevolutionary forces and their respective cohesion.

The combination of civilizational and structural conditions and historical contingencies that generated the great revolutions has been rather rare in the history of mankind. With all their dramatic importance, these revolutions certainly do not constitute the only, main, or even the most far-reaching types of such changes, whether in premodern or modern times. When other combinations of structural and institutional factors develop, for instance, in Japan, India, South Asia, or Latin America, they give rise to other processes of change and new political regimes. These are not just "faulted," would-be revolutions. They should not be measured by the yardstick of the great revolutions; rather, they denote different patterns of change, "legitimate" and meaningful transformation of societies, and they should be analyzed in their own right. Then again, as we shall see shortly, the case of Japan is of special interest.

XXII

These considerations also brought a reexamination of the vision of modernization and modernity. Such reexamination focused above all on the problem of the so-called convergence of industrial and modern societies—or, in a somewhat broader formulation, on whether what we witness on the contemporary scene is the development of one modern civilization encompassing most contemporary societies, but with local subvariations, or of several modern civilizations, that is to say, civilizations sharing common characteristics but which tend to develop as distinct civilizations with different ideological and institutional dynamics.[69]

Contrary to the vision implicit in the "classical" studies of modernization and the convergence of industrial society—behind which there loomed a conviction of the inevitability of progress towards modernity—whether political, industrial, or cultural, there slowly developed a growing recognition of the great symbolic and institutional variability and of the different modes of ideological and institutional dynamics attendant on the spread of modern civilization. A new perspective on the process of modernization emerged from a critical examination of these various theories—such as those which stressed the importance of traditions or the dynamics of international systems for the understanding of this variability—and from the comparative civilizational approach. Accordingly, the process of modernization should no longer be viewed as the ultimate end of the evolution of all known societies. This new perspective on modernization does not assume that the process of modernization brings out the evolutionary potential common to all societies. Rather, it considers that modernization or modernity is one specific type of civilization that originated in Europe and spread throughout the world, encompassing—especially after the Second World War—almost all of it.

The crystallization and expansion of this new type of civilization was not unlike that of the great religions or of the great imperial expansions in the past. But because the expansion of this civilization almost always combined economic, political, and ideological factors, its impact on the societies on which it spread was much more intensive than in these other historical cases. Just as when historical civilizations expand, so the expansion of modernity challenges the symbolic and institutional premises of the societies that are incorporated into them. This challenge calls for responses from within these societies, which has the effect, in turn, of opening up new options and possibilities. A great variety of modern or modernizing societies have developed out of these responses, out of the interaction between the expanding civilization of modernity and the various Asian, African, and Latin American civilizations. They share many common characteristics but also evince great differences among themselves. They share many common problems—such as those aris-

69. S. N. Eisenstadt, "A Reappraisal of Theories of Social Change and Modernization" in *Social Change and Modernity*, ed. H. Haferkamp and N. J. Smelser (Berkeley and Los Angeles: University of California Press, 1992), 412–29.

ing from urbanization, industrialization, the expansion of communication, and widespread politicization—but they differ in the institutional "solutions" to these problems, as we have seen in the definitions of the ways in which these problems or "needs" are defined. These differences crystallize out of the selective incorporation—hence, also the transformation—of the major symbolic premises and institutional formations of the original Western civilization as well as that of the traditions and historical experiences of their own civilization.

Here again the case of Japan is of special interest as it connects the analysis of the frameworks of revolutions with the crystallization of different cultural programs of modernity. The interesting point here is the Meiji Ishin, the so-called Meiji Restoration which was indeed very often compared with the great revolutions analyzed above.

The Meiji Ishin did indeed constitute a far-reaching, radical revolutionary breakthrough, but of very distinct type, one which gave rise to a distinct type of modernity not rooted in Axial civilization—even if it developed in response to the impact of Western modernity. The Meiji Ishin was not, contrary to many interpretations, a purely political event. Like the great revolutions, it was a process which, out of a more fluid vision and actions of multiple actors, gave rise to the crystallization and promulgation of a new cultural and political program—a vision of far-reaching transformation of society—which was to no small extent influenced by the impact of the West. But this program, and the discourse that developed during the revolutionary process, was characterized by some distinct features which bear on it being called a "restoration," or rather a renovation, and not a revolution.

True enough, the term "restoration" is not an accurate translation of "ishin," although some of the early ideological foundations have the "osei fukko" legitimized in terms of restoration. As Tetsou Najita has pointed out, its real connotation is to "pull together the disparate trends of society in a new direction." The discourse of the ishin implied the search for some basis of knowledge for ordering society and saving people and on the reexamination of the principles of reconstruction of social order.

The discourse that developed at the end of the Tokugawa period and during the Ishin and in the Meiji state contained several elements which can probably be found in all programs of modernity. Two potentially contradictory elements have been the more pragmatic of state formations and the more "social" egalitarian communal themes of social justice and participation. The tensions between these two components were to be found in other cultural programs of modernity—be they the "original" Western and American (including Latin American) ones as well as later Eastern European and Asian ones—and in the Meiji Ishin.

But the way in which these tensions worked out—ideologically and insti-

tutionally—differed greatly between the Meiji regime and the postrevolutionary regimes in societies which developed out of Axial civilizations.

The crux of this difference was indeed rooted in, or closely connected
with, the Axial or non-Axial roots of, respectively, the great revolutions and
the Meiji Ishin. Of special importance in this context was the nature of the
utopian components or orientations, especially the relative predominance of
universalistic, missionary, future-oriented orientations, which necessarily entailed a strong break with the past.

It is indeed here, in the cultural program promulgated in the revolution
and in the postrevolutionary regimes that some of the distinctive characteristics of the Meiji Ishin which distinguish it from the great revolutions are to be
found. This program differed greatly from that of most of the great revolutions.
It was in a way the reverse mirror image of those of the great revolutions—
although in many ways it was no less radical.

The new cultural program and the cosmology and ontology entailed in it
were promulgated as the renovation of an older archaic system (which in fact
never existed), not as a revolution aimed at changing the social and political
order in an entirely new universalistic direction. Utopian, future-oriented visions, rooted in a universalistic-transcendental vision, were, in contrast to the
other revolutions, very weak and almost nonexistent, although millenarian re-
storative themes were prominent in different sectors of the uprising before and
during the restoration.

Concomitantly in the Meiji Ishin there did not develop, as was the case
in the great revolutions in Europe, the United States, Russia, and China, a
universalistic, transcendental, missionary ideology, or any components of class
ideology—two elements which were also very weak in the peasant rebellions
and movements of protest of the Tokugawa period. Some elements of a universal civilizing mission developed in the late Meiji in attitudes towards Korea and
China, but these did not entail the conception of these societies constituting,
together with the Japanese ones, parts of a general universal civilization. The
Meiji Ishin was inward-oriented towards the Japanese people; it aimed at the
revitalization of the Japanese nation, at making it capable of taking its place in
the modern world, but it had no pretense to "save" the entire world—mankind
as a whole—in terms of a new universalistic, future-oriented utopian vision.
Many of the leaders of groups which were active in the restoration emphasized
the importance of learning and of promulgating universal knowledge, but very
few of them translated it into principles of overall political action, of ways to
reconstruct the Japanese polity and collectivity—and these leaders lost out
very early in the game. Similarly, explicit social symbolism—especially class
symbolism—was almost entirely absent and was certainly not incorporated
into the major symbols of the new regime—not even in connection with the
semiutopian, or rather "inverted utopian," restorationist themes.

XXIII

The researches on the different Axial civilizations and on the processes of revolution do indeed bear on the reappraisal of the major problems of sociological theory as they have developed in contemporary discourse. Such reappraisal was indeed incorporated within most of these researches, and I have addressed these problems in explicitly theoretical articles. One of them is in "The Order-maintaining and Order-transforming Dimensions of Culture" included in this collection as chapter 12.

In this article, I have systematically developed the insights about the relations between culture and social structure further as presented in "Charisma and Institution Building." In "Order-maintaining and Order-transforming Dimensions of Culture," I emphasize that the "order-maintaining" aspects of culture ("culture as opium for the people") and the "order-transforming" aspects of culture are both inherent in the very interweaving of culture and social structure in the process of crystallization of institutional formations. This double aspect of culture is best illustrated in the ubiquity of themes, movements of protest, and liminal situations in the construction of social formations[70] which I illustrate in this article, basing myself on more elaborate researches. It is indeed such themes, movements, and situations that provide—as I have hinted already in "Charisma and Institution Building"—one of the most important links between the charismatic dimension of human activities and institution building and between culture, social structure, and change.

"Order-maintaining and Order-transforming Dimensions of Culture" also explicates the point that culture and social structure are not, as has been assumed in recent controversies, two distinct ontological, easily reifiable, entities but, as was seen among the classics and in the structural-functional approach, two analytical dimensions of any pattern of social interaction. It is also made clear that the mode in which these two dimensions are interwoven in different situations and patterns of interaction, the reappraisal of the relations between culture and social structure, should constitute one of the major foci of sociological analysis, as has been more recognized in some recent developments in sociological theory.

XXIV

All these discussions also bear on the reevaluation of the problem of functional analysis—that analysis which has constituted the starting point and focus of most theoretical controversies in the social sciences since the sixties. In my

70. S. N. Eisenstadt, "Comparative Liminality: Liminality and Dynamics of Civilization," *Religion* 15 (1985). See also chapter 12, "The Order-Maintaining and Order-Transforming Dimensions of Culture."

short article on functional analysis,[71] I have attempted to present such a reevaluation, taking into account the numerous controversies around it but also trying not to throw out the baby with the bathwater.

The central point of such a reevaluation has been an examination of a concept central to structural-functional analysis—namely, that of so-called systemic needs or prerequisites. Basing myself on the various researches mentioned here, I have noted that all relatively continuous settings of social interaction exhibit strong systemic tendencies, and "needs" or "prerequisites" develop within them; they have to be, as it were, taken care of in order for such settings to continue. Contrary, however, to the assumptions of the structural-functional school, such systems are not closed, nor are their needs or prerequisites "given."

Construction of concrete systemic boundaries, of the "needs" and prerequisites of various patterns of social interaction, with their—even if very low— systematic tendencies, is effected through the cultural definition of political, economic, and religious activities and of various situations of interaction. Such definitions derive from the symbolic or ideological evaluations rooted in a society's basic ontological concepts of the unique elements of human experience. Culture mediates in the definition of sex, growth, and aging; of mental and physical capacities; and of the importance of time. It mediates definitions of the major arenas of social activity as well, specifying the ground rules that regulate social interaction and the flow of resources. Such definitions and regulations construct the broad meaning, contours, and boundaries of the major institutional formations, that is, the types of centers, the patterns of authority, the modes of social hierarchy, the modes of economic production and polity, and the like.

In other words, each institutional formation is shaped—to a very large extent—by a distinct cultural program or programs rooted in distinct ontological visions and conceptions of social order promulgated by different influential elites, often contested by different countercoalitions. The concrete institutional dynamics of each such society are shaped by the interaction between the attempts to implement such visions and the structural constraints of different political-ecological settings. Moreover, no setting of social interaction, excluding macrosocietal settings, is constructed as a "closed system"—its systemic boundaries are, in principle, rather loose and fragile, and no population is enclosed within any single system.

This reevaluation of the starting points of the structural-functional school—based as it is on the theoretical discussions and controversies and research analyzed above—bears very closely on some of the major theoretical

71. S. N. Eisenstadt, "Functional Analysis in Anthropology and Sociology: An Interpretative Essay," *Annual Review Anthropology* 19 (1980):243–60.

problems which became the point of controversy from the seventies on—mainly in "agency vs. structure," the relations between culture and social structure as well as in the very concept of social structure.

In the last essay, "Action, Resources, Structure, and Meaning"—which was written especially for this collection—I have taken up, in close relation to some of the more recent works in sociological theory, some of these problems, bringing together the major threads of analysis developed in these essays.[72]

72. See especially J. C. Alexander, ed., *Durkheimian Sociology: Cultural Studies* (Cambridge: Cambridge University Press, 1989); idem, *Action and its Environments* (New York: Columbia University Press, 1988); J. C. Alexander and S. Seidman, ed, *Culture and Society: Contemporary Debates* (Cambridge: Cambridge University Press, 1991); J. C. Alexander, B. Giesen, R. Munch, and N. Smelser, ed., *The Macro-Micro Link* (Berkeley and Los Angeles: University of California Press, 1977); B. Giesen, *Die Intellektuellen und die Nation: Eine deutsche Achsenzeit* (Frankfurt: Suhrkamp Verlag, 1993); R. Munch and N. J. Smelser, ed, *Theory of Culture* (Berkeley and Los Angeles: University of California Press, 1992).

One

THE PLACE OF ELITES AND PRIMARY GROUPS IN
THE ABSORPTION OF NEW IMMIGRANTS IN ISRAEL

I

THIS PAPER IS BASED on an extensive research project on the assimilation of new immigrants in Israel and is intended to provide an analysis of one particular significant aspect of the problem.

The fieldwork on which this material is based was carried out from October 1949 to November 1950, in ten centers of new immigrants' settlement—three urban quarters, three semiurban quarters, and four cooperative agricultural settlements—and dealt mainly with "new" immigrants, those who arrived after the establishment of the State of Israel. The average length of stay of the immigrant in Israel was, at the end of the fieldwork, about nineteen months.

The fieldwork was executed in the following way: In each place a fieldworker—or, in the urban centers, a group of two or three fieldworkers—established himself as a student of the problems of new immigrants. The fieldwork was based on three techniques: (1) continuous, systematic observation of the behavior of the new immigrants in various typical social situations—work, school, public life, religious life, relief agencies, and, to some degree, home life; (2) intensive "free," "open-ended" interviewing of a selected sample in each place (usually a random sample within each main "ethnic" group) according to prearranged schedules, which were not, however, distributed during the interviews;[1] and (3) more extensive and free conversations and interviews with a

Originally published in *American Journal of Sociology* 57 (1951):222–31. © 1951 by The University of Chicago. All rights reserved.

This research project has been sponsored jointly by the Jewish Agency and the Hebrew University (under a grant for sociological research from Mr. G. Wise) and executed at the research seminar in sociology of the university. All the quotations in this paper are from the interviews in the files of the research project. A detailed first report is being published in Hebrew, and more extensive reports in Hebrew and English are planned.

1. These interviews took place either in the immigrants' homes or on informal walks and usually included the adult and adolescent members of the family. The schedule dealt with a variety of topics, namely, their general background, motives for immigration, general identification, levels of aspiration in different spheres, social participation and identification, etc. This sample served also as a panel for repeated interviewing on different problems of attitudes and behavior, such as identi-

larger sample of immigrants, usually with a great part of the inhabitants of a given quarter. These latter were used for obtaining more general background information and for investigation of various points raised during the intensive interviews. All these interviews varied in the degree of their intensity. Altogether about nine hundred families were investigated in some systematic way. (This does not include all those touched upon during the general observations.)

This paper is based on general observation and acquaintance with about nine hundred families (about 2,500 persons), of which three hundred have been interviewed systematically and one hundred and eighty intensively on certain problems. The ethnic distribution of these families was as follows (it did not change to any great extent) in all these groups: Yemenite Jews, about 15 percent; North African Jews, 35 percent; Turkish Jews, 10 percent; Balkan (Yugoslav and Bulgarian) Jews, 25 percent; Central European Jews, 15 percent. These groups represented not only different ethnic origins but also different types of Jewish communities and tradition, and this fact was sometimes useful in checking the cultural limitations of different hypotheses.

The central problem of the investigation was to analyze the main ways and processes in which different groups of immigrants became integrated into the new social structure. Although these groups differed in size, extent of social relations, composition, and degree of cohesion, almost everywhere they could be designated as "primary groups,"[2] based mostly on kinship and previous neighborhood ties. Throughout the various dislocations caused by immigration, these groups were the immigrants' mainstay and the center of their most continuous and effective social relations and of their basic social identifications. It has been amply demonstrated in almost all our cases that any kind of integration into the new social system could be effected only by changing the roles, values, and social perspectives of these groups and not by breaking them up or neglecting them. This is in line with some conclusions of recent social research: that the identification of the members of any given social system with the values of this system are mediated through different primary groups and their specific identifications and values[3] and that the best way of effecting a

---

fication with the new country, participation in the new social setting, etc., in regard to which changes may have taken place during the year. The interviews were undertaken only after the field workers established themselves in the places and were extended in time and on many topics repeated three or four times, according to changing conditions and situations.

2. The term "primary group" is defined here essentially in the same way as by Kingsley Davis, *Human Society* (New York: Rinehart & Co., 1949), 289 ff.

3. See, for a summary of these findings, E. A. Shils, *The Present State of American Sociology* (Glencoe, Ill.: Free Press, 1948), pp. 40 ff.; and E. A. Shils and M. Janowitz, "Cohesion and Disintegration in the Wehrmacht in World War II," *Public Opinion Quarterly* 12 (1948).

change of an individual's behavior is by changing the values and patterns of behavior of the group(s) in which he participates.[4]

Although this general conclusion has been amply demonstrated throughout our investigation, it became quite clear that it could not, in its general form, account for the great diversity of degrees and types of integration and identification and that a more differentiated analysis was called for. On the one hand, we had to distinguish between these different types of integration and identification; and, on the other hand, we had to analyze the different types of "mediation" between the primary groups and the total social system which could account for this diversity. Special importance should have been attached to the location of the "mediators" and of the situations in which the mediation takes place. From the beginning of our investigation, the importance, from this point of view, of the elites and leaders stood out quite clearly. The relations of the members of the elite to the different primary groups of the immigrants and to the new social system seemed to be of great importance in determining the directions and types of integration of the new immigrants into the new social structure. The problem has been investigated systematically, and this paper reports in outline the results of this investigation. Because of the limitation of space, only the most necessary and basic outlines are given here.

We have defined here as elites those groups which occupy relatively high positions in the social strata and/or which hold positions of leadership, influence, and power. This definition assumes that, although the elites are distinct groups within the social system, they are not necessarily identical with "class positions" and that they may be, to some degree (which differs in different societies), dispersed among different social strata. The main emphasis in our definition is on recognized leadership and influence within different areas, which need not coincide with any specific stratum and does not necessarily appertain to *all* members of such a stratum. Our definition assumes also the plurality of elites—that the elites of a given social system need not be unified and organized. These assumptions were mainly based on our material, in which the existence of many different elites, often not identical with a specific social stratum, has been easily discerned. Some of such instances may be found among the different traditional, religious elites of rabbis, etc., and among leaders of Jewish communities in the Diaspora which did not always correspond with any social stratum. The diversity of elites was strongly emphasized in our case, owing to the disruption of the social fabric and the dislocations caused by immigration.

---

4. K. Lewin, *Resolving Social Conflicts* (New York: Harper & Bros., 1948), chap. iv; K. Lewin, "Group Design and Social Change," in T. Newcomb and E. Hartley, *Readings in Social Psychology* (New York, 1941), 330–45.

II

In order to analyze the importance of the elites in the process of integration of immigrants, we had, at first, to see what were the most important dimensions of participation within the new social structure and of identification with it. The following seemed to be most pertinent to our present analysis,[5] and, although they are mostly related to the specific situation of new immigrants, they appear to be of more general importance and applicable, to some degree, to a "stable social structure."

1. Participation in the Social Structure

1. *The extent of new social roles performed by the immigrants and the degree of their participation in the main institutional spheres of the social structure.*—Almost all immigrants had, of course, to assume from the beginning various roles in the economic sphere, but they greatly differed in their disposition to participate in other spheres—the civic, political, educational, cultural (in learning the new language, participating in festivals, cultural activities), etc.

2. *The degree of successful performance of these roles and of stabilization of social relations within the different spheres.*—This distinction is of great importance in our specific case, because of the great cultural heterogeneity of the immigrants. In many cases we found immigrants with strong aspirations toward the performance of civic, political, etc., roles who could not, however, realize these aspirations because of their complete ignorance of the different cultural assumptions underlying them.

2. Identification with the Social Structure

1. *Positive or negative identification with the new country and its main social values.*— This distinction was important because for many immigrants the new country was, as it were, "on trial" from the point of view of realizability of their aspirations.

2. *The "breadth" of identification and social orientations.*—This dimension may be best explained as related to the scope of social roles and values on the realization of which the positive identification with the country depends. On the one hand, there were those whose aspirations were mainly limited to the successful maintenance of their families and jobs and whose values and attachments were centered mainly on them. On the other hand, there were those whose aspirations were oriented toward broader clusters of roles and who judged the new country according to "broader," more inclusive systems of values—whether they be political, religious, etc. Our problem was, then, to find out whether

---

5. A different aspect of this problem has been analyzed by David F. Aberle in "Shared Values in Complex Societies," *American Sociological Review* 15, no. 4 (August 1950): 495–502.

any connection exists between different relations between the immigrants and their elites and the development of these various dimensions of participation and identification. The two main conclusions, which form the framework of our analysis, were found to be the following: (*a*) the extent of social participation and the breadth of identification of the immigrants with the new country are functionally related to the extent of relations existing between the immigrants and their members of their elites (e.g., the elites of their former social structure), and (*b*) the social and cultural orientations of the immigrants are to a very large extent identical with those of their elites.

Among the immigrants investigated by us, two main types could be distinguished from the point of view of the first conclusion. The first type consisted mainly of more or less isolated families, the members of which participated in almost no communal activities with other immigrants from the same country or town and whose main constant social relations were confined to family life. They perpetuated few of their former social relations and cultural activities, and any constant wider relationship was confined to neighbors, relatives, and in some—the most active—cases to regular attendance at a given synagogue. The relations between the members of these families and the elites of their former social structure were either nonexistent or minimal, confined to chance encounters without any stability or duration. (This was true of about 80 percent of the families of this type. About 15 percent of such isolated families themselves belonged to the elites and became disconnected from their former society either because of the destruction of Jewish communities in Europe or during migration.)

The second type consisted of families who lived in more or less close relations patterned after their old social structure and was mostly confined to immigrants from the same country who were known to one another in different degrees. Although their former social structures and relations could not, in any case, be wholly perpetuated in the new country, these families were trying, in different degrees, to perpetuate them at least in some spheres. The degree of this participation in communal groups varied among these families, but it was highly correlated with stable and intensive relations with their former elites. This relationship was maintained by about 73 percent of all these families, the percentage rising with a more intensive participation in communal groups.

The extent of relations with the elites was highly correlated with the extent of participation within the new social structure and with the "breadth" of identification with it. Among 78 percent of the families of the first type (i.e., most of the families who were not themselves members of the elites), the extent of participation within the new social structures was very small and rarely extended beyond the spheres of family, neighborhood, and sometimes their place of work. At the same time the breadth of their identification with the new social system was limited, and in about 70 percent of the families (which overlap largely with the families with limited participation) it was confined to achievement of stability for their families and in their jobs without any orientation toward other institutions and values. Within the second type, the picture was still more diversified. First, we see that here also those families whose contacts with the elites were less intensive showed, in general, a much higher tendency to less participation within the new structure and more limited breadth of identification with it than families whose relations with elites were more intensive and stable.

The crucial evidence for this conclusion comes from those families of immigrants who, through change of place of residence, either became disconnected from their former "ethnic" groups and elites or were brought in once more within its orbit. The number of these cases in our inquiry was not great—about twenty-five families in all—but in twenty-two a definite change in the extent of their participation and breadth of identification took place. Participation and identification subsided to a large extent among those who became disconnected from their elites, while those who came within the orbit of the elites increased also their participation and intensified their identification with the new society. As one of them has put it:

> In [their former place] we did not know anything about festivals, politics, etc. There was nobody to tell us, and we were not really interested. It was all so strange. Here, however, it is different; it is changed. There are here some very important people from our town, who have explained these things to all. They are very important here also, and it is now really very interesting to take part in all these activities . . . They should know, and they have helped us a lot. We do not feel so "alone" any more, and here is really our land.

In this type, however, the close relation between participation and identification, which we have encountered in the first type, did not exist to such a large extent. While the breadth of identification was large in about 85 percent of these families, only about 65 percent of them (on the average) showed a high degree of real, active participation within the various spheres of the new structure (outside the sphere of family). We see also that this participation was not equally distributed among the main different spheres of activities—the civic and political, the "educational" (participation in school committees), the religious, etc. These diversities bring us to our second conclusion. Almost all the families (the 20 percent of the second type) among whom there existed the discrepancy between participation in the new social structure and the breadth of identification with it were attached to traditional religious elites, the members of which showed little inclination to participate within those spheres of activities based on "modern" secular assumptions. At the same time, however, their identification with the new social structure was based on inclusive, usually religious-national, values which were oriented toward wider institutional spheres. An interesting example of this attitude is found in the following remarks in an interview:

> No, we are not interested in politics and parties. We have our rabbis, our synagogue, our friends—the whole "community." This is enough for us. Our rabbis and wise men are better than the "bosses" who do not know the Holy Law. We live according to our ancient laws which are the truly Jewish ones, and it would be better if all the Jews would live so. But if they do not, we do not want to get involved with them more than is necessary, as in work.

We see here that the social orientation of the new immigrants is to a large extent identical with that of the elites. This explains also the unequal distribution of activities within different spheres among different groups of immigrants. In most cases, it was found that the participation within any specific sphere was identical with that of their elites and that diversity was mainly accounted for by the cultural heterogeneity of both the elites and the whole body of immigrants. On the average about 75 percent, and in no case less than 55–60 percent, of the members of a given group of immigrants tended to concentrate their activities in the same field as their elites. (This holds, of course, only for the period of our investigation, i.e., the first year or eighteen months in the new country.)

III

These findings show us that the elites perform a very important function as "mediators" between the primary groups of the immigrants and the wider social structure and that the extent of the participation within it and identification with it is to a large measure dependent on the existence and permanence of this mediation. The identification of the immigrants with the new society is to a large extent effected through their identification with the elites, and the elites seem to influence the formation of the values and activities of the primary groups.

In what ways does this mediation take place? This problem can be analyzed from two related points of view—the structural and the psychological. From the structural point of view, we have to analyze the different types of activities and situations in which the meeting between the primary groups and the elites takes place and the importance of these in the social structure. From the psychological point of view, we have to analyze the problems and needs of the immigrants which are solved and fulfilled by these relations.

Structurally, these meeting points have two outstanding characteristics. First, among those who had a strong, active orientation on the new country, the elites usually tried to act as intermediaries between the new system and the immigrant. This was usually effected by trying to monopolize the distribution of most benefit accruing to the new immigrants—to organize work, rehabilitation, distribution of housing, allowances for "first arrangements," schooling facilities, etc. On the other hand, they began to organize their fellow countrymen within the new institutional framework so as to enable them to perform the main roles—civic, political, educational, cultural—incumbent on them. They were, as it were, the main linking points with wider and more diversified clusters of roles. The stability of the new participation and identification was to a large degree dependent on the successful performance of this double task. Wherever this success was not achieved, either because of cultural or of personal incompatibility or corruption, social disorganization developed.

Second, the success of the elites was also largely dependent on the extent to which they maintained close personal relations with their fellow countrymen. These relations were usually of two types—either traditional, rigorously defined situations, such as attendance at the synagogue, arbitration in disputes, laying-down of norms, etc., or more informal meetings, discussions, and explanations. In our investigation it has been clearly shown that only insofar as the elites maintained these contacts were they successful in directing and influencing the people and that, whenever they sought shelter behind formal bars or did not show great activity in these situations, their influence subsided to a large extent.

Throughout the interviews, and among themselves, the immigrants emphasized that their attachment to their leaders was dependent to a large extent on the maintenance of these close face-to-face relations. Whenever the leader did not maintain them, it was seen as a sign of estrangement and mutual distrust. This demand for personal relations did not assume any feeling of equality or of common participation in all spheres of activity. On the contrary, quite often they used to emphasize the superior status of the members of the elites and the necessity to confine the relations between them to specific situations and meetings. Their success and continuity depend, however, on the maintenance of close personal relations within these meetings.

We see, then, an extension here of primary relations, which are, however, confined to specific limited situations and which are based on a definite differential allocation of authority and influence and in which the relations obtaining between the leaders and the people are asymmetrical. It is through full participation in these situations that the elite fulfil the various needs and solve the problems of their fellow countrymen. Our interview material, based on intensive interviewing of a small sample (about 180), reveals to us what these functions are. The main functions which were mentioned in most interviews (although, of course, in different proportions) seem to be the following:

1. *Structuring and defining of new, wider fields of social relationship and explaining them in terms of the traditional values and attitudes.* —

> A. and C . . . know everything and understand all the problems of the government bureaus, the schools, the bureau of employment. It is so entirely different from the way things were in Morocco; we did not have such problems there. Everything was more or less settled there, and, wherever some difficulties arose, there were some people like A. who knew what it meant. It is very good that they are here also. When they explain all these things, they do not seem so strange and terrible . . .

> It is very good that we have our wise men here. Otherwise we would be lost, because only they can tell us what all these things are, why it is so different here. There came many other people who tried to tell us, but they were strangers, and we felt that they did not understand us, and we could not really believe them. At home it is all right, more or less as we used to be, but everything else is different, and it is good that they can tell us about it.

It is important to note here that, although this function is emphasized because of the necessity to adapt to the new country, it is at the same time usually seen as a continuation of a similar function in the "old" country. About 55–60 percent of the interviewees expressly mentioned and elaborated this theme.

2. *Help in solution of problems relating to participation in wider clusters of roles.* —This is, of course, an extension of the former function, but here the more active and behavioral aspect prevails. Here is demanded not only "explanation" and clarification of situations but active guidance in daily problems of behavior.

> Whenever we do not know what to do, we come and ask them . . . They are able to tell us what we have to do, how can we best get the work, to what schools to send our children. These parties and elections are also so confusing, and we do not know what they are for and how one should behave there . . . They explain it to us and advise what to do. If it were not for this, we would probably get lost and suffer a lot . . .

> I am a simple man and quite often do not know what to do . . . whether it is good or bad to go and ask for something in the bureau, how to get the things I need and want. Many people come and tell us—vote this way, send the children here, go and try to work here . . . It is good that we have got some of our people—they are really important—who know all this and advise us what to do. If they are good people, they usually know and help us.

Throughout the interviews many concrete instances of this help were told, and about 60 percent of the interviewees enlarged on this theme.

3. *Mediation of wider, inclusive value systems of the wider social structure.*—This function is, of course, of more complex character than the previous ones, and its existence is usually dependent on the successful performance of the others. The interviewees many times indicated that full understanding of the wider, ultimate values of the society and attachment to them was to a large extent dependent on their relations with the elites. As this problem was not directly connected with the difficulties of adjustment in the new country, it was more difficult to dwell on it, and only about 40 percent of the interviewees mentioned it one way or another; but it seems that its importance may be much greater. Some typical comment is the following:

> Whenever I talk with H . . . , he makes me understand better the great problems of our tradition, of the way of life we have to lead here and the issues at stake . . . I am a religious man myself, but it is different with him. He understands really the great problems, the important things and not only the small things.
>
> J. is of great help . . . He seems to make us feel the things we believe in . . . I am a good worker and believe in the rights of workers, in social equality, but somehow it is so far from daily life. It is when we meet with J. and M. we feel nearer to it.

Closely connected with this function is the next one.

4. *Symbolization of the social system and of belongingness to it.*—This function has been mostly emphasized by some of those immigrants coming from traditional settings, whose relations with the elites took place largely in clearly defined situations and usually have some symbolic meaning (religious ceremonies, etc.). The same theme was, however, also sometimes elaborated by immigrants coming from secular-formal societies in regard to some of their political leaders.

> When we take part in the meetings at the synagogues or at the different "committees" and see the rabbis and wise men, we really feel that we belong to the People of Israel. It is like seeing Ben-Gurion.
>
> I think that A. is for most of us the representative of the whole Jewish people. He is one of us, but at the same time he knows so well all the important people and matters . . .

From this it may be seen that, first, the elites serve as symbols of security and identification by bringing, as it were, the more inclusive values and the prerequisites of new roles within the orbit of the primary groups of the immigrant. Second, they are the main channels of communication connecting the immigrants, living in their primary groups, and the values and problems of the total social structure. Their crucial importance as channels of communication may be seen, in our case, from the fact that almost all cases in which various parties and organizations tried to bypass them proved a failure and did not succeed in organizing the immigrants within their folds or in arousing any great interest among the immigrants for their problems, issues, etc.

IV

The importance of the attachment to the elites in achieving a sense of security within the social structure and identification with it was emphasized in those cases when this attachment or relation was severed or endangered. Such occasions arise often in situations of flux-like immigration, and two typical cases have been encountered in our investigation. Quite often the members of the elites failed in insuring the immigrants the different benefits and rights accruing to them—either because of misunderstandings caused by cultural incompatibility or because of personal corruption. A second, and perhaps more important, case was the development of competition among different groups within the elites for the monopolization of the contacts with the government agencies or the emergence of new groups claiming status for themselves and competing with the old elites.

It is obvious that these developments are of great general importance in the breaking-down of the old social and cultural pattern in the new country. This last process is in itself of great importance for the understanding of the place of the elites in the social structure in general.

We shall dwell here, however, only on those aspects closely connected with our problem. In most of the cases, whenever one group did not succeed in establishing itself firmly, two developments usually took place. First, the extent of social participation in the different new organizations diminished, and within their own groups different tensions, leading sometimes to manifestations of aggression and disorganization, arose. Sometimes this was also combined with a decrease in the breadth of identification, although it was usually difficult to establish this through the interviews. Second, in most cases there emerged a definite negative identification with the new country. In most cases, the inadequacy of the elites (or competition between them) was definitely frustrating, diminishing the sense of security within the new social structure. About 60–65 percent of those interviewed on this expressed this feeling; more than half of the remainder consisted of "mobile" families who either tried to break independently into the new social structure or claimed for themselves the status of elites. The new country was usually identified as the source of this frustration, as being "strange," not providing security, and confusing. In some cases this feeling was also oriented toward leaders who did not fulfil their functions and gave rise to apathy and loss of interest. In other cases the new immigrants identified themselves with their leaders against the new country and the emergence of some embryonic "ethnic" group symbols. The exact analysis of all these processes is, however, outside the limited scope of this paper.

It would be worthwhile, however, to dwell briefly on an additional aspect of the problem—namely, some characteristics of the "mobile" families, that is, the families aspiring to the status of elites and competing for it. It is interesting to point out the attitudes of these families toward the functions of the elites. The "mobile" persons did not deny the necessity of fulfilling these functions for the nonelite groups. Their stand was that they themselves are more qualified to fulfil these tasks and that they do not need any further guidance in the wider social field. This was usually elaborated in several ways, the most important of which were the following: (a) The old elites cannot perform these functions in the new setting, as their cultural tradition is not adapted to it, and they can only hinder the full and speedy absorption of the immigrants in the new country. (b) They emphasize that their own identification with the new social system and participation in it are not dependent on the attachment to the old elites. They feel that their own understanding of the new system is a better one and that their identification with it is fuller and more intensive. (c) They emphasize that they are fully capable of participating in the new system "on their own" without the intermediary of the elites. To them this full participation in the important situations and roles is the most cogent symbolical expression of their belongingness to the new society, and they do not need any other groups to symbolize it for them. As one of them has put it: "We are more close to the government and to Ben-Gurion. Although we do not know them, we feel that we know them, that we know better than others what the Yishuv [the Jewish Community in Palestine] really needs and stands for. We do not need these 'old fools' to explain it to us." (d) At the same time, almost all emphasize their wish to lead their fellow countrymen and to establish themselves as the new elite. They emphasize that they are able to communicate the values of the new system and its problems to their fellow immigrants and their wish to do so.

These brief indications show that mobility and aspiration to elite status are closely connected not only with a fuller social participation but also, and perhaps mainly, with a more active and independent one, the main characteristics of which are the feeling of *closer* relation to the main social values, the emphasis on the symbolic importance of one's own performance of various roles connected with these values, and the wish to communicate these values (e.g., to symbolize them to some extent) to other people. This may indicate that, although the processes of mobility and the interchange of elites may change the personnel and the values of the elites and the social system, they tend to emphasize the importance of the elites and the functions they perform in the social system and are oriented not toward the abolishment of this function but toward its reorientation and reorganization according to different values.

V

This analysis is a preliminary one which has dwelt only on some aspects of the problem. First, the different "deviant" cases have not been fully analyzed, and the very important problem of mobility has been only briefly and inadequately mentioned. Second, we have been dealing with "people" and societies in flux, and our conclusions may need modification, or at least elaboration, when applied to stable social systems. It would be worthwhile, however, to state our conclusions and some of their ramifications, tentative as they may be. We have started from the general conclusion that the identification of the members of a given social system with its values is to a great extent mediated through the values of their primary groups. This conclusion could not account, however, for the great diversity in the breadth and intensity of identification and of extent of participation in the social system. It seems that in every social system there are, on the one hand, members whose roles and social perspective are closely related and oriented toward the ultimate values of the society and whose participation in it is more inclusive, confined not only to basic minimal social areas; and, on the other hand, people whose roles and perspective are much narrower and confused. Our problem has been to understand in what ways the ultimate values of the system are brought home to the members with a lower level of participation and how their identification with these values is maintained.

Our tentative conclusion is that the maintenance or breadth of identification with the ultimate values of the system is dependent on the existence of specific social situations in which these values are communicated to the members of the system. In these situations people of different degrees of intensity of identification and participation interact with one another, the more active serving as communicators of the ultimate values of the social system. We have explored here one type of interaction—namely, that between members of elites and their "followers," members of manifold basic primary groups. Although these situations are to some degree extensions of the primary groups, most of the roles enacted in them are outside the scope of these groups, and they bring in a definitely new element—the definite differential allocation of authority and prestige. These situations are extensions of primary groups in so far as they are largely based on personal relations and spontaneous identification. Identification with broader, inclusive social values is mediated here through identification with the members of the elites, whose roles are to be more closely related to these values. The identification with the elites supplies a feeling of security within the system and of belonging to it, and any process which undermines this identification is experienced as a definite frustration. The successful and effective performance of their roles as "communicators" seems to be largely dependent on the continuity of this identification, their ability to insure for the members of the different primary groups the different rights and benefits accruing from participation in wider clusters of roles and on the internal consensus within the elites.

It is not, of course, our assumption that the situations explored here are the only ones through which effective communication within a social system is maintained and the ultimate values mediated. Further exploration of the problem may go in the following directions: (1) the analysis of different types of "mediating" and "communicating" situations existing within the social system; (2) the analysis of the prevalence of these different types within different types of societies and social orders; and (3) the analysis of effects of the relative nonexistence of such definitely structured situations and channels of communications. Some aspects of the problem of communication in "mass society" are relevant here.[6]

6. See L. Wirth, "Consensus and Mass Communications," *American Sociological Review* 12, no. 1 (February 1948).

Two

REFERENCE GROUP BEHAVIOR AND SOCIAL INTEGRATION: AN EXPLORATIVE STUDY

RECENTLY, SOCIOLOGISTS HAVE SHOWN a renewed interest in the problems of reference groups. This is as it should be since reference groups are important determinants of an individual's behavior and social orientation and of the behavior of people in multiple-group contexts. Much attention has been focused on the question of why an individual will choose a particular reference group and how this choice is related to his status and status-aspiration.[1] Both Shils' and Merton and Kitt's commentary on the "American Soldier" contributed a great deal to our understanding of the relation between membership and primary groups on the one hand and of reference groups on the other hand.[2]

However, most of the research on reference groups tends to deal with them as determinants of some segments of individual behavior rather than the individual's behavior as related to the functioning and integration of the society. This paper will report on some tentative explorations in this direction. We will try to show how an investigation of reference groups can be interpolated into a systematic analysis of the functioning of a society. Among the questions concerning reference groups we will emphasize *three which seem important.*

First, there is the problem of the relation of the reference groups chosen by an individual to the institutional structure of the society. Are reference groups chosen fortuitously from a welter of existing groups or does there exist a tendency to choose them in terms of some of the values of the society and according to some of the institutional premises and arrangements of that soci-

Originally published in *American Sociological Review* 19 (1954):175–85.

The research reported here has been done under a grant for sociological research from Dr. G. Wise, President of the American Friends of the Hebrew University and Chairman of the Board of Governors of the University. The author is indebted to Dr. S. Klausner for help in the drafting and revision of this paper and for many suggestive comments and criticism.

1. See for most up-to-date presentation of the data, T. Newcomb, *Social Psychology,* New York: 1951, chs. 6, 7; and E. and R. Hartley, *Fundamentals of Social Psychology,* New York, 1952, pp. 465–77.

2. See their papers in R. Merton and P. Lazarsfeld (eds.), *Continuities in Social Research,* (Glencoe: Free Press, 1951).

ety? Most of the researchers on reference groups have clearly indicated that it is through this "referring" that an individual orients himself beyond his immediate roles toward some wider roles and parts of the society. We are still not clear, however, about the relation between such orientations and the values and organizations of the social system in which he participates, and their influence upon his identification with it.

Second, in order to study the influence of reference groups on an individual's participation within his society, we should investigate the relation between the various reference groups and the actual membership group roles which an individual performs. It can be postulated that orientation toward reference groups reflects the aspirations of an individual in regard to his various social roles. The realizability of levels of aspiration influences an individual's satisfaction with his social role and position and, consequently, his identification with the society in which he lives. Thus, it seems that it would be theoretically important for us to evaluate the individual's membership groups in terms of his reference groups and standards. It is not enough to indicate—as has often been done—the relative influence of reference or membership groups on a given segment of an individual's behavior or attitudes. We need to know the extent to which an individual finds his reference standards realizable within his actual roles. It is proposed here that the extent of this realizability is an important determinant of his identification with the social system, its values, and his conformity with its norms. Then we could investigate the way in which evaluation of membership groups in terms of reference groups influences an individual's identification with the society in which he participates and his conformity with its norms. The hypothesis that such a relation may exist at all is, however, based on the assumptions that (a) the various reference groups chosen by an individual are closely related to the institutional setting of the society in which he participates and (b) the choice of reference groups by an individual is not fortuitous but is definitely related to some of the most important aspects of his personality.

It is here that we touch on the *third* basic problem of reference groups, namely, the investigation of the determinants of an individual's reference groups in terms of his personality needs and the relation of these needs to the individual's place within the society.

THE RESEARCH

The analysis presented here is based on several research projects of the Research Seminar in Sociology at the Hebrew University. The importance of the relation between membership groups, reference groups, and identification with the social system was first discerned in a *general* way in the first stages of the research project on the Absorption of Immigrants in Israel.[3] Some of the insights and the systematic conclusions attained at that stage led us to attempt a special small-scale investigation to elucidate the problems in this field. This investigation served as a starting point for much wider research. At the same time it was found that some aspects of other research projects, mainly those on youth movements, deal with these problems. The following analysis is specifically based on our special small-scale investigation, which we will immediately describe, and on more general conclusions from other investigations.

The special research focused on problems of communication, leadership, and mobility.[4] The sample consisted of 187 new immigrants, who were participating in special courses for community leaders and professional people. We used an open-ended, focused interview, which concentrated on the following points: (a) satisfaction with present situation (economic, social, etc.); (b) aspirations to change and action to achieve these changes; (c) relations within the immigrants' main social groups (family, neighborhood, work, etc.); (d) extent of social participation, and relations with old inhabitants; (e) identification with the country; and (f) attitudes towards the main social norms, values, and groups.

These interviews served as a basis for a much wider investigation of the total population of participants in various training courses in Israel and of the population of certain selected local areas and ethnic groups.

THE CHOICE OF REFERENCE GROUPS

What did the choice of different reference groups mean to the individual? The people investigated not only identified their reference groups but they were also asked why they attach importance to them and why they have chosen these particular groups. There was no uniformity in the choice of particular concrete groups, although quite often several individuals would choose the same concrete groups. There was, however, a marked parallel between the explanations for the particular choices. A content analysis of the answers has revealed that the most important single reason for choice reflected by about 90 percent of the respondents was the importance of their groups in terms of status-conferral within the social structure.[5] Whenever the choice, it was usually made because it was thought that this particular group could confer some

3. See on this the author's papers on "The Process of Absorption of New Immigrants in Israel" and "Institutionalization of Immigrant Behaviour" in *Human Relations*, 5, Nos. 3, 4 (August and November 1953).

4. See the author's memorandum on this Research submitted to the Second International Congress of Sociology, Liege, 1953. (Mimeographed by the Research Seminar in Sociology, The Hebrew University, Jerusalem.)

5. See the above-mentioned memorandum.

prestige in terms of the institutional structure of the society. The following two excerpts from an interview may well illustrate this point: "I want to be like the old settlers in X . . . (a cooperative settlement); they seem to me to be nice people; they know how to live . . . and they are very much respected and honored. They have much influence; they can arrange matters and everybody listens to them . . . If we were like them, we would be important people." "I try always to go to town, to see the young people there, those who are in the clubs . . . I do not always understand them and sometimes they seem to me to behave badly, but they are important. They can get what they want; everybody seems to obey them . . . They behave as if they were important people . . . maybe they are . . . therefore we want to be like them."

Side by side with this rather general orientation toward status-conferral in the choice of reference groups, most of the interviewed differentiated between aspects of their status aspirations. Roughly speaking, the following differentiation was found among most of them (about 85 percent): (a) those aspects which are related to economic goals in the widest meaning—generally to the attainment of various instrumental goals (money, earnings, dwellings, job, various facilities); (b) those aspects relating to social participation and solidarity (the kind of people one lives with, and generally associates with, the extent of sharing values with them, etc.); and (c) those aspects related to a cultural evaluation with a general pattern of life. The interview material showed that the relation between (b) and (c) was a very close one. The extent to which this differentiation was clearly articulated varied. The following is an excerpt from a relatively nonarticulated interview:

"There are so many things I should like to have, like so many people over here. Some people are rich; they may also be nice, but not always. Sometimes I want to be like them, but sometimes they do not seem good pals to me; they do not like to help people. But it is good to know them, to have money and power like them. But their customs are also very strange . . . I think that our customs, the old customs, are best, but we do not get along very much with them."

Our exploration has so far indicated in a general way that the choice of given groups as reference groups is very much determined by the status-aspirations of an individual. Analysis of the interviews has also shown that aspirations are evaluated in terms of the institutional structure of the society in which he participates. Whatever the concrete variety of groups chosen, they tend to have a common denominator in terms of the way the individual evaluates them as status conferrers. The choice of reference groups seems, therefore, to be purely fortuitous—neither from the point of view of the individual nor from that of the social structure. It is the status-evaluation and aspiration that seem to be the focus of this choice from both points of view. Different individuals may, of course, have different status-evaluations and hence choose different groups for reference.

Status-aspiration is not, however, a unitary dimension and we have seen that among most of those investigated three different dimensions of such aspirations existed. It is in terms of this differentiation that the fact that many individuals may choose several reference groups can be easily explained. These findings are in line with those of Hyman's pioneer study on psychology of status, but tend to emphasize more the institutional aspect of status-aspirations and choices.[6]

THE EVALUATION OF MEMBERSHIP GROUPS IN TERMS
OF REFERENCE GROUPS AND ITS RELATION
TO CONFORMITY AND IDENTIFICATION WITH THE SOCIETY

On the basis of these explorations we can now proceed to our next problem, namely, to the evaluation of membership groups in terms of reference groups and its influence on identification with the society and conformity with its norms.

The following four types of evaluation were distinguished: (a) a totally positive one (i.e., the membership groups are seen as a repository, or representative, of the main reference standards and norms); (b) a totally negative one (total opposition); (c) and (d) partial opposition or congruity—only some membership groups succeed or fail to meet reference standards. Types (c) and (d) may be seen as two subtypes of partial evaluation with different overall emphases. It was found that there were 55 people with complete positive evaluation, 26 with complete negative evaluation, 62 with partially positive and 44 with partially negative ones.

We had, then, to find how the different types of evaluation relate to the extent of identification with the society and conformity with its norms. For this purpose, some of the more significant variables of identification and conformity found in the first research on immigrants[7] were explored and then more systematically elaborated.

On the basis of this elaboration, the following variables were systematically investigated in the interviews: (a) identification with the society—positive or negative; and (b) conformity with the main norms of the society, especially in intergroup relations, or deviancy from them, especially intergroup aggression. Table 1 shows us the relation between these factors.

6. It should be emphasized that in our study there were only 16 (about 9 percent) cases in which the choice of reference groups was not explained in terms of one of these status dimensions, and of these 5 were cases of inadequate answers, misunderstanding, etc.

7. See "Institutionalization of Immigrant Behaviour," *op. cit.*

TABLE 1.
RELATION BETWEEN EVALUATION OF MEMBERSHIP GROUP, IDENTIFICATION
WITH THE SOCIETY AND CONFORMITY WITH ITS NORMS

Type of Evaluation of Membership Group	Identification		Conformist or Deviant Tendency		
	Positive	Negative	Conformist Tendency	Deviant Tendency	Total
Positive	25	20	24	21	45
Negative	3	23	2	24	26
Partially positive	57	5	34	28	62
Partially negative	40	4	20	24	44
Total					177

This table shows us some interesting data from which it is clear that the relation between evaluation of membership groups in terms of reference groups is not a very simple one. Thus the simple, commonsense hypothesis that those satisfied with their membership groups tend to be conformist members of the society and to be strongly identified with it, and those who are dissatisfied are not, has to be rejected. We see that there exists some such consistency qamong those who have a wholly negative evaluation, but it does not hold for those with a partially negative (or positive) evaluation or for those with a wholly positive one. Those with a partially or negative evaluation tend mostly to have a positive identification with the society and to be divided on the conformist-deviant variable, while those with a positive evaluation are more or less equally divided on both variables.

SINGLE AND MULTIPLE REFERENCE GROUPS

The explanation of this great complexity of the data, and of the general difference between those with consistent and nonconsistent evaluations and attitudes could be made only with the help of an *intervening variable*. We found and explored one which proved to be of crucial importance in this respect. *This variable was the extent to which the individual's various reference groups were unitary or differentiated.*

Within any complex society there exist many groups and standards to which the individual may refer himself. Different individuals choose different reference groups in terms of their purposes and goals. But individuals may differ as to whether they *define* and evaluate these groups as different from one another or whether they tend to define them as constituting one rather undifferentiated cluster, or even to identify them entirely with one another. Both of these types were found in our research. It became obvious that the definition of the total reference group complex determined very much the extent of the actual choice of different groups. Those with a single group referent tended to limit their possibility of choice, focusing on a very limited number of actual groups that could be brought within the framework of their unitary rigid standards. Those with a multiple group referent evince a possibility of broader choice within the society.

The limitation of the choice of the first type was evident in the fact that they usually applied almost the same concrete standards to every type of group chosen by them. They looked for the identity between them, so that actually their perception of the possibilities of choice was limited. Of special interest is the fact that they usually applied the three main criteria—the instrumental, cultural, and "social" to the same cluster of groups—with almost no differentiation whatsoever.

It was found that those with totally positive evaluation were almost *equally* divided (24 and 21) among those with multiple and single reference groups, and that among those with totally negative evaluation, 23 (out of 26) were single-reference group centered while among all the other types there were about 102 (out of 107) which had multiple group references.

This extent of single or multiple group reference was shown to be crucial in determining the individual's identification with society and his conformist or deviant tendencies. Thus, within the totally positive group there was almost a complete correlation (with only 4 exceptions) between those who have a multiple group referent and positive identification and conformist tendencies and between those with a single group referent and deviant ones (and negative identification).

It may thus be provisionally postulated that a single group referent is very closely correlated with negative identification and deviant tendencies, while a multiple group referent is closely connected with positive identification (but not necessarily with conformist tendencies).

The mere correlation does not, however, provide the reasons for the choice of a single or multiple group referent.

RITUAL AND OPEN STATUS IMAGES

We have seen that the choice of reference group is closely related to the individual's status aspirations. Thus, it is within the individual's status image that we should look for some determinants of this choice. Which aspects of the organization of a status image are relevant? Obviously, it is not the *content* of the status aspirations (and the parallel reference groups) that is crucial here, as there existed a great variety of contents both among the single and the multiple referent group.

We found that a formal, organizing principle was the crucial one—a principle which we had already encountered in our first research on immigrants.[8] *This principle concerned the extent of openness or ritual closeness of the status image.* Let us explain the way in which we have been using these terms.

The status image of an individual is that hierarchy of values according to which he judges himself and his place within the society. Though values may be of different concrete contents, they always relate to some basic orientations of the individual. We have seen that there seem to be *three such basic orientations:* (a) the attainment of various goals; (b) the attainment of solidary primary group relations of mutual affection and response; and (c) the attainment of certain cultural goals, patterns of values, of a way of life. These are the main axes about which every status image of an individual revolves. One of the most important problems in the organization of the status image is the extent of interdependence among these three different orientations. Although some such interdependence may be necessary for the integration of the personality, they are also to some degree autonomous. The second and third orientations in particular may be to some degree independent of the first, that is, an individual may feel that he is acceptable socially and a "good man," even if he does not attain certain goals. On the other hand, an individual may perceive himself in such a way that his social acceptability and his goodness seem to him to be entirely dependent on the attainment of certain goals and amenities—such as money, dwelling, and type of job. These amenities become his symbols of status. It is this type of status image that we call ritual, while the former is an "open" one.[9]

It was found that most (about 90 percent) of the individuals with a ritual status image tended to focus their aspirations on one cluster of reference groups and to evaluate these groups as a unitary, undifferentiated field. This is closely and manifestly related to their lack of differentiation which they tend to focus on one undifferentiated field. It should be possible to find such people both among those with positive and with negative overall evaluation of their membership groups. However, within our sample, they tended to concentrate among the "negative" cases. Only half of the positive ones focused on a single group. Those with the "open" status images, on the other hand, were found

---

8. See S. N. Eisenstadt, "The Process of Absorption of New Immigrants in Israel," *op. cit.*

9. Within the situation of immigration and adaptation the distinction between these two types could become clearly distinguished because of the scarcity of many goals, and the needs of changing goal aspirations. They were empirically established by such questions as: "What is the most important thing you want to attain here?" "From what do you suffer most here?" "What were your main difficulties?" "How could they be helped?" "Who could help you?" "Would they like to help you?" and similar open-ended questions.

among half of the positive consistent ones, and among most of the inconsistent ones. Thus, it seems that there *is a very strong correspondence between the type of an individual's status image and his choice and organization of reference group.* This could explain some of the seeming contradictions encountered above. It is the organization of the status image which mediates between consistency of evaluation according to different reference standards and the focusing of their evaluation on single or multiple groups.

It seems now that the relation between the determinants of single or multiple group referents and positive or negative identification with the society and conformist or deviant tendencies also becomes clear.

Those with ritual status images could not distinguish very much between the attainment of the various types of goals and social relations. The attainment of social solidarity is, for them, conditioned by the attainment of a specific type of instrumental goals and pattern of life. Hence, they cannot differentiate to any large extent between various reference groups, finding within each one the satisfaction of a particular type of goal, but focus all their aspirations on one undifferentiated field with which they identify their overall status aspirations.

For those with a ritual status image it was found that the whole society is symbolized in this field and constitutes an almost unitary reference group. Their identification with the society is conditioned by the maintenance of this status image. This would help to explain their total negative attitude in case of nonrealizability, as well as the strong aggressive and deviant element in case of realizability of their status aspirations. Even when they are satisfied with their position, the implications of this satisfaction run counter to some of the normative aspects of a multiple group society, and they develop strong aggressive tendencies toward some subgroups of the society.

Thus, the dichotomy between open and ritual status images and single and multiple group referents provides us with important organizing principles of reference group behavior, and its relation to the integration of a social system. On the basis of this analysis, *it can be postulated that* those with a ritual status image tend to choose their reference groups and standards in such a way as to *maximize overall disintegrative* tendencies—whether manifest or latent—while those with an open status image tend to choose their reference group so as to spread out the risks between different types of disintegrative behavior and to maximize the possibilities of adjustment within the social system.

Our explorations show us, then, that merely positive or negative evaluation of membership groups in terms of reference groups, mere satisfaction or dissatisfaction with given roles is not, in itself, sufficient to determine the individual's basic attitudes towards his society. It is only insofar as this satisfaction or dissatisfaction is related to his basic status aspiration that it becomes an important determinant. But even here it was found that different individuals tend to be more or less flexible in their status aspirations and that insofar as they are more flexible, the possibilities of maximization of satisfaction and adjustment are greater.

Our analysis is not yet, however, complete. While it has explained the very marked correlation between ritual status aspirations and negative identification with the society and deviant tendencies, it has not yet explained all the variations among those with open status images. Truly enough most of them evince positive identification with the society. But there does not exist such a consistency in relation to the conformity-deviance dichotomy. There are among them about 52 cases with deviant tendencies. These are more or less proportionally distributed among those with a partial negative or positive evaluation of the membership groups. How can these facts be explained? Some general indications are borne out by our material.

The existence of some deviant tendencies among those with open status images could mean that dissatisfaction with even one sphere may sometimes be of such importance as to undermine, if not the individual's basic identification with his society, at least his conformity with its basic norms. May any kind of dissatisfaction be strong enough to influence an individual in a deviant way, or is it confined to dissatisfaction to a specific sphere? Our material suggests that negative evaluation of membership groups in the *solidary* sphere seems to be of special importance to an individual. Thus, among the deviant "open" ones there were 40 who insisted on a negative evaluation of their solidary sphere, while among the conformist "open" ones there were only 12 out of 54. In the interviews the importance of the solidary sphere has also been quite often emphasized by the individuals in several ways. The exact importance of this sphere in relation to others is not, however, yet fully clear, and all that has been said above is merely an indication to be yet fully investigated in further researches. It also seems that it would be worthwhile to differentiate in a more systematic way between various types of conformity and deviancy and their relation to the various spheres of social activities.

SOME INDICATIONS FROM RESEARCH ON YOUTH MOVEMENTS[10]

Let us now turn to the research on youth movements. What light can these results throw upon the variables investigated here?

Two of the problems investigated dealt with the motives for joining the

10. This research has been directed jointly by the author and Mr. J. Ben-David of the Department of Sociology of the Hebrew University to whom the author is indebted for discussion and help in regard to the problem analyzed here. We shall not present here the full data in regard to this research, the results of which will be separately published, but will only touch on some of the problems related to the main problems discussed in this paper.

movements and the types of identification with the social system which the different movements engendered.[11] Broadly speaking, we could distinguish between those movements which more or less accepted the main values of the society (though perhaps giving relatively more emphasis to their source, as with the pioneering values) and those which had a more deviant, rebellious character. Although such a distinction could be relatively easily made, it was found that to some extent this distinction cut across the different movements, as in most of them there were members who tended to put one interpretation or another on the values of their movements. It was also found that a rebellious attitude was usually directed towards members of out-groups and towards the general "renegade" adult society. We attempted to correlate these attitudes and types of identification with the movements with the main types of motivation for joining the youth movements. The common motivation was the feeling of some inadequacy in their family and school roles. They often felt that they could obtain full social acceptance as equals, expressive satisfaction, personal independence, and the like, through the movements since these were not fully gratified in the family and school life. In a way this is similar to the common motive for joining peer groups in most modern societies. In addition, however, there exists a special element in the Israeli scene. Most of the youth movements claim not only to satisfy various social needs of their members but also, and perhaps mainly, to represent the main collective values of the community. Thus, joining them is usually connected with some sort of desire to attain full social status and participation in respect to these common values and symbols of identification of the society. Consequently many members of these movements tend to evaluate the several roles which they perform in their various membership groups, school, family, and others, not only in terms of the satisfaction of immediate personal needs, but also in terms of their relation to the ultimate values of the society. In other words, these values and the status aspirations connected with them serve as one of the main reference standards of the adolescents.

From this point of view, it was found that but few of the members of the youth movements see their basic membership groups as fully representative of the standards and values of the society. But they differed greatly as to whether they thought these groups were relevant to some of the main values of the society and represented them or were basically incompatible with them. Thus, one member would say that good education and moral atmosphere is to be found at home; the school gives proper schooling while the movement in its

11. As we shall see, the various youth movements constitute, within Israeli society, one of the main institutional frameworks through which adolescents are referred to some of the goals and ultimate values of the society.

form gives him "social" education. Another would stress the total opposition of the family and school life to the values represented by the movements, which were seen as the only repositories of the central values of the society.

As could be expected a very high correlation was found between negative evaluation of their membership group and aggressive attitudes to nonmembers of the youth movements. But even more important is the fact that these were very clearly correlated with focusing on certain values and reference standards as the sole manifestations of collective values and the only proper channels for status attainment (or, in the terms of our former discussion, a ritual status image). Coupled with this was a tendency not to participate in many diverse membership groups, but to concentrate on one primary group (the nuclear primary group of the youth movements) as the sole or main group, the roles of which carry full cultural and status evaluation on the part of their members. All the other roles did not provide a basis for the evaluation and were of purely technical and instrumental importance for them. These they segregated from those roles which bore a full solidary expressive value. Among those members of the youth movements who evaluated the various role-clusters as complementary, such a complete segregation did not exist, although there were difficulties in emphasis on the different roles and role-clusters.

These conclusions tend to corroborate those of the previous section, but in addition, they provide dynamic analysis of the interaction between the type of status aspiration and images an individual develops in his behavior in respect to some of the basic institutional possibilities of participation open to him in the social system and their repercussions on his identification with the social system.

The researches on which this paper is based also shed some light on the internal structure of the membership groups which are evaluated by their members. Hitherto we have only concentrated on the evaluation, and have not yet analyzed how it is related to the actual structure of these membership groups, the interaction of their members, and their actual roles within these groups. Although a full analysis of this aspect must be postponed to a separate publication, we will indicate some of the more general conclusions. A high correlation was found between the negative evaluation of membership groups in terms of ritual status aspirations, and a nonsolidary structure of the membership group (a very small extent of mutual primary identification between the members and with the group as such). It is as yet difficult to say whether it is this nonacceptance in the group that motivates the member to seek reference goals beyond it, or vice versa, but there clearly exists some relation between the two. This conclusion corresponds very closely to that arrived at in the initial research on absorption of immigrants in which the concept of ritual status image was developed. There it was found that there was a functional relationship between nonsolidary families and ritual status aspirations, and that it was because of the lack of emotional security within the family that an individual clung to the ritual status image. We hope to be able to analyze this problem in greater detail in the subsequent stages of our research.

DISCUSSION AND CONCLUSIONS

What conclusions may be drawn from this material? What further possibilities and problems for research are indicated by them? It seems that there are at least two possible ways in which reference groups chosen by individuals and the institutional structure of the society are related. *First,* most of the choices of reference groups seem to be made in terms of *status aspirations* of the individual and his *evaluation of the status-conferral* possibilities of different groups within the institutional structure of the society. We have also seen that there may well exist several, but determinate, status dimensions of an individual—the instrumental, solidary, and cultural—in terms of which his choice of reference groups may be made. *Second,* the data on youth movements seem to show that within the society there are special institutional organizations and arrangements through which reference to the basic values of the society is developed and maintained. Within complex societies there are many such frameworks. The problem here concerns the relation between these institutional possibilities open to an individual and his actual choice of reference groups, the extent to which there exist some congruence between the two and the limits of variability of choice in this respect. This is a problem which still awaits further elaboration both in comparative and intensive small-scale investigations. We have only been able to begin to work on these problems.

We have distinguished two main types of choice and organization of different reference groups by an individual, namely, the *single group reference,* that is, all the different reference groups and standards being focused on one undifferentiated cluster of groups; and the *multiple group reference,* involving a greater differentiation and flexibility. We have seen that these types of choice and organization are closely related to ritual or open status images of an individual. It is through this organization that the individual refers himself to the total society in which he participates, minimizing or maximizing the possibilities of adjustment within it, and evaluating his participation in his identification with that society.

This last problem has been explored by analyzing the relation between the individual's evaluation of his membership groups in terms of his reference groups and his identification with the society and its norms. It has been shown that mere satisfaction or dissatisfaction with one's actual roles is not enough to determine one's identification and conformity. In general it has been shown that those individuals who, because of their ritual status image, focus their choices on one cluster of groups, tend to maximize deviant possibilities (even when satisfied, but of course much more when dissatisfied), while those with open status image and multiple group references, may spread out their dissatisfaction and hence minimize its influence on deviant behavior.

This distinction between single and multiple group referents and their influence on the interpretation of the social system is closely related to some suppositions developed by R. Williams and K. Lewin. In his work on intergroup tensions, Williams has submitted the proposition that a society ridden by many minor cleavages is in less danger of open mass conflict than a society with only one or a few major cleavages.[12] This supposition is closely related to K. Lewin's comparative analyses of American and German societies. Our analysis seems to corroborate these suppositions but it also shows the necessity of distinguishing more closely between various types of groups between which the choice can be made. It is from this point of view that the distinction between different types of integrative behavior becomes pertinent.

INDICATIONS FOR FURTHER RESEARCH

Further research might attack the cluster of problems relating to the determinants of the choice of reference groups by an individual. The importance of different types of status images for this choice has been demonstrated, but this leaves open the question as to the conditions which determine the development of these various types of status images and aspirations. In this respect it might be interesting to look into: (1) the structure of the various membership groups, the individual's position within them and their interrelation; and (2) the individual's and the group's position in the main institutional spheres of the social structure.

In addition these determinants of choice should be explored from the point of view of the personality structure of the individual. By combining these two approaches, we could study the relative importance of different reference groups for the individual and their influence on his participation in and identification with society.

We have discussed the ordering of the various reference groups in uniform or diverse clusters mainly from the point of view of the individual. A parallel analysis should be attempted from the point of view of the social structure. Do there exist within different social structures different ways of ordering of the framework of choice of reference groups and of the main interpretive mechanisms of the social structure? Here once more K. Lewin's analysis is indicated but many more systematic researches are needed. What is the mechanism existing within a society whose function it is to develop and maintain reference

12. R. Williams Jr., *The Reduction of Intergroup Tensions*, Social Science Research Council, Bulletin 57 (1947), pp. 56–7 ff.

orientations among its members? Though there has been but little systematic exploration in this direction, it seems that promising results are to be expected from connecting problems of reference groups with those of communication and leadership.[13] Through such an analysis, we could explore the institutional implications of reference group behavior.

We have only stated the problem of deviance and deviant behavior in a preliminary way. There are at least two directions in which it can be explored. First, the main components and types of deviance and of deviant behavior, as analyzed by Parsons in *The Social System*, should be systematically studied in their relation to various types of reference group behavior. Second, looking into the development of deviant reference group orientations and identification with them should prove fruitful. It seems that here, once more, an analysis in terms of communication, and similar terms, may be very profitable.

13. See the author's paper on the place of "Elites and Primary Groups in the Process of Absorption of New Immigrants," in *American Journal of Sociology* 57 (November 1951), pp. 222–31, and the report on this research submitted to the 2nd Congress, Sociology, *op. cit.*

Three

ARCHETYPAL PATTERNS OF YOUTH

YOUTH CONSTITUTES a universal phenomenon. It is first of all a biological phenomenon, but one always defined in cultural terms. In this sense it constitutes a part of a wider cultural phenomenon, the varying definitions of age and of the differences between one age and another.[1] Age and age differences are among the basic aspects of life and the determinants of human destiny. Every human being passes through various ages, and at each one he attains and uses different biological and intellectual capacities. At each stage he performs different tasks and roles in relation to the other members of his society: from a child, he becomes a father; from a pupil, a teacher; from a vigorous youth, a mature adult, and then an aging and "old" man.

This gradual unfolding of power and capacity is not merely a universal, biologically conditioned, and inescapable fact. Although the basic biological processes of maturation (within the limits set by such factors as relative longevity) are probably more or less similar in all human societies, their cultural definition varies from society to society, at least in details. In all societies, age serves as a basis for defining the cultural and social characteristic of human beings, for the formation of some of their mutual relations and common activities, and for the differential allocation of social roles.

The cultural definitions of age and age differences contain several different yet complementary elements. First, these definitions often refer to the social division of labor in a society, to the criteria according to which people occupy various social positions and roles within any society. For instance, in many societies certain roles—especially those of married men, full citizens, independent earners—are barred to young people, while others—as certain military roles—are specifically allocated to them. Second, the cultural definition of age is one important constituent of a person's self-identity, his self-perception in

Reprinted by permission of *Daedalus*, Journal of the American Academy of Arts and Sciences, from the issue "Youth: Change and Challenge," vol. 91, no. 1 (winter 1962).

1. A general sociological analysis of the place of age in social structure has been attempted in S. N. Eisenstadt, *From Generation to Generation* (Glencoe, Ill.: The Free Press, 1956).

terms of his own psychological needs and aspirations, his place in society, and the ultimate meaning of his life.

Within any such definition, the qualities of each age are evaluated according to their relation to some basic, primordial qualities, such as vigor, physical and sexual prowess, the ability to cope with material, social, and supernatural environment, wisdom, experience, or divine inspiration. Different ages are seen in different societies as the embodiments of such qualities. These various qualities seem to unfold from one age to another, each age emphasizing some out of the whole panorama of such possible qualities. The cultural definition of an age span is always a broad definition of human potentialities, limitations, and obligations at a given stage of life. In terms of these definitions, people map out the broad contours of life, their own expectations and possibilities, and place themselves and their fellow men in social and cultural positions, ascribing to each a given place within these contours.

The various qualities attributed to different ages do not constitute an unconnected series. They are usually interconnected in many ways. The subtle dialectics between the unfolding of some qualities and the waning of others in a person is not a mere registration of his psychological or biological traits; rather, it constitutes the broad framework of his potentialities and their limits throughout his life span. The characteristics of any one "age," therefore, cannot be fully understood except in relation to those of other ages. Whether seen as a gradually unfolding continuum or as a series of sharp contrasts and opposed characteristics, they are fully explicable and understandable only in terms of one another. The boy bears within himself the seeds of the adult man; else, he must as an adult acquire new patterns of behavior, sharply and intentionally opposed to those of his boyhood. The adult either develops naturally into an old man—or decays into one. Only when taken together do these different "ages" constitute the entire map of human possibilities and limitations; and, as every individual usually must pass through them all, their complementariness and continuity (even if defined in discontinuous and contrasting terms) become strongly emphasized and articulated.

The same holds true for the age definitions of the two sexes, although perhaps with a somewhat different meaning. Each age span is defined differently for either sex, and these definitions are usually related and complementary, as the "sexual image" and identity always constitute basic elements of man's image in every society. This close connection between different ages necessarily stresses the problem of transition from one point in a person's life to another as a basic constituent of any cultural definition of an "age." Hence, each definition of age must necessarily cope with the perception of time, and changes in time, of one's own progress in time, one's transition from one period of life to another.

This personal transition, or temporal progress, or change, may become closely linked with what may be called cosmic and societal time.[2] The attempt to find some meaning in personal temporal transition may often lead to identification with the rhythms of nature or history, with the cycles of the seasons, with the unfolding of some cosmic plan (whether cyclical, seasonal, or apocalyptic), or with the destiny and development of society. The nature of this linkage often constitutes the focus round which an individual's personal identity becomes defined in cultural terms and through which personal experience, with its anguish, may be given some meaning in terms of cultural symbols and values.

The whole problem of age definition and the linkage of personal time and transition with cosmic time become especially accentuated in that age span usually designated as youth. However great the differences among various societies, there is one focal point within the life span of an individual which in most known societies is to some extent emphasized: the period of youth, of transition from childhood to full adult status, or full membership in the society. In this period the individual is no longer a child (especially from the physical and sexual point of view) but is ready to undertake many attributes of an adult and to fulfill adult roles. But he is not yet fully acknowledged as an adult, a full member of the society. Rather, he is being "prepared," or is preparing himself for such adulthood.

This image of youth—the cultural definition of youth—contains all the crucial elements of any definition of age, usually in an especially articulated way. This is the stage at which the individual's personality acquires the basic psychological mechanism of self-regulation and self-control, when his self-identity becomes crystallized. It is also the stage at which the young are confronted with some models of the major roles they are supposed to emulate in adult life and with the major symbols and values of their culture and community. Moreover, in this phase the problem of the linkage of the personal temporal transition with cosmic or societal time becomes extremely acute. Any cultural definition of youth describes it as a transitory phase, couched in terms of transition toward something new, something basically different from the past. Hence the acuteness of the problem of linkage.

The very emphasis on the transitory nature of this stage and of its essentially preparatory character, however, may easily create a somewhat paradoxical situation. It may evolve an image of youth as the purest manifestation and repository of ultimate cultural and societal values. Such an image is rooted first

2. The analysis of personal, cosmic, and societal time (or temporal progression) has constituted a fascinating but not easily dealt with focus of analysis. For some approaches to these problems, see *Man and Time* (papers from the Eranos Yearbooks), ed. by Joseph Campbell (London: Routledge & Kegan Paul, 1958), especially the article by Gerardus van der Leeuw. See also Mircea Eliade, *The Myth of the Eternal Return*, trans. W. R. Trask (New York: Pantheon Books, 1954)(Bollingen Series).

in the fact that to some extent youth is always defined as a period of "role moratorium," that is, as a period in which one may play with various roles without definitely choosing any. It does not yet require the various compromises inherent in daily participation in adult life. At the same time, however, since it is also the period when the maximum identification with the values of the society is stressed, under certain conditions it may be viewed as the repository of all the major human virtues and primordial qualities. It may then be regarded as the only age in which full identification with the ultimate values and symbols of the society is attained—facilitated by the flowering of physical vigor, a vigor which may easily become identified with a more general flowering of the cosmos or the society.

The fullest, the most articulate and definitive expression of these archetypal elements of youth is best exemplified in the ritual dramatization of the transition from adolescence to adulthood, such as the various *rites de passage* and ceremonies of initiation in primitive tribes and in ancient civilizations.[3] In these rites the pre-adult youth are transformed into full members of the tribe. This transformation is effected through:

1. a series of rites in which the adolescents are symbolically divested of the characteristics of youth and invested with those of adulthood, from a sexual and social point of view; this investment, which has deep emotional significance, may have various concrete manifestations: bodily mutilation, circumcision, the taking on of a new name or symbolic rebirth;

2. the complete symbolic separation of the male adolescents from the world of their youth, especially from their close attachment to their mothers; in other words, their complete "male" independence and image are fully articulated (the opposite usually holds true of girls' initiations);

3. the dramatization of the encounter between the several generations, a dramatization that may take the form of a fight or a competition, in which the basic complementariness of various age grades—whether of a continuous or discontinuous type—is stressed; quite often the discontinuity between adolescence and adulthood is symbolically expressed, as in the symbolic death of the adolescents as children and their rebirth as adults;

4. the transmission of the tribal lore with its instructions about proper behavior, both through formalized teaching and through various ritual activities; this transmission is combined with:

5. a relaxation of the concrete control of the adults over the erstwhile adolescents and its substitution by self-control and adult responsibility.

Most of these dramatic elements can also be found, although in somewhat more diluted forms, in various traditional folk festivals in peasant communities,

3. For a fuller exposition of the sociological significance of initiation rites, see Mircea Eliade, *Birth and Rebirth* (New York: Harper & Brothers, 1958) and *From Generation to Generation* (ref. 1).

especially those such as rural carnivals in which youth and marriage are emphasized. In an even more diluted form, these elements may be found in various spontaneous initiation ceremonies of the fraternities and youth groups in modern societies.[4] Here, however, the full dramatic articulation of these elements is lacking, and their configuration and organization assume different forms.

The transition from childhood and adolescence to adulthood, the development of personal identity, psychological autonomy and self-regulation, the attempt to link personal temporal transition to general cultural images and to cosmic rhythms, and to link psychological maturity to the emulation of definite role models—these constitute the basic elements of any archetypal image of youth. However, the ways in which these various elements become crystallized in concrete configurations differ greatly from society to society and within sectors of the same society. The full dramatic articulation of these elements in the *rites de passage* of primitive societies constitutes only one—perhaps the most extreme and articulate but certainly not the only—configuration of these archetypal elements of youth.

In order to understand other types of such configurations, it is necessary to analyze some conditions that influence their development. Perhaps the best starting point is the nature of the social organization of the period of adolescence: the process of transition from childhood to adulthood, the social context in which the process of growing up is shaped and structured. There are two major criteria that shape the social organization of the period of youth. One is the extent to which age in general and youth in particular form a criterion for the allocation of roles in a society, whether in politics, in economic or cultural activity—aside from the family, of course, in which they always serve as such a criterion. The second is the extent to which any society develops specific age groups, specific corporate organizations, composed of members of the same "age," such as youth movements or old men's clubs. If roles are allocated in a society according to age, this greatly influences the extent to which age constitutes a component of a person's identity. In such cases, youth becomes a definite and meaningful phase of transition in an individual's progress through life, and his budding self-identity acquires content and a relation to role models and cultural values. No less important to the concrete development of identity is the extent to which it is influenced, either by the common participation of different generations in the same group as in the family, or conversely by the organization of members of the same age groups into specific, distinct groups.

The importance of age as a criterion for allocating roles in a society is closely related to several major aspects of social organization and cultural ori-

---

4. See Bruno Bettelheim, *Symbolic Wounds, Puberty Rites and the Envious Circle* (Glencoe, Ill.: The Free Press, 1954).

entation. The first aspect is the relative complexity of the division of labor. In general, the simpler the organization of the society, the more influential age will be as a criterion for allocating roles. Therefore, in primitive or traditional societies (or in the more primitive and traditional sectors of developed societies) age and seniority constitute basic criteria for allocating social, economic, and political roles.

The second aspect consists of the major value orientations and symbols of a society, especially the extent to which they emphasize certain general orientations, qualities, or types of activity (such as physical vigor, the maintenance of cultural tradition, the achievement and maintenance of supernatural prowess) which can be defined in terms of broad human qualities and which become expressed and symbolized in specific ages.

The emphasis on any particular age as a criterion for the allocation of roles is largely related to the concrete application of the major value orientations in a society. For instance, we find that those primitive societies in which military values and orientations prevail emphasize young adulthood as the most important age, while those in which sedentary activities prevail emphasize older age. Similarly, within some traditional societies, a particular period such as old age may be emphasized if it is seen as the most appropriate one for expressing major cultural values and symbols—for instance, the upholding of a given cultural tradition.

The social and cultural conditions that determine the extent to which specific age groups and youth groups develop differ from the conditions that determine the extent to which age serves as a criterion for the allocation of roles. At the same time, the two kinds of conditions may be closely related, as we shall see. Age groups in general and youth groups in particular tend to arise in those societies in which the family or kinship unit cannot ensure (it may even impede) the attainment of full social status on the part of its members. These conditions appear especially (although not uniquely[5]) in societies in which family or kinship groups do not constitute the basic unit of the social division of labor. Several features characterize such societies. First, the membership in the total society (citizenship) is not defined in terms of belonging to any such family, kinship group, or estate, nor is it mediated by such a group.

Second, in these societies the major political, economic, social, and religious functions are performed not by family or kinship units but rather by various specialized groups (political parties, occupational associations, etc.), which individuals may join irrespective of their family, kinship, or caste. In these societies, therefore, the major roles that adults are expected to perform in the wider society differ in orientation from those of the family or kinship

5. A special type of age groups may also develop in familistic societies. See *From Generation to Generation* (ref. 1), ch. 5.

group. The children's identification and close interaction with family members of other ages does not assure the attainment of full self-identity and social maturity on the part of the children. In these cases, there arises a tendency for peer groups to form, especially youth groups; these can serve as a transitory phase between the world of childhood and the adult world.

This type of the social division of labor is found in varying degrees in different societies, primitive, historical, or modern. In several primitive tribes such a division of labor has existed,[6] for example, in Africa, among the chiefless (segmentary) tribes of Nandi, Masai, or Kipigis, in the village communities of Yako and Ibo, or in more centralized kingdoms of the Zulu and Swazi, and among some of the Indian tribes of the Plains, as well as among some South American and Indian tribes.

Such a division of labor likewise existed to some extent in several historical societies (especially in city states such as Athens or Rome), although most great historical civilizations were characterized mainly by a more hierarchical and ascriptive system of the division of labor, in which there were greater continuity and harmony between the family and kinship groups and the broader institutional contexts. The fullest development of this type of the social division of labor, however, is to be found in modern industrial societies. Their inclusive membership is usually based on the universal criterion of citizenship and is not conditioned by membership in any kinship group. In these societies the family does not constitute a basic unit of the division of labor, especially not in production and distribution, and even in the sphere of consumption its functions become more limited. Occupations are not transmitted through heredity. Similarly, the family or kinship group does not constitute a basic unit of political or ritual activities. Moreover, the general scope of the activities of the family has been continuously diminishing, while various specialized agencies tend to take over its functions in the fields of education and recreation.

To be sure, the extent to which the family is diminishing in modern societies is often exaggerated. In many social spheres (neighborhood, friendship, informal association, some class relations, community relations), family, kinship, and status are still very influential. But the scope of these relations is more limited in modern societies than in many others, even if the prevalent myth of the disappearance of the family has long since been exploded. The major social developments of the nineteenth century (the establishment of national states, the progress of the industrial revolution, the great waves of intercontinental migrations) have greatly contributed to this diminution of scope, and especially in the first phase of modernization there has been a growing discontinuity between the life of the children, whether in the family or the traditional school, and in the social world with its new and enlarged perspectives.

6. For fuller details, see *From Generation to Generation*, especially chs. 3 and 4.

Youth groups tend to develop in all societies in which such a division of labor exists. Youth's tendency to coalesce in such groups is rooted in the fact that participation in the family became insufficient for developing full identity or full social maturity, and that the roles learned in the family did not constitute an adequate basis for developing such identity and participation. In the youth groups the adolescent seeks some framework for the development and crystallization of his identity, for the attainment of personal autonomy, and for his effective transition into the adult world.

Various types of youth organizations always tend to appear with the transition from traditional or feudal societies to modern societies, along with the intensified processes of change, especially in periods of rapid mobility, migration, urbanization, and industrialization. This is true of all European societies, and also of non-Western societies. The impact of Western civilization on primitive and historical-traditional peoples is usually connected with the disruption of family life, but beyond this it also involves a change in the mutual evaluation of the different generations. The younger generation usually begin to seek a new self-identification, and one phase or another this search is expressed in ideological conflict with the older.

Most of the nationalistic movements in the Middle East, Asia, and Africa have consisted of young people, students, or officers who rebelled against their elders and the traditional familistic setting with its stress on the latters' authority At the same time there usually has developed a specific youth consciousness and ideology that intensifies the nationalistic movement to "rejuvenate" the country.

The emergence of the peer group among immigrant children is a well-known phenomenon that usually appears in the second generation. It occurs mainly because of the relative breakdown of immigrant family life in the new country. The more highly industrialized and urbanized that country (or the sector absorbing the immigrants) is, the sharper the breakdown. Hence, the family of the immigrant or second-generation child has often been an inadequate guide to the new society. The immigrant child's attainment of full identity in the new land is usually related to how much he has been able to detach himself from his older, family setting. Some of these children, therefore, have developed a strong predisposition to join various peer groups. Such an affiliation has sometimes facilitated their transition to the absorbing society by stressing the values and patterns of behavior in that society—or, on the contrary, it may express their rebellion against this society, or against their older setting.

All these modern social developments and movements have given rise to a great variety of youth groups, peer groups, youth movements, and what has been called youth culture. The types and concrete forms of such groups varies widely: spontaneous youth groups, student movements, ideological and semipolitical movements, and youth rebellions connected with the Romantic movement in Europe, and, later, with the German youth movements. The various social and national trends of the nineteenth and twentieth centuries have also given impetus to such organizations. At the same time there have appeared many adult-sponsored youth organizations and other agencies springing out of the great extension of educational institutions. In addition to providing recreative facilities, these agencies have also aimed at character molding and the instilling of civic virtues, so as to deepen social consciousness and widen the social and cultural horizon. The chief examples are the YMCA, the Youth Brigades organized in England by William Smith, the Boy Scouts, the Jousters in France, and the many kinds of community organizations, hostels, summer camps, or vocational guidance centers.

Thus we see that there are many parallels between primitive and historical societies and modern societies with regard to the conditions under which the various constellations of youth groups, youth activities, and youth images have developed. But these parallels are only partial. Despite certain similarities, the specific configurations of the basic archetypal elements of the youth image in modern societies differ greatly from those of primitive and traditional societies. The most important differences are rooted in the fact that in the modern, the development of specific youth organizations is paradoxically connected with the weakening of the importance of age in general and youth in particular as definite criteria for the allocation of roles in society.

As we have already said, the extent to which major occupational, cultural, or political roles are allocated today according to the explicit criterion of age is very small. Most such roles are achieved according to wealth, acquired skills, specialization, and knowledge. Family background may be of great importance for the acquisition of these attributes, but very few positions are directly given people by virtue of their family standing. Yet this very weakening of the importance of age is always connected with intensive developments of youth groups and movements. This fact has several interesting repercussions on the organization and structure of such groups. In primitive and traditional societies, youth groups are usually part of a wider organization of age groups that covers a very long period of life, from childhood to late adulthood and even old age. To be sure, it is during youth that most of the dramatic elements of the transition from one age to another are manifest, but this stage constitutes only part of a longer series of continuous, well-defined stages.

From this point of view, primitive or traditional societies do not differ greatly from those in which the transition from youth to adulthood is not organized in specific age groups but is largely effected within the fold of the family and kinship groups. In both primitive and traditional societies we observe a close and comprehensive linkage between personal temporal transition and societal or cosmic time, a linkage most fully expressed in the *rites de passage.*

Consequently, the transition from childhood to adulthood in all such societies is given full meaning in terms of ultimate cultural values and symbols borne or symbolized by various adult role models.

In modern societies the above picture greatly changes. The youth group, whatever its composition or organization, usually stands alone. It does not constitute a part of a fully institutionalized and organized series of age groups. It is true that in many of the more traditional sectors of modern societies the more primitive or traditional archetypes of youth still prevail. Moreover, in many modern societies elements of the primitive archetypes of youth still exist. But the full articulation of these elements is lacking, and the social organization and self-expression of youth are not given full legitimation or meaning in terms of cultural values and rituals.

The close linkage between the growth of personality, psychological maturation, and definite role models derived from the adult world has become greatly weakened. Hence the very coalescence of youth into special groups only tends to emphasize their problematic, uncertain standing from the point of view of cultural values and symbols. This has created a new constellation of the basic archetypal elements of youth. This new constellation can most clearly be seen in what has been called the emergence of the problems and stresses of adolescence in modern societies. While some of these stresses are necessarily common to adolescence in all societies, they become especially acute in modern societies.

Among these stresses the most important are the following: first, the bodily development of the adolescent constitutes a constant problem to him (or her). Since social maturity usually lags behind biological maturity, the bodily changes of puberty are not usually given a full cultural, normative meaning, and their evaluation is one of the adolescent's main concerns. The difficulty inherent in attaining legitimate sexual outlets and relations at this period of growth makes these problems even more acute. Second, the adolescent's orientation toward the main values of his society is also beset with difficulties. Owing to the long period of preparation and the relative segregation of the children's world from that of the adults, the main values of the society are necessarily presented to the child and adolescent in a highly selective way, with a strong idealistic emphasis. The relative unreality of these values as presented to the children—which at the same time are not given full ritual and symbolic expression—creates among the adolescents a great potential uncertainty and ambivalence toward the adult world.

This ambivalence is manifest, on the one hand, in a striving to communicate with the adult world and receive its recognition; on the other hand, it appears in certain dispositions to accentuate the differences between them and the adults and to oppose the various roles allocated to them by the adults. While they orient themselves to full participation in the adult world and its values, they usually attempt also to communicate with this world in a distinct, special way.

Parallel developments are to be found in the ideologies of modern youth groups. Most of these tend to create an ideology that emphasizes the discontinuity between youth and adulthood and the uniqueness of the youth period as the purest embodiment of ultimate social and cultural values. Although the explicitness of this ideology varies in extent from one sector of modern society to another, its basic elements are prevalent in almost all modern youth groups.

These processes have been necessarily accentuated in modern societies by the specific developments in cultural orientations in general and in the conception of time that has evolved in particular. The major social developments in modern societies have weakened the importance of broad cultural qualities as criteria for the allocation of roles. Similarly, important changes in the conception of time that is prevalent in modern societies have occurred. Primordial (cosmic-mythical, cyclical, or apocalyptical) conceptions of time have become greatly weakened, especially in their bearing on daily activities. The mechanical conception of time of modern technology has become much more prevalent. Of necessity this has greatly weakened the possibility of the direct ritual links between personal temporal changes and cosmic or societal progression. Therefore, the exploration of the actual meaning of major cultural values in their relation to the reality of the social world becomes one of the adolescent's main problems. This exploration may lead in many directions—cynicism, idealistic youth rebellion, deviant ideology and behavior, or a gradual development of a balanced identity.

Thus we see how all these developments in modern societies have created a new constellation of the basic archetypal elements of youth and the youth image. The two main characteristics of this constellation are the weakened possibility of directly linking the development of personality and the personal temporal transition with cosmic and societal time, on the one hand, and with the clear role models derived from the adult world, on the other.

In terms of personality development, this situation has created a great potential insecurity and the possible lack of a clear definition of personal identity. Yet it has also created the possibility of greater personal autonomy and flexibility in the choice of roles and the commitment to different values and symbols. In general, the individual, in his search for the meaning of his personal transition, has been thrown much more on his own powers.

These processes have provided the framework within which the various attempts to forge youth's identity and activities—both on the part of youth itself and on the part of various educational agencies—have developed. These attempts may take several directions. Youth's own activities and attempts at self-expression may first develop in the direction of considerable autonomy in the choice of roles and in commitment to various values. Conversely, they may develop in the direction of a more complete, fully organized and closed ideology connected with a small extent of personal autonomy. Second, these attempts may differ greatly in their emphasis on the direct linkage of cultural values to a specific social group and their view of these groups as the main bearers of such values.

In a parallel sense, attempts have been made on the part of various educational agencies to create new types of youth organizations within which youth can forge its identity and become linked to adult society. The purpose of such attempts has been two-fold: to provide youth with opportunities to develop a reasonably autonomous personality and a differentiated field of activity; and to encompass youth fully within well-organized groups set up by adult society and to provide them with full, unequivocal role models and symbols of identification. The interaction between these different tendencies of youth and the attempts of adult society to provide various frameworks for youth activities has given rise to the major types of youth organizations, movements, and ideologies manifested in modern societies.

These various trends and tendencies have created a situation in which, so far as we can ascertain, the number of casualties among youth has become very great—probably relatively much greater than in other types of societies. Youth's search for identity, for finding some place of its own in society, and its potential difficulties in coping with the attainment of such identity have given rise to the magnified extent of the casualties observed in the numerous youth delinquents of varying types. These failures, however, are not the only major youth developments in modern societies, although their relatively greater number is endemic in modern conditions. Much more extensive are the more positive attempts of youth to forge its own identity, to find some meaningful way of defining its place in the social and cultural context and of connecting social and political values with personal development in a coherent and significant manner.

The best example in our times of the extreme upsurge of specific youth consciousness is seen in the various revolutionary youth movements. They range from the autonomous free German youth movements to the less spectacular youth movements in Central Europe and also to some extent to the specific youth culture of various more flexible youth groups. Here the attempt has been made to overcome the dislocation between personal transition and societal and cultural time. It is in these movements that the social dynamics of modern youth has found its fullest expression. It is in them that dreams of a new life, a new society, freedom and spontaneity, a new humanity, and aspirations to social and cultural change have found utterance. It is in these youth movements that the forging of youth's new social identity has become closely connected with the development of new symbols of collective identity or new social-cultural symbols and meanings.

These movements have aimed at changing many aspects of the social and cultural life of their respective societies. They have depicted the present in a rather shabby form; they have dubbed it with adjectives of materialism, restriction, exploitation, lack of opportunity for self-fulfillment and creativity. At the same time they have held out hope for the future—seemingly, the not very far off future—when both self-fulfillment and collective fulfillment can be achieved and the materialistic civilization of the adult world can be shaken off. They have tried to appeal to youth to forge its own self-identity in terms of these new collective symbols, and this is why they have been so attractive to youth, for whom they have provided a set of symbols, hopes, and aims to which to direct its activities.

Within these movements the emphasis has been on a given social group or collectivity—nation, class, or the youth group itself—as the main, almost exclusive bearer of the "good" cultural values and symbols. Indeed, youth has at times been upheld as the sole and pure bearer of cultural values and social creativity. Through its association with these movements, youth has also been able to connect its aspiration for a different personal future, its anxiety to escape the present through plans and hopes for a different future within its cultural or social setting.

These various manifestations have played a crucial part in the emergence of social movements and parties in modern societies. Student groups have been the nuclei of the most important nationalistic and revolutionary movements in Central and Eastern Europe, in Italy, Germany, Hungary, and Russia. They have also played a significant role in Zionism and in the various waves of immigration to Israel. Their influence has become enormous in various fields, not only political and educational but cultural in general. In a way, education itself has tended to become a social movement. Many schools and universities, many teachers, have been among the most important bearers of collective values. The very spread of education is often seen as a means by which a new epoch might be ushered in.

The search for some connection between the personal situation of youth and social-cultural values has also stimulated the looser youth groups in modern societies, especially in the United States, and to some extent in Europe as well—though here the psychological meaning of the search is somewhat different. The looser youth groups have often shared some of the characteristics of the more defined youth movements, and they too have developed an emphasis on the attainment of social and cultural change. The yearning for a different personal future has likewise become connected with aspirations for changing the cultural setting, but not necessarily through a direct political or organized expression. They are principally important as a strong link with various collective, artistic, and literary aspirations aimed at changing social and cultural life. As such they are affiliated with various cultural values and symbols, not with any exclusive social groups. Thus they have necessarily developed a much greater freedom in choice of roles and commitment to values.

Specific social conditions surround the emergence of all these youth groups. In general, they are associated with a breakdown of traditional settings, the onset of modernization, urbanization, secularization, and industrialization. The less organized, more spontaneous types of youth organization and the more flexible kind of youth consciousness arise when the transition has been relatively smooth and gradual, especially in societies whose basic collective identity and political framework evince a large degree of continuity and a slow process of modernization. On the other hand, the more intensive types of youth movements tend to develop in those societies and periods in which the onset of modernization is connected with great upheavals and sharp cleavages in the social structure and the structure of authority and with the breakdown of symbols of collective identity.

In the latter situation the adult society has made many efforts to organize youth in what may be called totalistic organizations, in which clear role models and values might be set before youth and in which the extent of choice allowed youth is very limited and the manifestations of personal spontaneity and autonomy are restricted. Both types of conditions appeared in various European societies and in the United States in the nineteenth and early twentieth centuries, and in Asian and African societies in the second half of the twentieth century. The relative predominance of each of these conditions varies in different periods in these societies. However, with the progress of modernization and the growing absorption of broad masses within the framework of society, the whole basic setting of youth in modern society has changed—and it is this new framework that is predominant today and in which contemporary youth problems are shaped and played out.

The change this new framework represents is to some extent common both to the fully organized totalistic youth movements and to the looser youth groups. It is connected mainly with the institutionalizing of the aims and values toward the realization of which these movements were oriented, with the acceptance of such youth organizations as part of the structure of the general educational and cultural structure of their societies.

In Russia youth movements became fully institutionalized through the organization of the Komsomol. In many European countries the institutionalizing of youth groups, agencies, and ideologies came through association with political parties, or through acceptance as part of the educational system—an acceptance that sometimes entailed supervision by the official authorities. In the United States, many (such as the Boy Scouts) have become an accepted part of community life and to some extent a symbol of differential social status.

In many Asian and African countries, organized youth movements have become part of the nationalistic movements and, independence won, have become part of the official educational organizations.

This institutionalizing of the values of youth movements in education and community life has been part of a wider process of institutionalizing various collective values. In some countries this has come about through revolution; in others, as a result of a long process of political and social evolution.

From the point of view of our analysis, these processes have had several important results. They have introduced a new element into the configuration of the basic archetypal elements of youth. The possibility of linking personal transition both to social groups and to cultural values—so strongly emphasized in the youth movements and noticeable to some extent even in the looser youth culture—has become greatly weakened. The social and sometimes even the cultural dimension of the future may thus become flattened and emptied. The various collective values become transformed. Instead of being remote goals resplendent with romantic dreams, they have become mundane objectives of the present, with its shabby details of daily politics and administration. More often than not they are intimately connected with the processes of bureaucratization.

All these mutations are associated with a notable decline in ideology and in preoccupation with ideology among many of the groups and strata in modern societies, with a general flattening of political-ideological motives and a growing apathy to them. This decline in turn is connected with what has been called the spiritual or cultural shallowness of the new social and economic benefits accruing from the welfare state—an emptiness illustrated by the fact that all these benefits are in the nature of things administered not by spiritual or social leaders but, as Stephen Toulmin has wittily pointed out, "the assistant postmaster." As a consequence, we observe the emptiness and meaninglessness of social relations, so often described by critics of the age of consumption and mass society.

In general, these developments have brought about the flattening of the image of the societal future and have deprived it of its allure. Between present and future there is no ideological discontinuity. The present has become the more important, if not the more meaningful, because the future has lost its characteristic as a dimension different from the present. Out of these conditions has grown what Riesman has called the cult of immediacy. Youth has been robbed, therefore, of the full experience of the dramatic transition from adolescence to adulthood and of the dramatization of the difference between present and future. Their own changing personal future has become dissociated from any changes in the shape of their societies or in cultural activities and values.

Paradoxically enough, these developments have often been connected with a strong adulation of youth—an adulation, however, which was in a way

purely instrumental. The necessity of a continuous adjustment to new changing conditions has emphasized the potential value of youth as the bearers of
continuous innovation, of noncommitment to any specific conditions and values. But such an emphasis is often couched in terms of a purely instrumental
adaptability, beyond which there is only the relative emptiness of the meaningless passage of time—of aging.[7]

Yet the impact on youth of what has been called postindustrial society
need not result in such an emptiness and shallowness, although in recent literature these effects appear large indeed. It is as yet too early to make a full and
adequate analysis of all these impacts. But it should be emphasized that the
changes we have described, together with growing abundance and continuous
technological change, have necessarily heightened the possibility of greater
personal autonomy and cultural creativity and of the formation of the bases of
such autonomy and of a flexible yet stable identity during the period of youth.

These new conditions have enhanced the possibility of flexibility in linking cultural values to social reality; they have enhanced the scope of personal
and cultural creativity and the development of different personal culture. They
have created the possibility of youth's developing what may be called a non-
ideological, direct identification with moral values, an awareness of the predicaments of moral choice that exist in any given situation, and individual responsibility for such choices—a responsibility that cannot be shed by relying on
overarching ideological solutions oriented to the future.

These new social conditions exist in most industrial and post-industrial
societies, sometimes together with the older conditions that gave rise to the
more intensive types of youth movements. They constitute the framework
within which the new configuration of the archetypal elements of youth and
the new possibilities and problems facing youth in contemporary society develop. It is as yet too early to specify all these new possibilities and trends:
here we have attempted to indicate some of their general contours.

---

7. For an exposition of this view, see Paul Goodman, "Youth in Organized Society," *Commen-*
tary, February 1960, pp. 95–107; and M. R. Stein, *The Eclipse of Community* (Princeton: Princeton
University Press, 1960), especially pp. 215 ff.; also, the review of this book by H. Rosenberg,
"Community, Values, Comedy," *Commentary,* August 1960, pp. 150–7.

Four

INSTITUTIONALIZATION AND CHANGE

THIS PAPER ILLUSTRATES the combination of systematic institutional analysis with the analysis of change, showing that the explication of change is inherent in the systematic analysis of concrete societies or parts thereof.

Claims have long been made that structural or "structural-functional" analysis, with its stress on systems, equilibrium, common values and boundary-maintenance, not only neglects problems of change, but is analytically incapable of dealing with them. In response, many sociologists have recently asserted that not only is there no necessary contradiction between structural analysis and the analysis of change, but that on the contrary the two are basically compatible.

As formulated, for instance, by Moore, the argument is that every society (or social system) is inherently predisposed to change because of basic problems to which there is no overall continuous solution.[1] These problems include uncertainties of socialization , perennial scarcity of resources relative to individual aspirations, and contrasting types of social orientation or principles of social organization (e.g., *Gemeinschaft* vs. *Gesellschaft*) within the society. While this general view has been accepted to some extent, it has given rise to the contrary claim that it is couched in terms too general to explain the specific directions of change in any concrete society, that such specificity is beyond the province of "structural" analysis, and that such analysis can explain any

Originally published in *American Sociological Review* 29 (1964):235–47. This paper was written in 1962–3 when I was Carnegie Visiting Professor of Political Science at M.I.T. I am indebted to Professor R. N. Bellah for detailed comments on earlier versions of this paper. Parts of this paper were presented at the Fifth International Congress of Sociology, Washington, D.C., in September 1962.

1. See Wilbert E. Moore, "A Reconsideration of Theories of Social Change," *American Sociological Review* 25 (December 1960), pp. 810–18, and Kingsley Davis, "The Myth of Functional Analysis as a Special Method in Sociology and Anthropology," *American Sociological Review* 26 (December 1959), pp. 752–72.

concrete change only by reference either to very general and hence inadequate causes, or to forces external to the system.[2]

These difficulties can be at least partially overcome by recognizing that the general "predilections" to change inherent in any social system become "concretized" or "specified" through the process of institutionalization. Our major point is that the institutionalization of any social system—be it political, economic or a system of social stratification or of any collectivity or role— creates in its wake the possibilities for change. The process of institutionalization is the organization of a societally prescribed system of differentiated behavior oriented to the solution of certain problems inherent in a major area of social life.[3]

The organization of such systems of behavior involves the creation and definition of norms to regulate the major units of social behavior and organization, criteria according to which the flow of resources is regulated between such units, and sanctions to ensure that such norms are upheld. All these involve the maintenance of the specific boundaries of the system, i.e., the maintenance of the units that constitute it, of its relations with outside systems, and of the norms that delineate its specific characteristics.

And yet the very attempt to institutionalize any such system creates in its wake the possibility for change. These are possibilities not only for general, unspecified change but for more specific changes, which develop not randomly but in relatively specific directions, to a large extent set by the very process of institutionalization. Hence a systematic structural analysis is a prerequisite for an adequate analysis of change.[4]

II

We shall illustrate this general point by analyzing the process of institutionalization in one type of political and one type of religious system, drawing on recent work on the social and political structure of the historical centralized bureaucratic Empires, i.e., the Sassanid, Roman, Byzantine, Chinese, Caliphate

2. See, for instance, Ronald Philip Dore, "Function and Cause," *American Sociological Review* 26 (December 1961), pp. 843–53; Kenneth E. Bock, "Evolution, Function and Change," *American Sociological Review* 28 (April 1963), pp. 229–37.

3. Following Alvin W. Gouldner and Helen P. Gouldner, *Modern Sociology, An Introduction to the Study of Human Interaction* (New York: Harcourt, Brace, 1963), p. 484; see also Harry M. Johnson, *Sociology, A Systematic Introduction* (New York: Harcourt, Brace, 1960), ch. 2; Talcott Parsons, *The Social System* (Glencoe, Ill.: The Free Press, 1951), chs. 2 and 5.

4. Some parallel indications can be found in Thomas F. O'Dea, "Sociological Dilemmas, Five Paradoxes of Institutionalization," in Eduard A. Tiryakian (ed.), *Sociological Theory, Values and Sociocultural Change, Essays in Honor of Pitirim A. Sorokin* (New York: The Free Press, 1963), pp. 71–91; see also Neil J. Smelser, *Theory of Collective Behavior* (New York: The Free Press, 1963), esp. chs. 2 and 3.

and Ottoman Empires, and the European states in the period of absolutism,[5] and on the development of religious institutions within them.[6]

The majority of these empires developed from (a) patrimonial empires such as Egypt or the Sassanid Empire; (b) dualistic nomadic-sedentary empires (necessarily sharing many characteristics with the patrimonial ones); (c) feudal systems, such as the European absolutist states; or (d) city-states (the Roman and Hellenistic Empires). Despite the great variety in historical and cultural settings, we may designate some common features in the first stages of establishment of such polities.

The empires were first established through interaction between the political goals of the rulers who established them, and the broader conditions prevailing in their respective social structures. The initiative for the establishment of these polities came, in all cases, from the rulers—emperors, kings, or members of a patrician ruling elite (like the more active and dynamic element of the patrician elite in Republican Rome). These rulers came, in most cases, from established patrician, patrimonial, tribal, or feudal families. Some were usurpers, coming from lower-class families, who attempted to establish new dynasties or to conquer new territories, and some were conquerors who attempted to establish their rule over various territories.

In most cases such rulers arose in periods of strife and turmoil during dismemberment of the existing political system or during acute strife within it. Usually their aim was to reestablish peace and order. They did not, however, attempt to restore the old order in its entirety, although for propagandist reasons they sometimes upheld such restoration as political ideology or slogan. They sought to establish a more centralized, unified polity in which they could monopolize and set the political goals, without being bound by traditional aristocratic, tribal, or patrician groups. Even the conquerors—as in the Roman, Islamic, or Spanish American Empires—had some vision of distinctly political goals and attempted to transmit it to at least part of the conquered population. These aims were very often oriented against, and opposed by, various social and political groups. However great the turmoil, unrest, and internal strife, some groups always either benefited from it (or hoped to do so) or aimed to reestablish the "old" order in which they held positions of power and influence.

To implement their aims against aristocratic patrician forces, the rulers found allies, active or passive, among the strata whose interests were opposed to those of the aristocratic groups and who could benefit from weakening the

5. See Shmuel N. Eisenstadt, *The Political Systems of Empires* (New York: The Free Press, 1963), and "The Causes of Disintegration and Fall of Empires—Sociological and Historical Analyses," *Diogenes* 34 (Summer 1961), pp. 82–158.

6. See Shmuel N. Eisenstadt, "Religious Organizations and Political Process in Centralized Empires," *The Journal of Asian Studies* 21 (May 1962), pp. 271–94, and *The Political Systems of Empires, op. cit.*

aristocracy and establishing a more unified polity. These allies were, basically, of two kinds. The first were the more active (mostly urban) economic, cultural and professional groups who, by origin or by social interest and orientation, or both, were opposed to the traditional aristocratic groups. The second were the larger, politically and socially more passive strata, including especially peasants and also lower urban groups who could benefit, even if indirectly, by the weakening of the aristocratic forces.

To implement their aims the emperors attempted to establish a relatively centralized administration and to mobilize the resources needed for the neutralization, weakening or destruction of their enemies.

III

The successful institutionalization of the organizations through which the rulers could realize their aims was thus dependent first on the emergence of political entrepreneurs, the emperors, and their immediate entourage, who had the vision and ability to create new political entities.

Second, it depended on the existence, within the broader society, of certain specific conditions. Briefly, the most important of these conditions was the development, in all major institutional spheres, of a certain level of differentiation, i.e., the development of specific collectivities and roles in the major institutional spheres, such that the activities and resources of large parts of the population were freed from ascriptive (kinship, lineage, aristocratic) commitments and thus could be made available to the rulers.

These different social groups were willing to provide resources and support mostly because they perceived these emperors as the best available choice among the various existing possibilities (as compared to more traditional aristocratic pretenders or to a state of continuous disorder). They may have identified themselves to various degrees with the goals and symbols of the emperors; they may have hoped that the emperors would help them attain some of their own goals, and in maintaining their values, establish norms and organizations to help regulate some of their internal problems, or they may have seen these emperors as the least evil among the available choices.

To the degree that both sets of conditions developed in a given society, the possibility that a new imperial political system would be institutionalized was relatively great.

These conditions developed, for instance, though in varying degrees, in China from the beginning of the Han dynasty, in Byzantium and the Roman Empire in their formative stages, and in the Caliphates at the initial stages of their development.

In the Greek city-states, on the other hand, while the broader social conditions did develop, there arose no group of leaders or entrepreneurs capable of forging a new polity. In other historical cases—e.g., those of Charlemagne or Genghis Khan—such leaders did arise but the broader social conditions were lacking.[7]

IV

But even when such conditions were propitious, and the new political leaders could obtain enough support, such support was of varying quality and intensity.

Several basic attitudes of the major strata toward the premises of the political systems of these empires and toward the rulers' primary aims can be distinguished. The first attitude, evinced chiefly by the aristocracy, was one of opposition to the premises of the political systems. The second, passivity, was manifested mainly by the peasantry and sometimes also by other groups interested only in maintaining their limited local autonomy and their immediate economic interests.

The third attitude, found mostly in the bureaucracy, in some urban groups, and in part of the professional and cultural elite, consisted of basic identification with the premises of the political system and willingness to fight for their interests within the framework of existing political institutions. The fourth attitude, developed mainly by the more differentiated urban groups and by the professional and intellectual elite, favored changes in the scope of the political system.

These attitudes often overlapped in concrete instances, and the attitudes of each group and stratum varied in different societies and periods. Moreover, the attitudes of any one group were never homogeneous and stable, and they could change according to the conditions or the demands made by the rulers. The concrete constellations of these various political attitudes of the major social groups greatly influenced the extent of their political participation.

V

Out of the interaction between these goals of the rulers on the one hand, and the broader social conditions and the varied attitudes of the various social strata on the other, the specific characteristics of these empires became institutionalized.

Whatever the differences between the aims of various rulers and whatever the attitudes of the various groups, once the major contours of the empires were institutionalized, various organizations developed within them—mostly through the efforts of the rulers—to implement policies designed to maintain

7. For a fuller exposition of this statement, see Eisenstadt, *The Political Systems of Empires.*

the specific external and internal boundaries of the system, that is, its specific institutional contours and characteristics.

The most important characteristic of these empires was the coexistence, within the same political institutions, of traditional, undifferentiated political activities, orientations and organizations with more differentiated, specifically *political* goals. Or in more general terms, the autonomy of the political as a distinct institutional sphere was limited. Autonomy of the political sphere was manifest first in the tendency toward political centralization, second, in the development by the rulers of autonomous political goals and third, in the relatively high organizational autonomy of executive and administrative organs and activities.

But the differentiation of political activities, organizations and goals was, in these political systems, limited by several important factors. First, the rulers were usually legitimated in terms of basically traditional-religious values, even where they stressed their own ultimate monopoly of such values. Second, the subject's political role was not fully distinguished from other basic societal roles—such as, for instance, membership in local communities; it was often embedded in local groups, and the citizen or subject did not exercise any direct political rights through a system of voting or franchise. Third, many traditional ascriptive units, such as aristocratic lineages or territorial communities, performed crucial political functions and served as units of political representation. As a consequence, the scope of political activity and participation was far narrower than in most contemporary political systems.

Let us briefly analyze the policies of the rulers. First, they were interested in the limited promotion of free resources and in freeing them from commitments to traditional aristocratic groups. Second, the rulers wished to control these resources, to commit them, as it were, to their own use. Third, they tended to pursue various goals—e.g., military expansion—that could, in themselves, have exhausted many of the available free resources.

Perhaps the most interesting example of these policies is the rulers' attempts to create and maintain an independent free peasantry with smallholdings and to restrict the big landowners' encroachments on these smallholdings, in order to assure both the peasants' independence and the provision of resources to the rulers.

Of special importance too was the establishment of colonies and settlements of peasant soldiers, to make certain that the state would have sufficient military manpower. These colonies were not necessarily state-owned: they were closely associated with more complicated economic measures and policies, like various types of taxation. The policy of establishing such colonies evolved particularly in societies whose problems of frontier defense were of paramount importance. In Byzantium one purpose of the famous system of themes, supposedly evolved by the Emperor Heraclius (A.D. 610–41), was to

provide adequate manpower for frontier garrisons. This was achieved by starting colonies of free peasants from which soldiers were involuntarily recruited.
A similar pattern was established in the Sassanid Empire by Khousru the Great.
The T'ang Emperors of China also organized the peasant militia on similar
lines.[8]

VI

But the initial institutionalization of these political systems did not, in itself,
assure their continuity. The very process of institutionalizing these empires
created new problems—mainly because maintaining the conditions necessary
for these institutions became a more or less continuous concern of the rulers,
so that special policies, activities, and organizations had to be set up to ensure
their perpetuation. Because the rulers had to pursue continuously certain policies oriented against some social groups and in favor of others, the contradictions among their various goals and in the attitudes of various groups to the
basic premises of the system were evoked, and the negative orientations of
certain groups were intensified. Though not always consciously grasped by
the rulers, these contradictions were nevertheless implicit in their structural
positions, in the problems and exigencies with which they dealt, and in the
concrete policies they employed to solve these problems.

These internal contradictions developed in almost all the major institutional spheres, but perhaps especially in the sphere of legitimation and stratification. As we have seen, the rulers often attempted to limit the aristocracy's
power and to create new status groups such as the free peasantry, a nonaristo-
cratic officialdom, and so on. But these attempts faced several obstacles. Re-
gardless of the number of new titles created or of the degree to which new or
lower strata were encouraged, the symbols of status used by the rulers were
usually very similar to those borne by the landed, hereditary aristocracy or by
some religious elites. To create an entirely new secular and "rational" legitimation based on universalistic social principles was either beyond their capacities
or against their basic political interest, or both. To do so would necessarily
have enlarged the sphere of political participation and consequently increased
the influence of various strata in the political institutions. The rulers, therefore,
were usually unable to transcend the symbols of stratification and legitimation
represented by the very strata whose influence they wanted to limit.

Thus the ability of the rulers to appeal to the lower strata of the population
was obviously limited. Even more important, because of the emphasis on the
superiority and worth of aristocratic symbols and values, many middle or new

8. *Ibid.*, ch. 7.

strata and groups tended to identify with them and consequently to "aristocratize" themselves.

Contradictions in the rulers' policies and goals developed in another direction as well. However tradition-bound the ruling elite may have been, its policies required the creation and propagation of more flexible "free" resources in various institutional fields, and the propagation of free resources gave rise to or promoted many religious, intellectual, and legal groups whose value orientations differed from the traditional ones. Although in many societies all these groups were weak and succumbed to the influence of more conservative groups, in other cases—as in Europe—they developed into relatively independent centers of power, whose opposition to the rulers was only stimulated by the latter's conservative policies.

Similar contradictions also existed in the military, economic, and cultural spheres. Thus, for example, the growing needs of the Sassanid and Byzantine Empires in the last centuries of their respective empires for military manpower and economic resources caused them to weaken the independent peasantry through mobilization and taxation and to increase the power of the landed aristocracy. These policies undermined the very bases of their empires.[9]

VII

But contradictions in the activities of the rulers and in the attitudes of the various strata did not constitute the only important foci of potential change in these political systems. Of no less importance was the possibility that the very organs created to implement the goals and policies of the rulers could develop goals and activities opposed to the basic premises of these political systems. The most important problem of this kind arose from the tendency of members of the bureaucratic administration to develop autonomous political orientations and activities.

First, the power that these bureaucracies acquired in societies in which there were usually but few "constitutional" limits on power, and in which access to power was relatively limited, put the members of the bureaucracy in an especially privileged position. Second, the great emphasis, in these societies, on ascriptive symbols of status necessarily "tempted" the members of the bureaucracy to use their power to acquire such symbols or to convert their positions into ascriptive, often hereditary status symbols. Third, the relatively low level of economic development and social differentiation permitted only limited development of special professional roles and only inadequate remuneration for them. The fact that in most of these societies the sale of offices was a very common expedient fully attests to this.

9. *Ibid.*, ch. 12.

As a result of these conditions, members of the bureaucracies often tended to distort many of the customary or explicit rules and to divert many services to their own benefit or to that of some social groups with whom they were identified, and they tended to be both alienated from other groups in the society and oppressive toward them. In other words, they displaced the goal of service to the rulers and the various social strata, emphasizing goals of self-interest and aggrandizement instead.

On the other hand, the relative weakness of many political groups, and the great dependence of the bureaucracy on the rulers, often weakened and undermined the relative autonomy of the bureaucracy and brought about its total subjugation to the rulers. The latter could divert all the activities of the bureaucracy to their own exclusive use and prevent it from upholding any general rules for providing services to other strata in the society.

Thus the bureaucratic administration in these societies could, potentially, develop political orientations which were to some extent opposed to the basic premises of these polities and which generated changes that could not be contained within the institutional framework of the polity.

VIII

In these ways the very process of institutionalizing the political systems of these empires created the possibility of change—change that could be absorbed within the institutional structures as well as change that undermined them.

The concrete reasons for these changes were usually series of events closely related to the various contradictions described above, the impingement of external events (such as wars, invasions, or fluctuations of trade routes), or interaction between internal and external processes.

In more concrete terms, the main factors generating processes of change in these empires were (a) the continuous needs of the rulers for different types of resources and especially their great dependence on various "flexible" resources; (b) the rulers' attempts to maintain their own positions of control, in terms of both traditional legitimation and effective political control over the more flexible forces in the society; (c) the development in most of these societies, of what has been called *Primat der Aussenpolitik*[10] and the consequent great sensitivity of the internal structure of these societies to various external pressures and to international political and economic developments; and (d) the development of various autonomous orientations and goals among the major strata and their respective demands on the rulers. These changes were more

10. This term has been often used by F. Altheim in his studies of Roman and Sassanid History; see for instance, F. Altheim, *Gesicht von Abend und Morgen* (Frankfurt: Fischer Verlag, 1955), *passim.*

intensive so far as the rulers emphasized very "expensive" goals that exhausted the available economic and manpower resources, or different strata developed strong, autonomous political orientations.

In such situations, the rulers' tendency to maintain strong control over the more differentiated strata could become predominant, thus increasing the power of traditional forces and orientations and sharpening the conflicts between the traditional and the more flexible, differentiated strata, so that the latter were destroyed or alienated from the rulers. The excessive demands of the rulers in such situations, the growing public expenditures and the consequent increase of taxation and inflation, if not checked, often struck hardest at those groups whose economic organization was based on more flexible resources.

At such times, a continuous flux of foreign elements—mercenaries, hirelings, and personal helpers of the rulers—often invaded the centers of the realms. With the depletion of the native strata and the growing external and internal exigencies, they succeeded in infiltrating some of the most important political posts (such as those of eunuchs, military commandments, and viziers) and finally in totally usurping the ultimate power. Foreign merchants sometimes played a similar role, as in Byzantium or the Ottoman Empire, where they gradually succeeded in monopolizing all the tradeposts abandoned by the depleted indigenous merchants.

Where, as in Europe, these economically and socially more active strata were not depleted, they became alienated from the rulers, their policies, and the political institutions of the society, becoming hotbeds of revolt and change.

Such developments usually intensified the great sensitivity of the rulers and the society to various external economic and political changes (in trade routes or in international price movements, or through the intrusion of foreign elements). Usually, some combination of external and internal pressures and exigencies precipitated changes in the political systems of these empires. Hence, the greater the intensity of these internal contradictions and the greater the pressure of external exigencies that could not be dealt with by internal forces, the more quickly changes accumulated in these societies.[11]

IX

Some salient features of these changes were: First, interaction between internal and external events was greatly dependent on the special systemic characteristics of these political systems. While naturally enough many external events, such as invasions, were entirely beyond the control of any given empire, each

---

11. See Eisenstadt, *The Political Systems of Empires*, chs. 7 and 10.

polity constituted part of a relatively "international" environment. Because of its basically expansionist goals and its great dependence on free economic resources, each empire was especially sensitive to various specific developments in its broader environment. Moreover, external events and influences could very easily become closely interwoven with many of the internal problems of these empires.

Second, while some such exigencies and problems are common to all political systems, their *specific* nature depends on the structure of the institutional system. Thus, the special sensitivity of the centralized bureaucratic empires to such exigencies and pressures and to international economic fluctuations was rooted first in their rulers' great emphasis on military and expansionist goals and second in their need for various "free" resources, the availability of which depended on the international economic situation.

Similarly, while all political systems are influenced by and dependent on the efficiency and political loyalty of their administrative personnel, these empires were especially sensitive to the possibility that the bureaucracy might become " aristocratized," "parasitic," and inflated. This sensitivity was due first to the fact that the bureaucracy was the ruler's main instrument for implementing his goals and overcoming his political opponents, and second, to the constant danger that the free resources so necessary for the implementation of his goals might be depleted by the encroachments of various aristocratic or traditional groups and by the aristocratic tendencies of the bureaucracy.

These specific sensitivities also determined the location of the foci from which the impetus to change developed. Such foci tended to develop, in these political systems, mainly though certainly not only, in two basic spheres. One was that of economic and social organization. The level of differentiation of this sphere and the nature of its internal, autonomous organization was crucial to the development of different levels of resources on the one hand and different levels of political demand on the other.

The other sphere was that of values, or "culture." This sphere encompassed the legitimation of the system and of the ruler and, because the active cultural elites regulated many aspects of communication in the society, it greatly influenced the level of demands made on the central political institutions. While in many cases cultural values kept the level of such demands within the confines of the system, in other cases, as in the Islamic or European countries, values became a very important focus of charismatic innovations that might easily have undermined the existing system and created entirely new perceptions of the political sphere among many social groups.

Both economic organization and special cultural values strongly influenced the specific sensibilities of these systems and the generation of change within them. And when the two developed simultaneously, in the direction of either increasing or diminishing differentiation, their impact on the destiny of these political systems was of crucial importance.

Finally, the directions of change and the outcomes of the processes of change were to a very large extent set by the nature of the institutional systems of these Empires and by their internal problems. The range of political systems that arose on the ruins, as it were, of these Empires was relatively limited. Short of total disorganization, they could either "recede" into some type of relatively uncentralized patrimonial or feudal system (but not, for instance, into a city-state or a primitive system) or become a relatively more differentiated oligarchic modern system (but not a mass democracy or a "canton-democracy").

X

The preceding analysis has drawn on illustrations only from the political sphere. But the same problems of institutionalization are found in any other major social sphere. We shall briefly illustrate this by analyzing the problems of institutionalization of religions and religious organizations in the empires analyzed above.[12]

The religions that developed within the confines of these empires were among the major world religious systems: the Mazdean religion in Iran; Confucianism, Taoism and Buddhism in China and India; Islam; Eastern Christianity in Byzantium; Catholicism in Europe and Spanish America, and, later in Europe, Protestantism. These religions were usually developed through the activities of great religious innovators—either outstanding individuals or small groups of intense religious devotees—who attempted to create new cults and doctrines, and to spread and establish them in their respective societies.

Despite the great variety among these religions, they share important characteristics in some aspects of their value orientations, especially in their orientations to social reality.

The first such aspect is the breadth of the "group referent" of these religions; in most cases it was wider than any ascriptive or territorial group in these empires. The basic religious group referents were the total society as the bearer of religious values, the specific religious community, and such wider potential religious collectivities as "all believers" or "all mankind."

The second major characteristic of these religious value orientations is their emphasis on individual moral or religious activism, stressing the devotee's commitment to certain religiously prescribed tenets and lines of action and to the endeavor to implement them in social life.

Third, each of these value systems developed relatively independent ideo-

---

12. See Eisenstadt, "Religious Organizations and Political Process," *op. cit.*

logical systems, attempting to organize and evaluate, in terms of ultimate values, the social reality in which they grew up, to shape the world in terms of religious values and purposes, and to convert others to the same endeavor. The commitments imposed by these ideological systems were not simply embedded in ritual and religious acts but implied the development of more specific social or political activities.

All of these orientations denote the detachment of religious orientations from basic ascriptive symbols and communities. They were developed mainly in the centers of religious activity by the more active religious leaders and innovators. Among the broader strata the differentiation of religious activities and organizations was much more limited. Nevertheless these orientations did develop to some extent, constituting the basis for the potential willingness of these groups to join the new religions and for the possibility of their institutionalization.

From the interaction of the major religious orientations with the religious leaders' concrete goals and with the broader social and religious conditions prevalent in the society, as well as from the more specific relations with the rulers and other groups, developed the specific institutional characteristics of these religions, their organization into churches, orders, and sects or the more diffuse organizational patterns characteristic of China.

But in all these empires, the distinctiveness of the religious sphere was limited. On the one hand, there were many specialized religious organizations, such as temples, religious "foundations," priestly associations, sects, churches, and monastic orders, many of which were organized in a bureaucratic manner, and, in conjunction with these, many specialized religious roles—priests, preachers, monks, and occupants of different positions in ecclesiastical organizations and hierarchies. On the other hand, however, the worshipping community was, to a very large extent, either identical with local groups or closely related to them. Only within the various sects and monastic orders did a special type of religious community develop.

Neither the institutionalization nor the continuity of these religious systems was assured. The religious leaders who aimed to establish and institutionalize them within their respective societies faced several basic problems. The most general problem stemmed from the existence of relatively free-floating cultural and religious orientations and activities which were not embedded in ascriptive units. To maintain their place in the cultural order, religious organizations had to shape and direct these resources. They not only had to ensure the loyalty and adherence of their members, but they also had to compete for economic resources, manpower, allegiance and support, both with other religious groups and with other social spheres, especially the political and economic ones.

Thus, the leaders of these religions were faced with the internal problems of formulating and formalizing their creeds and traditions so as to articulate and organize them on a relatively differentiated cultural level, and also with the necessity of regulating and channelling the diverse dynamic orientations and elements that could develop within them.

In connection with these internal problems several policies and patterns of activity were developed by the religious elites and organizations in these societies. Perhaps the most important of these was the very extensive formalization and codification of religious traditions, as manifested in the codification of sacred books, in the development of schools devoted to interpretation of the texts, in the growth of special educational organizations for the spread of religious knowledge, and in the elaboration of comprehensive ideologies.

The religious leaders also faced more concrete organizational and external problems. Because they depended, in all their endeavors, on both the rulers and the broader strata in the society, they developed several basic aims. The first was to gain full official recognition and protection from the state as the established religion or, at least as a secondary but recognized and protected one. The second aim was to maintain independence and autonomy in the performance of the major religious functions, especially in internal government, organization of activities, and recruitment of members. This meant relative autonomy in the propagation of the creed and the maintenance of shrines, temples, and educational institutions, as well as independent determination and transmission of the major religious values and dogma. The demands for autonomy were directed mainly against the rulers and the bureaucracy who, as we have seen earlier, usually aspired to control the activities of the religious elite and to incorporate them into the general framework of their administrative activities.

The third major political objective of the religious elite, closely related to the first, was to preserve and extend the material bases (i.e., property) of the religious groups and institutions and to enhance their general social positions. A fourth objective, at least for some members of the religious elite, was to obtain positions of political and administrative influence.

XI

Whatever the success of the religious leaders in achieving these aims, the very institutionalization of these religions within the framework of their respective societies and polities could create continuous tension and give rise to several new problems.

The religious organizations needed the protection and help of the political institutions to establish and maintain their positions, organizations, and property, just as the political institutions needed the basic legitimation and support that could be provided only by the religious elite. This mutual dependence of relatively autonomous spheres could easily create many tensions, since each aimed to control the structural positions of the other and thus provide for its own needs. But whatever the scope of such conflicts and tensions, some *modus vivendi* was usually established, constituting a basic aspect of the institutionalization of these religions.

Thus in all of the societies studied, the religious elite upheld both the traditional legitimation of the rulers and supported, in principle, at least some of their political orientations and policies, despite the numerous conflicts over concrete issues arising between themselves and the political elite. Moreover, in most of the societies studied, the political participation of religious groups was, at least for certain periods of time, contained well within the basic framework of bureaucratic policy and institutions. In such cases these groups furthered the development of legitimate political struggle and contributed in this way to the continuity of the regime. The Mazdean Church in Persia, the Byzantine Church, and especially the Confucians and Buddhists in the Chinese Empire actively participated in politics and cooperated with the rulers. Thus they contributed, directly or indirectly, to the continuity of these systems. At the same time, the state provided important protection for the religious organizations.

But whatever the concrete *modus vivendi* between the rulers and any given religious elite or organization, in almost none of these societies—with the partial exception of Confucianism in China—did such mutual accommodation persist throughout the life of the empire or the religious organizations.

The very institutionalization of any such *modus vivendi* created the possibility for change both within the religions themselves and in their relations with other institutional spheres. The process of institutionalizing these religions and the necessity for continuous maintenance through varied policies and accommodations could easily enhance the contradictions inherent in the orientations of the religious leaders.

These contradictions were of several, often overlapping, kinds. One was between a "conservative" orientation that accepted the existing social order and the place of religion within it, on the one hand, and, on the other hand, a more radical orientation aiming to extend the autonomy of religious orientations and activities. Another was between an "other-worldly" emphasis stressing the perfection of purely religious attitudes and activities, and a more active, this-worldly orientation aiming at the transformation of the world.

Such contradictions were rooted in the relative autonomy and independent historical origins of the religious sphere, in its continuous interaction with the political sphere and in the nature of its value orientations. All these characteristics could serve as foci of crystallization for new religious groups—sects, groups of devotees, or "freelance" religious intellectuals upholding one or another of these orientations in its purity as against the more "compromise-ridden" activities of the established religious leaders and organizations. The religious elites, in the course of working out and implementing their various *modi vivendi* with the rulers, and in attempting to maintain their own interests, tended to alienate some of the religiously active elements as well as some of the broader strata.

Moreover, the relatively complex organizations of these religions, and the great importance of a formal written tradition and its exegesis, were fertile ground for the rise of various sectarian movements and orders. The possibility of sectarian development was also enhanced by the fact that in many of these societies several religious bodies and organizations competed with one another for predominance.

Hence within all these religions there developed many processes of change, which created new forms of religious organization. Some of these could be contained within the established religious framework, while others completely undermined it.

The same factors frequently also predisposed some of the religious groups and elites to develop more extreme political orientations and to participate—as in China, Persia, or Byzantium—in radical political and social movements, such as peasant uprisings, urban movements, and conspiracies. Cooperation between popular movements and leaders of religious secret societies was a common characteristic of rebellions in China and to some extent Byzantium and of peasant uprisings in France.

In still other cases—or in the same societies under changing circumstances—these religious organizations could also influence processes of change in the political system by instigating or furthering the withdrawal of active social and political support from the ruling elites. In this way they undermined the political frameworks of the empires and indirectly also the bases of the *modus vivendi* between political and religious institutions.

The exact strength and direction of these processes of change depended greatly on the basic value orientations and institutional characteristics of the religions and on the nature of their struggles and accommodations with the rulers and other centers of power in the society.

But the direction of these changes was not random, nor were these changes limitless. Organizationally, religious institutions could either undergo what might be called the "ossification" and "indrawing" of existing churches, as in the case of the Eastern Church after the fall of the Byzantine Empire, or, through the development of various sects and more independent religious activities, be transformed into less homogeneous and monolithic, more differentiated structures, as was the case in Western Christianity, especially in Protestantism, and to a lesser extent in early and "middle" Islam. The effect of these changes on religious orientations is either to enhance the tendency towards "other-worldliness," social passivity, withdrawal, and mysticism, or to encourage more active and differentiated this-worldly activity.[13]

XII

The preceding analysis of the processes of change in the centralized empires and in the major religions that developed within them is intended to illustrate the ways in which the institutionalization of a political, a religious, or any other social system in itself creates the potentialities and directions of change.[14]

The institutionalization of any social system means that certain norms, sanctions and organizations must be set up, and that policies through which these norms can be upheld and applied to a relatively large and complex variety of social situations must be implemented. These things are done by people who are placed in or attempt to achieve strategic positions and who aspire to certain goals. The new norms regulate the provision of various resources from other parts of the society to these power positions and to the new organizations, some of the relations among the different groups in the society, and the obligations of the occupants of these positions toward various groups in the society.

While the occupants of these positions naturally attempt to set up norms in accord with their own values, goals, and interests, they also define certain norms shared by a number of groups. Very often they legitimize these norms by values that are purportedly shared, to some extent, by a large part of the society and symbolized by themselves. Hence, such values tend to be binding on the rulers themselves.

But whatever the success of such attempts to establish common norms and legitimize them in terms of common values and symbols, these norms are probably never fully accepted by the entire society. Most groups within any society or collectivity tend to exhibit some autonomy in terms of their attitudes toward any such institutionalization, and they vary greatly in the extent of their willingness or ability to provide the resources demanded by the system. While for very long periods of time a great majority of the members of a given society may be to some degree identified with the values and norms of the system and willing to provide it with the resources it needs, other tendencies also develop. Some groups—like the aristocracy in the case of the empires

13. *Ibid.*

14. The same basic considerations are applied to role analysis in Shmuel N. Eisenstadt, Dov Weintraub and Nina Toren, "Analysis of Role Change," Jerusalem: The Hebrew University, Department of Sociology, Technical Note No. 7, Contract No. AFGI (052)-480 (mimeo.), 1963.

discussed above—may be greatly opposed to the very premises of the institutionalization of a given system, may share its values only to a very small extent, and may accept these norms only as the least among evils and as binding on them only in a very limited sense.

Others may share these values and accept the norms to a greater degree but, like the cultural and economic elites or sects, may look on themselves as the more appropriate repositories of these same values, may oppose the concrete level at which the norms are institutionalized by the elite in power, and may attempt to interpret them in different ways. Others again may develop new interpretations of existing values and strive for a change in the very bases of the institutional order. Hence any institutional system is never fully "homogeneous," that is, fully accepted or accepted to the same degree by all those participating in it, and these different orientations all may become foci of conflict and of potential institutional change.

Even more important, from the point of view of our analysis, is that whatever the initial attitudes of any given group to the basic premises of the institutional system, these may greatly change after the initial institutionalization of the system. Any institutionalization necessarily entails efforts to maintain the boundaries of the system, through continuous attempts to mobilize resources from different groups and individuals, and to maintain the legitimacy of the values, symbols and norms of the system. But continuous implementation of these policies may affect the positions of different groups in the society, giving rise to continuous shifts in the balance of power among them and in their orientations to the existing institutional system and its values.

Moreover, the institutionalization of any system usually creates new collectivities and organizations, such as the bureaucratic organizations in the centralized empires. These organizations necessarily develop needs, interests, and orientations of their own which may impinge on various other groups and institutional spheres.

Similarly, changes in the balance of forces within the system also facilitate the development and "maturation" of certain inherent tendencies in the structure and orientation of key groups and elites, as in the tendencies of some religious groups to develop and establish wider universalistic orientations and membership units, which may then develop beyond the basic premises of the system.

These processes may be intensified by the systemic relations between any given institutional framework or sphere and other spheres within the society. Whatever the degree of integration of the "total" society, systemic relations between, e.g., the political and the economic, or the political and the kinship systems, are inherent in any ongoing society. But as has been so often pointed out, the basic or predominant orientations and norms regulating each of these institutions differ to some extent. For example, family and kinship units tend to emphasize particularistic, diffuse, and ascriptive orientations while economic units emphasize universalism and achievement.[15]

These different institutional spheres, represented by the structurally patterned activities of occupants of the major positions within them, attempt to maintain their autonomy and tend to make contradictory demands on different groups to provide them with the necessary resources. Each may look for support from different groups in the society, thus exacerbating potential conflicts among the various groups, changing their relative strengths, and possibly undermining the premises of a given institutional system.

These contradictions, conflicts, and shifts in the balance of power may lead to the depletion of the resources needed to maintain a given system or give rise to the crystallization of new foci of resources and orientations which may in turn seek to create a new institutional system.

Events leading to different processes of change, as has been pointed out before, also affect the relations between any given institutional system and its external environment. Each institutional system is especially sensitive, in terms of dependence on resources and maintenance of its own boundaries, to certain aspects of its relations with its environment.

XIII

Thus we conclude that the institutionalization of a system creates the possibility that "antisystems," or groups with negative orientations toward its premises, will develop within it. While the nature and strength of such antisystems may vary, as between different institutional (i.e., religious, political) systems and between different types within each, and while they may often remain latent for very long periods of time, they also constitute important foci of change, under propitious conditions.

The existence of such contradictions or conflicts among the different institutional spheres and among different groups does not, of course, preclude the possibility that the system will maintain its boundaries more or less continuously, through a hierarchy of norms and accommodation or partial insulation of different subsystems, and that a definite order and stable relations among the system's parts will persist. But the possibility of conflict and potential change is always present, rooted in the very process of institutionalization, and the direction and occurrence of change depend heavily on the nature of this process.

Just as the predilection for change is necessarily built into any institutional

15. See Alvin W. Gouldner, "Reciprocity and Autonomy in Functional Theory," in Llewellyn Gross (ed.), *Symposium on Sociological Theory* (Evanston, Ill.: Row Peterson, 1959), pp. 241–71, and Gideon Sjoberg, "Contradictory Functional Requirements and Social Systems," *The Journal of Conflict Resolution* 4 (June 1960), pp. 198–258.

system, so the direction and scope of change are not random but depend, as we have shown in discussing the processes of change in the empires and in the great religions, on the nature of the system generating the change, on its values, norms and organizations, on the various internal forces operating within it and on the external forces to which it is especially sensitive because of its systemic properties. These various forces naturally differ between religious and political institutions and among different societies, but sensitivity to these forces and the tendency to change are inherent in all of them.

The analysis presented above does not pretend to solve all the problems in analyzing social change; we have not discussed the mechanisms of change, nor the relations between changes at different institutional levels of a given society. But at least we have indicated that for conceptual tools adequate to the analysis of change we need not necessarily go beyond systematic sociological analysis; rather, a full explication of systematic sociological concepts can provide a fruitful initial step for the analysis of change.

Five

SOCIAL CHANGE, DIFFERENTIATION, AND EVOLUTION

EVOLUTIONARY THEORY DOMINATED sociological thought in the nineteenth and early twentieth centuries, but since about 1920 interest in it has, on the whole, given way to preoccupation with systematic analysis of social systems, analysis of broad social and demographic trends, and investigation of the social determinants of behavior. The recent tentative revival of interest in an evolutionary perspective is closely related to growing interest in historical and comparative studies. It does not, of course, denote a mere "return" to the assumptions of the older schools, but it does imply revision and reappraisal of evolutionary theory in the light of recent advances in sociological theory and research.

The older evolutionary models broke down mainly on two stumbling blocks. The first was the assumption that the development of human societies is unilinear, and the major "stages" of development universal.[1] The second stumbling block was the failure to specify fully the systemic characteristics of evolving societies or institutions, as well as the mechanisms and processes of change through which the transition from one "stage" to another was effected. Most of the classical evolutionary schools tended, rather, to point out general causes of change (economic, technological, spiritual, etc.) or some general trends (e.g., the trend to complexity) inherent in the development of societies. Very often they confused such general tendencies with the causes of change or assumed that the general tendencies explain concrete instances of change.[2]

Originally published in *American Sociological Review* 29 (1964):375–86.

1. One of the best expositions of the strength and limitations of the classical evolutionary approach was written by a prominent contemporary sociologist identified with that approach. See Morris Ginsberg, "On the Concept of Evolution in Sociology" in *idem, Essays on Sociology and Social Philosophy,* Vol. 1 (London: William Heinemann, 1957), and *idem, Diversity of Morals* (London: William Heinemann, 1956), chs. 11 and 12. For a more recent summary, see T. B. Bottomore, *Sociology, A Guide to Problems and Literature* (London: Unwin University Books, 1962), chs. 7 and 16.

2. See Kenneth E. Bock, "Evolution, Function and Change," *American Sociological Review* 28 (April 1963), pp. 229–37. The use of general causes or trends for explanation of evolution can be found also in Marshall D. Sahlins and Elman R. Service (eds.), *Evolution and Culture* (Ann Arbor, Mich.: University of Michigan Press, 1960) who follow Leslie A. White, *The Evolution of Culture*

Hence, reappraisal of an evolutionary perspective is contingent on systematic explanation of the processes of change within a society, the processes of transition from one type of society to another, and especially the extent to which such transition may crystallize into different types or "stages" that evince some basic characteristics common to different societies. Despite contrary claims, the conceptual tools recently developed for the analysis of systematic properties of societies and social institutions may be used to analyze the concrete processes of change within them.

First, tendencies to change are inherent in all human societies, because they face basic problems to which no overall continuous solutions exist. These problems include uncertainties of socialization, perennial scarcity of resources relative to individual aspirations, and different, contrasting, types of social orientation or principles of social organization (e.g., *Gemeinschaft* vs. *Gesellschaft*) within the society.[3] Second, specific processes of change in any concrete society are closely related to the specific characteristics of its institutional structure and can be explained largely in terms of the crystallization of this structure and the problem of maintaining it. Moreover, the directions of change in any given society are greatly influenced and limited by its basic systematic characteristics and by the specific problems resulting from its institutionalization.[4]

From the point of view of reappraising evolutionary theory, however, the more crucial problem concerns the extent to which change from one type of society to another is not accidental or random but evinces overall evolutionary or "developmental" trends in the society's adaptability to an extending environment. In other words, the main problem here is the extent to which such changes may be envisaged as crystallizing into developmental "stages"—the key concept in classical evolutionary thought.

In the older evolutionary school such stages have been construed mostly in terms of "specialization" and "complexity." In recent works these concepts have been to a large extent replaced by that of "differentiation."[5] This replacement is not merely semantic: it reflects an important theoretical advance in the study of society—an advance that greatly facilitates critical reevaluation of the evolutionary perspective in the social sciences.

Differentiation is, like complexity or specialization, first of all a classifica-

---

(New York: McGraw-Hill, 1959). However, their distinction between general and specific evolution indicates that they are aware at least of some of the difficulties in such an assumption.

3. See Wilbert E. Moore, "A Reconsideration of Theories of Social Change," *American Sociological Review* 25 (December 1960), pp. 817 ff.

4. See Shmuel N. Eisenstadt, "Institutionalization and Change," *American Sociological Review* 29 (April 1964), pp. 49–59.

5. See, for instance, Robert M. MacIver and Charles Page, *Society* (New York: Rinehart, 1947); Talcott Parsons, *The Social System* (Glencoe, Ill.: The Free Press, 1951), chs. 4, 5; and Marion J. Levy, Jr., *The Structure of Society* (Princeton: Princeton University Press, 1952), especially ch. 7.

tory concept. It describes the ways through which the main social functions or the major institutional spheres of society become disassociated from one another, attached to specialized collectivities and roles, and organized in relatively specific and autonomous symbolic and organizational frameworks within the confines of the same institutionalized system.

In broad evolutionary terms, such continuous differentiation has been usually conceived as a continuous development from the "ideal" type of the primitive society or band in which all the major roles are allocated on an ascriptive basis, and in which the division of labor is based primarily on family and kinship units.[6] Development proceeds through various stages of specialization and differentiation.

Specialization is manifest first when each of the major institutional spheres develops, through the activities of people placed in strategic roles within it, its own organizational units and complexes, and its specific criteria of action. The latter tend to be more congruent with the basic orientations of a given sphere, facilitating the development of its potentialities—technological innovation, cultural and religious creativity, expansion of political power or participation, or development of complex personality structure.[7]

Secondly, different levels or stages of differentiation denote the degree to which major social and cultural activities, as well as certain basic resources— manpower, economic resources, commitments—have been disembedded or freed from kinship, territorial and other ascriptive units. On the one hand, these "free-floating" resources pose new problems of integration, while on the other they may become the basis for a more differentiated social order which is, potentially at least, better adapted to deal with a more variegated environment.

DIFFERENTIATION AND PROBLEMS OF INTEGRATION

The more differentiated and specialized institutional spheres become more interdependent and potentially complementary in their functioning within the same overall institutionalized system. But this very complementarity creates more difficult and complex problems of integration. The growing autonomy of each sphere of social activity, and the concomitant growth of interdependence and mutual interpretation among them, pose for each sphere more difficult problems in crystallizing its own tendencies and potentialities and in regu-

6. For a recent discussion of primitive societies from an evolutionary point of view, see Elman R. Service, *Primitive Social Organization, An Evolutionary Perspective* (New York: Random House, 1962).

7. For an earlier approach, see Pitirim A. Sorokin, *Society, Culture and Personality* (New York: Harper, 1947), and for one of the fullest recent analytic approaches, see Talcott Parsons and Edward A. Shils (eds.), *Toward a General Theory of Action,* (Cambridge, Mass.: Harvard University Press, 1951), p. 2.

lating its normative and organizational relations with other spheres.[8] And at each more "advanced" level or stage of differentiation, the increased autonomy of each sphere creates more complex problems of integrating these specialized activities into one systemic framework.[9]

Continuous regulation of these more specialized units and of the flow of "free-floating" resources among them necessitates the institutionalization of certain symbolic, normative, and organizational patterns[10]—written language, generalized legal systems, and various types of complex social organization— which evince, at each more complex level of differentiation, a greater scope of generalization.

Perhaps the best indication of the importance of these macrosocietal integrative problems is the emergence of a "center," on which the problems of different groups within the society increasingly impinge.[11] The emergence of a political or religious "center" of a society, distinct from its ascriptive components, is one of the most important breakthroughs of development from the relatively closed kinship-based primitive community. In some of the archaic societies of the ancient Near East, pre-Han China, and various preliminary stages of city-states, the center in these first stages of differentiation was not only structurally differentiated from the major ascriptive groups but also distinct from them, being largely identical with relatively closed but already differentiated higher-status groups.

With growing differentiation in later city-states and in feudal and centralized imperial systems, impingement of the broader groups and strata on the center increased somewhat. This is most clearly visible at the onset of modernization, when broader groups and strata tend to be drawn into the center, demanding greater participation.

Recognition of the integrative problems that are attendant on new levels of differentiation constitutes the main theoretical implication of the concept

---

8. For an analysis of these problems in one major cultural and social sphere, see Robert N. Bellah's companion article in this issue on evolution in religion.

9. For an analysis of one such case see Shmuel N. Eisenstadt, *The Political Systems of Empires* (New York: The Free Press, 1963).

10. Talcott Parsons describes these as "evolutionary universals" in his companion article in this issue.

11. On the concept of "center of society" and on the problems of macrosociological analysis, see Edward A. Shils, "Epilogue," in Talcott Parsons, Edward A. Shils, Kaspar D. Naegele, and Jesse R. Pitts (eds.), *Theories of Society* (New York: The Free Press, 1961), Vol. 2, especially pp. 1441–1445. For special developments in modern societies see Daniel Lerner, *The Passing of Traditional Society* (Glencoe, Ill.: The Free Press, 1958); Talcott Parsons, *Structure and Process in Modern Societies*, (Glencoe, Ill.: The Free Press, 1960), ch. 4; Edward A. Shils, *Political Development in New States* (The Hague: Mouton, 1963); and Shmuel N. Eisenstadt, *Modernization, Growth and Diversity*, The Carnegie Faculty Seminar on Political and Administrative Development, Indiana University, Bloomington, Ind., 1963.

of differentiation. How does this analytical implication affect the possibility of reappraising the evolutionary perspective in sociological theory?

Such a reappraisal is contingent on the explication of three major problems. First, the occurrence of changes that facilitate growing differentiation must be explained. Second, we must understand the conditions that ensure institutionalization of more differentiated, generalized, and adaptable systems, and third, the possibility that parallel systems will develop within different societies should be evaluated. We are as yet far from any definitive answers to these questions, but at least we can point out some of the most important problems.

The passage of a given society from one stage of differentiation to another is contingent on the development within it of certain processes of change which create a degree of differentiation that cannot be contained within the preexisting system. Growing differentiation and the consequent structural breakthroughs may take place through a secular trend of differentiation, or through the impact of one or a series of abrupt changes, or both. These tendencies may be activated by the occupants of strategic roles within the major institutional spheres as they attempt to broaden the scope and develop the potentialities of their respective spheres. The extent to which these changes are institutionalized, and the concrete form they take in any given society, necessarily depend on the basic institutional contours and premises of the preexisting system, on its initial level of differentiation, and on the major conflicts and propensities for change within it.[12]

But we need not assume that all changes in all societies necessarily increase differentiation. On the contrary, the available evidence shows that many social changes do not give rise to overall changes in the scope of differentiation, but instead result mainly in changes in the relative strength and composition of different collectivities or in the integrative criteria of a particular institutional sphere. Largely because the problem has not yet been fully studied we do not know exactly what conditions facilitate or precipitate these different types of change in different societies.[13]

Similarly we need not assume that the successful, orderly institutionalization of a new, more differentiated social system is a necessary outcome of every instance of social change or of increased social differentiation within a society. Moreover, the concrete contours of such institutionalization may greatly vary among different societies at similar or parallel stages of differentiation.

The degree of differentiation refers mainly to the "division of labor" in any social system. It denotes the extent to which a society has been transformed

12. See Eisenstadt, "Institutionalization and Change," *op. cit.*
13. But see Fred Eggan, "Cultural Drift and Social Change," *Current Anthropology* 4 (October 1963), pp. 347–60. For a preliminary attempt to analyze this problem in one case, see Eisenstadt, *The Political Systems of Empires, op. cit.*, ch. 12.

from something approximating Durkheim's "mechanical" model to a potentially more "organic" one; it also denotes the extent to which new regulative or integrative problems cannot be dealt with by preexisting institutions. Growing differentiation entails extension of the scope and depth of internal problems and of external environmental exigencies to which any social system is sensitive and with which it may or may not be able to deal.

The growing autonomy of the different institutional spheres, and the extension of their organizational scope, not only increases the range and depth of "social" and human problems, but it opens up new possibilities for development and creativity—for technological development, expansion of political power or rights, or cultural, religious, philosophical, and personal creativity. Growing differentiation also enhances systemic sensitivity to a much wider physical-technical environment and to more comprehensive intersocietal relations. But the growth of systemic sensitivity to a broader and more variegated environment, to new problems and exigencies, does not necessarily imply the development of the ability to deal with these problems, nor does it indicate the ways in which these problems may be solved. At any given level of differentiation, an institutional sphere may or may not achieve an adequate degree of integration, and the potentialities unfolded through the process of differentiation may be "wasted"—i.e., fail to become crystallized into an institutional structure.

RESPONSES TO GROWING DIFFERENTIATION

The possibility that similar processes of change and institutionalization of different levels of differentiation may occur in different societies can be explained only so far as the available evidence bears out the assumption that the tendencies of major social spheres to autonomy and some of the basic potentialities for development in these spheres are characteristic of all societies.

Unlike the classical evolutionary writers, however, most "recent" theorists, from Weber on, do not assume that the types of social system characteristic of a given level of differentiation take on the same concrete institutional contours in all societies.[14] But the implications of this position have not yet been fully explicated.

At any level of development, response to the problems created by the

14. See Max Weber, *The Theory of Social and Economic Organization* (London: William Hodge, 1941), especially ch. 3. More recent works dealing with these problems include Robert Redfield, *The Primitive World and Its Transformations* (Ithaca, N.Y.: Cornell University Press, 1953); MacIver and Page, *op. cit.*, especially chs. 2 and 3; Talcott Parsons, *Structure and Process in Modern Societies, op. cit.*, ch. 3; and Verne F. Ray (ed.), *Intermediate Societies, Social Mobility and Communication*, Proceedings of the 1959 Annual Spring Meeting of the American Ethnological Society (Seattle: University of Washington Press, 1959).

process of differentiation may take one of several different forms. The most extreme outcome is failure to develop any adequate institutional solution to the new problems arising from growing differentiation. Aside from biological extinction, the consequences may be total or partial disintegration of the system, a semiparasitic existence at the margin of another society, or total submersion within another society.

Thus, for instance, the Greek city-states at the end of the Periclean period—in contrast to the late Roman Republic—did not produce a political leadership capable of building new types of political regime; as distinct sociopolitical units they became extinct. Similarly, many societies undergoing modernization lack the ability to crystallize new, viable regimes in the economic, political or cultural fields. In Bulgaria, for instance, Gerschenkron has analyzed an interesting case of what he calls "missed opportunity." The Congo constitutes perhaps the most extreme instance of this problem among contemporary new states.[15]

A less extreme type of response tends to lead to "regression," i.e., to the institutionalization of less differentiated systems. Examples include the establishment of small patrimonial or semifeudal chiefdoms on the ruins of the Ahmenid Empire, the development of dispersed tribal-feudal systems at the downfall of the Roman Empire, and similar developments on the ruins of Greek city-states.[16] Many such regressive developments are only partial in the sense that within some parts of the new institutional structure some nuclei of more differentiated and creative orientations may survive or even develop. Sometimes, but certainly not always, these nuclei "store" entrepreneurial ability for possible—but not inevitable—future developments.

Another possibility, which perhaps overlaps with the last one but is not always identical to it, is the development of a social system in which the processes of differentiation and change go on relatively continuously in one part or sphere of a society without yet becoming fully integrated into a stable wider framework. In such situations a continuous process of unbalanced change may develop, resulting either in a breakdown of the existing institutional framework, or in stabilization at a relatively low level of integration.

Perhaps the best examples of such developments can be found in various dual conquest societies (e.g., conquest of the sedentary population by nomads in the Mongol Empire) and especially in the preindependence stages of modern colonial societies. In the colonial societies, changes in the "central" areas have not been congruent with changes at the local level. Most changes intro-

15. See Alexander A. Gerschenkron, *Economic Backwardness in Historical Perspective* (Cambridge, Mass.: Harvard University Press, 1962), ch. 8, and also Shmuel N. Eisenstadt, "Breakdowns of Modernization," *Economic Development and Cultural Change*, forthcoming.

16. For analysis of some of the relevant societies, see Eisenstadt, *The Political Systems of Empires, op. cit.*, including full bibliographical references.

duced either directly or indirectly by the colonial powers have been focused on the central political or economic institutions of the society. Central political structures and orientations have been greatly altered by the introduction of unitary systems of administration, the unification or regularization of taxation, the establishment of modern court procedures, and at later stages, the introduction of limited types of representation. Similarly, many changes have been effected in the economy, notably the change to a market economy.

At the same time, however, the colonial powers (or indigenous traditional rulers) saw it as part of their task to effect these changes only within the limits set by the existing institutions and their own interests. The rulers tried to contain the changes taking place in the local rural and urban communities within the preexisting traditional systems, and at the local level most of their administrative efforts were aimed at strengthening existing organizations and relations, maintaining peace and order, and reorganizing the system of taxation. Thus, while the administration attempted to introduce innovations—particularly new taxes and improved methods of revenue administration—it did so within a relatively unchanged social setting, with the implicit goal of limiting changes to technical matters.

These processes of uneven change in colonial societies, unlike parallel but less intensive and continuous processes in the older conquest societies, could not be frozen at a given stage. Attempts at indirect rule, on the one hand, and the widespread efforts of indigenous rulers to limit changes to purely technical matters, on the other, reflect attempts to stop development at a particular stage, but such devices did not usually have different structural results and needs of the colonial powers or the indigenous ruling groups, their growing dependency on continuously changing international markets and international political organization, precluded any freezing of development, and tended to draw wider strata of the colonial societies into the orbit of modern institutional settings. This in turn facilitated the development of social movements that tended to focus on solidary symbol to the exclusion of other problems.[17]

A fourth, and perhaps the most variegated, type of response to growing differentiation consists of some structural solution which is on the whole congruent with the relevant problems. But within this broad type a wide variety of concrete institutional arrangements is possible. Such different solutions usually succeed for a long time. Each solution denotes a different structure crystallized according to different criteria, and different modes of interpenetration of the major social spheres.

Thus, drawing again on examples from the great centralized empires, we

17. On the Nomad Empires, see Owen Lattimore, *Studies in Frontier History* (London: Oxford University Press, 1962), especially chs. 3 and 4. On the processes of unbalanced change in colonial societies see Shmuel N. Eisenstadt, *Essays on Sociological Aspects of Political and Economic Development* (The Hague: Mouton, 1961).

see that although the initial stages of socioeconomic differentiation were relatively similar in Byzantium, in the later (Abbasside) Caliphate, and in post-Han China, each of these societies developed different overall institutional structures. The Byzantine Empire became a highly militarized and politically oriented system, while in the Caliphate a theocratic structure, based on continuous attempts to institutionalize a new type of universalistic politico-religious community, developed. China developed a centralized system based, at the center, on the power of the Emperor and the bureaucracy, and at the local level, on the relative predominance of the gentry. The selective channels of the examination and the literati were the major mechanisms integrating the local and central levels.[18]

Among modern and modernizing societies an even wider variety of concrete institutional types can be found at all stages of modernization. Modern societies differ, as is well known, not only in the degree of economic or political differentiation, but also in the basic integrative criteria and symbols in the political, economic, or cultural spheres. At each level of differentiation a great variety of institutional patterns occurs.[19]

One very interesting and intriguing possibility is the development of a relatively stable system in which the major institutional spheres vary in degree of differentiation. One of the most important examples of such variation occurs in feudal systems, which are characterized by a relatively high degree of differentiation in some of the central cultural roles as against a much smaller degree of differentiation in the economic and political roles.[20] Similar instances of "uneven" differentiation which have not yet crystallized into stable overall institutional systems exist in some of the more differentiated tribal and patrimonial societies.

One interesting aspect of uneven differentiation is that the more differentiated units of such related societies (e.g., the church in feudal or patrimonial systems) develop a sort of international system of their own apart from that of their "parent" societies.

Similarly, various aspects of modernization may develop in different degrees in the major spheres of modernizing societies. As one example, in many new states today—especially in Africa but also in Asia—we witness a continu-

18. See Eisenstadt, *The Political Systems of Empires, op. cit.*

19. On the varieties of modern societies see Parsons, *Structure and Process in Modern Societies, op. cit.*, ch. 3, and "A Revised Analytical Approach to the Theory of Social Stratification," in *Essays in Sociological Theory* (rev. ed.) (Glencoe, Ill.: The Free Press, 1954), pp. 386–441; Clifford Geertz (ed.), *Old Societies and New States* (New York: The Free Press, 1963); and Eisenstadt, *Modernization, Protest and Change* (Englewood Cliffs: Prentice Hall, 1966).

20. See Otto Hintze, Wesen un Verbreitung des Feudalismus," *Sitzungsberichte der Preussischen Akademie der Wissenschaften, Phil. Hist. Klasse,* 1929, 5, 321–347, and Rushton Coulborn (ed.), *Feudalism in History* (Princeton: Princeton University Press, 1956), p. 1. C. L. Cahen, "Réflexions sur L'usage du mot de 'Féodalite,'" *Journal of the Economic and Social History of the Orient* 3 (April 1960), pp. 1–20.

ous extension of political modernization, which is not usually accompanied by anything approaching a similar degree of development in the economic sphere, even where economic development is an important slogan. In many of these societies these varying degrees of modernization seem to coalesce into ongoing social and political systems, though at a minimal level of efficiency and integration.[21] This structural type may sometimes be similar to, or a derivative of, the product of continuous "unbalanced" change described above. But much more research is needed to elucidate the exact relations between the two.

The variety of integrative criteria and institutional contours at any level of differentiation is, of course, not limitless. The very notion of interdependence among major institutional spheres negates the assumption that any number of levels of differentiation in different institutional spheres can coalesce into a relatively stable institutionalized system. The level of differentiation in any one sphere necessarily constitutes, within broad limits, a precondition for the effective institutionalization of certain levels of differentiation in other social spheres. But within these broad limits of mutual preconditioning a great deal of structural variety is possible.

CONSTRICTED DEVELOPMENT

Not only may different institutional contours and integrative mechanisms develop at each level of differentiation, but each such structure, once institutionalized, creates its own boundary-maintaining mechanisms, its own directions of change, and its potential for further development or for breakdown and regression. Each such institutional system tends to develop specific tendencies toward "de-differentiation," or the constriction of the new potentialities for further development. The growing differentiation and increasing interdependence among the various more autonomous and diversified institutional spheres increases the probability that one sphere will attempt to dominate the other coercively, by restricting and regimenting their tendencies toward autonomy.

This probability is especially strong with respect to the political and religious (or value) spheres, because these spheres are especially prone to "totalistic" orientations that tend to negate the autonomy of other spheres. Religious and political elites may attempt to dominate other spheres, imposing rigid frameworks based on their own criteria. The aim of such policies is usually an effective de-differentiation of the social system, and they may result in rigidity and stagnation, or precipitate continual breakdown of the system. These tendencies to de-differentiation are usually very closely related to the specific processes of change that may develop within any institutionalized system.

21. See Eisenstadt, *Modernization, Growth and Diversity, op. cit.*

Thus, in the Byzantine Empire, the centralistic tendencies of the monarchs and the Church alternated with the more centrifugal tendencies of the aristocracy and some peasant groups, while the relatively high levels of political commitment demanded by the polity conflicted with the strong tendencies toward passivity and "otherworldliness" among elements within the Church. In the long run, the predominance of the latter alternatives contributed to the downfall of the Byzantine Empire and the "ossification" of the Eastern Church.

This outcome was also facilitated by the weakness of later emperors who oscillated between repressive policies and giving in to the aristocratic forces, in both cases without developing a consistent new institutional framework.

The situation was different in the early Caliphate. On the one hand there was a strong universalistic emphasis on the state as the framework of the religious community but in a way subordinate to it. On the other hand, no comprehensive, independent, and cohesive organization of the religious groups and functionaries developed. Political participation was confined mostly to court cliques, and neither participation in the bureaucracy nor the religious check on political authority was effective because no machinery other than revolt existed to enforce it. Indeed, various religious sects and movements continually arose, very often contributing to the downfall of the state.

This aspect of the early Caliphates gave rise to a continual oscillation between "totalistic" political-religious movements, aiming at the total transformation of the political regime through various illegitimate means—assassinations, rebellions—and an other-worldly passivity that only helped to maintain the despotic character of the existing political regimes.

In the later Caliphate, various sects tried to overthrow the more differentiated polity and establish simple, de-differentiated political communities; these attempts alternated with military-bureaucratic usurpations. These movements, which often overlapped, blocked further political development.[22]

Similarly, breakdowns of relatively differentiated frameworks and attempts to "de-differentiate" have also occurred in various modern modernizing societies. In the more recent period such processes have developed in several "new states" like Burma, Indonesia, or Pakistan. These developments are not entirely dissimilar from other less recent examples. The initial modernization of China, so often used as a negative example in comparison with the more successful initial modernization of Japan, comes to mind here. Similarly, the long histories of several Latin American countries represent a similar process. Although in many of them only the very minimal structural or socio-demographic features of modernization developed over a very long time, in other cases, as in

22. See Eisenstadt, *The Political Systems of Empires, op. cit.*, and "Institutionalization and Change," *op. cit.*

Chile and especially in pre-Peron Argentina, evident progress toward modernization was halted or reversed.

Lastly, the rise of militarism in Japan and especially the European Fascism and Nazism of the twenties and thirties should be mentioned here as perhaps the most important case of a breakdown of modernization at a much more advanced level of development.

In each of these cases we witness the breakdown of a relatively differentiated and modern framework, the establishment of a less differentiated framework or the development of blockages and eruptions leading to institutionalized stagnation, rigidity, and instability.[23]

Thus, specific processes of institutional change open up some potentialities but may block others, and in some cases the institutionalization of a given solution may "freeze" further development or give rise to stagnation or continual breakdown. In these cases the new systems are unable to adapt effectively to the wider and more variegated environments to which they became exposed as a result of the differentiation they have undergone.[24]

CAUSES OF DIFFERENT EVOLUTIONARY PATHS

The great variety of institutional and integrative countours of different societies arriving at similar levels or stages of differentiation may be due to several different, yet interconnected, reasons. First, different societies arrive at the same level of differentiation through different historical paths and through a variety of concrete structural forms. Thus, for instance, the political systems of centralized empires could develop from city-states, or from patrimonial or feudal regimes. These different antecedents greatly affected the social composition and the concrete organization of the new centralized structure as well as the basic orientations and problems of its rulers.

Similarly, the process of modernization may begin in tribal groups, in caste societies, in different types of peasant society, and in societies with different degrees and types of prior urbanization. These groups differ greatly with regard to resources and abilities for setting up and implementing relatively differentiated goals, and for regulating the increasingly complex relations among different parts of the society.

One aspect of the variety among these antecedents of differentiation is of special interest. Within many relatively undifferentiated societies exist en-

23. See Eisenstadt, "Breakdowns of Modernization," *op. cit.*

24. One of the most interesting recent comparative analyses of the development of different institutional structures and different potentialities for further change, at a similar level of differentiation is Marshal D. Sahlins, "Poor Man, Rich Man, Big Man, Chief: Political Types in Melanesia and Polynesia," *Comparative Studies in Society and History* 5 (April 1963), pp. 285–304.

claves of much more differentiated and specialized activities, especially in the economic and cultural spheres. Thus, cities function in many societies not only as administrative or cultural centers but very often as distinct entities, to some extent separated from the rest of society evincing a much higher degree of differentiation and specialization in the cultural or economic field. Similarly, monasteries and monastic orders, sects and academies, and very often special ethnic and religious minorities and special religious-tribal federations, may to some extent be detached from the wider society and evince, at least in certain spheres, a higher degree of differentiation. In more modern times various political, religious, and intellectual sects and elites may constitute important enclaves of more differentiated activities.[25]

Very often enclaves of this sort constitute parts of an international system of their own which transcends, at any given time, the confines of the total society to which they belong as well as its own international system.

Such enclaves may be very important sources of innovation within a society. Their presence or absence in any "antecedent" stage may greatly influence the scope and nature of the different integrative solutions that may be institutionalized at a later stage of differentiation.

Third, the variability of institutional contours at the same level of differentiation also stems from differences among predominant elites. Elites may develop either in different institutional spheres or in the same sphere but with different ideologies and orientations of action. Some of them may be more influential than others in establishing the detailed contours of the new institutional system.

Thus, to return to our earlier example, the major differences in the institutional contours among the Chinese, Byzantine, and Abbaside Empires has been to no small degree influenced by the different types of predominant elites—the bureaucratic-literati in China, the separate military and religious elites in Byzantium, and the militant sectarian elite in the Caliphate.

Similarly, Shils' analysis of the different institutional patterns of modern and modernizing societies—political democracy, tutelary democracy, modernizing oligarchy, totalitarian oligarchy, and traditional oligarchy—shows how the crystallization of each such type is influenced not only by the broad structural conditions of these societies but also, to a very large degree, by the composition and orientation of the leading elites in each type of society.[26] Kerr and

25. For an analysis of some modern intellectual sectarian groups see, in addition to Weber's classical analysis of the Protestant Ethic, Franco Venturi, *Roots of Revolution* (New York: Alfred A. Knopf, 1960); Vladimir C. Nahirny, "The Russian Intelligentsia From Men of Ideas to Men of Convictions," *Comparative Studies in Society and History* 4 (July 1962), pp. 403–36; Harry J. Benda, "Non-Western Intelligentsia as Political Elites," in John H. Kautsky (ed.), *Political Change in Underdeveloped Countries, Nationalism and Communism* (New York: Wiley, 1962), pp. 235–52.

26. Shils, *Political Development in the New States, op. cit.*

associates have shown in a recent analysis that different modernizing elites tend to develop different strategies with regard to some major problems of social and economic policy, such as the pace of industrialization, sources of funds, priorities in development, pressures on enterprises and managers, the educational system, policies of agriculture, methods of allocation of labor, and many others.[27]

INNOVATING ELITES

These considerations—especially recognition of the complex relations between the processes of social change and structural differentiation, on the one hand, and viable institutionalization of different types of structure, on the other—are crucial to the critical reevaluation of the evolutionary perspective in the social sciences.

How can we explain the variability of institutionalized solutions to the problems arising from the development of a given level of structural differentiation? We must first recognize that the emergence of a solution, i.e., the institutionalization of a social order congruent with the new range of problems, is not necessarily given in the process of differentiation. We must discard the assumption—underlying, even if only implicitly, many studies of comparative institutions in general and of modernization in particular—that the conditions giving rise to structural differentiation, and to "structural sensitivity" to a greater range of problems, also create the capacity to solve these problems or determine the nature of such solutions.

The crucial problem is the presence or absence, in one or several institutional spheres, of an active group of special "entrepreneurs," or an elite able to offer solutions to the new range of problems. Among modern sociologists Weber came closest to recognizing this problem when he stressed that the creation of new institutional structures depends heavily on the "push" given by various "charismatic" groups or personalities and that the routinization of charisma is critical for the crystallization and continuation of new institutional structures. The development of such "charismatic" personalities or groups constitutes perhaps the closest social analogy to "mutation."

A number of questions pertaining to such elites and their relation to the broader social strata and structure in which they operate should be considered here, as possible guides to further research.

First, under what conditions do leaders or entrepreneurs with the requisite vision and organizational ability appear at all? Second, what is the nature of this "vision," or the proposed institutional solution to the problems attendant

27. Clark Kerr, *et al., Industrialism and Industrial Man* (Cambridge, Mass.: Harvard University Press, 1960).

on growing differentiation? This problem has two aspects. One has to do with the particular institutional sphere within which an elite develops and is most active, or the values and orientations it especially emphasizes and attempts to institutionalize or "impose" as the dominant values of the new social structure. The other aspect is the nature of the concrete solution that the emerging elite proposes within this particular institutional framework. At any level of differentiation a given social sphere contains not one but several, often competing, possible orientations and potentialities for development. Again, Weber saw this most clearly when he showed that religious institutions may take several forms, often contradictory, at any level of differentiation of the religious sphere from other institutions. Thus, at the stage when autonomous religious orientations and organizations break away from the relatively closed "primitive" community, prophets or mystagogues may arise, and at higher levels of differentiation, sectarian developments may compete with tendencies to establish Churches, or strong "other-worldly" orientations, with "this-worldly" ones.[28]

Finally, we should consider readiness of competing elites and various wider segments of the society to accept the new elite's solutions, i.e., to provide at least the minimal resources necessary for the institutionalization of the proposed solutions. Within broad limits, the degree of correspondence between the elite's "vision" and the needs of other groups varies; it is not fully determined by the existing or developing level of differentiation.

As yet, we know little about the specific conditions, as distinct from the more general trend to structural differentiation, that facilitate the rise of new elites, and which influence the nature of their basic orientations, on the one hand, and their relations with broader strata, on the other. Available indications, however, are that factors beyond the general trend to differentiation are important. For example, various special enclaves, such as sects, monasteries, sectarian intellectual groups, or scientific communities, play an important role in the formation of such elites. And a number of recent studies have indicated the importance of certain familial, ideological, and educational orientations and institutions.[29]

28. See Max Weber, *The Sociology of Religion*, trans. Ephraim Fischoff (Boston: Beacon Press, 1963), especially chs. 4, 10, 11. For an interesting modern case study bearing on this problem see Ernest Gellner, "Sanctity, Puritanism, Secularism and Nationalism in North Africa," *Archives de Sociologie des Religions* 15 (January–June 1963), pp. 71–87.

29. See David C. McClelland, *The Achieving Society* (Princeton: Van Nostrand, 1960), and "National Character and Economic Growth in Turkey and Iran," in Lucien W. Pye (ed.), *Communication and Political Development* (Princeton: Princeton University Press, 1963), pp. 152–82; and Everett Hagen, *On the Theory of Social Change* (Homewood, Ill.: The Dorsey Press, 1962); Clifford Geertz, "Modernization in Moslem Society: The Indonesian Case," in *Cultural Motivation to Progress and the Three Great World Religions in South and South East Asia*, An International Seminar sponsored by the University of the Philippines, Manila, and The Congress for Cultural Freedom, Manila, 1963 (mimeo.), and *idem. Peddlers and Princes* (Chicago: University of Chicago Press, 1963).

Within this context the whole problem of the extent to which institutional patterns are crystallized not through "independent invention" within a society but through diffusion from other societies, should be reexamined. Cases of diffusion might be partially due to the successful "importation," by entrepreneurial groups on the margins of a given society, of acceptable solutions to latent problems or "needs" within that society.

Thus, at any given level of differentiation the crystallization of different institutional orders is shaped by the interaction between the broader structural features of the major institutional spheres, on the one hand and, on the other hand, the development of elites or entrepreneurs in some of the institutional spheres of that society, in some of its enclaves, or even in other societies with which it is in some way connected.

The variability in the concrete components of such interaction helps to explain the great—but not limitless—variety of structural and integrative forms that may be institutionalized at any given level of differentiation. It indicates also that while different societies may arrive at broadly similar stages of evolution in terms of the differentiation of the major institutional and symbolic spheres, the concrete institutional contours developed at each such step, as well as the possible outcomes of such institutionalization in terms of further development, breakdown, regression or stagnation, may greatly differ among them.

SUMMARY

The considerations presented above constitute the background for a reappraisal of the evolutionary perspective within the framework of recent sociological theory. An evolutionary perspective makes sense, as we have seen, only so far as at least some of the processes of change that are inherent in the very nature of any social system, create the potentialities for institutionalization of more differentiated social and symbolic systems. But recognition of the relation between such changes and institutionalization of more differentiated social orders must be tempered by several systematic considerations.

First, the preceding analysis does not imply that all processes of social change necessarily give rise to changes in overall institutional systems. While the potentialities for such systematic changes (as distinct from changes in patterns of behavior, or in the composition of subgroups, or in the contents of the major integrative criteria of different spheres), exist in all societies, the tempo and direction of such changes vary.

Second, we need not assume that all systemic changes that alter the scope of differentiation within the major spheres of a society necessarily result in the institutionalization of a new, more differentiated social order, better adapted to a wider and more variegated environment. Under certain circumstances, differentiation may also lead to "regression," stagnation, attempts to dedifferentiate, or breakdown.

Third, even when structural differentiation is institutionalized, the concrete contours of the new institutional and symbolic structure may greatly vary; many concrete structural and cultural crystallizations are possible at each "stage" of differentiation.

Thus, the degree of differentiation within a given society or institutional field does not in itself determine the concrete contours of the system. The institutionalization of greater ranges of differentiation, of a wider scope of autonomy for each major social sphere, and the successful regulation of free-floating resources may rise to new types of social, political or cultural structure, each of which has different potentialities for further change, for breakdown, or for development.

The concepts of differentiation and of "stages" are important guides for identifying the crucial breakthroughs at which different spheres of social and cultural activity are freed from various ascriptive frameworks, and the potential for crystallization of more differentiated social and symbolic systems is enhanced. But these concepts neither describe nor explain the concrete crystallizations that appear at these junctures.[30]

Because the conditions giving rise to structural differentiation differ from those that encourage the formation of new elites who can provide solutions for the problems attendant on such differentiation, the assumption that evolution is undirectional at any given stage of differentiation is untenable.

These different types of concrete institutional crystallization are not, however, entirely random. Study of the interaction between processes of differentiation and the formation and activities of different elites may help to explain systematically the possibilities for institutionalization of such different integrative principles and concrete structures at a given level of societal differentiation. Systematic analysis of the interaction between these different types of condition may provide an approach to the explanation of specific historical constellations. But in this endeavour broad evolutionary considerations only indicate ranges of possibilities and types of potential breakthroughs.

30. The distinction between general and specific evolution, as laid out by Sahlins and Service, *Evolution and Culture, op. cit.,* is in some ways similar to the point of view taken up here. But their insistence on the preponderance of technological factors in evolution leads them to neglect the internal dynamics of change in different social and cultural systems. Even more questionable, from the point of view of the present discussion , is their assumption—as phrased by Eggan—"that these specific, particular developments necessarily add up to the succession of culture through stages of overall progress, which is general evolution." See F. Eggan, "Cultural Drift and Social Change," *op. cit.,* p. 355.

Six

SOCIETAL GOALS, SYSTEMIC NEEDS, SOCIAL INTERACTION, AND INDIVIDUAL BEHAVIOR: SOME TENTATIVE EXPLORATIONS

PARSONS' AND HOMANS' THEORIES may seem to constitute completely antithetic approaches to the nature of the social order, in the tradition of many older social philosophical controversies. Homans attempts to explain the social behavior of individuals and the crystallization of social organization and institutions as derivable from individual drives, goals, and aspirations, as governed by a set of principles derived from the laws of supply and demand, on the one hand, and of Skinnerian psychology on the other. Parsons, however, is often said to conceive social order as rooted in the systemic nature of social organization, in its normative focus, and in the systems of societal needs, phases, and roles that regulate the behavior of individual members of any group or society. Each of these approaches has been subjected to continuous criticism which is derived largely from the basic premises of the other.

The major criticisms leveled against Homans and some of his followers refer to what has been called their psychological reductionism, that is, to their attempts to explain or to derive patterns of institutional organization and behavior from laws of individual behavior—attempts that have proven rather unsuccessful, as can be seen in the last chapter of his book, *Social Behavior.*[1]

From the other direction, Homans and others have directed certain basic

Reprinted with permission of Macmillan College Publishing Company from *Institutions and Social Exchange: The Sociology of Talcott Parsons and George C. Homans*, edited by Herman Turk and Richard L. Simpson, © 1971 by Macmillan College Publishing Company, Inc.

In this paper I have tried to develop further some points of view presented earlier in my chapter called "The Study of Processes of Institutionalization, Institutional Change and Comparative Institutions," in S. N. Eisenstadt, *Essays on Comparative Institutions* (New York: John Wiley & Sons, 1965), especially pp. 16–40; in my introduction to S. N. Eisenstadt (ed.), *Max Weber on Charisma and Institution Building* (Chicago: University of Chicago Press, 1968); and in my articles on "Sociological Thought" and "Social Institutions" in the *International Encyclopedia of the Social Sciences* (New York: The Macmillan Company and The Free Press, 1968). I am indebted to Herman Turk for helpful comments on an earlier draft.

1. George C. Homans, *Social Behavior: Its Elementary Forms* (New York: Harcourt, Brace & World, 1961), chap. 18.

arguments against the "systemic" or "functional-structural" approach repre-sented by Parsons and others. Leaving aside the more personal aspects of these polemics, their major criticism is that the "functional-structural" school tends to "reify" the social system, its goals, and its needs to an extent that denies the autonomy of individual behavior within the social setting and of the various parts of social systems and organizations. Because of this, sociologists of the functional-structural school, such as Parsons, are allegedly unable to explain both the variability of behavior by individuals and subgroups and their contri-bution to the crystallization of collectivities and institutional frameworks.

From the variety of arguments that have been raised to support this gen-eral contention it might be worthwhile to mention, first, the accusation that this approach upholds the "oversocialized conception of man," a term coined by Dennis Wrong.[2] This view holds that through the process of socialization most individuals in a society (except "deviants") do accept the roles, norms, and tasks "assigned" to them by the society and that hereby their activities fit the "needs" of the system, that is, they fulfill the functions necessary for the working of the given system.

Second is the allegation that the functional-structural approach assumes that it is the common values or "goals" of a society on the one hand, and its basic functional needs on the other, that determine the working of the social system and regulate the behavior of the individuals who participate in it and assure their compliance with the major societal needs.

The "functional-structural" approach is seen as assuming, first, that there exists, within any group or society, a central value system that is accepted, more or less, by most participants, determining the criteria and scales of differ-ential evaluation of roles and assuring the acceptance of these criteria by the participants in the system; second, it is seen to assume that such evaluation and the concomitant division of labor also reflect the specific organizational needs or exigencies of a society.

Opposed to these assumptions or theories, many critics of this approach (for instance Dahrendorf, Rex, and others[3]) have claimed that both the central values and the presumed needs of any society are neither given nor to be found within it in some natural way, but are mostly imposed by those people or groups that succeed in seizing and monopolizing positions of power within it. It is therefore the distribution of power, and not the "objective" needs of any society nor any common values and norms, that is the main determinant of the differential allocation of roles or positions in a society, or of access to these positions.

2. See Dennis Wrong, "The Oversocialized Conception of Man in Modern Sociology," *American Sociological Review* 26 (1961), pp. 183–93.

3. Ralf Dahrendorf, "Out of Utopia," *American Journal of Sociology* 64 (1958), pp. 115–27; and John Rex, *Key Problems of Sociological Theory* (London: Routledge and Kegan Paul, 1961).

Closely related to such stress upon the power element are observations concerning the ubiquity of conflict and consequent developments, mainly within those groups or individuals that do not accept the predominant values or the existing institutional arrangements, that may constitute foci of social change.[4]

SOCIAL DIVISION OF LABOR AND INDIVIDUAL INTERACTION: MICRO AND MACRO SOCIETAL SETTINGS

The heated controversy that has often erupted between the protagonists of these approaches attests, as is so often the case, that the arguments of both sides tend to converge around similar topics—in this case topics that have been in the very forefront of social thought from its very beginnings. First among them is one of the roots or bases of individuals' acceptance of the social order or of their attempts to change it and, second, that of the relations between what may be called societal needs, that is, systemic needs of social organization or groups on the one hand and individual behavior and interaction within the social context on the other.

Both approaches "admit" the existence of the two sides of the problem—that is, that on the one hand social groups or systems do have "needs" and that on the other, the various social arrangements that constitute the crux of the social division of labor are upheld   or changed—by the behavior of individuals within these social frameworks.

Thus Homans, who on the whole does not like to talk in terms of such needs, did base his earlier work *The Human Group*[5] on an analysis conceived in these very terms. He showed how some organizational needs have to be met through some division of the labor that takes care of them, in order for such a group to survive, although indeed there is no preordained reason why it should.

Then again, throughout Parsons' work—whether in his general studies of personality, of cultural systems, or of changing institutional patterns, or in his exposition of the work of some of the classics, especially Weber—it is easy to find illustrations of how the activities of individuals in the social context, and especially of various subgroups within any system, are among the most important foci of institutional change and innovation.

Thus it is indeed the process of emergence of social division of labor as

---

4. Some of these arguments are not dissimilar from those that have been raised in the controversies around stratification, especially those of Davis and Moore, and Tumin. See, for instance, Kingsley Davis and Wilbert E. Moore, "Some Principles of Stratification," *American Sociological Review* 10 (1945), pp. 142–49; and Melvin Tumin, "Some Principles of Stratification: A Critical Analysis," *American Sociological Review* 18 (1953), pp. 387–94, and the ensuing discussion.

5. George C. Homans, *The Human Group* (New York: Harcourt, Brace & Co., 1950).

related to behavior of individuals who participate in this process that constitutes the crux of the problems that may be seen as common to these two approaches and to which both address themselves.

It is not impossible to trace the process through which personal interactions lead to a division of labor that takes care of various societal needs in the context of small groups, be they laboratory or natural small groups. This, it is well known, has been done in many sociopsychological and small group studies, and it is indeed one of the great attainments of Homans' work to explore these processes within the framework of informal groups. However, the basic weakness of his analysis lies in his assumption concerning an almost total homology between these processes as they occur in such groups and those which occur in the macrosocietal setting.[6]

Homans' analysis deals almost exclusively with exchanges of personal attitudes, sentiments, and activities within relatively restricted, face-to-face, informal settings, such as work groups, which exist wider institutional and organizational frameworks, whose existence, for the purpose of this analysis, he usually takes for granted. Beyond its contribution to the study of such interpersonal relations, Homans also claims that the type of exchange found in relations of this type can serve both as the prototype of and as the starting point for the crystallization of broad institutional settings and norms. The major differences between "preinstitutional" exchange (that is, informal, interpersonal) and the fully institutionalized version according to him, seem to be that adherence to institutional norms is based upon the assurance of secondary as well as primary rewards (through such media as money or political power) and upon investment by the leaders or norm setters of different resources, such as money, manpower, time, or effort, which they are able to use as capital for providing both short- and long-term rewards to their followers.

Thus in Homans' analysis it is clear on the whole that the commodities exchanged in interpersonal and institutional settings differ from one another. The major commodities exchanged in interpersonal relations are mainly personal, "informal," attitudes or activities: help in some tasks, such as the execution of work assignments set up by the more formalized settings; personal esteem; or power with regard to these relations. The commodities of exchange in the broader institutional social setting are mainly money, institutionalized "prestige," and formalized status. According to Homans, however, a close similarity or homology exists between these two types of commodities *qua* the means of exchange.

This claim of similarity or homology between the processes of exchange

---

6. The following exposition is based on my article, "The Study of Processes of Institutionalization, Institution Change and Comparative Institutions," in S. N. Eisenstadt (ed.), *Essays on Comparative Institutions* (New York: John Wiley & Sons, 1965).

of interpersonal relations and the processes of institutionalization necessarily rests on several assumptions. First, it rests on the assumption that the commodities exchanged in both types of situations and the norms that regulate such exchanges are analytically similar (that is, in the points crucial to the process of exchange), except that they are more fixed and are based on "capital" in the broad institutional fields of societies. Second, it rests on the assumption that these different types of commodities are interchangeable, in a way, that is, the interpersonal attitudes crystallize into the various kinds of institutional commodities, even if the two never merge entirely. Third, it is based on the assumption that the basic goals (or "drives") of individuals in informal, interpersonal, and institutional settings are also either similar or easily interchangeable.

However, closer examination of these assumptions will show us that some very crucial differences exist between both the commodities exchanged in interpersonal and institutional settings and the norms that regulate these exchanges. Two such differences are of special importance. One is that symbolic desiderata and institutionalized commodities have a much wider scope of generality, even within a primitive society in which exchange is relatively restricted and fixed. They can be applied to wider sets of situations, and they are relatively interchangeable between different groups and situations in the society. A second difference is that most of this exchange is *indirect*—it is not of a "barter" character in limited face-to-face relations. It takes place between people who are not in direct contact, and it involves the use of generalized media of exchange to an extent unconceivable in an informal group. From the psychological point of view, such media of exchange become *direct* rewards or reinforcements for the persons concerned. However, from the organizational view they have an autonomy of their own (evident for instance in the specific rule of different markets—merit for money or labor), and their becoming primary rewards only reinforces this autonomy.

Third, and closely connected with the former, is the fact that the flow of these media and of the respective commodities is controlled by sets of formalized norms which regulate in a fairly continuous way the rates of exchange between different commodities, and uphold the legitimacy of the generalized media of exchange. Last, the variety of the commodities exchanged within any wider institutional setting such as the economy or the polity, and between such settings is necessarily much greater than within interpersonal relations.[7]

Here Parsons' work, which emphasizes the institutional nature of the major media of exchange—power, money, influence, and value-commitments—and which has large parts devoted to distinguishing the analytical properties of

---

7. It is no pure chance that Homans has often engaged in controversy with Lévi-Strauss, because Lévi-Strauss represents, in a way, the other extreme position in the analysis of cultural exchange, a position that emphasizes the purely symbolic and cognitive exchange and largely neglects the organizational, institutional, and motivational aspects of such exchange.

these media and the structural relations among them, provides very important indications in this direction.

It also indicates that although some similarities do indeed exist between the process of development of social division of labor in informal interpersonal groups and on the macrosocietal level, the macrosocietal division exhibits much more "fixed" organizational and normative features; it is therefore much more difficult at this level to trace the development of division of labor in relation to the behavior of individuals. At this level we have to accept, to some extent, the existence of some social division of labor as a basic given of any organized social life.

But even if we have to take some degree of existence of a division of labor for granted and to view it as an "evolutionary universal" of any human society, we must consider the *development* of a division of labor within any concrete group, organization, or society as a question to be answered.

Here the illustrations of the medieval manor or the Bank of England used by Homans at the end of his book, or any other illustration of institutional change, challenge us with the problem of explaining the emergence of the concrete contours of such division of labor and of the development of any such concrete institutional setting in more than descriptive historical terms.

SOCIETAL GOALS AND SYSTEMIC NEEDS VIS-A-VIS INDIVIDUAL GOALS: AN ILLUSTRATION AND SOME PROBLEMS

Given such convergence of both approaches around the central problem of the interrelations between the emergence of patterns of division of labor and the behavior of individuals who participate in this process, perhaps the best way to profit from the confrontation would be by attempting to derive from it a series of more detailed problems that can be subjected to critical and empirical analysis.

We might start with the problem of relations between societal goals and needs and individual social behavior. The industrialization of Soviet Russia might serve as an illustration for the analysis of this problem. It—like almost any other case of institutionalization of a certain type of economic, political, or religious system—shows beyond a doubt that once the push to industrialization had been given, the process gave rise to a series of "needs" or prerequisites without which industrialization could not go on. These needs or prerequisites included, among others, developing a labor force capable of performing some industrial tasks; new types of organizational structures and managerial skills; and some marketing, planning, or banking procedures and frameworks.

Several of these prerequisites seem to be more or less common to all types of industrial systems. Others, such as the establishment of explicit political control of the industrialization process, were probably more characteristic of the specifically Soviet type.

Thus the illustration of Soviet industrialization, as would be the case for any new social, economic, or political system, shows that the specific needs of the system—distinguished from more general "societal" needs that may seem part of the definition of any social system—appear to be generated by those goals that become institutionalized in some way within any society as "its own." It shows that once such institutionalization takes place—even if, as is usually the case, only to a very limited extent—there do indeed arise several systemic types of needs that must be met by the development of some specific type of division of labor, if the implementation of such goals is to prove feasible.

However, the Soviet case also brings another aspect of the relations between goals and needs into very sharp relief, namely, that the very decision to industrialize does not have to be taken for granted in any society but constitutes in itself a very important aspect of the process of institution-building. Moreover, the institutionalization of such goals is not assured in itself even when the "objective" conditions for it are given, as it were—that is, when resources exist to help implement such goals and even when enough people exist who might be willing or coerced into giving up resources at their disposal for the implementation of such goals.[8]

Similarly the history of the Soviet system, as that of many other systems, indicates that even once the initial push to industrialization has been given with the decision to industrialize the other consequences (development of various arrangements that assure the fulfillment of the various needs and prerequisites) are not automatic. It is well known that the Soviet process of industrialization encountered many obstacles and problems.

These problems and difficulties are not unique to the process of Soviet industrialization. They are common to all processes of institutionalization, the institutionalization of societal goals included; and they all point out some of the most important problems in studying the relation between the emergence of various concrete types of social division of labor and behavior patterns of individuals who participate in these processes. Particularly, they point out some of the problems in the relations between these broader societal goals and "needs" and the goals, aspirations, and activities of individuals.

First, there is the problem of the place of these societal goals in the universe of the individual's goals and wishes. Second, there is the problem of how

8. From this point of view Gerschenkron's analysis of Bulgaria's failure to institutionalize is very instructive. See Alexander Gerschenkron, *Economic Backwardness in Historical Perspective* (Cambridge, Mass.: Harvard University Press, 1962), pp. 198–234; see also the analysis of cases of unsuccessful attempts to institutionalize imperial systems in Shmuel N. Eisenstadt, *The Political Systems of Empires* (New York: The Free Press, 1963), especially chap. 6.

and by whom such goals are crystallized and formulated. Third, there is the problem of the conditions for successful institutionalization of such goals or the conditions under which those who propose them are able to make them acceptable to other groups and also to organize the social mechanisms necessary for their implementation or institutionalization, that is mechanisms that take care of the "needs" or prerequisites of any such concrete system.

We have only first glimmerings of answers to most of these problems, owing to no small extent to the fact that the relevant questions have not been fully and systematically posed. In the following paragraphs we shall attempt to point out some of these problems and, in a very preliminary way, to indicate some possible directions for exploring them.

The Place Held by Conceptions of Social Order and Societal Goals in the Universe of Individual Goals

Let us start with the first problem, namely the place of broad societal goals that may imply some conception of a social order in the universe of an individual's goals. Although this may seem a rather naïve or simple question at first glance, it does in fact contain a reorientation of the major question about the nature of the social order. Instead of assuming that such order and certain more concrete societal goals that "represent" it are given by external forces imposed on the individuals in some way and on their own wishes, or that it is only an outcome of the rationally premeditated and selfish evaluation by individuals of their own interests or of the exigencies of social and economic division of labor engendered by these interests, it emphasizes that among the basic wishes or orientations of people exists some quest for such an order, not only in organizational but also in symbolic terms. This implies that a very important part is played among the egoistic wishes of people by their quest for and conception of the symbolic social order or of the "good" society, and by their quest for participation in such an order. The structural focus of such a quest is to be found in charismatic activities, groups, or symbols.

In other words, among the various goals or needs of individuals in society, the quest for some meaningful order brings goals into being that define the nature of such an order or some of its basic aspects. This quest plays a very significant part in individual and collective participation in that order. It constitutes a basic, although differential, component in the whole panorama of individuals' social and cultural activities, orientations, and goals. It also calls for a rather special response from those who may be able to respond. Such response to this quest tends to be located in specific, distinct parts or aspects of the social structure.

The search for such a broader order constitutes the major focus of the orientation to the charismatic in a society and of the possibility that such charismatic orientations can be institutionalized.[9] This does not mean, of course, that the search for a meaningful order of this kind is the only, or even the main, individual goal. Obviously there are always others, such as avoiding trouble from those in power or selecting what is thought to be the "least of evils."

Beyond this it is necessary to emphasize that a large portion of the goals and desires of individuals are discrete and segregated. Individual goals comprise those types of activity that are oriented toward ends not connected together in some great pattern or "grand design"; that are oriented mostly to goals instrumental to other goals or aims; and that are also mostly oriented toward adaptation to any given natural or human (social) environment, to persistence and survival within it.

Much of the daily activity of human beings in society is probably organized in such a way and oriented to such goals. Their implementation necessitates the development of many specific organizations and structures, which tend to coalesce into varied institutional patterns. In a sense, it is these goals and activities that constitute the crux of the institutional nexus within any society.

True, all these goals and patterns also tend to become related somehow to a broader, fundamental order, rooted in the orientations to charismatic symbols or structures and focused around the different situations and centers in which the charismatic is more fully embedded and symbolized.

Yet, in these various "orderly" activities oriented to discrete, instrumental, and adaptive goals the charismatic orientations may become greatly attenuated. The various concrete goals may be perceived as rather distant from the sources of the charismatic. Nevertheless some such relation or orientation to the charismatic tends to persist in these activities, even in the most attenuated and passive form.

Here the view proposed by Coleman[10] may also be of special importance: that at least part of an individual's interest in a special type of social order is rooted in his perception of the future, that is, in the expectation of benefits that will accrue to members (whether present or future generations) and in his acknowledgment that certain types of institutional arrangements and investment of his own resources may be important in order to assure the members' future.

Whatever the exact details of such attitudes toward the conception of a broader center, admitting that the quest for such order, for participation in it, and for the possible implementation of goals that can "manifest" it constitutes an important dimension of the universe of individuals' goals and adds a new

9. For greater detail see Edward Shils, "Charisma, Order, and Status," *American Sociological Review* 30 (1965), pp. 199–213.

10. See James S. Coleman, "Collective Decisions."

and crucial dimension to the conception of the individuals' wishes. This dimension seems to go beyond Homans' analytical scheme. It not only emphasizes
both the symbolic orientation and the definition of many of these wishes but
also stresses the close interrelation between such symbolic orientation and the
evaluation of concrete institutional arrangements and frameworks.[11] However,
the existence of some such interrelation does not in itself assure the ability
of individuals to be able to formulate the more concrete goals, or to develop
organizations and mechanisms necessary for collective implementation of such
order or goals.

Charismatic Elites and Entrepreneurs as
Bearers of the Conception of Social Order
and as Propagators of Societal Goals

This brings us to the second problem, that of how and by whom such broader
goals or conceptions are formed and institutionalized.

All the available data seem to indicate that the crucial problem is the presence or absence, in one or several institutional spheres, of an active group of
special "entrepreneurs," or an elite able to offer solutions to the new range of
problems. Among modern sociologists Weber came closest to recognizing this
problem when he stressed that the creation of new institutional structures depends heavily on the "push" given by various "charismatic" groups or personalities and that the routinization of charisma is critical for the crystallization and
continuation of these new structures.

The development of such charismatic or entrepreneurial personalities or
groups constitutes what is perhaps the closest social analogy to "mutation." It
is the possibility of such mutation that explains why at any level of differentiation a given social sphere contains not one but several, often competing, possible orientations and potentialities for development.

In other words, all available indications show that a crucial role is played
in the crystallization of institutional frameworks by people who evince a special capacity to set up broad orientations, to propound new norms, to articulate
goals, to establish organizational frameworks, and to mobilize such resources
necessary for all these purposes as the readiness to invest in the appropriate
activities.

The preceding discussion does not necessarily imply that such innovations
or new types of broader societal goals are formed only through the activities
of one central group. They may emerge through a more dispersed range of

---

11. The closest that Homans comes to recognizing this problem is his use of the concept of
distributive justice. See Homans, *Social Behavior*, especially chap. 12; and also see Peter M. Blau,
"Justice in Social Exchange."

activities of different entrepreneurial and elite groups, or even through the accumulation of more dispersed discrete exchange activities. But whatever the exact process through which such goals are formed, it seems that at most levels of social life a crucial part is played by some entrepreneurial groups—either those oriented to the establishment of broad charismatic order or those oriented to the implementation of more discrete goals.

However, the availability of such entrepreneurs, or their concrete orientation and activities, is not always assured or determined by the development of the varying "needs" among different groups in a society. Moreover, even if some such charismatic leaders or more mundane entrepreneurs do emerge, the ways in which they will act and the types of institutions they will build are not given or predetermined, because the concrete broad orientations and goals that they develop may vary greatly.

We still know very little about conditions of development of such charismatic leaders and institutional entrepreneurs, about their psychological and behavioral attributes, or about the conditions under which they may be able to implement their vision. There exist data and several descriptive studies, but as yet relatively few systematic analyses[12] of this problem or of the nature of the process through which specific charismatic symbols and orientations become embedded in the more "ordinary" institutional activities and exchange.

SOME GENERAL CHARACTERISTICS OF INSTITUTION-BUILDING PROCESSES

Existing analyses do provide several important indications about some of the conditions of successful or unsuccessful institutionalization of various societal goals. In a general way it may be said that organizations and institutions are built up through the varied responses and interactions between different people or groups who, in order to implement their varied goals, undertake processes of exchange with other people or groups.[13]

However, the individuals or groups who engage in such exchange are not distributed randomly in any society or the same in all societies. Such exchange takes place between people in structurally different positions (that is, in different cultural, political, family, or economic positions). These positions may in themselves be outcomes of former processes of institutional exchange. Aspirations and goals are greatly influenced by differential placement in the social structure and the power which can thereby be exercised. The resources at indi-

---

12. See for one attempt in this direction, David C. McClelland, *The Achieving Society* (Princeton: D. Van Nostrand Co., 1961). Also see the various works on religious and social movements quoted above.

13. See this in greater detail in my essay, "Processes of Institutionalization," especially pp. 16–40.

viduals' or groups' disposal—such as manpower, money, political support, or religious identification—are determined by these institutional positions and vary according to the specific characteristics of the different institutional spheres. Such resources serve as means of implementing individual goals, and they may in themselves become goals or objects of individual endeavor. They always evince some tendency to become organized in specific, autonomous ways, according to the specific features of their different institutional spheres. This tendency can be seen, for instance, in the fact that the exchange of economic resources in any society is organized in ways different from the exchange of political or religious resources.

The terms of exchange, however—the criteria of what is regarded as valuable, or which things are conceived as equivalent—are at least partially derived from the charismatically charged goals and norms, from the broader and more fundamental conceptions of social order. Hence, as we have already pointed out, a crucial part is played in the crystallization of institutional frameworks by those people who evince a special capacity to set up broad orientations to propound new norms and to articulate new goals.

In other words, institution-building is not only based on the direct or indirect exchange of various institutional resources between individuals or groups that attempt to use such resources to implement their discrete, instrumental goals. Institution-building also requires interaction between those individuals or groups who are able to articulate varied collective goals and crystallize acceptable norms, on the one hand, and, on the other, those individuals, groups, or strata that are willing to accept such regulations and norms. The crystallization and upholding of these norms provide some sort of response to the quest for a degree of general stability and order and attests to a capability of providing some broader meaning to more varied specific needs that may arise in different situations. Hence, the capacity to create and crystallize such broader symbolic orientations and norms or to articulate various more concrete societal goals, to establish organizational frameworks, and to mobilize the resources necessary for all these purposes (such as the readiness to invest in the appropriate activities) is a basic aspect of institution-building in any society.

INDIVIDUALS' GOALS AND SOCIETAL ORDER: A TENTATIVE RESTATEMENT

The preceding exposition seems to come very close to Homans' and Blau's formulations but in fact goes beyond them and underlies some of the basic limitations of their approaches (analyzed above)—because of the sharp emphasis on the institutional bases and characteristics of exchange. At the same time, however, it also emphasizes the importance of confronting or combining analysis of the symbolic-normative, systemic, and power aspects of institution-building with analysis of the continuous interaction and creativity of individuals in such processes.

In one sense, the preceding exposition does indeed assume that both the social division of labor and the autonomy of individuals' goals and aspirations are given, basic data for the analysis of any society or of any process of institution-building. However, it does not assume that society and the social order are external to individuals' wishes and goals or to their basic nature, but rather that orientation to social and cultural order is part of the individual's basic orientation.[14] Neither does it assume that this fact in itself assures the stability and continuity of any given social order. In other words, it does not posit that the relations between these basic data of human existence and social order are fixed. Instead of taking any such relation between them as given, the present formulation considers it to be a variable.

This can perhaps best be seen if we briefly examine the implications of our exposition for the so-called "oversocialized conception of man." This conception is right to the extent it assumes that any relatively successful process of socialization inculcates orientations to values, symbols, norms, and more concrete roles into individuals, although of course the degree to which this process is successful varies greatly among different individuals.

However, this does not mean that the process also assures an individual's acceptance of any given social system or of any of its concrete arrangements. To be sure, the preceding discussion fully brings out that some such evaluation is made, in very large degree, in terms of "symbolic" and "charismatic" conceptions and broader values. Needless to say, individuals acquire these very values and orientations in the process of their socialization, but socialization does not necessarily ensure individuals' acceptance of the specific institutional goals or of the specific features of the institutional order. On the contrary, the development of these orientations may inculcate critical attitudes toward the social order, including orientations favorable to a different type of order. It is the individual's evaluation of the contribution made to his own goals by a given group or by certain institutional settings or tasks and his conceptions of social order that seem of crucial importance in influencing his adherence to a given institutional order. As a result, when any such evaluation is rooted in orientation to the charismatic conception of social order, the evaluation may very well serve as a point of dissension and change.

It is well known that an initial assumption of many sociological analyses of charisma has been that it is disruptive and contributes to the destruction of existing institutions and to social change. The recognition that charismatic

14. This follows of course, to a very large extent, both Durkheim and Weber, and Parsons' critical appraisal of their place in the development of sociology. See Talcott Parsons, "Unity and Diversity in the Modern Intellectual Disciplines: The Role of the Social Sciences," *Daedalus* 94 (1965).

activities or symbols also constitute a part of the solidary institutional frame-work does not negate this basic insight. It only enables us to approach the relation between charisma and social change and transformation in a much more differentiated and systematic way. It enables us to see that the very quest for participation in a meaningful order may be related to processes of change and transformation, that it may indeed constitute—at least in certain circum-stances—the very focus of processes of social transformation.

The starting point of this approach is the recognition of the inherent ten-sion that the charismatic builds into any social system.[15] Such tensions or con-flicts not only are rooted in the clashes of different interests in a society, but also in the differential distribution of what is charismatic in the symbolic and organizational aspects of any institutional system. It is the combination of this with conflicts of interests that may indeed constitute the major focus of both continuity and potential changes in any social system.[16]

CONDITIONS OF THE INSTITUTIONALIZATION OF SOCIETAL ORDER AND GOALS: THE CALCULUS OF CONSENSUS

Because of the preceding exposition's twin emphases upon the givenness of the social division of labor and of individuals' autonomous social commitment as well as focus upon the variable relation between the two, the problem of the place of individual behavior in the processes of institution-building and in social change in general may be approached in a differentiated way.

This brings us back to our third problem—namely the conditions under which different types of societal goals can be institutionalized. Also here only some preliminary indications can be given for further research. At the crux of this problem lie the conditions under which various social groups are willing to accept certain conceptions of social order and societal goals as binding and the conditions under which they, together with the entrepreneurial groups that formulate and present such goals, are capable of developing the requisite orga-nizational mechanisms that can assure meeting needs generated by such goals.

The first part of this problem may be designated as that of the calculus of consensus in a society, of the ways in which individuals evaluate different as-pects of the social order and of the ways in which such evaluation tends to influence their acceptance of any such given order and its basic institutional frameworks in general and of their own positions within it in particular. This evaluative calculus of consensus has two basic components. One is the object of the evaluation, the second is composed of the bases of the evaluation.

15. See this in greater detail in Reinhard Bendix, "Max Weber's Sociology Today," *International Social Science Journal* 17 (1965), pp. 9–20.

16. See Shmuel N. Eisenstadt, "Institutionalization and Change," *American Sociological Review* 29 (1964), pp. 49–59.

Taking the object of evaluation first, we might distinguish three levels at the present state of our discussion. The given social and sociocultural order and its central institutional frameworks and symbols constitute the most general level. Evaluations of various discrete and concrete institutional arrangements and frameworks within the sociocultural order occur at the second level. The third level object is the individual's own place within that order.

Turning to the bases of evaluation, two levels can be discerned which are closely related to those just discussed. One is the individual's conception of the proper nature and contents of the "good social order," broadly defined, and of its basic institutional rules. The other is the set of goals or desires held by the individual.

In any such calculus of consensus a continuous interplay takes place between these two bases of evaluation and the three major objects of evaluation. Thus—even on the purely symbolic level—the calculus of consensus not only includes the conception of a desirable "total" social and moral order, but also the joint evaluation of a given broad order and concrete institutional arrangements in terms of the more discrete and segregated goals of individuals.

The possible range within the evaluative calculus of consensus of any broad institutional system or more discrete institutional framework is much greater in terms of such goals than it is when "total" social order is considered in terms of what is "ideal" or "good." However, we know little as yet about the conditions under which different degrees or types of such consensus tend to develop and the ways in which they influence the process of institutionalization.

MECHANISMS OF INSTITUTIONALIZATION: SIMULATION OF DESIDERATA AND CREATION OF ARTIFICIAL SCARCITIES

To be able to approach these problems one must inquire into the nature of the mechanisms that influence the development of consensus. General social reflection and sociological theory have pointed out some of these mechanisms for some time in a very general way. Three social techniques have been distinguished: persuasion, coercion, and profitability.

The persuasive mode is oriented by definition to maximizing the individual's identification with a given social order in terms of his own conception of order or his more specific wishes. Coercive means are symbolically or cognitively oriented, in the main, to the acceptance of a given social order as the least of evils. The third mode of interaction, that of profitability, appears to be especially important in the case of the more discrete, segregated goals of individuals; the degree to which participation in a given social or institutional activity seems profitable to different individuals depends upon their varied interests.

These techniques do not only operate on the symbolic or cognitive plane. In order to be effective even on these planes they must also be very closely interwoven with specific structural mechanisms. These general structural mechanisms have also long since been identified and even formalized in sociological literature. The most important ones are, first, to be sure, socialization—including the various mechanisms of secondary socialization—through which the various desiderata and goals become internalized by individuals; second, processes of communication, which tend to influence the individual's evaluation of a social system; third, a diversity of market or barter mechanisms; fourth, the various mechanisms of social control, ranging from the formal application of political power to those forms of informal social influence, and social interaction, which generate their own modes of coorientation around common foci and norms.[17]

We know many of the ways in which these mechanisms operate in social systems. But we do not know enough about the ways in which these orientations or modes of activity tend to become connected with the mechanisms of socialization, communication, economic transactions, and social control and interaction, or how they may influence the various foci of the calculus of consensus which have been pointed out. These questions should indeed constitute topics of further research. At this point of our discussion it might be worthwhile to indicate some very general possibilities for such research.

Taking as our point of departure the importance of interaction and exchange among individuals as they attempt to maximize their goals and desiderata and to institute certain types of social order or societal goals, but emphasizing institutional and symbolic aspects of this exchange, it could prove instructive to point some mechanisms out through which exchange of this kind is regulated on both its demand and its supply sides.

The main mechanisms are, first, the attempted simulation, mostly by certain elite or entrepreneurial groups, of specific goals and desiderata held within other groups and, second, the attempted monopolization by the former groups of the provisions for such needs.

Let us begin to explicate these mechanisms. On the demand side of this process, we may first note the various mechanisms through which attempts are being made within any given society to regulate the wants or desiderata of different groups. Socialization and communication are probably of greatest importance here. Beyond what may be called charismatic persuasion on the broadest level—that is, beyond attempts to convert various groups to the conception of social and cultural order envisaged by the elites—the most im-

17. See Thomas J. Scheff, "Towards a Sociological Model of Consensus," *American Sociological Review* 32 (1967), pp. 32–46.

portant mechanism is made up of attempts to convince social groups that the provision of certain needs is instrumental to their personal desires, or that it provides a more general "atmosphere" of conditions through which pursuit of the broader conceptions of social order held by such groups can be realized. In this way the provision of such needs may become secondary goals—or a series of secondary goals—for the different groups of people within a society. Also to be noted, however, are attempts to restrain different groups from attaining certain goals and to limit the accessibility of such desiderata to only some people who are close to the elite and who would not, by sharing these desiderata, endanger the elites' own positions.

On the supply side of these exchange patterns the most important ones are elite attempts to monopolize the possibility of providing such needs. Beyond direct coercion the major mechanism is one of creating artificial scarcity of skills through which these needs are fulfilled.

Both the channelization or regulation of goals and desiderata and the creation of artificial scarcities constitute inherent parts of the process through which the internal pattern of exchange and of social differentiation becomes crystallized in any society. Each of the different modes of social technique, as well as the different structural mechanisms which have been discussed are operative in the regulation of both demand and supply. Both of these regulative processes can also create the types of interaction through which modes of coorientation to common foci tend to develop. There is, however, an important difference between them.

In the creation of artificial scarcities the scope for the exercise of power and coercion seems to be very large—although even here it is clear that there are many limitations on the use of sheer force or even power, because such power has to be legitimized at least to some extent. In the simulation of "needs" or "goals" the scope of coercion or use of power is much more limited, not only because of this general "need" for legitimation, but mainly because the level of member commitment to goals and needs beyond the minimal ones that can be developed through the use of power seems to be too low and hence worth little to those interested in simulating them for any length of time, in any stable way.

Here, in the channelization of needs and desiderata, the appeal has to be made either in terms of some of the individual's goals and aims—such as the wish for power, money, or a recognized position within the system—or in terms of what may be good, appropriate, or beneficial for the group as such.

These suggestions are necessarily only very tentative and need to be explored more fully in analytical and comparative research. They bring us to the last part of our problem: namely, the organizational aspects of institutionalizing societal goals.

The Organizational Aspects of Institutionalizing Societal Goals: Some Unexplored Problems

Even assuming that certain goals have, by some calculus of consensus, been accepted within large parts of a population, such acceptance does not mean that the organizational needs and prerequisites necessitated by the implementation of these goals are automatically taken care of, or that the necessary organizations and arrangements will automatically develop and become institutionalized.

The example of Soviet industrialization—or of institutionalization of any other social, economic, political, or religious system—shows that the development of appropriate organizational means cannot be assured by the mere success of an elite—or series of elites—in imposing their own conception of social order or some more specific goals.

Admittedly we often tend toward the assumption that the incumbents of elite positions who formulate these various societal goals or aspire to them are especially sensitive to what may be called societal "needs" and that they may attempt to take care of the activities and problems in a manner required for the maintenance and continuity of given social organizations and institutions.

Yet the evidence tends to show that any link between formulation of goals—be they broad conceptions of social order, more specific macrosocietal goals, or the diverse goals of subgroups in a society—and perception of various societal "needs," let alone the ability to take care of them, is not automatic and has to be explored more fully.

Many problems and difficulties may arise as a result of sheer inability or because lack of knowledge gives rise to varying processes of trial and error and the concomitant "natural" selection of organizational patterns. This is not, of course, unique to Soviet industrialization. Something like it, as more recent researchers in economic history tend to indicate, has been happening throughout the processes of industrialization in all societies.[18]

Paradoxically, however, this problem has perhaps been least explored in systematic sociological analysis. We need to explore a variety of different mechanisms through which some linkage among the acceptance of goals, the perception of the organizational needs necessary for the implementation of such goals, and the willingness and ability to institute the appropriate organizations and mechanisms is effected.

We know very little as yet about such mechanisms largely because most sociological analysis postulates the relation between goals and needs and the

---

18. See, for instance, Ronald Cameroun in collaboration with Olga Crisp, Hugh T. Patrick, and Richard Tilly, *Banking in the Early Stages of Industrialization* (New York: Oxford University Press, 1967).

automatic development of the necessary organizational frameworks to meet them.

Neither do we know enough about the relations of these mechanisms to the processes through which various calculi of consensus tend to develop in different societies and how the processes are related to effecting the links between acceptance of certain goals and the establishment of the appropriate institutional settings.

We do not exactly know as yet how individuals' lack of identification or satisfaction with an organizational setting affects its functioning. Such a state itself does not necessarily lead to immediate disorganization or to the "disappearance" of norms. It probably tends to have more indirect effects. It may alter the relative accessibility of various resources to different groups. It may greatly influence predispositions to enter into some types of exchange rather than others and, thus, also influence the chances of having competing leaders and norm setters. Hence, the processes through which individuals are sensitized to the symbol norms and goals of various groups in society and the ways in which they internalize and maintain the norms and criteria of evaluation may be of crucial importance for interlinking their attitudes and sentiments with the establishment and maintenance of institutional norms and frameworks.

Here several findings are of special interest from small-group study and from investigations based on game theory, which indicate that the very processes of situational interaction may indeed engender tendencies to perceive common norms.[19] It is probably in this research area that some of the most fruitful contributions have been made by microsocietal and "situational" studies to the understanding of macrosocietal processes.

All of these processes may well constitute foci for further exploration and exposition. They bring us back to several basic problems we have encountered throughout our discussion: conditions of the development of charismatic and noncharismatic entrepreneurs in different institutional spheres; the varied types of consensus; the relation between these and the perception of systemic "needs"; and the conditions and range of institutional innovations, whether through processes of trial and error or through certain processes of interaction and selection. The exploration of all these problems seems crucial to me for further systematic investigations of the nature of social order and of the processes of institution-building. The very possibility of formulating some of these problems has itself been derived from reexamining some of the central problems of social order in the light of the confrontation between Parsons' and Homans' approaches.

19. See Scheff, "Towards a Sociological Model of Consensus."

Seven

Symbolic Structures and Social Dynamics with Special Reference to Studies of Modernization

I. The Premises of Structuralism and Its Confrontation with Problems of Social Organization

A DISCUSSION OF SOME of the possibilities and limitations of the structuralist approach to the analysis of societies is of interest. In the last 20 years there have been debates and controversies in social sciences which dealt with the place of symbolic dimension in the construction of social life and its relationship to the organizational aspects and workings of social groups and systems.

The structuralist approach, to some degree initially developed as a contrast to the then-prevailing emphasis in anthropological literature on the integrative role of rituals and symbols in the functioning of social systems. It stressed the autonomy, and possibly the predominance, of the symbolic sphere in the construction of social and cultural reality.

Structuralism, as developed by Lévi-Strauss (1963, 1966, 1969); Hayes and Hayes (1970); Lane (1970); Scholte (1973), however, goes beyond the mere emphasis on autonomy, importance, or even predominance of the symbolic dimension in the construction of culture and society. (See, for instance, Boon 1972). It combines such emphasis with more specific assumptions about the structure and working of the symbolic sphere and its relations to human behavior and to social organization (MacRae 1968; Hammel 1972).

The crux of the structuralist claim (Lane 1970; Leach 1965; Hayes and Hayes 1970) is, first, that there exists within any society or culture some "hidden structure" which is more real and permeating than the overt social organization or behavioral patterns. Second, the rules according to which this structure is constituted are crystallized in code in the "human" mind. They are not concrete rules of social organization, nor are they derived from organizational or institutional needs or problems. Third, the most important of these rules (at least according to Lévi-Strauss and his followers) are those of binary oppositions and consequent rules of transformation which govern the ways these oppositions are resolved. Fourth, it is these rules which are the constitutive ele-

Originally published in *Structural Sociology*, edited by I. Rossi, © Columbia University Press, New York.

ment of culture and society, and which provide the deeper ordering principles of social and cultural realms. Fifth, these principles constitute the real models of any society—those according to which society is structured. They need not be identical with the conscious models represented in the minds of its participants or symbolized in various concrete situations and representations (like myths) although it is mostly through a structural analysis of these representations that such rules can be analyzed and understood.

The discussions between the structuralists and the more "orthodox" anthropologists, although very heated, were often rather unproductive. Because of the mixture of "principled" philosophical, ontological, metaphysical, and sociological assertions, they tended to talk past one another. (For analysis and illustration of some of these discussions see H. Geertz 1965; P. E. Josselin de Jong 1965a, b; Kobben 1966; Pouwer (1966a, b, c); Scholte 1966; Rotenstreich 1972; Rossi 1973.)

Lévi-Strauss and his followers were often criticized for a failure to provide empirical evidence for their assumptions. These were countered by arguments about "irrelevance" of evidence based on empirical "positivist" assumptions as against the importance of discovering "hidden" models of societies in which the working of the basic rules of human mind is manifest (Maybury-Lewis 1960; Needham 1960; Lévi-Strauss 1966). Each side tended often to dismiss the other as "irrelevant" or as dealing with a different level of reality. And yet the structuralist approach presented a major challenge to anthropologists and sociologists of all camps. First, is it possible to specify the concrete institutional loci and derivatives of the symbolic systems and orientations of the so-called general rule of the human mind (beyond the concrete and immediate organizational exigencies and processes) by means of studies in "conventional" sociological analysis? (See, for instance, Parsons 1961; Mayhew 1971; Parsons and Platt 1973). Second, how do these rules impinge on the actual working of social systems? To which aspects of the institutional structure are they related?

Some preliminary answers have developed in recent sociological and anthropological literature in two directions. One, the indication of the ways "deeper" symbolic principles may influence the working of institutions, could indeed be found in several recent studies in anthropology and sociology. They could be found first in the work of the Dutch anthropologists of the Leyden school (J. P. B. Josselin de Jong 1922; P. E. Josselin de Jong 1951, 1960, 1964, 1965a, 1971; Schulte-Nordholdt 1971; Pouwer 1964, 1966c), all of whom attempted to indicate how various symbolic orientations may explain different patterns of kinship and territorial arrangements.

Similarly the work of Louis Dumont (1971) on India attempts (however great the criticism of detail) to derive at least some of the organizational aspects of Indian society from the symbolic structure of Indian civilization; Luc de Heusch (1971) studied the interweaving of symbolic realm and of social organization in African tribes; E. Leach, Lévi-Strauss' major critical follower among the senior group of the British anthropologists, worked on the succession of Solomon (Leach 1968) and on Burma and Ceylon (Leach 1954, 1960, 1961), and stressed the importance of such symbolic orientations in defining the boundaries of the different ethnic, religious, and political collectivities.

Similarly, one may also include some attempts by Marxists like Maurice Godelier (1973) or Lucien Sebag (1964) to specify the institutional loci of principles of a society's "hidden structure" which are of great interest for our discussion. In this context D. M. Schneider's (1968, 1972; Schneider and Smith 1973) efforts to clearly distinguish the symbolic from the more behavioral and organizational aspects of kinship in general and the American one in particular (while at the same time indicating the ways in which the two are interwoven) have been extremely significant.

A second major direction toward which the search for the institutional anchorages and specifications of the symbolic dimension developed was, as in the case of scholars like C. Geertz, V. Turner, or T. O. Beidelman in anthropology, in the analysis of how symbolization of social and cultural orders takes place in special social situations. Among sociologists, important studies are E. Shils' (1961, 1965) analyses of the nature of the charismatic identification in particular, as well as E. Tiryakian's (1970) attempts to combine the "structural"-symbolic with the structural-functional approach. Tiryakian's attempt was based on designating the sphere of the sacred or the symbolic as the crucial element in the construction of the boundaries and identity of a society. This provides the "meaning" (the normative and cognitive focus) through which the "structuralization" of social organization takes place. In addition, he emphasized the concept that social structures are normative phenomena of intersubjective consciousness which frame social space. Finally, he indicated various institutional and subinstitutional loci (whether the more fully ritualized situations or the less formalized but very pervasive "esoteric" situation of social relation) where symbolic orientations may be especially visible.

II. The Institutional Impact of Cultural Orientations: Some Comparative Data

A. Institutional Continuities in Traditional and Modern Societies

These indications about the institutional anchorage of symbolic orientations may now be systematized on the basis of more recent comparative sociological analysis. Comparative macrosocietal studies in general, and those of modernization in particular, have provided some highly pertinent insights about these institutional problems. The revisions of the initial model of modernization has, among other factors, given rise to a very strong stress on tradition and continuity that has some important relevance to our concern about both the possible institutional anchorages of symbolic orientations and the implications of such orientations for the working of social systems.

In these studies two major aspects of social order were indicated as potentially important from these points of view. First was the possible importance of some "abstract" or symbolic principles which tend to influence the organizational patterns of societies—very often cutting across changes in regimes, in organizational patterns, or in levels of social modernization or economic development—thus coming seemingly very close to the structuralists rules of the "hidden structure." Second, there developed an emphasis (in a way not dissimilar from Tiryakian's analysis of the importance of understanding the nature of society) on the portrayal of a society's own "real," often "unconscious," self-image in some symbols of collective identity. Such symbols, most fully enacted in symbolic ritual occasions, are also pervasive in more "dispersed" situations.

With respect to the first area, comparative research has identified some aspects in institutional spheres in which some continuity (which may be indicative of some broader cultural orientations) could be discerned. Some of these continuities have indeed been identified in central aspects of two focal institutional complexes of a society: the political sphere and that of social stratification. Striking similarities were found in how central institutional-regulative problems in these two areas were dealt with in the "same societies" (in their traditional and "modern" phases) and in different traditional and modern societies.

In the political sphere the most important were the nature of the loci of centers of political decision and innovation, the types of center-periphery relations prevalent within a society, the relative emphasis by the rulers or elites on different types of components of centers or activities of centers, the types of policies developed by the ruler and the types of public goods developed in a society, and some aspects of political struggle and organization.

Within the field of stratification the most important of such institutional aspects found to be relatively continuous are the type of attributes emphasized as constituting the basis of societal evaluation and hierarchy, the degree of status autonomy of different groups (as manifested in their access to such attributes irrespective of centers of the society), and the degree of broader status association as opposed to status segregation of relatively close occupational and professional groups.

B. The Coalescence of Institutional Features into Patterns of Social and Political Systems

These characteristics tend to coalesce into some broader institutional complexes, or patterns of sociopolitical orders. One may cite those which have been designed as "absolutist," "estate," and "nation-states" models in Western Europe; the autocratic-imperial and revolutionary-class models of Russia or

China; and various patrimonial and neopatrimonial models. Others, such as those which crystallized in, say, the Japanese or Turkish complexes may also be noted. Each of these complexes or broader patterns shows evidence of specific continuous structural characteristics.

Thus, for example, the modern sociopolitical order of Western Europe has been characterized by a high degree of congruence between the cultural and political identities of the population as well as a high level of symbolic and affective commitments to the political and cultural centers. There has been a marked emphasis on politically defined collective goals for all members of the national community, while access of broad strata to symbols and centers has been relatively autonomous.

Many of these characteristics of the European nation-states are similar to those which existed in their premodern sociopolitical traditions—those of the imperial, city-state, and feudal systems. The strong activism characteristic of these nation-states derives from the traditions of city-states, while the conception of the political order as being actively related to the cosmic or cultural order has its origin in many imperial traditions or in the traditions of great religions. The strong emphasis on the autonomous access of different groups to the major attributes of social and cultural orders prevalent in these regimes find their sources, at least in part, in the pluralist-feudal structure. Continuation and expansion of these premodern structures and orientations have been greatly facilitated by the commercial and industrial revolutions as well as by the development of absolutism on the one hand, and of Protestantism on the other.

In the imperial eastern societies such as Russia, Japan, or China, the pluralistic elements have been much weaker than those found in the feudal or city-states of the traditional western European order (for greater detail, see Eisenstadt 1973b). Their political traditions have rarely entailed a dichotomy between state and society. Rather, they have tended to stress the congruent, but often passive, relations between the cosmic order and the sociopolitical order. The interrelation between the political and the social orders is not stated in terms of an antithesis between these entities, but envisaged as the coalescence of different functions within the same group or organization with a common focus in the cosmic order. In Russia, for example, this constellation of attitudes has encouraged neither the conception of relatively autonomous access to the political and cultural centers for the major strata nor the autonomy of the social and cultural orders in relation to the political one.

In traditional as well as modern patrimonial regimes (Eisenstadt 1973c) the broader social or cultural order is perceived mostly as something to be mastered or accommodated, not as something commanding a high level of commitment. Within these societies, acceptance of the givenness of the cultural and social order tends to be strong, while the possibility of active autonomous participation is barely perceived by any social groups that could shape the contours of that order—even to the extent that such shaping is possible in traditional systems. Tension between a "higher" transcendental order and the social order seldom appears; and when it does, it constitutes an important element in the "religious" sphere, but not in the political or social ones.

Such societies place little emphasis on the autonomous access of the major groups or strata to the predominant attributes of these orders. Such access is usually seen as mediated by ascriptive individual groups or ritual experts who represent the "given" order and are mostly appointed by the center or subcenters. The connections between broader universalistic percepts—be they religious or ideological—and the actual social order tends to be weak. Ritualistic participation in the society's broad orientations plays a more prominent role than deep commitment to such concepts. The basic premises of the cultural order are accepted with relative passivity, while the givenness of that order often goes unquestioned.

As a result of these perceptions of the sociopolitical order, the inclination to active participation in the centers of these societies is weak. And the center is depended upon to provide resources and to regulate internal affairs insofar as these are related to the broader society. In such situations the development of autonomous mechanisms of self-regulation is inhibited.

In these societies demands on the center have nevertheless abated with the spread of the basic assumptions of modernity. But such demands have not usually focused on control of the center, but on change in its contents and symbols or on the possible creation of new types of social and cultural orders by the center.

III. SYMBOLIC ORIENTATIONS AND PATTERNS OF CODES AS "HIDDEN STRUCTURE" OF SOCIAL ORDER

These patterns point out broad institutional similarities that persist in the "same" society in different periods of its development. The patterns also cut across different levels of social differentiation, as well as changes of regimes, boundaries, collectivities, and symbols of collective identity. All of this attests to similarities in the ways of coping with problems specific to traditional and modern settings—even though the concrete organizational problems themselves vary greatly between such settings. Crucial to our analysis of these different institutional patterns is that.these ways of coping with societal problems are related to some type of symbolic orientation.

The available comparative macrosociological analyses and studies indicate that there is a rather close relation between the broad principles of institutional patterns or constellations analyzed and some cultural orientations. Two types of cultural orientations seem to have a great impact on institutional life.

One type of orientation refers to the "cosmic," existential problems of human life: (1) (and above all) the relative evaluation of these problems of the major dimensions of human existence (the ritualistic, the political, and the economic); (2) the conception of the degree of autonomy or interrelations of the cosmic, cultural, social, and political orders and of their mutual relevance and the concomitant problems of theodicy; (3) the relative emphasis on active or passive attitudes toward participation in the social and cultural orders and their formation; (4) the different conceptions of change, attitudes to change, and the possibility of an active rather than passive participation in the formation of such changes in the major social and cultural spheres; (5) the bases of legitimation of cosmic social orders, especially with regard to the degree in which the relations to these orders are mostly adaptive ones, as opposed to an attitude of commitment.

Another set of such orientations is those related to symbolic evaluation of the fundamental dilemmas of social life and the bases of acceptance of social order—i.e., to the relative emphasis on power, solidarity, or instrumental relations and the underlying bases of social order; or the conception of social life as being harmonious or conflict-ridden; or the relative emphasis on equality or hierarchy and on individualism or communalism.

These themes or problems constitute some of the major loci of the symbolic domains in human culture. Of course, they are manifested in the most speculative and intellectually articulated symbolic expression of human creativity in the fields of aesthetics, philosophy, or theology. But they also constitute some of the major symbolic foci of the quest for the construction of a good or just social and cultural order, and of participation in it. In such an order, people's discrete social activities would be brought into some patterns of meaningful experience, encompassing the maintenance of a meaningful personal life in some relation to these orders.

The impingement of such orientations on the working of institutions is effected through the transformation or crystallization of such general broad orientations into what may be called cultural codes. Such codes are very close to what Max Weber (1947, esp. p. iv, 1958; 1964) has called *Wirtschaftsethik* generalized modes of "religious" or "ethical" orientation to a specific institutional sphere and its problems—the evaluation of this sphere, the provision of guidelines for its organization and for behavior within it in terms of the perception of major problems of human existence outlined above. In a somewhat different paraphrase, such *Ethik* or "code" connotes a general mode of orientation to a given sphere of social life, based on, or derived from, the "answer" to the basic symbolic problems mentioned above.

It is through the institutional derivatives of the programmatic specification of these codes that the symbolic and organizational dimensions of the structuring of human activities are most closely interwoven in the process of institutionalization and in all these ways they may seem to provide different principles of the hidden structure of any given social order.

Support for this supposition can be found, first of all, in the fact that some regularity can be discerned in the way any such specific orientation influences certain aspects of the institutional structure. To give a few initial and random illustrations based on the materials presented above, it seems that when (as in Western Europe) the social and cultural orders are perceived as relevant to one another and mutually autonomous, the greater will be the degree of political autonomy of different groups and of the development of independent foci of political struggle, and of the ideological dimension in politics. The more the access to these orders is, as in Russia, fused, or the more they are dissociated from one another (as in many patrimonial societies), the smaller will be the degree of such autonomy. In the first case the center will tend to permeate the periphery without permitting independent impingement by the periphery on the center; while in the second (and third) cases adaptive relations will tend to develop between the center and the periphery.

Similarly, the more the center is conceived of as the single focus of broader cultural order, the more the emphasis tends to be on functional attributes of status and on closed segregated status groups. The greater the "adaptive" attitude to the center, the greater also the degree of status segregation and emphasis on restricted prestige of closed communities. The greater the commitment of broader groups to the social order, the greater the center's permeation on the periphery.

Emphasis on power usually tends to create, among other things, a greater distinction between center and periphery, a very strong control on social mobility by the center, and dissociation between kinship groups and status units. The autonomy of strata is minimized. An emphasis on solidarity, however, tends to minimize the distinctions between center and periphery, to increase the formation of autonomous strata, and to strengthen the relations between strata and kinship units. (For greater detail, see Eisenstadt 1971b.)

IV. Patterns of Codes and Institutional Order: The Establishment of the Ground Rules of Social Interaction and the Development of Systemic Sensitivities of Social Organizations

Several questions crucial to our analysis are raised here. What is the place of the institutional derivatives of these orientations in the context of institutional social order? What is the relation of these principles to other aspects of social organization, especially to organizational problems, "needs," and exigencies of social groups, collectivities, or systems with which sociological analysis has been so greatly concerned? (Parsons 1961; Mayhew 1971; Parsons and Platt

1973). What are the mechanisms through which these orientations are concretely institutionalized?

The preceding illustrations (as well as the data in the various researches referred to above) indicate that the basic institutional derivatives of the symbolic orientations are the specifications of the following: goals "appropriate" for different categories of people in major types of societal situations; attributes of similarity and of criteria of membership in different collectivities; criteria of regulation of power over resources in different social situations and institutional spheres; interrelations among them all; and legitimation in terms of criteria of distributive justice which are perceived as incumbent in such different situations and in different collectives of social and cultural orders (see Eisenstadt and Curelaru 1976).

Such programmatic derivatives of codes provide the normative and evaluative specification—in terms of some of the tensions inherent in major problems of human existence analyzed above—of a range of goals or of desiderata available or permitted to the members of a certain group or social-cultural category (sex, age, occupation, territorial belongingness) and of the combinations of discrete "goals" into some broader styles of life.

In addition, such programmatic derivatives of codes define the basic attributes of social and cultural similarity which constitute the criteria of membership in different collectivities, including the symbolic and institutional boundaries of these collectivities. The establishment of attributes of similarity involves the definition of the contents of the sociocultural orders, of the rules of access to them, and of their legitimation in terms of some broader "charismatic" conceptions of justice, order, or appropriateness.

These attributes provide the starting points for the definition of criteria of membership in various collectivities and orders; for the specification of the rights and limitation of access to such attributes and the consequent rights of participation in the order or community; of the range of conditional and unconditional obligations and rights accruing through membership in such collectivities or orders; and of the consequent terms of conditional and unconditional access to the various resources and positions which are available according to such criteria. Thus membership in collectivities entitles one to benefit from and participate in certain rules of distributive justice, to be subject to certain rules of exchange. And it defines the duties symmetric to these rights, which are interlinked in the process of interaction that makes a clear distinction between members' and nonmembers' rights to participation (Eisenstadt 1971c).

Thus, side by side with the specification of attributes of membership and solidarity, the programmatic derivatives of codes also specify the general principles of distribution of power within the major institutional spheres of a society. Indeed, the major focus of the institutional derivatives of such codes is on membership criteria and boundaries of collectivities with regulation of power over resources and with the major mechanism and criteria of allocation of roles, rewards, and principles of integration in the various institutional spheres. This connection is effected by establishing the major criteria according to which public and semipublic goods—as well as of institutional credit in institutional spheres (Kuhn 1963, ch. 9; Olson 1968; Coleman 1971)—are organized. Or, in greater detail, it sets up the criteria of the differential payment of the costs of the payment of such goods—of the public distribution of semipublic and private goods (i.e., the direct allocation of various resources and rewards to different groups of the population according to criteria which differ greatly from those of pure exchange). These criteria also specify the ways in which different groups, organizations, and institutional spheres enjoy institutional credit—i.e., the degree to which resources provided to any such group or institution are not channeled into immediate exchange, but relinquished unconditionally to a certain group or institutional complex. Thus such group or institution is provided with what may be called "credit autonomy," which supplies the prerequisites of any long-range working of such institution.

A closer look at these various institutional derivatives of the major cultural codes indicate that they are not randomly distributed in social interaction, but are found in some specific institutional locations and that they work through specific institutional mechanisms. The programmatic derivatives of such codes touch especially on those areas of institutional life within which, in principle, there exists a strong possibility of randomness, uncertainty, and potential conflict of the original Hobbesian state of war of all against all.

The major institutional derivatives of the various codes provide some of the mechanisms through which these areas of potential randomness and conflict became structured in ways which can then assure some continuity of frameworks of interaction. They circumscribe those uncertainties inherent in any social interaction which are taken for granted and which have to be overcome in order to assure the continuity of any interaction. And they provide some of the rules according to which the boundaries of any given collectivity or of social interaction are structured *vis-à-vis* their respective internal and external environments.

These programmatic specifications of codes and their derivatives impose some limitations on what may be called free exchange between people interacting in institutional frameworks, thus setting up some of what, in Durkheim's terminology, can be called the precontractual elements of social life, the bases of mechanical solidarity (Durkheim 1933; Davis 1963; Bloch 1974). Or, to use Schneider's (1968, 1972) nomenclature: they combine the construction of "identity" and membership in different collectivities with the range of "codes" incumbent on those participating in such collectivities.

In this way the precondition for the effective participation of members of a society in terms of broader rules of ethics and criteria of justice prevalent in such a society is also established (Piaget 1932; Mead 1934; Parsons 1961, 1973a; Kohlberg 1971).

In the language of game theory, these limitations of free exchange and interaction which are set up by programmatic specification of codes define, first, "the ground rules that structure the basic frameworks within which decision-making in different areas of social life is possible, and, second (albeit in various degrees in different societies or parts thereof) some of the broad criteria of the rules that guide choices among the options which such frameworks allow" (Buchler and Nutini 1969).

Similarly the institutional specification of the codes defines the range of concrete needs of a society. Even if we accept that groups and societies do have general common needs or problems, such as those of allocation or regulation, or the famous Parsonian problems of adaptation, goal orientation, and pattern maintenance (Parsons and Shils 1951), the nature of any concrete definition of such a particular group or society's needs is not simply given by the coalescence of the people and the resources generated and available in any situation into some patterns of division of labor—i.e., in groups, role sets, and institutional spheres. Within each concrete situation, such needs or problems can be defined in different ways and different answers can be given to them (Eisenstadt 1971a). These definitions are crystallized through the specification of the institutional derivatives of the codes. Such crystallization is effected firstly by specifying the range of "permissible" questions and answers about some of the basic problems of social and cultural existence. Second, it is effected by relating these questions and answers to the definition of criteria for boundaries and membership of collectivities, and combining them with the principles of criteria of allocation of power within societies.

All these specify the broader parameters within which the organizational problems of any such group are set—i.e., the boundaries of the environment of the respective groups and the ranges of possible responses to the "pressures" of such environment. Above all they play a central role in the cybernetic mechanisms of any social system—both primary and secondary cybernetics (Maruyama 1964)—and in the crystallization of the specific morphostatic and morphogenic tendencies of any such system (Buckley 1967).

Above all, they influence the ways in which the general functions necessary for the working of social systems will perform within any concrete setting. In this way they also influence, once such systems or congeries of codes are institutionalized, the range of their systemic sensitivities, the salience of different potential conflicts and problems of the continuity of the given systems, and the ways in which different systems cope with the specific range of problems and crises they face, as well as the possible outcome of such crises—

especially of modes of "incorporation" or various dimensions of social and political expansion.

These patterns of codes influence the conception of the major political problems: the specific types of conflicts to which they are especially sensitive, the types of conditions under which the potentialities for such conflicts become articulated into more specific "boiling points" which may threaten the stability of any regime, the ways in which the regimes cope with these problems of conflict, and especially the ways of incorporating various types of political demands—those of growing participation in the political order. In particular, such codes influence the intensity of these types of conflicts and the perception of their acuteness—the range of "flexibility" or of rigidity in response to them and the relative importance of regressive (as against expansive) policies in coping with them (a fuller exposition of such differential systemic sensitivities of one type of politics is given in Eisenstadt 1973c). Different patterns of codes do also shape the mode of change that develops in different societies; thus it has been shown that revolutionary changes develop only in those civilizations within which there is prevalent a strong perception of tension between the transcendental and the mundane order, and a this-worldly, or combined this- and other-worldly mode of resolution of such tension (Eisenstadt 1978).

V. The Openness of Systems of Codes in Relation to Concrete Institutionalization

The preceding analysis bears out in fuller detail the assertion made earlier that these basic institutional derivatives of codes which constitute the ground rules of social interaction and "hidden structure" are not concretized through some sort of direct "emanation" of the institutional rules derived from symbolic premises of the codes and models of social structure, or from some general laws of the human mind. The process of their concrete crystallization or institutionalization involves elements of openness, choice, and uncertainty.

This can be demonstrated even more forcefully by the fact that there exists no simple one-to-one relation between such cultural models or patterns of codes and any specific regime or macrosocietal order. The ways in which basic problems and dilemmas are defined and resolved in an articulated cultural model, or in the broad pattern of codes, do not necessarily correspond only to one specific pattern of institutionalization.

Within any tradition or social order, the possible relations among its different components are not exhausted by their actual coalescence in the existing institutionalized system. Within each such order there exist several ranges of freedom with respect to the concrete possibilities of institutionalization of the various derivatives of codes.

Concretely, such openness of different cultural models and systems of codes is evident in the fact that the same cultural model or pattern of codes can be institutionalized in different—if not endless—types of political regimes or economic systems. Thus, for instance, codes that specify the general types of relations between, let us say, the political and social or cultural order can leave undefined the concrete settings or boundaries of such organizations and units. For example, while an emphasis on the importance of the fusion of the political and cultural communities is basic to all of Islam, the way it can be institutionalized has varied greatly from one situation to another—from the tribal setting of Arabia, to the centralized empires of the Middle East, to the more shifting centers of North Africa (Gellner 1973; Mardin 1973; Yalman 1973). Within each such situation, rather different societal orientations may operate and different cultural themes emphasized.

Even in the more "compact" traditional societies, like China, Japan, and Burma, where there is greater coalescence between the cultural and political orders, these codes have been institutionalized in various ways (Bellah 1972; Wakeman 1972). Thus in China, the tension between the ideals of sociopolitical involvement of the individual and of inner harmony can be played out in the distinction between the lonely scholar and the bureaucrat on the one hand, and between the legalistic official and the Taoist-Buddhist mystic on the other (Wakeman 1972).

The fact that there is great choice in the institutionalization of codes is manifest on several levels. To begin with, there exists some openness in the coalescence between the two major types of codes—those oriented to the existential problems of human life and those oriented to the symbolism of the special dilemmas of social life. Thus any specific institutional concretization of, let us say, a strong emphasis on the political dimension of human life, together with conceptions of a very strong correlation—and tension—between the cosmic and cultural order may be defined in a strongly ritualistic, third world manner, as in China, or transcendentally, as in Islam. The concretization may be combined in different historical situations, in different concrete regimes, and with varying emphasis on hierarchy or equality, conflict or harmony; and great or small value may be placed upon the relative importance of power, solidarity, or instrumental attributes of social order.

Second, any such institutionalization of a model or pattern of codes entails the specification of the appropriate "here and now"—the concrete setting, groups, or collectivity—as distinct from other such groups; the *concrete* criteria of membership, with an emphasis on a specific group with its primordial symbols, or its particular dogma.

Such specification is very closely related to the other major type of institutional derivative of symbolic orientations—to the concretization of the symbols of collective identity which are taken up and crystallized in any such situation. The various symbols of collective and personal identity which are constructed in the process of institutionalization of such models and patterns of codes—even if they are taken out of the reservoir of traditional symbols—are rarely simply given. They are continuously being reconstituted and reconstructed. This becomes especially vivid in situations of far-reaching social and cultural change. In such situations, cultural traditions, symbols, artifacts, and organizations become more elaborate, more rationally organized, or at least more formalized and articulated, as different groups and individuals in a society become increasingly aware of these traditions and symbols. That is, "tradition" becomes differentiated in layers. Simple "given" usages or patterns of behavior may become quite distinct from these more articulated and formalized symbols of the cultural order—such as the great ritual centers and offices, theological codices, or special buildings. The layers of tradition tend also to vary in the degree and nature of their prescriptive validity and in their relevance to different spheres of life. These processes are often related to a growing "partialization" and privatization of various older existing traditions or customs. Even if the "old" customs and symbols are not negated or "thrown out" they undergo far-reaching changes (Eisenstadt 1973b; Yalman 1973).

VI. The Special Characteristics and Mechanisms of the Process of Institutionalization of the Ground Rules of Social Interaction: The Conditionalities, Titles, and Institutional Entrepreneurs

It is only through all these processes of selection, through the combination of these different elements—each with its own tendencies or rules—that any model of cultural and social order, as well as of patterns of codes, can become concretized and impinge on the working of concrete social groups or collectivities.

Such concretization is effected through processes of institutionalization with very strong elements of struggle, choice, and coalition making. But the processes of institutionalization of the institutional derivatives of codes, of the ground rules of social interaction, contrast rather sharply with relatively free exchange of resources in open institutionalized markets regulated either by rules of supply and demand or rules of operant psychology or with the "direct" provision for the "needs" of social groups. We are only beginning to analyze these problems, and only some very preliminary indications can be discerned.

The most general mechanism of the regulations of the patterns of interaction and of the flow of resources in a society (Coleman 1971), through which these aspects of institutional life are regulated is the specification of unconditionalities—of patterns of interaction in social institutional settings which are not based on the direct conditional but rather on indirect giving and receiving of services, resources, and rewards, and on the setting up of "titles" (Eisenstadt 1971c). The construction of unconditionalities takes place through the institutionalization of various ascriptive limitations on institutional interaction or exchange on access to positions as well as on the use of resources for establishing the rules of such access. Ascriptive restrictions on exchange mean that an actor, even if he possesses the commodities relevant to a given exchange and is willing to enter into the exchange, is excluded because he belongs to some group or category of people.

The most important aspect of such restrictions, from the point of view of the regulation of the flow of resources, is the combination of economic resources and power with prestige—not only with prestige as a symbolic dimension of interpersonal relations but, above all, as the structural principle which regulates the access to participation in some relatively "exclusive" order: membership in a collective, in societal centers, or in the cultural orders (Eisenstadt 1973b). The pursuit of discrete goals—whether for economic gain, power, or interpersonal prestige—is linked to such participation in various societal and cultural orders. This linkage creates the structural, as distinct from the purely interpersonal, aspects of prestige and underlies the central role of prestige as the potential transformer or regulator of other media (Eisenstadt 1973b).

The formation of these institutional patterns is effected in special frameworks and through interaction among the occupants of special types of social positions. Thus the establishment of such unconditionalities and their continuous regulation takes place, in contrast to markets based on barter or on the free interchange of various media and resources, in special hierarchical frameworks. Among such frameworks are ritual and communicative situations (analyzed above) in which reference orientations of different population groups are set up. Various legal and political frameworks are included as well (see also Williamson 1973a, b).

These unconditionalities and organizational frameworks and the consequent restrictions on exchange they entail are constituted by the cross-cutting of two levels of social interaction. The first is interaction (cooperative or conflictual) between those people, holders of different positions or members of different groups, who can be designated as institutional entrepreneurs (Barth 1963; Eisenstadt 1973a, b, c). Such people articulate models of social order, set up new norms and organizational frameworks, and mobilize the necessary public resources. Second is the interaction between social units (or their representatives). They are mostly oriented to the assuring the flow of some mutual solidarity and of the establishment of continuity of social interaction among those individuals, strata, and groups who are ready to provide such resources— i.e., those who are willing to pay something for these entrepreneurial activities.

(See also Cartwright and Schwartz 1973 for one of the few concrete analytical studies of the development of such norms.)

It is through these types of interaction that the ground rules of social interaction are institutionalized and, above all, combinations of membership with principles of power—of "codes and identity"—are institutionalized. They are derived from the "meeting" of the symbolic with the organizational aspects of social life. They differ from "regular" institutional interaction in that they regulate not only the flow, exchange, and conversion of organizational resources (especially economic resources and power), but also that they combine— above all through the different mechanisms of prestige—such resources with the symbolic orientations in general, and with different symbols of identity in particular.

The institutionalization of these ground rules does not "solve" the problems of social order. Rather it transposes it and its ambivalences to the meeting of the symbolic and the organizational aspects of social life. The nature of these ambivalences and their selection to the institutionalization of the ground rules of social interaction can be best seen in the situations in which such institutionalization is symbolized.

VII. The Symbolization of Models of Social Order and Their Institutionalization in Ritual and Communicative Situations

Any such normative specification and legitimation inherent in the institutionalization of the selection of the derivatives of patterns of codes involves the prohibition and sanctioning of some patterns of behavior, as well as the exclusion of other situations and groups. Hence it is only natural that such specification also creates a very strong ambivalence about the concrete "resolution" of human predicaments provided in any such model and about the consequent exclusion of other possibilities. Ambivalence is also created about the need to employ sanctions through which these models and the norms derived from them are maintained.

Hence, each model or system or complexes of codes contains within it several points of tension, which are inherent in the contradictions that develop within any such system itself and in its application to the creation of institutional complexes.

These contradictions tend to cluster around certain themes or poles, according to their perception and formulation on the symbolic level. Among such themes the most important are the varying ways of structuring the differences in human life between nature and culture; the perennial encounter between the quest for solidarity and the exigencies of division of labor and political struggle; the tension between the givens of power and its exercise and the search for more transcendental types of legitimation of the social order; and the degree to which various models of cosmic, human, and social order can provide foci for meaningful human endeavor. Such themes tend to coalesce in different ways in different models.

These ambivalences are most fully and dramatically played out in special social situations (Geertz 1973, ch. 15; Peacock 1968b; Eisenstadt 1965, section V)—in plays, public displays, private encounters, jokes, and various types of myths (Peacock 1968a, b; Munn 1973b). But they tend to be most fully articulated in those ritual occasions which are most closely related to individual and collective *rites de passage*—be they rituals of birth, initiation, wedding, and death; or of first-fruits collective ceremonies, and those occasions in which routine is to some extent broken or disturbed (Eisenstadt 1968). Rites of passage tend to become fully articulated in (a) situations where there is some transition from one institutional sphere to another; contemporaneous activity in several institutional spheres, or in several subsystems of a society; (b) situations where various subsystems must be directly connected with the central values and activities of a society; (c) situations where people are faced with a choice among various roles; (d) situations where the routine of a given role of an individual or group is endangered or disrupted.

In all such situations the individual is placed in potentially ambiguous, undefined, and conflicting conditions in which his identity and status image and the continuity of his perception of other actions are endangered.

These various situations—the more structured individual and collective rites of passage reported in anthropological studies, and the less structured "communicative situations" of modern societies—have a common denominator: people or groups involved in these situations experience some shattering of the existing social and cultural order to which they are bound. Hence they become more sensitive to symbols or messages that attempt to symbolize such order, and are more ready to respond to people who are able to present new symbols to them. Such new symbols could give meaning to their experience in terms of some broader fundamental, cosmic, social, or political order; they may prescribe the proper norms of behavior, relate the individual to collective identification, and reassure him of his status and in place in a given collectivity.

Such situations do not arise only in catastrophic conditions. They constitute part of any orderly social life—of the life of individuals as they pass from one stage in their lifespan to another, or from one sphere of activities to another. They also occur in organizations of groups and societies.

In all these situations the cognitive, evaluative, and affective aspects of such symbolization are focused on the ambivalences inherent in the concretization of the models of social and cultural order, and around the dilemmas of human existence and social life. In such situations these dilemmas, and the various subconscious orientations toward them, serve as focal points of the meeting between the cultural evaluation of different attributes (natural and cultural) of people and of the organizational problems of social division of labor and of participation in it, and of the tensions inherent in any such meeting. Especially important here are the tensions between the ideal models of social and cosmic orders and the possibilities of their actualization in life; between different dimensions of prestige; between dimensions of solidarity and between the givens of social division of labor (Turner 1968; Geertz 1973).

Thus in such situations the models of cosmic, social, and cultural orders, and the choices of action they imply, are often focused around the evaluation of interpersonal relations in basic groups—family, work, etc.—the tensions involved and their resolution are formulated in terms of the evaluation of life and death or sexual prowess, age, or symbols of purity and pollution. Hence such symbolization is also focused around the major primordial symbols of personal and collective identity (Douglas 1966, 1970; Turner 1968; Silverman 1971; Munn 1973b).

In the construction of such answers, the objects closest to these problems—bodily characteristics and functions, some basic aspects of the natural environment, as well as of the major attributes of solidarity, or power—become foci of evaluative symbolism, of purity, and pollution. They become components and symbols of personal and collective identity and guides in performance of many social tasks and activities (Douglas 1966, 1970; Schneider 1968, 1972; Schneider and Smith 1973).

Hence in all such communicative and ritual situations, what may be called the natural givens of any of the respective institutional spheres—sex, age, and procreation in the family, power and force in politics, or the extraction of resources from nature in economics—are usually dramatized, evaluated, and related to the organizational problems of each sphere. In fact, however, there is no "natural" predestined correspondence between any organizational problem and any given fixed set of symbols (Schneider 1968, 1972; Silverman 1971; Meggit 1972). For instance, although in most societies there is a predilection toward combining the placement of new members with symbols of procreation, this need not always be the case. Similarly, although some symbols of blood do indeed enter into the definition of familial identity, in some societies such natural biological data may be crystallized as symbols of polity, or of different types of cultural orders, and not of family or kinship (Ossowski 1948).

All such situations are characterized by a very high element of ritualization. Such ritualization highlights two strongly connected functions of the ground rules of social interaction that are derived from the meeting between the symbolic and the organizational aspects of social life. The strong element of formalization inherent in ritualization restricts the freedom potentially given in any human discourse (Bloch 1974). In this way it defines and symbolizes the given environment of any group or society and maintains some cybernetic control within it (Rappaport 1971; Munn 1973b).

VIII. Conclusion: The Possibilities and Limitations of the Application of Structural Analysis to Social Organization

The preceding analysis has illustrated in relatively detailed ways that the "hidden structure" of social order, as presumably represented by the programmatic derivatives of codes, is not just a set of abstract rules of the "human mind" which are somehow reflected in social organization. Hidden structure is effected through complicated institutional processes and mechanisms. This analysis has indicated that, as in other spheres of symbolic patterning of human experience, it is the "schemata" of the respective sphere and not the "objective" contents of the objects of such experience that provides the decisive principles of cognitive and evaluative organization of human behavior, of the hidden structure or contexts of such behavior. (Munn 1973b; Turner 1973; and for a classical exposition, Cassirer 1953). But the schemata operative in the social field are not purely cognitive, "prelogical" or logical ones. They are (Geertz 1973, chs. 1, 13) closely combined with the more existential dimension of human life and social organization.

It may be true of course that on a very high level of abstraction some very common general tendencies of such coding or structuring—like those of "mediation" between polar opposites—are common to all systems of human creativity and activity. But this, in itself, does not tell us about the ways in which these principles influence the construction and operation of different concrete spheres of human activity. Whatever the degree or scope of such universal rules, their concrete crystallization (and hence the possibility of creation of new contents and combinations) is possible only when they unfold in concrete interaction.

The most crucial aspect of such interaction (probably contrary to the exposition of some structuralists) is the openness of both "models" and "codes" with respect to the ranges of their concretization in institutional life. Such openness implies that the concretization of such rules and models entails some potentialities of innovation, and that it is effected through some concrete processes of human activity—which have some rules or tendencies of their own. Hence the concretization of such codes and models is mediated by those different problems specific to these different spheres of activity.

Thus, insofar as it is meaningful to talk about hidden structure with respect to social organization, the meaning of the term structure here is much nearer to the way Piaget (1970) tends to use it, as Terry Turner has put it (1973: 371): "Structures . . . are not conceived as directly fulfilling functions, or indeed, as 'acting.' They consist rather, in generalized codes or mechanisms for regulating the functional activities of 'subjects.' . . .

"As against this concept Lévi-Strauss' concept of structure, as Piaget notes is static, atemporal, anti-functionalist, and leaves no place for the activity of the subject." (See also Geertz 1973, ch. 13.)

But here we encounter some limitation of Piaget's own analysis in general and its bearing on the problems of social organization in particular. Piaget's definition of structure does not distinguish between different types of structure that are specific to different types of objects and organizations—mathematical or logical operations as contrasted with, for instance, social organization.

Our analysis has provided some indications about these problems. We have discussed the nature of the specific symbolic orientations and of the problems of these models and codes, oriented to the working of systems and the institutional loci on which they impinge.

We have also discussed the relations between such rules and the organizational aspects of social life. It has shown that these orientations and rules are indeed related to such problems—but at the same time they are not identical with the concrete organizational "functional" problems of any specific social group or system.

Thus, the influence of cultural models and systems of codes in the social field does not automatically stem from some natural emanation of these models and codes. It constitutes a crucial—although special—aspect of the process of institutionalization, with very strong elements of power struggle, choice, resolution of conflicts, and coalition-making. But these elements refer to a level, or aspect, of institutionalization which differs from concrete organizational interaction and from the concrete organizational interaction of groups and collectivities. It therefore entails possibly different rules, carriers, and modes of continuity. We do indeed encounter one of the most difficult problems of our analysis—the identification of the different social carriers and mechanisms through which distinct levels of the institutional order are crystallized. The analysis of the different characteristics of these levels of institutionalization and of their interrelation constitutes one of the basic challenges for sociological and anthropological analysis in general, and for the further elucidation of structuralist approaches to social organization in particular. In the preceding pages we have attempted to provide some initial indications in this direction.

REFERENCES

Barth, F. 1963. *The Role of Entrepreneur in Social Change in Northern Norway*. Bergen: Artok.

Bellah, R. N. 1972. "Intellectual and society in Japan." *Daedalus* (Spring 1972):89–117.

Bloch, Maurice. 1974. "Symbols and songs, dance and features of articulation;

or, Is religion an extreme form of traditional authority?" *Archives Europeens de Sociologie* 15:55–82.

Boon, J. A. 1972. *From Symbolism to Structuralism*. Oxford, Basil Blackwell.

Buchler, Ira R., and Hugo G. Nutini, eds. 1969. *Introduction to Game Theory in the Behavioral Sciences*, pp. 1–23. Pittsburgh: University of Pittsburgh Press.

Buckley, W. 1967. *Sociology and Modern Systems Theory*. Englewood Cliffs, N.J., Prentice-Hall.

Cartwright, B. C., and R. D. Schwartz. 1973. "The invocation of legal norms: An empirical investigation of Durkheim and Weber." *American Sociological Review* (June) 38:340–54.

Cassirer, E. 1953. *The Philosophy of Symbolic Forms*. New Haven: Yale University Press.

Coleman, J. S. 1971. *Resources for Social Change*. New York: Wiley.

Davis, J. A. 1963. "Structural balance, mechanical solidarity and interpersonal relations." *American Journal of Sociology* 68:446–62.

Douglas, M. 1966. *Purity and Danger*. London: Routledge & Kegan Paul.

———— 1970. *Natural Symbols*. Harmondsworth, Middlesex: Penguin Books.

Dumont, L. 1971. *Homo Hierarchicus*. Chicago: University of Chicago Press.

Durkheim, E. 1933. *On the Division of Labor in Society*. New York: Macmillan.

Eisenstadt, S. N. 1965. *Essays on Comparative Institutions*. New York: Wiley.

———— 1968. *Charisma and Institution Building: Max Weber and Modern Sociology*. Chicago: University of Chicago Press.

———— 1971a. "General introduction: The scope and problems of political sociology." In Eisenstadt, ed. *Political Sociology*. New York: Basic Books.

———— 1971b. *Social Differentiation and Stratification*. Glenview: Scott, Foresman.

———— 1971c. "Societal goals, systemic needs, social interaction and individual behavior: Some tentative explanations." In Herman Turk and Richard R. Simpson, eds. *Institutions and Social Exchange—The Sociologies of Talcott Parsons and George C. Homans*, pp. 36–56. New York: Bobbs-Merrill.

———— 1973a. "Post-traditional societies and the continuity and reconstruction of tradition." *Daedalus* (Winter), pp. 1–29.

———— 1973b. *Tradition, Change and Modernity*. New York: Wiley.

———— 1973c. "Traditional patrimonialism and modern neopatrimonialism." *Sage Research Papers in the Social Sciences* 1 (90–003). (Studies in Comparative Modernization Series.) Beverly Hills: Sage Publications.

———— 1978. *Revolution and the Transformation of Societies*. New York: The Free Press.

Eisenstadt, S. N. and M. Curelaru. 1976. *The Form of Sociology—Paradigms and Crises*. New York: Wiley.

Geertz, C. 1973. *The Interpretation of Cultures*. New York: Basic Books.

Geertz, H. 1965. Comment on Professor P. E. Josselin de Jong [1965a]. *Journal of Asian Studies* 24(2):294–97.

Gellner, C. 1973. "Post-traditional forms in Islam: The turf and trades, and votes and peanuts." *Daedalus* (Winter), pp. 191–207.

Godelier, M. 1973. *Horizons, Trajets Marxistes en Anthropologie.* Paris: E. Anthropos.

Hammel, D. 1972. "The myth of structural analysis." Addison-Wesley Modules in the Social Sciences. New York: Addison-Wesley.

Hayes, E. N. and T. Hayes, eds. 1970. *Claude Lévi-Strauss, The Anthropologist as Hero.* Cambridge: MIT Press.

de Heusch, L. 1971. *Pourquoi s'epouser.* Paris: Gallimard.

Josselin de Jong, J. P. B. 1922. "De Couvade." *Mededeelingen der Koninklijke Akademie Van Wetenschappen* 54(B):53–84.

Josselin de Jong, P. E. 1951. *Minanqkaba and Negri Sembilan. Socio-Political Structure in Indonesia.* Leiden: Eduard Ijdo.

———— 1960. "Cultural anthropology in the Netherlands." *Higher Education and Research in the Netherlands,* 4:13.

———— 1964. "Circulerent connubium en het dubbelunilineals principe." *Bijdragen Tot de Taal-, Land-en Volkenkunde* 120:181–94.

———— 1965a. "An interpretation of agricultural rites in Southeast Asia, with a demonstration of use of data from both continental and insular areas." *Journal of Asian Studies* 24(2):283–91.

———— 1965b. Reply to Professor Hildred Geertz [1965]. *Ibid.,* pp. 297–98.

———— 1971. "Presumed behavior: Comments on Cara E. Richards' brief communication." *American Anthropologist* 73:270–73.

Kobben, A. J. F. 1966. "Structuralism versus comparative functionalism: Some comments." *Bijdragen Tot de Taal-, Land- en Volkenkunde* 122:145–50.

Kohlberg, L. 1971. "Stage and sequence: The cognitive developmental approach to socialization." In David A. Goslin, ed. *Handbook of Socialization Theory and Research,* pp. 347–481. Chicago: Rand McNally.

Kuhn, A. 1963. *The Study of Society—A Unified Approach.* Homewood, Illinois: Dorsey.

Lane, M., ed. 1970. *Structuralism.* London: Jonathan Cape.

Leach, E. 1954. *Political Systems of Highland Burma.* London: C. Bell & Sons.

———— 1960. "The frontiers of Burma." *Comparative Studies in Sociology and History* 3(11):49–68.

———— 1961. *Paul Eliya. A Village in Ceylon.* Cambridge: Cambridge University Press.

———— 1965. "Claude Lévi-Strauss—anthropologist and philosopher." *New Left Review* 34:12–28.

———— 1968. *Genesis as Myth and Other Essays,* eds. W. Lepenies and H. Ritter. London: Jonathan Cape.

———— 1972. *Orte des Wilden Denkens.* Frankfurt: Suhrkamp.

Lévi-Strauss, C. 1963. *Structural Anthropology.* New York: Basic Books.

———— 1966. *The Savage Mind.* Chicago: University of Chicago Press.

——— 1969. *The Elementary Structures of Kinship*, ed. Rodney Needham. London: Eyre & Spottiswoodle.

MacRae, D. 1968. Introduction to Raymond Boudon, *The Uses of Structuralism*. London: Heinemann.

Mardin, S. 1973. "Center periphery relations: A key to Turkish politics? *Daedalus* (Winter), pp. 169–91.

Maruyama, M. 1963. "The second cybernetics: Deviation amplifying mutual causal processes." *American Scientist* 51:64–79.

Maybury-Lewis, D. 1960. "The analysis of dual organisation: A methodological critique." *Anthropologica. Bijdragen Tot de Taal-, Land- en Volkenkunde* 116:17–45.

Mayhew, L. 1971. *Society, Institutions and Action*. Glencoe, Ill.: Scott Forseman.

Mead, G. H. 1934. *Mind, Self, and Society*. Chicago: University of Chicago Press.

Meggit, M. 1972. "Understanding Australian Aboriginal society: Kinship systems or cultural categories." In P. Reining, ed. *Kinship Studies in the Morgan Centennial Year*. Washington, D.C.: Anthropological Society of Washington.

Munn, Nancy D. 1973a. *Waibiri Iconography. Graphic Representation and Cultural Symbols in a Central Australian Society*. Ithaca, N.Y.: Cornell University Press.

——— 1973b. "Symbolism in ritual context—aspects of symbolic action." In J. Honigman, ed. *A Handbook of Social and Cultural Anthropology*, pp. 579–613. Chicago: Rand McNally.

Needham, R. 1960. "A Structural Analysis of Aimol Society." *Antropologica. Bijdragen Tot de Taal-, Land- en Volkenkunde* 116:81–109.

Olson, M. Jr. 1968. *The Logic of Collective Action*. New York: Schocken.

Ossowski, S. 1948. *Wiez Spoleczna I Dziedzichwo Krwi* (Social Bond and Block Inheritance). Warsawa: Ksiazka.

Parsons, T. 1951. *The Social System*. Glencoe, Ill.: The Free Press.

——— 1961. "Introduction to culture and the social system." In T. Parsons and E. Shils, eds. *Theories of Society*, part 4, 2:963–992. Glencoe, Ill.: The Free Press.

——— 1973a. "Durkheim on religion revisited: Another look at the elementary forms of the religious life." In Charles Y. Glock and Phillip E. Hammond, eds. *Beyond the Classics*, pp. 156–80. New York: Harper & Row.

Parsons, T. and G. Platt. 1973. *The American University*. Cambridge: Harvard University Press.

Parsons, T. and E. Shils, eds. 1951. *Toward a General Theory of Action*. Cambridge: Harvard University Press.

Peacock, J. L. 1968a. "A problem in the study of ideals: Lévi-Strauss' statistical and mechanical models." Paper prepared for Symposium No. 41, Wenner-Gren Foundation for Anthropological Research.

——— 1968b. *Rites of Modernization: Symbols and Social Aspects of Indonesian Proletarian Dramas*. Chicago: University of Chicago Press.

Piaget, J. 1932. *The Moral Judgement of the Child*. London: Routledge & Kegan Paul.
———— 1970. *Structuralism*. New York: Basic Books.
Pouwer, J. 1964. "A social system in the star mountains: Toward a reorientation of the study of social systems." *American Anthropologist* 66: 133–61.
———— 1966a. "Referential and inferential Reality. A rejoinder." *Bijdragen Tot de Taal-, Land-en Volkenkunde*, 122:151–57.
———— 1966b. "Structure and flexibility in a new society." *Ibid*. pp. 158–69.
———— 1966c. "The structural and functional approach in cultural anthropology: Theoretical reflections with reference to research in western New Guinea." *Ibid*. pp. 129–44.
Rappaport, R. 1971. "The sacred in human evolution." *Annual Review of Ecology and Systematics* 2:23–24.
Rossi, I. 1973. "The unconscious in the anthropology of Claude Lévi-Strauss." *American Anthropologist* 25:20–49.
Rotenstreich, N. 1972. "On Lévi-Strauss' concept of structure." *The Review of Metaphysics* 25(3):489–526.
Schneider, D. M. 1968. *American Kinship: A Cultural Account*. Englewood Cliffs, N.J.: Prentice-Hall, Inc.
———— 1972. "What is kinship all about?" In P. Reining, ed. *Kinship Studies in the Morgan Centennial Year*, pp. 32–64. Washington, D.C.: Anthropological Society of Washington.
Schneider, D. M., and R. T. Smith. 1973. *Class Differences and Sex Roles in American Kinship and Family Structure*. Englewood Cliffs, N.J.: Prentice-Hall.
Scholte, B. 1966. "Epistemic paradigms: Some problems in cross-cultural research on social anthropological history and theory." *American Anthropologist* 68:1192–1200.
———— 1973. "The structural anthropology of Claude Lévi-Strauss." J. Honigman, ed. In *A Handbook of Social and Cultural Anthropology*, pp. 637–717. Chicago: Rand McNally.
Schulte-Nordholdt, G. H. 1971. *The Political System of the Atoni of Timor*. The Hague: Martinus Nijhoff.
Sebag, L. 1964. *Marxisme et Structuralisme*. Paris: Payot.
Shils, E. 1961. "Center and periphery." In *The Logic of Personal Knowledge: Essays Presented to M. Polanyi*, pp. 117–31. London: Routledge and Kegan Paul.
———— 1965. "Charisma, order, and status." *American Sociological Review* 30(2):199–213.
Silverman, Martin G. 1971. *Disconcerting Issue: Meaning and Struggle in a Resettled Pacific Community*. Chicago: The University of Chicago Press.
Tiryakian, E. A. 1970. "Structural sociology." In J. C. McKinney and E. A. Tiryahian, eds. *Theoretical Sociology: Perspectives and Developments*, pp. 112–35. New York: Appleton, Century-Crofts.

Turner, T. 1973. "Piaget's structuralism." *American Anthropologist* 75:351–73.

Turner, V. 1968. "Myth and symbol." *International Encyclopedia of the Social Sciences*, pp. 576–82. New York: Collier Macmillan.

Wakeman, F. J. 1972. "The Price of autonomy: Intellectuals in Ming and Ching politics." *Daedalus* (Spring), p. 351.

Weber, M. 1947. *From Max Weber, Essays in Sociology*. London: Routledge & Kegan Paul.

———— 1958. *The Religion of India: The Sociology of Hinduism and Buddhism*. New York: The Free Press.

———— 1964. *The Religion of China: Confucianism and Taoism*. New York: Macmillan.

Williamson, D. E. 1973a. "Some notes on the economics of Atmosphere." Fels Discussion Paper No. 29. University of Pennsylvania, The Fels Center of Government.

———— 1973b. "Markets and hierarchies: Some elementary considerations." *American Economic Review*, pp. 316–25.

Yalman, N. 1973. "Some observations on Secularism in Islam: The cultural revolution in Turkey." *Daedalus* 1:139–69.

Eight

CHARISMA AND INSTITUTION BUILDING: MAX WEBER AND MODERN SOCIOLOGY

I

WEBER'S WORK DOES NOT NEED an introduction to the English-speaking sociological world. Most of his major works—all the *Aufsätze für Religionsoziologie*,[1] his *General Economic History*,[2] many of his essays on methodology of the social sciences,[3] and large parts of his monumental *Wirtschaft und Gesellschaft* have been translated in special collections, in the *Theory of Social and Economic Organization*,[4] in parts of *Essays from Max Weber*,[5] in *The Sociology of Religion*,[6] and in *The City*[7] and in the volume *On Law*,[8] to be followed by a full-fledged translation by G. Roth. So also have several of his essays—the famous essays on politics and science as vocation, as well as some of his articles on economic history.[9] The major works missing in English are most of his empirical researches, collected in his *Gesammelte Aufsätze zur Soziologie und Sozialpolitik*[10] and several of the concrete his-

Originally published in *Max Weber on Charisma*, edited by S. N. Eisenstadt (University of Chicago Press), © 1968 by The University of Chicago. All rights reserved.

1. *The Protestant Ethic and the Spirit of Capitalism*, trans. by Talcott Parsons (London: Allen & Unwin, 1930); *The Religion of China: Confucianism and Taoism*, trans. and ed. by H. H. Gerth (Glencoe, Ill.: Free Press, 1951); *Ancient Judaism*, trans. and ed. by H. H. Gerth and Don Martindale (Glencoe, Ill.: Free Press, 1952); *The Religion of India: The Sociology of Hinduism and Buddhism*, trans. and ed. by H. H. Gerth and Don Martindale (Glencoe, Ill.: Free Press, 1952); *The Sociology of Religion*, trans. by Ephraim Fischoff (Boston: Beacon Press, 1963) (mostly from *Wirtschaft u. Gesellschaft*).

2. *General Economic History*, trans. by Frank H. Knight (Glencoe, Ill.: Free Press, 1927).

3. *Max Weber on the Methodology of the Social Sciences*, trans. and ed. by Edward A. Shils and Henry A. Finch (Glencoe, Ill.: Free Press, 1949).

4. Trans. by R. A. Henderson and Talcott Parsons, ed. by Talcott Parsons (New York: Oxford University Press, 1947).

5. *Essays from Max Weber*, trans. and ed. by H. H. Gerth and C. Wright Mills (New York: Oxford University Press, 1946).

6. *Sociology of Religion*.

7. *The City*, trans. and ed. by Don Martindale and Gertrud Neuwirth (Glencoe, Ill.: Free Press, 1958).

8. *On Law in Economy and Society*, trans. by Edward A. Shils and Max Rheinstein (Cambridge, Mass.: Harvard University Press, 1954).

9. *Essays from Max Weber*.

10. Tübingen, J. C. B. Mohr, 1924.

torical analyses, mostly collected in his *Gesammelte Aufsätze zur Sozial und Wirtschaftsgeschichte.*[11]

Even before most of these translations became available his work was introduced to the English-speaking and, especially to the American sociological world through the writings of Talcott Parsons.[12] In Parsons' *Structure of Social Action* he fully explored the place of Weber in the development of modern sociological thought and analysis and at the same time presented a very detailed examination of most of the major aspects of Weber's work. In further works and essays, especially in his introductions to the *Theory of Social and Economic Organization* and to the *Sociology of Religion,* Parsons has continued to explore the significance of Weber's work for the development of sociological theory in general and for various fields of sociology in particular. Perhaps the most succinct presentation of Weber's place in the history of sociology can be found in Parsons' recent paper "Unity and Diversity in the Modern Intellectual Disciplines: The Role of the Social Sciences."[13]

Aside from Parsons' works, exposition of Weber's works could be found in the thirties and forties in the historical exposition of Barnes and Becker,[14] in A. Salomon's articles in *Social Research,*[15] in several articles by Edward A. Shils,[16] and in the comprehensive presentation of his work and intellectual orientation given by R. Bendix in *Max Weber—An Intellectual Portrait.*[17] In connection with the centenary of Weber's birth in 1964 additional analyses of his significance in the history of sociology and of German cultural life have appeared.[18]

All this does not mean, of course, that there is no place for further detailed analysis of Weber's work in sociology and comparative history and of his place in European *Geistesgeschichte* in general and in German social and political

11. Tübingen, J. C. B. Mohr, 1924.

12. E.g., Introduction to Weber's *Theory of Social and Economic Organization,* 1–70: *The Structure of Social Action* (New York: Free Press, 1968); Introduction to Weber's *Sociology of Religion,* pp. ix–lxvii; "Unity and Diversity in the Modern Intellectual Disciplines: The Role of the Social Sciences," *Daedalus,* vol. 94 (Winter, 1965).

13. *Ibid.,* especially 55–61.

14. H. E. Barnes and H. Becker, *Social Thought from Lore to Science* (New York: Dover Publications, 1952, originally published in 1936).

15. "Max Weber's Methodology," *Social Research,* 1 (1934) 147–68; "Max Weber's Sociology," *ibid.,* 2 (1935):60–73; "Max Weber's Political Ideas," *ibid.,* 368–84.

16. "Some Remarks on the Theory of Social and Economic Organization," *Economica,* 15 (1948):36–50; Foreword to *Max Weber on the Methodology of the Social Sciences,* iii–x; "Charisma, Order and Status," *American Sociological Review,* 30 (1965):199–213.

17. R. Bendix, *Max Weber—An Intellectual Portrait* (New York: Doubleday, 1960).

18. E.g., Wolfgang Mommsen, *Max Weber und die deutsche Politik, 1890–1920* (Tübingen: J. C. B. Mohr, 1959); Otto Stammer, ed., *Max Weber und die Soziologie heute: Verhandlungen des 15. deutschen Soziologentages* (Tübingen: J. C. B. Mohr, 1965); the April, 1965, issue of *The American Sociological Review* (vol. 30): Karl Engisch, Bernhard Pfister, and Johannes Winckelmann, eds., *Max Weber: Gedächtnisschrift der Ludwig-Maximilians Universität München* (Berlin, 1966).

thought in the late nineteenth and early twentieth century in particular. The study of his influence in all these areas poses problems of research mainly for the historian of social thought, for those concerned with any of the many concrete fields of research in which Weber worked, and for the historian of German intellectual life in the nineteenth and twentieth centuries.

The importance of Weber, however, is not only as a major figure in the history of sociology or in the *Geistesgeschichte* of the nineteenth and twentieth centuries. Nor is Weber's work of significance today only as a mine of varied concrete hypotheses and analyses—many of them unsurpassed in the study of bureaucracy, of sociology of law, and sociology of religion or in the analysis of different types of capitalism. True enough, in many fields of sociology—the more analytical inquiry into the nature of social relations, general methodological writings, the analysis of social organization or social systems, the analysis of economic sociology, the study of bureaucracy and of different types of political systems, and to a lesser degree several aspects of sociology of religion and of law—sociological analysis has reached a stage in which, while building on Weber it may soon go beyond him—if not in the richness of details, then at least in analytical and conceptual elaboration. Thereby sociology may perhaps be able, in Whitehead's famous formulation, to forget its founders.

All the developments in these fields, important as they are, do not, however, yet confront us with the basic substantive and analytical problems which Weber's manifold analysis has posed, even if sometimes only implicitly, before sociological analysis and theory. This implicitness is due mostly to Weber's general reluctance to engage in full, systemic, formal analysis of social relations, to his predilection for pursuing thoroughly a single line of thought, and to his preoccupation with many current political and ideological issues in their unique contemporary historical setting. Therefore, in order to explore his contribution to central problems of sociological analysis, we shall not concentrate on the exposition of his conceptual and methodological approaches, which has already been abundantly treated in the literature.[19] Instead, we shall concentrate on the exposition of some of the major substantive problems implied in his analysis, and the purpose both of the selections from Weber's work included here and of this brief introduction is to attempt to present and analyze some of these problems.

II

The best way to explicate the central problems implied in Weber's work is through the confrontation of his major substantive contribution to sociology,

19. See, for example, Alexander von Schelting, *Max Weber's Wissenschaftslehre* (Tübingen, J. C. B. Mohr, 1934); R. Bendix, *Max Weber—An Intellectual Portrait* (New York, 1960); Talcott Parsons, *The Structure of Social Action* (New York: Free Press, 1968).

on the one hand, and his major philosophical, "value," or intellectual orientations which directed his scientific analysis, on the other. From the point of view of substantive contribution, Weber's greatness and uniqueness lay in the manner in which he combined historical and sociological analysis. The unparalleled richness and variety of the materials which he mastered and his training in legal, economic, and social history made him fully aware of the various methodological problems of each of these fields. His ability to master the history of far-away religions and civilizations made him stand out among all sociologists—and such mastery in itself could be enough to assure him a unique place in their company. But his greatest contribution to comparative historical sociology lay in the ways in which he made use of this great richness. He did not use it to erect great evolutionary schemes of world history or of the progress of the human mind—although, as we shall yet see later, many of the concerns or preoccupations of the evolutionary schools and of German *Geistesgeschichte* and *Kulturgeschichte* were very close to Weber's heart. Neither did he use it to illustrate or elaborate a classificatory schema of different types of social activities and organizations—an approach which was very much in vogue in German sociology at the period of Weber's activity—although here again some of the central problems of such classification and typology were also very close to his concerns. Rather Weber employed all this richness to analyze systematically the great variety of human creativity in its social context, to analyze the most salient of the common characteristics and problems of different spheres of human endeavor, and to explore the conditions of emergence, continuity, change, and stagnation of different types of social organization and cultural creativity.

Analytically, his greatest contribution to comparative studies was based on the application of general categories to the systematic study of whole societies both inside and outside Europe. But he did not use these rich historical materials to "illustrate" his broad analytical categories. He used the broad analytical categories either to explain, on a comparative canvas, some of the distinct characteristics of a single society or to analyze some broader types of societies, institutions, collectivities, and patterns of behavior. It was this continuous use of both these approaches and their continuous combination in his work that constitute the uniqueness and strength of his work.

But the wide range and great vitality of his historical and comparative analysis can be fully understood only when we examine how it was related to his basic philosophical or value orientations and concerns. The foci of these concerns were the problems and predicaments of human freedom, creativity, and personal responsibility in social life in general and in modern society in particular. In this respect he was not, of course, unique among modern sociologists. All the classical figures of modern sociology—Marx, Tocqueville, Lorenz von Stein, Durkheim—were deeply concerned with these problems. The rise of sociological analysis has often been attributed to the growing awareness of the specific ways in which these problems became manifest in the context of modern society. The uniqueness of Weber—and his importance for the development of systematic sociological analysis—lies in the way in which he dealt with these problems and related them to his scientific analysis. While deeply concerned with analyzing the condition of freedom, he did not conceive the search for freedom—or its suppression—as the only constituent of social life or as the only mainspring of human motivation; nor did he construct grandiose developmental or historical schemes which assured, as it were, the ultimate victory of freedom.

True enough, the problem of alienation—central in Marx's early thought—was of no less concern to Weber. He did not, however, see alienation as derived from only one aspect of social relations, but rather as immanent in all such relations in all institutional fields.[20] Weber perceived that it is possible for alienation to be rooted in several basic aspects of social and cultural life. By its very nature, social life imposes on those who participate in it the possibility or even the necessity of gradual withdrawal from the mainsprings of social and cultural creativity and thereby creates not only the possibility of their losing contact with these mainsprings, but also the possibility of hatred towards those who represent such creativity either in their own persons or in the offices of which they are incumbents. It is here that the close and paradoxical relation between creativity, freedom, and organized social life stands out most fully.

III

For Weber, freedom, creativity, and personal responsibility did not lie outside the scope of society, of social relations and activities. On the contrary, interpersonal relations, organizations, institutional structures, and the macrosocietal setting constituted the arena in which freedom, creativity, and responsibility could become manifest. But they also imposed severe limitations and constrictions on such creativity, thus creating the possibility of alienation not only in the economic sphere, but in all spheres of social relations. Hence his most general concern, permeating all his work, was with what may be called, in the terminology of modern sociology, the processes of institution building, social transformation, and cultural creativity. These processes involve crystallization, continuity, and change of major types of institutions, cultural symbols, and macrosocietal settings, and the analysis of the possibilities (and limits) of transforming existing institutional and cultural complexes and building new ones.

20. S. M. Lipset stresses this point in "Social Class," an article in the *International Encyclopaedia of the Social Sciences* (New York: Macmillan, 1968).

On the one hand, Weber perceived face-to-face relations, social groups and organizations, and macrosocial and cultural frameworks as massive organizational and structural forces within which human beings enjoy but little freedom and few possibilities of creative change and activity, or even of full development and exercise of personal responsibility. On the other hand, however, face-to-face relations, organizations, institutions, the societal macrostructure, and cultural creations alike emerge as the result of the common endeavor of people in society, even if the ultimate outcome of such endeavor differs greatly from the original aims of their perpetrators.

These creations may be of at least two different kinds. First, they may be the result of the accretion or accumulation of long series of activities of many people in different walks of life in peripheral spheres of society, each of whom takes up something from the tradition he inherits and changes it imperceptibly by living in it and by transmitting it to new generations. Second, they may be the fruits of great dramatic innovations in the society or cultural organization or of innovations in the more peripheral spheres of society which succeed to impinge on such centers. Great religions and religious organizations and new types of legal norms and systems, of political leadership, of economic organization, and of artistic expression—all these are among such great, dramatic expressions of human creativity.

Thus, on all these levels of social life, the possibility of creativity and freedom does not exist outside the institutional framework; it is rather to be found in certain aspects of social relations and organization, of institution building and—paradoxically enough—very often in the process of destruction of institutions. But this very creativity is not lacking in structure. It is subject to organizational limitations and structural exigencies and itself creates possibilities of new organizational pressure and constriction. It contains within itself tendencies toward constriction and rigidity, and toward the destruction of institutions, symbols, and macrosocietal settings.

These constrictions and destructive tendencies may be rooted, first, in the fact that once an innovation is accepted it may as a result become routine, "deflated," more and more removed from its original impetus. Those who participate in its perpetuation—its originators and their initial close collaborators—tend to become less interested in it; indeed, their whole relation to these mainsprings of creativity may become attenuated. But such constrictions may also be rooted in the fact that the originators of these cultural innovations— of great religions, of new political systems, or of new economic enterprises— may become afraid of the further spread of the spirit of such free creativity, may attempt to impose limitations on such spread, on the attempts of other people or groups to participate in such creativity or to extend its scope. In this way the innovators may engender among such outside groups hostility and alienation toward the very acts of creativity and toward the destruction of institutions. It is this continuous tension between what may be called the constrictive and the creative aspects of institutions and of social organization that is of central interest to Weber.

According to Weber, this tension was closely related, as we shall yet see in greater detail later, to the whole process of rationalization and of demystification (*Entzauberung*) of modern social life. Hence the possibility of attaining freedom, creativity, and personal responsibility seemed very doubtful and problematic to him, particularly under modern conditions. Weber certainly did not share the optimism which much later Karl Mannheim expressed in his last works on the possibility of democratic planning.[21] But his deep pessimism was matched only by the depth of his concerns with these problems and by his attempts to evaluate soberly yet passionately the possibilities of creativity and freedom in different types of social relations and organizations. And it was through the continuous confrontation of this concern with his analytical apparatus on the one hand and his vast comparative sociological and historical knowledge on the other that Weber reformulated and transformed some of the basic problems of sociology.

IV

Weber developed his study of the problem of individual freedom and creativity around the concept of *charisma*. As is well known, his most explicit definition of charisma was presented with regard to different types of legitimation of authority but, as we shall see, this definition is not really confined to the political sphere but stretches far behind it. Weber describes charisma as "a certain quality of an individual personality by virtue of which he is set apart from ordinary men and treated as endowed with supernatural, superhuman, or at least specifically exceptional qualities."[22] It is essential that the charismatic individual be recognized or regarded as such; "this recognition is a matter of complete personal devotion arising out of enthusiasm, or of despair and hope."[23]

Hence social or political systems based on charismatic legitimation exhibit certain characteristics which reflect the intense and personal nature of the response to charisma. First, recognition of the leader is an especially compelling duty, even if it be formally voluntary. As Parsons puts it, "the authority of the leader does not express the 'will' of his followers, but rather their duty or obligation."[24] Consequently, there is a distinctive moral fervor that is sharply opposed to the forms of traditional morality and sober rational calculation. Char-

21. *Freedom, Power and Democratic Planning* (London: Routledge & Kegan Paul, 1951).
22. *Theory of Social and Economic Organization*, 329.
23. *Ibid.*, 359.
24. *Theory of Social and Economic Organization*, 65.

ismatic groups do not have elaborate systems of roles, rules, and procedures to guide the performance of administrative functions. They disdain "everyday economizing," the attainment of a regular income by continuous economic activity devoted to this end.[25] Thus it has been claimed that the charismatic situation is the total antithesis of "routine," of organized social institutions and relations. It is not only that charismatic authority is formally contrasted with "traditional" and "rational" authorities. Beyond this formal distinction, pure charisma has some inherent antinomian and anti-institutional predispositions. Given the absolutistic moral fervor, the revolutionary disdain of formal procedures, and the inherent instability of the lack of provision for succession, charismatic activities and orientations, because of their close relation to the very sources of social and cultural creativity, contain strong tendencies toward the destruction and decomposition of institutions.

This charismatic fervor is rooted in the attempt to come into contact with the very essence of being, to go to the very roots of existence, of cosmic, social, and cultural order, to what is seen as sacred and fundamental. But this attempt may also contain a strong predisposition to sacrilege: to the denial of the validity of the sacred, and of what is accepted in any given society as sacred. The very attempt to reestablish direct contact with these roots of cosmic and of sociopolitical order may breed both opposition to more attenuated and formalized forms of this order, as well as fear of, and hence opposition to, the sacred itself.

It is these tendencies that constitute the focus of both the creative and destructive tendencies of charisma. If, on the one hand, the charisma may lead to excesses of derangement and deviance, on the other hand charismatic personalities or collectivities may be the bearers of great cultural social innovations and creativity, religious, political, or economic. It is in the charismatic act that the potential creativity of the human spirit—a creativity which may perhaps in some cases be deranged or evil—is manifest; and it is not only the potential derangement, but such creativity by its very nature and orientation tends to undermine and destroy existing institutions and to burst the limits set by them. Similarly, on the personal level, charismatic predispositions may arise from the darkest recesses and excesses of the human soul, from its utter depravity and irresponsibility of its most intensive antinomian tendencies; while, on the other hand, charisma is the source of the fullest creative power and internal responsibility of the human personality.[26]

And yet the antithesis between the regular flow of organized social relations and of institutional frameworks on the one hand, and of charismatic qual-

25. *Ibid.*, 332.

26. This aspect of charisma has been especially stressed by Wolfgang Mommsen in "Max Weber's Political Sociology and his Philosophy of World History," *International Social Science Journal*, 17 (1965):23–46.

ities and activities on the other, is not as extreme or total as might be deduced from the foregoing discussion. While analytically this distinction between "organized" (traditional, legal, or bureaucratic) routine and charisma is sharp, this certainly does not imply total dichotomy between concrete situations. True enough, in some very special situations—extreme social change, breakdowns and attempts to transform such crumbling frameworks—this dichotomy between orderly institutional life and the destructive or the innovative and constructive potentials of charismatic activities could become sharply articulated.

But even in such situations the analytical distinction between the charismatic and the routine is not complete or extreme. Throughout his discussion of charisma Weber emphasizes not so much the charismatic leader, but the charismatic group or band, be it the religious sect or the followers of a new political leader. The first meeting point between the charismatic predisposition toward the destruction of institutions and the exigencies of orderly social organization is demonstrated in the necessity of the charismatic leader or group to assure some continuity for this very group, that is, to assure the succession of its leadership and the continuity of its organization. Such transformation of a great charismatic upsurge and vision into some more continuous social organization and institutional framework constitutes the first step in the routinization of charisma. But routinization of charisma does not necessarily imply only the process through which a great upsurge of charismatic vision loses, as it were, its initial impetus and becomes flattened, diffused, and in a sense obliterated. There is another equally important aspect to this process, the key to which lies in the concepts of "charisma of the office" (*Amtcharisma*), of kinship (*Geltilcharisma*), of hereditary charisma (*Erbcharisma*),[27] or of "contact charisma."[28] As is well known, these concepts, especially that of the charisma of the office, have been used by Weber to denote the process through which the charismatic characteristics are transferred from the unique personality or the unstructured group to orderly institutional reality.

The very coining of these terms indicates that the test of any great charismatic leader lies not only in his ability to create a single event or great movement, but also in his ability to leave a continuous impact on an institutional structure—to transform any given institutional setting by infusing into it some of his charismatic vision, by investing the regular, orderly offices, or aspects of social organization, with some of his charismatic qualities and aura. Thus here the dichotomy between the charismatic and the orderly regular routine of social organization seems to be obliterated—to be revived again only in situations of extreme and intensive social disorganization and change.

The obliteration of this dichotomy which seems to take place is deceptive.

27. Max Weber, *Theory of Social and Economic Organization*, 334–42.
28. This concept has first been used by Shils in "Charisma, Order, and Status," 201.

Thus the concepts of charisma of the office, of kinship, of hereditary or contact charisma, constitute the first step in the replacement of the classification which defines purely charismatic and purely routine actions or structures as pure and incompatible by a classification which sees charismatic activities and orientations as analytical elements which are inherent, even if in varying degrees, in all social relations and organizations.

Thus we face the necessity of defining the nature of the charismatic quality of activities and orientations in a way that can account for both its distinctness from ordinary, routine activities as well as the possibility of its interweaving in concrete situations.

V

Perhaps the best way to approach the resolution of this problem is through the analysis of the appeal of the charismatic, of the desire to participate in the charismatic act and group, and of the nature of the social situation in which people may become especially sensitized to such appeal. What is it in the charismatic that appeals to people, that makes them willing to follow a charismatic leader, to accept his call to give up some of their resources—wealth, time, energy, or existing social bonds and commitments—for the implementation of his vision? And when are people most willing to follow his appeal?

In Weber's own writings this problem is not explicitly dealt with. For the most part, he takes for granted the nature of the appeal of the charismatic. This taking for granted of the appeal of the charismatic is even more common—without Weber's insights—in subsequent analyses. One approach, often employed in sociological and psychological research, stresses the general abnormality of the predisposition to the charismatic, an interpretation in line with Weber's emphasis on the extraordinary character of charisma. These analyses often attribute the predisposition to acceptance of charismatic leadership to some semipathological or sociopsychological cause. Weber's own formulation could seemingly lend itself to such an interpretation; he suggests that charisma "may involve a subjective or internal reorientation born out of suffering, conflicts or enthusiasm," and that this may take place "in times of psychic, physical, economic, ethical, religious, political distress."[29] Thus it may seem that it is mainly the disturbed, the disoriented, the alienated that tend to respond to such appeals—and they necessarily will become most prominent in extreme situations of social change and disturbances. It is in situations of stress or, to use Durkheim's term, of anomie, that more and more people tend to feel helpless, alienated, and disoriented and feel that the society in which they live is meaningless and normless; thus their own pathogenic tendencies become

29. *Theory of Social and Economic Organization,* 333.

strengthened and the more pathological personalities may become prominent and find a wider scope for their activities.

Several trends of sociological research tended indeed to emphasize this approach. For instance, many of the earlier attempts to apply psychoanalytic theory to social phenomena seemed to imply that any predilection to some identification with charismatic symbols was rooted in early deformations of some "natural" familial relations—especially those between parents and children.[30]

Many of the more recent studies of social and religious movements or of processes of conversion have followed a similar line; likewise, many studies of political leaderships, attitudes, and ideologies, for instance, the studies of "authoritarian personality."[31] Even much of the recent usage[32] of the term charisma in the literature on new countries has tended to emphasize the importance of charismatic symbols and personality in abnormal situations, in situations of crisis or of stress and tended to interpret the charismatic saviors, symbols, and leaders as a panacea for the disturbed situations in which these countries found themselves.

True enough, many of these studies, especially the latter ones, do indeed contain many important insights into our problem. And yet their implicit tendency to see the predisposition to the acceptance of the charismatic as rooted in some pathological state cannot explain the potentially continuous appeal of the charismatic in seemingly orderly and routine situations. Does charisma appeal only to some pathological predispositions potentially always present among all or most people? Even if we assume that some such pathological tendencies do really always exist, does any charismatic quality appeal equally to all of them? And what does this appeal mean? Does it simply feed these pathological tendencies, reinforcing them, or does it attempt to resolve some of them? And what does such resolution entail? Does any situation of stress or of anomie intensify such pathological tendencies? What are the conditions under which leaders arise who possess only those charismatic qualities which

30. See for instance, Harold D. Lasswell, *The Analysis of Political Behaviour* (London: Routledge & Kegan Paul, 1948), 180–245.

31. See, among others, T. W. Adorno, *The Authoritarian Personality* (New York: Harper & Row, 1950); Norman Cohn, *The Pursuit of the Millenium* (New York: Harper & Row, 1961); Leon Festinger, Henry W. Riecken, and Stanley Schachter, *When Prophecy Fails* (Minneapolis: University of Minnesota Press, 1946); Yonina Talmon, "Pursuit of the Millenium—the Relation between Religious and Social Change," *European Journal of Sociology*, 3 (1962):125–49; *idem.*, "Millenarian Movements," *ibid.*, to be published; Anthony F. Wallace, "Revitalisation Movements," *American Anthropologist*, 58 (1956); and *idem.*, *Culture and Personality* (New York: Random House, 1962).

32. See, for instance, David Apter, *The Politics of Modernization* (Chicago: University of Chicago Press, 1966); and for a critical appraisal of the uses of this concept in this context see Claude Ake, "Charismatic Legitimation and Political Integration," *Comparative Studies in Society and History*, 9 (1966):1–13.

are destructive of institutions, as against those who are also capable of building up new institutions?

All these problems have in some way constituted foci of diverse trends of research in the social sciences from Weber on. But as yet our knowledge about all these problems is limited—and not only because of the naturally intermittent and haphazard course of any scientific enterprise. It is also because the crucial differentiating variables relevant to these problems have not been fully and explicitly stated and formulated. Perhaps the most important missing link in this whole area was the lack of systematic exploration of the nature of the charismatic orientation and bond as a distinct type of social action. It is only when it is fully recognized that this bond is not something abnormal, that the differences between the more extreme and the more routine expressions of charisma can be more fully recognized and systematically studied. This has lately been done by Edward A. Shils.[33] We may quote here from him:

> The charismatic quality of an individual as perceived by others, or himself, lies in what is thought to be his connection with (including possession by or embedment of) some *very central* feature of man's existence and the cosmos in which he lives. The centrality, coupled with intensity, makes it extraordinary. The centrality is constituted by its formative power in initiating, creating, governing, transforming, maintaining, or destroying what is vital in man's life. That central power has often, in the course of man's existence, been conceived of as God, the ruling power or creator of the universe, or some divine or other transcendent power controlling or markedly influencing human life and the cosmos within which it exists. The central power might be a fundamental principle or principles, a law or laws governing the universe, the underlying and driving force of the universe. It might be thought to reside in the ultimate principles of law which should govern man's conduct, arising from or derived from the nature of the universe and essential to human existence, discerned or elucidated by the exercise of man's most fundamental rational and expressive powers. Scientific discovery, ethical promulgation, artistic creativity, political and organizational authority (*authoritatem, auctor,* authorship) and in fact all forms of genius, in the original sense of the word as permeation by the "spirit," are as much instances of the category of charismatic things as in religious prophecy . . .
>
> This extended conception of a charismatic property (as perceived by one who is responsive to it, including the "charismatic person" himself) refers to a vital, "serious," ultimately symbolic event, of which divinity is one of many forms. Presumptive contact with the divine, possession by the divine, the possession of magical powers, are only modes of being

33. "Charisma, Order, and Status," 199–213.

charismatic. Contact with this class of vital, "serious" events may be attained through reflective wisdom or through disciplined scientific penetration, or artistic expression, or forceful and confident reality-transforming action. All these are also modes of contact with, or embodiment of, something very "serious" in Durkheim's sense, which is thought to be, and therewith becomes, central or fundamental to man's existence . . .

Most human beings, because their endowment is inferior or because they lack opportunities to develop the relevant capacities, do not attain that intensity of contact. But most of those who are unable to attain it themselves are, at least intermittently, responsive to its manifestations in the words, actions, and products of others who have done so. They are capable of such appreciation and occasionally feel a need for . . . Through the culture they acquire and through their interaction with and perception of those more "closely connected" with the cosmically and socially central, their own weaker responsiveness is fortified and heightened.

All of these charismatic "connections" may be manifested intensely in the qualities, words, actions and products of individual personalities. This was emphasized by Weber and it has entered into contemporary sociology. But they may also become resident, in varying degrees of intensity, in institutions—in the qualities, norms, and beliefs to which members are expected to adhere or are expected to possess—and in an attenuated form, in categories of strata of the members of a society . . .

Here the gap between the charismatic as an extraordinary event or quality and as a constituent element of any orderly social life is at least partially bridged. The search for meaning, consistency, and order is not always something extraordinary, something which exists only in extreme disruptive situations or among pathological personalities, but also in all stable social situations even if it is necessarily focused within some specific parts of the social structure and of an individual's life space.

VI

This general contention is borne out by various researches in the social sciences which—although they were not consciously dealing with these problems and not even fully aware of them—do yet touch on them; and if reexamined in the light of our questions may indeed contribute to their elucidation. Two kinds of research are of special importance from this point of view: first, anthropological studies bearing on the place of rituals in social life, and second, studies of communication in modern societies. Different as the nature of the problems with which these two kinds of research are concerned, they seem to point to parallel conclusions with regard to the nature of the social situations in which the appeal to the charismatic becomes especially articulated and the predisposition to respond to some charismatic symbols becomes especially intensive.

Anthropological literature shows first how charismatic symbols are especially articulated in those ritual occasions most closely related to individual and collective rites of passage—birth, initiation, marriage, and death, or various collective ceremonies. Second it shows how receptiveness to such charismatic qualities and activities permeates more routine types of social activities—economic or community affairs or regular political or administrative activities—but especially on those occasions or situations in which their routine is to some extent broken or disturbed.

This becomes even more fully borne out from modern studies of communication, a field which may seem to have little to do with charisma. Some of the initial approaches implicit in these studies shared the assumption to which we have previously alluded, namely, that a sensitivity to charismatic forms of communication is of a semipathological nature, rooted in psychic stress and deformation.[34] The results of these researches indicated that such predispositions are not something abnormal, that they do not arise only in very extraordinary circumstances, but that they become articulated in certain definite types of social situations.[35]

An analysis of these various researches indicates that the most important among such situations are (a) those in which there takes place some transition from one institutional sphere to another, or situations of simultaneous activity in several institutional spheres, or in several subsystems of a society; (b) situations in which such various subsystems have to be directly connected with the central values and activities of a society; (c) situations in which people are

34. See, for instance, Rudolph Arnheim, "The World of Daytime Serial," in Paul F. Lazarsfeld and Frank K. Stanton, eds., *Radio Research 1942–43* (New York: Duell, Sloan and Pearce, 1943), 507–48; Eliot Freidson, "Communications Research and the Concept of the Mass," in W. L. Schramm, ed., *Process and Effects of Mass Communications* (Urbana: University of Illinois Press, 1954), 380–89; Joseph T. Klapper, *The Effects of Mass Media: A Report to the Public Library Inquiry* (New York: Bureau of Applied Social Research, Columbia University, 1949); Ernst Kris and Nathan Leites, "Trends in Twentieth Century Propaganda," in Bernard Berelson and Morris Janowitz, eds., *Reader in Public Opinion and Communication* (Glencoe, Ill.: Free Press, 1950), 278–88; Lloyd Warner and William Henry, "The Radio Daytime Serial: A Symbolic Analysis," in Berelson and Janowitz, *Public Opinion and Communication*, 423–34. For instances of more differentiated approaches to the problem see Robert K. Merton, "Mass Persuasion: The Moral Dimension," in Berelson and Janowitz, *ibid.*, 465–68; Hans Speier, "The Future of Psychological Warfare," in Berelson and Janowitz, *ibid.*, 381–96.

35. See S. N. Eisenstadt, "Conditions of Communicative Receptivity," *Public Opinion Quarterly,* 17 (Fall 1953):363–75 and "Communication and Reference-Group Behavior," in his *Essays in Comparative Institutions* (New York: John Wiley, 1965), 309–43.

faced with a choice among various roles; (d) situations in which the routine of a given role or group is endangered or disrupted. In all such cases the individual is placed in potentially ambiguous, undefined, and conflicting situations in which his identity and status image and continuity of the perception of other actions are endangered. The common denominator of these various situations, of the more structured individual and collective rites of passage reported in anthropological studies, and of the less structured "communicative situations" of modern societies, is that people or groups participating in them experience some shattering of the existing social and cultural order to which they are bound. Hence in such situations they become more sensitive to those symbols or messages which attempt to symbolize such order, and more ready to respond to people who are able to present to them new symbols which could give meaning to their experiences in terms of some fundamental cosmic, social, or political order, to prescribe the proper norms of behavior, to relate the individual to collective identification, and to reassure him of his status and of his place in a given collectivity.[36]

Moreover, all these studies indicate that such situations do not arise only in catastrophic conditions, but that they constitute part of any orderly social life—of the life of individuals as they pass from one stage in their lifespan to another, or from one sphere of activities to another, and of the organization of groups and societies. But the recognition of the fact that some predisposition to the acceptance of charismatic appeals and some quest for meaning and order exists in most social situations does not only pose again the problem of the relations between the charismatic and the ordinary in the structure of any social relation, organization, and institution, but adds a new dimension to this problem. Especially, it raises more sharply the problem of the different foci of the charismatic in the institutional structure. The preceding analysis of the processes of institutionalization of the charismatic and of the nature of the situations in which people are especially sensitized to the appeal of the charismatic has mainly been focused on more dispersed, microsocietal situations. And yet the most common emphasis in Weber's own work, as well as in much of the subsequent sociological analysis, was that the charismatic tends to become more fully embedded in more central societal locations and in the broader macrosocietal frameworks and that these frameworks tend to become directed by the charismatic symbols. Hence it is necessary to analyze in greater detail the problem of the nature of the broader macrosocietal, institutional frameworks or foci within which the charismatic orientations, symbols, or activities are centered.

As is well known, sociological analysis has continuously stressed that it is the religious and the political spheres that are the most natural foci or institu-

36. *Ibid.*

tional abodes of such charismatic qualities and symbols. This contention has often been presented in a rather routine way as deriving mainly from the specific organizational needs of these spheres for legitimation or for keeping people quiet and obedient, thus reinforcing the "semi-conspiratorial" theory of charisma or of ideology.

Once again, Shils' expositions provide the most important developments beyond this line of analysis, especially his exposition of the "center" as a distinct aspect of any institutional framework, and as the structural locus of the macrosocietal institutionalization of charisma. To quote Shils again:[37]

> Society has a center. There is a central zone in the structure of society. This central zone impinges in various ways on those who live within the ecological domain in which the society exists. Membership in the society, in more than the ecological sense of being located in a bounded territory and of adapting to an environment affected or made up by other persons located in the same territory, is constituted by relationship to this central zone.
>
> The central zone is not, *as such,* a spatially located phenomenon. It almost always has a more or less definite location within the bounded territory in which the society lives. Its centrality has, however, nothing to do with geometry and little with geography.
>
> The center, or the central zone, is a phenomenon of the realm of values and beliefs. It is the center of the order of symbols of values and beliefs, which govern the society. It is the center because it is the ultimate and irreducible; and it is felt to be such by many who cannot give explicit articulation to its irreducibility. The central zone partakes of the nature of the sacred. In this sense, every society has an "official" religion, even when that society or its exponents and interpreters conceive of it, more or less correctly, as a secular, pluralistic, and tolerant society. The principle of the Counter-Reformation: *Cuius regio, eius religio,* although its rigor has been loosened and its harshness mollified, retains a core of permanent truth.
>
> The center is also a phenomenon of the realm of action. It is a structure of activities, of roles and persons, within the network of institutions. It is in these roles that the values and beliefs which are central are embodied and propounded.

This close relation between the charismatic and the center is rooted in the fact that both are concerned with the maintenance of order and with the provi-

---

37. "Centre and Periphery" in *The Logic of Personal Knowledge: Essays Presented to Michael Polanyi* (London: Routledge & Kegan Paul, 1961), 117–31.

sion of some meaningful symbolic and institutional order. But this close relation between the two does not imply their total identity. Rather, it raises many new questions and problems. What is the structure of such centers and what are their structural relations to the periphery? How many centers which embody such charismatic orientation are there in a society, for instance, political, cultural, religious or ideological, and other centers? What is the relation between the "ordering" and "meaning-giving" (charismatic) functions of such centers, on the one hand, and of their more organizational and administrative activities, on the other?

Especially it brings us to the problem of the ways in which both the symbolic and the organizational aspects of routinization of charisma vary among the major institutional spheres of a social order. Given that the quest for order is evident throughout the major spheres of a society and that it is not something purely abstract or symbolic, but closely related to the organizational needs and problems of these spheres, it necessarily follows that the process of routinization of charisma and the charismatic qualities may differ greatly among different institutional spheres. This problem of the different charismatic qualities which are appropriate to different types of institutional spheres has been dealt with by Weber only indirectly, by way of illustration or by analysis of some aspects of charismatic leadership in the different spheres of social life. He has drawn the fullest "ideal-typical" description of charismatic personalities and activities from the religious and political spheres, and has presented there some of the obvious differences between the charismatic qualities or orientations in these two spheres. Thus, the prophet or the mystagogue, different as they are in their basic orientations, have to be able especially to organize purely symbolic-emotive spheres and to restructure the emotional components of personality, while the political leader has to exhibit different qualities or orientations, in combining a symbolic ordering of the *social* stability with more detailed daily problems of administration.

Similarly, although less explicitly, we find allusions to or illustrations of the charismatic qualities needed by the innovator in the legal or economic fields. Throughout his work on sociology of law, Weber's analysis points out the specific characteristic of the legal conception of order as differing in both its symbolic and organizational implications from the political or the religious, although they are, of course, often very closely interrelated. Perhaps of special interest here are Weber's analyses of the economic entrepreneur, in general, and of the modern capitalist, in particular. Through his analysis of the relation between Protestantism and capitalism, he attempts to show that even in this seemingly most "material" of all social spheres, real change, innovation, or transformation are greatly dependent not only on the objective forces of the market or of production but on a charismatic reformulation of the *meaning* of economic activities.[38] All these are only allusions or indications for further research. But they point out in a general way that such differences between the charismatic qualities most appropriate to different institutional spheres are rooted both in the difference in the organizational needs and problems of these spheres as well as in the specific symbolic problems, or problems of symbolic order inherent in each such sphere. One major structural meeting point between these two is the nature of the quest for participation in the central aspects of each such institutional sphere, that is, of participation in those aspects of such spheres which seem to be most fundamental, most closely related to the essence of cosmic, cultural, or social order.

Weber's works also point out that the nature of the symbolic and organizational problems, and hence the nature of the charismatic qualities necessary for finding new appropriate answers to these problems, differs not only between different institutional spheres but also in different types of societies, between a primitive country and a great historical empire, between a traditional religious community and a modern scientific organization. Moreover, the nature of these problems may well change under the very impact of such different charismatic personalities, and of the new institutional settings set up by them. All these constitute problems for further research, problems with regard to which sociological research has not yet fully taken up Weber's challenge.

VII

But whatever the results of such researches will be concerning such differences between different institutional spheres and between different societies, the very formulation of this problem implies the existence of some quest for such order and for participation in those symbols, organizations, and frameworks in which this order may be embedded. This in turn raises the questions of the nature of the quest for such participation and of the relations between the center or centers and the periphery, especially in terms of the aspiration of members of a society to participate in such centers and the possibilities of access to them. In Weber's own work the nature of such centrality has not, paradoxically enough, been fully explored in its relation to the political and religious fields. In a way, Weber took it for granted. He took up more fully the structural aspects and implications of such centrality in his analysis of social stratification. Although greatly influenced by Weber, subsequent analyses of stratification have not fully caught up with the implications of his work. The central concept in later sociological analysis of stratification, largely derived from Weber, is that of prestige.[39] As is well known, prestige has been presented

38. *The Protestant Ethic and the spirit of Capitalism.*
39. Max Weber, *Theory of Social and Economic Organization,* 393–94.

in most analyses of stratification as one of the three major dimensions of stratification, power and wealth being the other two. But at the same time prestige
was the least analytically specified dimension. Both the bases (or criteria) of
prestige and the structural implications of its differential distribution have been
abundantly described but not fully explored in their basic analytical implications. They were to some extent taken for granted, often subsumed under, or
related to, the concept of "style of life," which often served, like the concept
of prestige itself, as a sort of general residual category in the studies of stratification.

However, important implications for these problems can be derived from
Weber's own work and from the preceding analysis of charisma. Among the
most important of these implications is that the sources of prestige, of the
deference which people render to others, are rooted not only in their organizational (power, economic, etc.) positions, but also in their differential proximity
to those areas which constitute the institutional foci of charisma, that is, the
various types of centers (political, cultural, etc.) and in the degree of their
participation in those areas. But if the roots of prestige are to a large extent
defined through such differential and varied participation in the charismatic
foci of institutions and symbols, then the *control* of the degree of such participation, of the access to these centers, becomes a crucial aspect of social structure
in general and of stratification in particular. In this way prestige is no longer
manifest only in symbolic difference and behavior, as many analysts other than
Weber have sometimes assumed, but in addition, it implies control of the differential access to participation in such centers. Hence, such participation is
not only a goal in its own right and may also become a medium of exchange
through which other goals, other media, such as money or power, may
be obtained. This insight opens up many additional problems in sociological
analysis which may be elucidated by further research.

VIII

Throughout the preceding discussion I have continuously alluded to the distinction between the ordinary and the charismatic, a distinction which seems
to be implicit in Weber's approach and in the later derivations from it, and
have assumed that both are basic components of any concrete social relation,
organization, or macrosociety, and that both are present in any process of institution building. I have not, however, explicated the nature of this distinction
between the ordinary and the charismatic and of the relations between them.
We may start perhaps by attempting to see what was Weber's own approach
to this problem.

Weber's most general exposition of the relations between the ordinary and the charismatic was probably given in his definition of the relations between "interests" and ideas. In Mommsen's translation:[40]

"Interests" (material and ideal) directly govern the acts of men. Nevertheless, "views of life" created by ideas, have frequently, as pointed, indicated the lines along which the dynamic power of interest propels action. The "view of life" will determine from what and for what one wants to be—be it said—can be "saved." Whether from political or social bondage to some messianic future kingdom, or from some absolute evil and bondage to some Messianic future Kingdom on this side of the grave, or from absolute evil or bondage to sin into a perpetual free state of bliss in the bosom of some divine Father; or from the chains of the finite and the threat of Hell manifested in pain, disease and death into ever-lasting bliss in some earthly or paradisal future existence?

A somewhat more detailed definition of the various ordinary or routine aspects of social relations can be found in those parts of Weber's work, in the well-known passages in *Wirtschaft und Gesellschaft*, translated in *Theory of Social and Economic Organization*, in which are given his conceptions of human activity in general and of social relations in particular, which were of such crucial importance in the development of sociological thought. "Social" action is defined by him as "action oriented to the past, present or future behavior of others," while "social relationships denotes the behavior of a plurality of actors in so far as, in its meaningful content, the action of each takes account of that of others and is oriented in these terms."[41] From this relatively simple yet basic conception, Weber's analysis of social relations and organization gradually branches out in two complementary directions. One is the analysis of the nature of what may be called, in more recent sociological parlance, the systemic properties and exigencies of social relations, organizations, and institutions. The other is the analysis of the major analytical aspects or types of social relations, what we call today the major institutional spheres of a society—economic, political, legal, stratificational, and religious or cultural spheres. Weber builds into his definition the various aspects of social relations in such a way as to bring out the different elements of more complex continuous and stable social relations. It is here that he develops the major orientations of action: *Zweckrational* and *Wertrational*, affective and traditional ones; their crystallization into different types of uniformities, customs, fashion, convention, etc.; the analysis of the major types of solidarity, communal, and associational relations.[42] In a similar vein he brings out the second aspect of organized social relations, that is, the

40. *International Social Science Journal*, 30.
41. *Theory of Social and Economic Organization*, 102–7.
42. *Theory of Social and Economic Organization*, 104–5.

definition of the different institutional fields of social activity—economic, political, religious. Thus, for instance, "Action will be said to be 'economically oriented' in so far as according to its subjective meaning . . . it is concerned with the satisfaction of a desire for 'utilities.' Economic action is a peaceful use of actor's control over resources which is primarily economically oriented."[43] Then he shows how each such aspect of social behavior, each institutional sphere, creates, beyond the very general needs or systemic problems which are inherent in any social relation or organization as such, the specific problems of each type of social relation or institutional sphere. Thus, in economic relationships the organizational problems of division of labor, of mobilization and processing of resources, and of marketing the products of economic activities are most predominant. In political relations it is the assurance of loyalty and of administrative expertise that are of crucial importance; likewise with regard to other major spheres of society, religion, culture, education, or social stratification. The specificity of each such aspect or sphere lies in the nature of its systemic interdependence on the other sphere or aspects. Any such aspect constitutes a problem from the point of view of its own sphere, as for instance the maintenance of order or of obedience for the political sphere constitutes a prerequisite from the point of view of economic activities.

True enough, with regard to all these problems, we do not find in Weber's work a systematic analysis of the "nature" or "problems" of social organization or system in terms of "systemic" needs or exigencies, and it is perhaps in this field of the exploration of the systemic qualities of social relations that the greatest advances and progress beyond Weber have been attained in sociological analysis.[44] But it is out of these indications that the nature of the distinction between the charismatic and the ordinary can be brought out. The noncharismatic or the ordinary activity seems to compromise those activities which are oriented to various discrete, segregated goals not connected together in some great pattern or "grand design," which are oriented mostly to goals which are instrumental to other goals or aims, and which are also mostly oriented toward adaptation to any given natural or human social environment and to persistence and survival within it.

A very large part of the daily activities of human beings in society is probably organized in such a way and oriented to such goals. The implementation of such goals necessitates the development of many specific organizations and structures which tend to coalesce into varied institutional patterns. In a sense, it is they that constitute the crux of the institutional nexus within any society. And yet, as we have seen above, all these goals and patterns tend also to be-

43. *Ibid.*, 145. For the definition of the political action, of "imperative control," see *ibid.*, 139.

44. See especially Talcott Parsons, *The Structure of Social Action: idem., The Social System* (Glencoe, Ill.: Free Press, 1951); Talcott Parsons, Robert F. Bales, and Edward A. Shils, *Working Papers in the Theory of Action* (Glencoe, Ill.: Free Press, 1953).

come somehow related to a broader, fundamental order, rooted in the charismatic and focused around the different situations and centers in which the charismatic is more fully embedded and symbolized. True enough, in these various "orderly" activities oriented to discrete, instrumental, and adaptive goals, the charismatic orientations may become greatly attenuated; they may become very distant and the various concrete goals may be perceived as rather distant from the sources of the charismatic. And yet some such relation or orientation to the charismatic tends somehow to persist in these activities, even if in the most attenuated and passive form.

This persistance of the charismatic is rooted in some of the basic characteristics of the major institutional spheres which have been stressed by Weber. Throughout his work he indicated that the political, economic, legal, religious, and stratification spheres are not only organizational aspects of any relatively stable social relations or institutions; they do not only constitute means for the attainment of goals which are, as it were, outside of them. They constitute also realms of goals, of "ends" of potentially broader, overall "meanings" toward which the activities of the participants are oriented. They constitute part of, to use Geertz's nomenclature,[45] the "symbolic" templates for the organization of social psychological processes.

IX

It is this double aspect of social institutions—their organizational exigencies on the one hand, and their potential close relations to the realm of meaning on the other—which may provide us with clues as to how the ordinary and the charismatic are continuously interwoven in the process of institution building. New organizations and institutions are built up through the varied responses and interactions between people or groups who, in order to implement their varied goals, undertake processes of exchange with other people or groups.[46] But the individuals or groups who engage in such exchange are not randomly distributed in any society. Such exchange takes place between people placed in structurally different positions, that is, in different cultural, political, family, or economic positions which in themselves may be outcomes of former processes of institutional exchange. Their very aspirations and goals are greatly influenced by their differential placement in the social structure and the power they can thereby exercise. The resources that are at their disposal— for instance manpower, money, political support, or religious identification—

45. C. Geertz, "Ideology as a Cultural System," in D. Apter, ed., *Ideology and Discontent* (Glencoe, Ill.: Free Press, 1964), 62–63.

46. S. N. Eisenstadt, "The Study of Processes of Institutionalization, Institutional Change and Comparative Institutions," in his *Essays on Comparative Institutions* (New York: John Wiley, 1965), especially 16–40.

are determined by these institutional positions and vary according to the specific characteristics of the different institutional spheres. These resources serve as means for the implementation of various individual goals, and they may in themselves become goals or objects of individual endeavors. Such resources always evince some tendency to become organized in specific, autonomous ways, according to the specific features of their different institutional spheres; this can be seen, for instance, in the fact that the exchange of economic resources is organized in any society in different ways than that of political or religious resources.

But the terms of exchange, that is, the criteria of what is regarded as valuable or of which goals or means are equivalent, are at least partially derived from the charismatically charged goals and norms, from the broader and more fundamental conceptions of order. Hence, in the crystallization of institutional frameworks a crucial part is played by those people who evince a special capacity to set up broad orientations, to propound new norms, and to articulate new goals. In other words, institution building is based not only on the direct or indirect exchange of various institutional resources between individuals or groups which attempt to use these resources for the implementation of their discrete, instrumental goals but in addition also necessarily includes interaction between, on the one hand, those individuals or groups who are able to articulate varied collective goals and crystallize acceptable norms and, on the other, those individuals, groups, or strata that are willing to accept such regulations and norms. The crystallization and upholding of such norms seemingly provides some sort of response to a felt need for some general stability and order and attests to the ability to provide some broader meaning to more varied specific needs which may arise in different situations. Hence, the capacity to create and crystallize such broader symbolic orientations and norms, to articulate various goals, to establish organizational frameworks, and to mobilize the resources necessary for all these purposes (for example, the readiness to invest in the appropriate activities) is a basic aspect or constituent of the flow of institution building in any society.

It is presumably people in such positions or aspiring to them who are especially sensitive to what may be called societal "needs," and who may be oriented to taking care of those activities and problems which may be necessary for the maintenance and continuity of given social organizations and institutions. But they are always interested in the maintenance and continuity not only, or mainly, of the society in general, but of some specific type of organization which best suits their own orientation and goals. The concrete institutional framework which emerges in any given situation is thus the outcome not only of some general appropriateness of a given solution proposed by such people to the groups acting in this situation but also of the relative success of different competing groups of such leaders and entrepreneurs who attempt to impose, through a mixture of coercive, manipulative, and persuasive techniques, their own particular solution on a given situation.[47]

But the availability of such people, or their concrete orientation and activities, is not always assured or determined by the development of the varying needs among different groups in a society. Moreover, even if some such groups or entrepreneurs do emerge, the ways in which they will act and the type of institutions they will build are not given or predetermined because the concrete broad orientations and goals which they may develop may vary greatly. The development of such "charismatic" personalities or groups constitutes perhaps the closest social analogy to "mutation," and the degree of their ability to forge out a viable symbolic and institutional order may be an important factor in the process of survival, or selection of different societies or cultural creations. This analysis brings out again the fact that a crucial aspect of the charismatic personality or group is not only the possession of some extraordinary, exhilarating qualities, but also the ability, through these qualities, to reorder and reorganize both the symbolic and cognitive order which is potentially inherent in such orientations and goals and the institutional order in which these orientations become embodied; and that the process of routinization of charisma is focused around the ability to combine the reordering of these two spheres of human existence and of social life.

We know as yet very little either about conditions of development of such entrepreneurial, charismatic people, of their psychological and behavioral attributes, and about the conditions under which they may be capable of implementing their vision. There exist several descriptive studies and data, but as yet but relatively few systematic analyses,[48] which deal with this problem or with the nature of the processes through which specific charismatic symbols and orientations become embedded in the more ordinary institutional activities and exchange. All these aspects still constitute an essential part of the challenge of Weber's work for modern sociological analysis—and problems for further analysis and research.

X

The preceding reformulation of the nature of the charismatic and of its relations to the process of institution building implies a reorientation of the major questions about the nature of the social order. Instead of assuming that such order is given by some external force imposed on the individuals and on their own wishes, or that order is only an outcome of their rational premeditated

47. S. N. Eisenstadt, "The Study of Processes of Institutionalization."

48. See, for one attempt in this direction, David C. McClelland, *The Achieving Society* (Princeton, N.J.: Princeton University Press, 1961) and also the various works on religious and social movements cited above.

selfish evaluation of their interests or of the exigencies of social economic division of labor engendered by these interests, this formulation emphasizes that the existence of some quest for some such order, not only in organizational but also in symbolic terms, is among the basic wishes or orientations of people.[49] In other words, this implies that among the "egoistical" wishes of human beings a very important part is comprised by their quest for and conception of the symbolic order, of the "good society," and of the quest for participation in such an order. This quest constitutes a basic, although differential, component in the whole panorama of social and cultural activities, orientations, and goals. It calls for rather special response from those able to respond to this quest, and this response tends to be located in specific, distinct parts or aspects of the social structure. The structural focus of this quest is to be found in the charismatic activity, group symbol, or institutional focus.[50]

But this quest for participation in such order does not necessarily constitute a focus of consensus—it may easily become a focus of dissension, conflict, and change. As we have seen, the initial assumption of many of the sociological analyses of charisma has stressed its disruptive effects, that is, its contribution to the destruction of existing institutions and to social change. The recognition that charismatic activities or symbols constitute also a part or aspect of the solidary institutional framework does not negate this basic insight; it only enables us to approach the relation between charisma and social change and transformation in a much more differentiated and systematic way. It enables us to see that the very quest for participation in a meaningful order may be related to processes of change and transformation; that it may indeed constitute, at least in certain circumstances, the very focus of processes of social transformation.

The starting point of this approach is the recognition of the inherent tension that the charismatic builds into any social system. Bendix has put this succinctly in the following words:

> . . . each system of domination remains "valid" only within limits, and when these are ignored or exceeded for too long, the type of domination either changes its form or loses its original, authoritative character altogether. Charisma is a "supernatural quality of a personality," which in its original meaning proved itself by miracles, thereby gaining recognition

49. Talcott Parsons, "Culture and the Social System: Introduction," in Talcott Parsons, *et al.*, *Theories of Society* (Glencoe, Ill.: Free Press, 1961), 2:963–93 and S. N. Eisenstadt, "Sociological Theory," in *International Encyclopaedia of Social Sciences* (New York: Macmillan, 1968).

50. This is, of course, not dissimilar from Durkheim's exposition of the "social" as distinct from the "individual" volitions, except that his very emphasis on this distinction did not facilitate the perception of the commitment to the social order as *one* among the individuals' "egoistical" wishes. See Emile Durkheim, *The Elementary Forms of Religious Life* (Glencoe, Ill.: Free Press, 1954); *idem.*, *Sociological Philosophy* (Glencoe, Ill.: Free Press, 1953).

from the ruled and in turn making that recognition their sacred duty. True, charismatic authority unconditionally demands acceptance of its claims to legitimacy, but the belief in its legitimacy is by no means unconditional. For, if the test of this claim remains forever wanting, then the "person favoured by the gift of grace is shown to be forsaken by his God or his magic or heroic powers."

Seen from the point of view of the ruled, this means that their belief in the lawful claims of this authority may well spring from "enthusiasm" or "necessity and hope" [*Begeisterung oder Not und Hoffnung*] but that secretly they desire or hope for tests which will confirm its legitimacy. It is certainly characteristic of charismatic domination that the ruler interprets these desires or hopes as disbelief and demands unconditional acceptance of this interpretation. But the desire of the ruler for signs of confirmation remains. The same applies to the other types. The legitimacy of traditional domination rests on the "sanctity of established structures and powers of command" [*Heiligkeit altüberkommener Ordnungen und Herrengewalten*]; accordingly, authority is exercised by the person of the ruler, not by means of status. However, the commands of a ruler are legal not only when they conform to tradition but also when they proceed from the "arbitrary will of the master. Hence, traditional domination possesses a charismatic duality of rule that is tradition bound as well as free from tradition." This freedom from tradition refers to the arbitrary will of the personal ruler, who may have the right to ignore tradition since his will is absolute, but who can thereby imperil his own traditional authority . . . [51]

Perhaps the most important aspect of this analysis is that such tensions or conflicts are rooted not only in the clashes of different interests in a society, but in the differential distribution of the charismatic in the symbolic and organizational aspects of any institutional system, and that it is the combination of this differential distribution and conflicts of interests that may indeed constitute a major focus both of continuity and of potential changes in any social system.

Whatever the success of the attempt of any institutional entrepreneurs to establish and legitimize common norms in terms of common values and symbols, these norms are probably never fully accepted by the entire society. Most groups tend to exhibit some autonomy in terms of their attitudes toward these norms and in terms of their willingness or ability to provide the resources demanded by the given institutionalized system. For very long periods of time a great majority of the members of a given society or parts thereof may be identified to some degree with the values and norms of the given system and willing

51. R. Bendix, "Max Weber's Sociology Today," *International Social Science Journal*, 17 (1965):19–20.

to provide it with the resources it needs; however, other tendencies also develop.[52] Some groups may be greatly opposed to the very premises of the institutionalization of a given system, may share its values and symbols only to a very small extent, and may accept these norms only as the least among evils and as binding on them only in a very limited sense. Others may share these values and symbols and accept the norms to a greater degree, but may look on themselves as the more truthful depositories of these same values. They may oppose the concrete levels at which the symbols are institutionalized by the élite in power, and may attempt to interpret them in different ways. Others may develop new interpretations of existing symbols and norms and strive for a change in the very bases of the institutional order. Hence, any institutional system is never fully "homogeneous" in the sense of being fully accepted or accepted to the same degree by all those participating in it. These different orientations to the central symbolic spheres may all become foci of conflict and of potential institutional change.

Even more important is the fact, that whatever the initial attitudes of any given group to the basic premises of the institutional system, these may greatly change after the initial institutionalization of the system. Any institutionalization necessarily entails efforts to maintain, through continuous attempts to mobilize resources from different groups and individuals, the boundaries of the system, and to maintain the legitimacy of its values, symbols, and norms. But continuous implementation of these policies may affect the positions of various groups in the society, and give rise to continuous shifts both in the balance of power among them and in their orientations to the existing institutional system. Thus, the very nature of the setting up of an institutional system, of the differential distribution in a society of the major charismatic symbols and centers and of differential access to them, creates the possibility that "anti-systems" may develop within the system; and while such anti-systems may often remain latent for very long periods, they may also constitute important foci of change under propitious conditions. The existence of such contradictions or conflicts among the different symbolic centers and institutional spheres and among different groups in their relations to these centers does not, of course, preclude the possibility that the system will maintain its internal subboundaries more or less continuously, and achieve accommodation or partial insulation of different subsystems. But the possibility of conflict and potential change is always present, rooted in the very process of crystallization and maintenance of institutional systems, of the structure of their symbolic and organizational centers, of the relations of these centers to the periphery's conceptions of centrality. These various forces naturally differ between different institutional spheres and

---

52. For further exposition see S. N. Eisenstadt, "Institutionalization and Change," *American Sociological Review*, 29 (April 1964):235–47.

between different societies—and should constitute foci of further research—but the very sensitivity of these forces and the tendency to change are inherent in all of them.

XI

It is here that we come to what is probably the central focus of the analysis of the relations between charisma and social change—the analysis of the self-transformative power of charismatic symbols and activities and of their power to transform the societies in which they are embedded. In what respect does such transformation differ from simple secular trends of structural or demographic change? What types of charisma are able to transform societies, and under what conditions? As with regard to so many other fields, although this problem is inherent in his work, Weber himself did not explicate it fully. However, the preceding analysis of some of the implications of his work may indeed help us in identifying the central characteristics of such transformation.

A central aspect of any process of social transformation is the recrystallization of the centers of any society—not only of the rates of access to such centers but of the very content and the definition of the central charismatic symbols and of the modes of participation in them. It is perhaps this dimension which constitutes the difference between stychic, structural, or demographic change on the one hand, and the transformation of social systems on the other. Throughout his studies Weber looked for those movements which are indeed capable of effecting such far-reaching institutional transformation. Which types of charismatic activities and orientations do indeed have such transformative powers, and under what conditions are they effective? In all his studies of systems—political, legal, or religious—Weber dealt with this problem. But only in his famous treatment of the problem of the Protestant ethic did he come close to a full systematic exposition of this problem, although even here most of the broader analytical implications have to be extrapolated from Weber's presentation.

What is it in the Protestant ethic or symbolic system and in the social setting of its bearers that facilitated its development in the direction of such transformation? On the basis of both Weber's analysis and of later work in this field,[53] it may be suggested that the aspects of the Protestant value orientation which are most important from the point of view of our discussion are: (1) its strong combination of "this-worldliness" and transcendentalism—a combination which orients the individual behavior to activities within this world but at the same time does not ritually sanctify any of them, either through a mystic

---

53. S. N. Eisenstadt, "The Protestant Ethic Thesis in an Analytical and Comparative Framework" in S. N. Eisenstadt, ed., *The Protestant Ethic and Modernization* (New York: Basic Books, 1968).

union or any ritual act, as the final point of religious consummation or worthiness; (2) the strong emphasis on individual activism and responsibility; (3) the unmediated, direct relation of the individual to the sacred and to the sacred tradition, an attitude which, while strongly emphasizing the importance and direct relevance of the sacred and of tradition, yet minimizes the extent to which this relation and individual commitment to the sacred can be mediated by any ritual institutions, organization, or professional textual exegesis. Hence it opens up the possibility of continuous redefinition and reformulation of the nature and scope of such tradition—a possibility which is further enhanced by the strong transcendental attitude which minimizes the sacredness of any "here and now."

These religious orientations of Protestantism and Protestants, especially Calvinists, were not, however, confined only to the realm of the sacred. They were closely related to, and manifest in two major orientations in most Protestant groups' conception of the social reality and of their own place in it, that is, in what may be called their status images and orientations. Most of the Protestant groups developed a combination of these two types of orientations. First was their openness toward the wider social structure, rooted in their "this-worldly" orientation which was not limited only to the economic sphere but which also, as we shall see later, could be expressed in other social fields. Second, they were characterized by a certain autonomy and self-sufficiency from the point of view of their status orientation. They were relatively little dependent for the validity of their own status symbols and identity on the existing political and religious centers. These aspects of the Protestant ethic were conducive to its great transformative capacities and the ability of the Protestant groups to influence the behavior of people and the shape of institutions.

But the extent to which these beliefs could indeed become influential depended to no small degree on the social organization of their bearers and of the broader social setting within which they were operative. Here, in general, it seems that such transformative tendencies of religious and ideological systems and movements tend to be greater the more they are borne and promoted by relatively cohesive élites with a strong sense of self-identity, and especially by secondary élites which, while somewhat distant from the central ruling one, yet maintain positive solidary orientations to the center and are not entirely alienated from the preexisting élites and from some of the broader groups of the society. Similarly, the effects of such transformative potentials of the religious and ideological movements tend to be greater insofar as the existing social structure in its totality or in those of its parts within which these religious and ideological developments are intensive, is characterized by some extent of autonomy or distinctiveness of the social, cultural, and political orders, and by relatively strong cohesiveness of the more active broader strata. Similarly, the existence within broader social strata and family groups of relatively strong internal cohesion of some status-autonomy and flexibility, together with openness toward the center, may greatly facilitate the internal transformation of these groups and the development within them of positive orientations to the new centers and of willingness to provide these centers with the support and resources they need. Conversely, insofar as such autonomy is small, and the self-closeness of wider social groups is great, they can, through withdrawal of resources and through the development of intensive unregulated demands on the center, undermine the very conditions of the functioning of these new institutional centers.

It was by virtue of the combination of these value orientation and structural characteristics that there emerged within the Protestant countries some psychosocial mechanisms through which the influence of ideas on behavior became operative. The most important of these seems to have been a new type of personal identity that has a degree of reference to a given collective identity. This identity generated a very strong, although flexible, emphasis on the personal commitment to do something for the community. At the same time, this identity was not entirely bound up with any one political system, state, or community. In addition, it entailed a strong connection between personal commitment, personal identity, and several types of institutional exchange activities—economic, political, administrative. In this way it opened up the connections between these personal and collective identities to a great variety of concrete, "this-worldly" activities.

Thus, if we look closely at Weber's Protestant ethic thesis, we see that, whatever the correctness of its details, it is an attempt to explain the transformation of a whole social or cultural system through a change in the type of relations between personal and collective identities, on the one hand, and between them and various concrete institutional activities on the other hand. And it was this symbolic transformation which thus facilitated, even if it did not cause, the emergence of some new institutional developments. This review of Weber's Protestant ethic thesis shows us that it contains important indications, not only about the particular historical problem it deals with, but also for the analysis of processes of transformation of social structures in general and for the relative importance in such processes of the charismatic push as against the purely secular or stychic structural organizational or demographic change.[54]

XII

The preceding analysis brings us to the problem of the relation between charisma and social change in comparative and historical perspective and to the

---

54. In Weber's own work perhaps the most interesting analysis of this problem is that of the causes of decline of the Ancient World. See Max Weber, "Die sozialen Gründe des Untergangs

problems of charisma in the modern world. Weber based his vast comparative work on great concern with problems of historical development in general and with the historical development of Western civilization in particular. Moreover, one of his major analytical contributions to sociological-historical studies lay in the way in which he was able to insert the temporal dimension as a category inherent in the very structure of social systems and of social life—not as something irrelevant to the major forms of social organization, or as an external force directing the destiny of societies. He saw that within social systems there is some inherent tendency to change over time and to perceive such change as an element of their cosmic, social, or cultural order. Did he, however, find beyond the great variety of concrete instances of change any guiding principles according to which the variety of different types of institutionalized relations, groups, or collectivities tend to develop in different societies?

True enough, Weber's analytical and methodological work was to a large extent oriented against much of current idealistic German *Geistesgeschichte*, historical materialism, and evolutionism alike; out of this reaction he developed a rather negative attitude to any overall scheme of human history—and this negative attitude became transferred to much of modern sociological theory. Therefore, it may seem as if many of the concrete types of social organizations which he classified in this grandiose enterprise of explanation of the nature of historical development, built allegedly in his "ideal-typical" way, are constructed either in a "random," "ad hoc" way, or in terms of the historical uniqueness of each society, without there being any more general guiding principle in the classification of these types. However, this would be only a partial view. Just as he was opposed to any definite and comprehensive schemes of universal history, so he was also opposed to historicism.[55] Hence, beyond the great variety of the concrete types with which he dealt, there tend to emerge some broader and more inclusive considerations and orientations. On the one hand, most of the major types which he constructs in almost all institutional spheres are distinguished according to what may be called the extent or scope of their structural differentiation. Thus, for instance, he distinguishes between primitive and historical communities, between small patrimonial and larger more complex historical bureaucratic structures. Moreover, a close examination of Weber's writings, especially his *Sociology of Religion* or in his studies in political sociology,[56] readily reveals that he draws most of his illustrations of the development of charismatic types and of their institutionalization from periods of

---

der antiken Kultur," in his *Gesammelte Aufsätze zur Sozial- und Wirtschaftsgeschichte* (Tübingen, 1924), 289–311.

55. For a somewhat different view see R. Bendix, "Max Weber's Sociology Today," *International Social Science Journal*, 17 (1965):9–22.

56. See Talcott Parsons, introduction to Max Weber, *Sociology of Religion*.

what may be called breakthroughs from one stage of social differentiation to another. In all these studies he indeed fully recognized the importance of structural differentiation in creating the conditions under which new problems of order and meaning emerge and in creating, through some charismatic innovation or transformation, the possibilities of breakthroughs to new types of social organization. But at the same time he was fully aware that neither the general possibilities of the institutionalization of such breakthroughs nor their concrete contours are fixed simply through the very process of structural differentiation. Nor did he assume that there will necessarily be any similarity in the nature of the contents of the charismatic innovation which may develop in different societies at similar stages of differentiation. However, he certainly did not negate the possibility of comparing such contents. Indeed, it can be legitimately claimed that most of his historical-sociological work was devoted to such comparisons. Although the starting points of many of his comparisons were rooted in specific historical situations, this did not negate the comparability of the problems and the wider comparative applicability of the concepts he developed—rather it emphasized such applicability.

It is in this context that the general problem of the contents of the various charismatic symbols and orders as they evolve in different types of societies and in human history becomes pertinent. Are the different types of charismatic activities and symbols which tend to develop in different types of societies purely random and accidental, or can one discern here also some more general pattern or trend? Or, to use again more modern sociological parlance, can one discern some trends or comparable developments, not only with regard to the process of structural differentiation, but also with regard to the principles of integrative order that tend to develop at similar stages of differentiation? It seems that Weber did indeed assume that some such comparable developments and problems can be discussed in a meaningful way. He focused this comparison in his work around the concepts of rationality and *Entzauberung*.[57]

The concept of rationality, as developed by Weber, has, as is well known, at least two different, even if interrelated, meanings or aspects. One is the more formal, organizational meaning, the *Zweckrationalität*, later designated by Mannheim as "functional rationality."[58] This aspect of rationality is very closely related to the process of structural differentiation and complexity; in many ways the possibility of the extension of such rationality is largely necessitated by the very process of structural differentiation. But rationality pertains also to the realm of meaning, of values, of *Wertrationalität*, of what has been called in

57. *Entzauberung* refers mainly to the "contents" aspects of culture and describes the demystification of the conception of the world connected with growing secularism, with the rise of science, and with growing routinization of education and culture.

58. K. Mannheim, *Man and Society in an Age of Reconstruction* (London: K. Paul, Trench, & Trubner, 1940).

Mannheim's terminology "substantive rationality." This rationality can be manifest and its scope may continuously expand in all spheres of human endeavor, of culture, and of social organization—in religion, education, and scientific endeavor, in political life, and in social and interpersonal relations. The broadening of the scope of substantive rationality becomes especially evident at the most crucial breakthroughs from one level of social differentiation to another. It becomes evident in the nature of the problems posed and answers given in all these spheres of human endeavor and social organization. At each such breakthrough there emerges the tendency, or at least the potentiality, to extend the scope of rationality in posing the basic problems of the major symbolic and cultural spheres in a more rational way, that is, in terms of growing abstraction in their formulation, of growing logical coherence and general phrasing, and to some extent also in the ranges of answers attempted to these problems.[59] Such possibilities of extension of rationality are to a very large extent tantamount to the extension of the potential of human creativity and ranges of human freedom. True enough, Weber does not succumb to the optimistic postulate that all charismatic answers (or types of order) which develop at the time of any such breakthroughs are always necessarily rational. On the contrary, in several parts of his work, and especially in his *Sociology of Religion* and in the analysis of modern political developments, he does most clearly postulate the possibility of what may be called irrational answers—magical, demonic, constrictive of freedom, and "alienated"—to such new problems. But although the establishment of such rational ordering is not automatically assured in any situation of growing social differentiation, yet the possibility of such development indeed lies within it. Such extension of substantive rationality is not confined to articulation of abstract ideas. It has some very definite structural-organizational consequences implied in the preceding analysis of the nature of the charismatic in general and of the routinization of charisma as a major aspect of institution building in particular.

Seemingly charismatic qualities, with their emphasis on the extraordinary, constitute the very opposite of any rationality. But it is indeed within the realm of meaning that the greatest potentials for the extension of substantive rationality are to be found. Therefore, given the basic affinity of the charismatic to the provisions of order and of meaning, such extension of rationality may indeed be very often the outcome of charismatic activities of personalities and groups who evolve new conceptions of order and goals and who are able to routinize these charismatic qualities and orientations through the crystallization of new societal centers and institutional frameworks.

59. Weber did not assume that the concrete contents of the questions raised, and especially of the answers given, in such situations was necessarily the same in different societies. But at the same time his work does imply the comparability of such answers and questions in terms of extension of rationality.

But this charismatic, transformative extension of substantive rationality contains also many paradoxes, especially in its relations to problems of creativity and freedom in general and in modern societies in particular. According to many prevalent views, the most important constrictions on such freedom and creativity, and hence also the most important sources of change, instability, and alienation in societies in general and in modern societies in particular, are rooted in the contradiction between the structural implications of the two types of rationality. According to such views, these constrictions are rooted in the contradiction between the liberating or creative potential given in the extension of substantive rationality as against the potentials for constriction and compulsion inherent in the organizational extension of functional rationality most clearly seen in the growing tendencies to bureaucratization inherent in modern societies. This contradiction, which has sometimes been seen as parallel to that between the liberating power of charisma as against the more constrictive tendencies of the process of its routinization, is not abated by the fact that often it is the very extension of substantive rationality (as evident, for instance, in the broadening of the scope of the political community, or in the extension of scientific knowledge) that creates the conditions for the intensification of the more constrictive tendencies inherent in extension of functional rationality in almost all spheres of human endeavor and of social life.

And yet, these more constrictive conflict-oriented tendencies which develop in modern societies are not only rooted in the extension of functional rationality and in its structural effects. They may also be rooted, especially in the modern world, in some of the aspects or consequences of the very extension of substantive rationality—and especially in those aspects of this expansion which are most closely related to *Entzauberung*—a concept which denotes the demystification and secularization of the world, the attenuation of charisma, and a sort of charismatic neutralism. The tendencies to such *Entzauberung* are rooted not only in the encounter between the dynamic qualities of charisma on the one hand and the organizational exigencies of its selective institutionalization in the social structure on the other hand, but also in some of the very basic implications of the transformation of the creative, charismatic qualities of the centers and of the quest for participation in these centers as they developed in modern societies.

Weber indicated, even if often only implicitly, that modern societies are characterized not only by certain structural characteristics such as growing differentiation and specialization, which necessarily lead to specialization of bureaucratization, but also by far-reaching changes in the structure of the social centers, in the pattern of participation in them, and of access to them. Modern societies are also characterized by a growing differentiation and autonomy of various centers, growing demands for access to them, and for participation in them, culminating in tendencies toward the obliteration of the symbolic difference between center and periphery. He sensed, even if he did not make it fully explicit, that, while in the first stages of modernity most social tensions and conflicts evolved around the broadening of the scope of participation and channels of access to the centers, later, when many of these goals may have indeed been attained, a new series of problems, tensions, and conflicts may arise. These problems are focused around the possibility of development of growing apathy toward the very central values, symbols, and centers, not because of the lack of possibility of access to them but because of, in a sense, overaccess to them. Thus the demystification of the world may come about in the phenomenon that the attainment of participation in many centers may indeed be meaningless, that the centers may lose their mystery, that the King may be naked indeed. This process may, of course, be greatly intensified by the increase of bureaucratization and of growing specialization in modern societies. But it would be erroneous to assume that these trends in themselves would produce such new problems and tensions. Rather it is the combination of these trends to bureaucratization with the changing structure of participation in the centers that may account for these results of demystification and of the routinization of the charismatic in modern settings.

This approach may add a new dimension to studies of change and conflict and may throw an additional light both on the study of the great social and political trends and problems of the twentieth century and on various contemporary phenomena, such as the new types of revolt of youth, or the transformation of problems of leisure. The common denominator of all these phenomena is in the attempts to dissociate one's predisposition to the charismatic from the societal centers and from the traditions of the larger culture and to associate it more and more only with the sphere of private, face-to-face relations and activities—and even here to emphasize tendencies toward secularization, negation of purity, and dissociation of seriousness and any normative commitment. Here again all these are only preliminary illustrations or indications. But they, as all the other preliminary indications outlined in the preceding paragraphs, are derived from that reformulation of the basic problems of social order which can be derived from a reexamination of Weber's work. They all constitute a challenge and guide line for further sociological analysis.

Nine

PATRON-CLIENT RELATIONS AS A MODEL OF STRUCTURING SOCIAL EXCHANGE

S. N. EISENSTADT AND LUIS RONIGER

THE STUDY OF PATRON-CLIENT RELATIONS

I.

THE STUDY OF PATRONAGE and of patron-client relations has come lately to the fore in anthropology, political science, and sociology, and has exerted a great fascination for scholars in these spheres. From a topic of relatively marginal concern it has become a central one, closely connected to basic theoretical problems and controversies in all the social sciences.

In the late fifties and early sixties the study of patron-client relations was in a rather marginal position in most of the social sciences: anthropology, sociology, and political science. It dealt with types of social relations or organizations that were seen as differing widely both from the "corporate," kinship and territorial groups so strongly emphasized in anthropological literature and from the universalistic-bureaucratic or market frameworks usually portrayed in sociology or political science as the epitomes of modernity and rationality. Patron-client relations, although fascinating, were seen as somewhat marginal in their respective societies and were studied in the framework of traditional concepts and concerns of these disciplines.[1] Since then the study of patronage

Originally published in *Comparative Studies in Society and History* 22 (1980):42–77. Reprinted with permission of Cambridge University Press, © 1980 Society for Comparative Study of Society and History.

The origins of this paper are in a seminar on Comparative Patron-Client Relations in the Department of Sociology of The Hebrew University, given in 1974–75 by S. N. Eisenstadt and J. Azmon, in a framework of seminars on Comparative Civilizations. Two papers based on this seminar have already been published: V. Burkolter, *The Patronage System, Theoretical Remarks*, Basel, Social Strategies, 1976; and Anita Brumer, "O Sistema Paternalista no Brasil," *Revista do Instituto de Filosofia e Ciencias Humanas da Universidade Federal do Rio Grande do Sol*, IV (1976), 57–79. Prof. J. S. Coleman of the University of Chicago and Prof. R. Breiger of Harvard University have commented in detail on earlier drafts of this paper, and problems have been discussed by S. N. Eisenstadt with Patti Cox and Beth Hevens at Harvard. Preliminary presentations of this paper have been made by the senior author at Cambridge University and the University of Manchester. He is greatly indebted to the discussions there.

1. Thus in anthropology they were connected with the study of such phenomena as ritual kinship or friendship, and anthropologists tended to concentrate on the institutionalized types of

and patron-client relations has burgeoned into central importance. This change came first of all from the extension of the objects of these studies from relatively limited, dyadic, interpersonal, semi-institutionalized relations between a single patron and one or several clients to a broader variety of social relations and organizations. These ranged from semi-institutionalized personal dyadic or triadic relations in small communities or in more organized settings like various bureaucratic agencies to relatively loose, less rigidly prescribed social relations, often organized in complex networks and connected by brokers, as well as to loose cliques and factions in political

---

personal patron-client relationship, above all in tribal settings or in small rural communities. Among the best-known studies are S. W. Mintz and E. R. Wolf, "An Analysis of Ritual Coparenthood (Compadrazgo)." *Southwestern Journal of Anthropology*, 6: 4 (Winter 1950). 341–68; G. M. Foster, "Cofradia and Compadrazgo in Spain," *ibid.*, 9:1 (Spring 1953), 1–28; H. Tegnaeus, *Blood Brothers*, New York, Philosophical Library, 1952; I. Ishino, "The Oyabun-Kobun: A Japanese Ritual Kinship Institution," *American Anthropologist*, 55:1 (1953), 695–707; J. Pitt-Rivers, *The People of the Sierra*, London, Weidenfeld and Nicholson, 1954; idem. "Ritual and Kinship in Spain." *Transactions of the New York Academy of Sciences*. Series 2:20 (1958), 424–31; M. Kenny, *A Spanish Tapestry: Town and Country in Castile*, New York. Harper and Row, 1966 (1961); H. W. Hutchinson, *Village and Plantation Life in Northeastern Brazil*, Seattle, University of Washington Press, 1957; S. H. Freed, "Fictive Kinship in a North Indian Village," *Ethnology*, 2 (1963), 86–104; G. M. Foster, "The Dyadic Contract: A Model for the Social Structure of a Mexican Peasant Village," *American Anthropologist*, 63:6 (1961), 1173–92; and idem, "The Dyadic Contract in Tzintzuntzan II: Patron-Client Relationship," *ibid.*, 65:6 (1963), 1280–94. In sociology, the study of patronage was closely related to "primary" groups and relations in more formalized settings such as bureaucracies. See the Hawthorne Studies in the 1930s: F. J. Roethlisberger and W. J. Dickson, *Management and the Worker: An Account of a Research Program, conducted by the qWestern Electric Co., Hawthorne Works*, Cambridge, Harvard University Press, 1970 (1939); L. W. Warner and P. S. Lunt, *The Social Life of a Modern Community*, New Haven, Yale University Press, 1941; W. F. Whyte, *Street Corner Society: The Social Structure of an Italian Slum*, Chicago, University of Chicago Press, 1958; E. Shils, "Primordial, Personal, Sacred and Civil Ties," in idem. *Center and Periphery*, Chicago, University of Chicago Press, 1975, 111–26; idem. "Primary Groups in American Army," in *ibid.*, 384–405; E. Katz and P. F. Lazarfeld, *Personal Influence*, Glencoe, IL. The Free Press, 1955. In political science the study of patronage was initially concentrated on political machines and "bossism" in more developed societies, gradually extending to the study of corruption in developing countries. See for instance H. J. Carmen and R. J. Luthin, *Lincoln and the Patronage*, New York, 1943; F. J. Sorauf, "Patronage and Party," *Midwest Journal of Political Science*, 3:2 (May 1959); J. Q. Wilson, "The Economy of Patronage," *Journal of Political Economy*, 69:4 (Aug. 1961), 369–80; S. Mandelbaum, *Boss Tweed's New York*, New York, Wiley and Sons, 1965; E. Banfield and J. Q. Wilson, *City Politics*, Cambridge, Harvard University Press and M.I.T. Press, 1963. In the literature on those phenomena in developing countries at this stage see R. Wraith and E. Simkins, *Corruption in Developing Countries*, London, G. Allen and Unwin, 1963; M. G. Smith, "Historical and Cultural Conditions of Political Corruption among the Hausa," *Comparative Studies in Society and History*, 6:1 (Jan. 1964), 164–94; J. D. Greenstone, "Corruption and Self-Interest in Kampala and Nairobi," *ibid.*, 8:1 (Jan. 1966), 199 210; M. Nash, "Party Building in Upper Burma," *Asian Survey*, 3:4 (April 1963), 197–202; and idem. *The Golden Road to Modernity*, New York, Wiley and Sons, 1965; C. H. Landé, *Leaders, Factions and Parties: The Structure of Philippine Politics*, New Haven, Yale University Press, Southeast Asian Studies, 1965.

machines. In the latter, a less structured exchange of diverse services and resources took place, while the element of solidarity between patron and client was much weaker.[2]

Second, these studies encompassed a wide range of societies throughout the world, in the Mediterranean, the Near East, Latin America, India, Southeast Asia, among others.[3]

2. For illustrations of the conceptualization of patron-client relationships since the late sixties see for instance E. Wolf, "Kinship, Friendship, and Patron-Client Relationships in Complex Societies," in M. Banton, ed., *The Social Anthropology of Complex Societies*, London, Tavistock, 1966, A.S.A. Monographs, 1–22; A. Weingrod, "Patrons, Patronage, and Political Parties," *Comparative Studies in Society and History*, 7:4 (Oct. 1968), 377–400; the issue of *Sociologische Gids* that deals with patron-client relations, 16:6 (Nov.–Dec. 1969); R. Lemarchand and K. Legg, "Political Clientelism and Development: A Preliminary Analysis," *Comparative Politics*, 4:2 (Jan. 1972), 149–78; W. T. Stuart, "The Explanation of Patron-Client Systems: Some Structural and Ecological Perspectives," in A. Strickon and S. Greenfield, eds., *Structure and Process in Latin America: Patronage, Clientage and Power Systems*, Albuquerque, New Mexico University Press, 1972, 19–42; R. Kaufman, "The Patron-Client Concept and Macropolitics: Prospects and Problems," *Comparative Studies in Society and History*, 16:3 (July 1974), 284–308; L. Grazziano, *A Conceptual Framework for the Study of Clientelism*, New York, Cornell University Western Societies Program Occasional Papers, 4 1975; J. S. La Fontaine, "Unstructured Social Relations," *The West African Journal of Sociology and Political Science*, 1:1 (Oct. 1975), 51–81; E. Gellner and J. Waterbury, eds., *Patrons and Clients in Mediterranean Societies*, London, Duckworth, 1977, esp. the following papers: E. Gellner, "Patrons and clients," 1–6; J. Scott, "Patronage or exploitation?," 21–40; A. Weingrod, "Patronage and power," 41–52; and J. Waterbury, "An attempt to put patrons and clients in their place," 329–42; J. Davis, *People of the Mediterranean. An Essay in Comparative Social Anthropology*, London, Routledge and Kegan Paul, 1977, ch. 4; S. W. Schmidt, L. Guasti, C. H. Landé and J. C. Scott, eds., *Friends, Followers, and Factions*, Berkeley, University of California Press, 1976.

3. The wide occurrence of patron-client relationships encompassed a great variety of links. Multipurpose, diffusely defined clusters of multiple dyadic ties were found between landholders and landless strata in search of share-cropping arrangements in the agrotowns of Italian latifundist Mezzogiorno; in Central Italy Mezzadrian *signori* and *mezzadri* paternalistic patronage; in Spain, where the link was either normatively anchored in the moral values of the pueblos and confused with friendship or was oppressive and labeled as *caciquismo*; in the Middle Eastern *smiyya* patronage with its stress on the social visibility of the patron and his power in institutional markets, as shown in Egyptian *futuwwa* as *ibn el-balad*, Lebanese *muqati'ji* and Iraqi *al-Taba'iyya*. Patrons can use the links in many markets or center their use upon a single institutional sphere as happened with South Italian political single *clientelismo* of the Notables or with the Spanish *caciques*. For these patterns see M. Rossi-Doria, "The Land Tenure System and Class in Southern Italy," *American Historical Review*, 64 (1958), 46–53; P. Schneider, "Honor and Conflict in a Sicilian Town," *Anthropological Quarterly*, 42:3 (July 1969), 130–54; idem, "Coalition Formation and Colonialism in Western Sicily," *Archives Européennes de Sociologie*, 13 (1972), 255–67; S. G. Tarrow, *Peasant Communism in Southern Italy*, New Haven, Yale University Press, 1967; L. Grazziano, "Patron-Client Relations in Southern Italy," *European Journal of Political Research*, 1:1 (1973), 3–34; P. A. Allum, *Politics and Society in Postwar Naples*, Cambridge, Cambridge University Press, 1973; S. F. Silverman, "Patronage and Community-Nation Relationship in Central Italy," *Ethnology*, 4:2 (1965), 172–89; idem, "Exploitation in Rural Central Italy: Structure and Ideology in Stratification Study," *Comparative Studies in Society and History*, 12:3 (July 1970), 327–39; J. Pitt-Rivers, *The People of the Sierra*; M. Kenny, "Patterns of Patronage in Spain," *Anthropological Quarterly*, 33 (Jan. 1960), 14–23; idem, *A Spanish Tapestry*; R. Aya, *The Missed Revolution. The Fate of Rural Rebels in Sicily and Southern Spain, 1840–1950*, Amsterdam University, Papers

Third, the centrality of these studies sprang from the growing awareness that patron-client relations were not destined to remain on the margins of society nor to disappear with the development and establishment of democracies with well-functioning political and economic systems marked by economic development and modernization, or with the growth of class consciousness

on European and Mediterranean Societies, No. 3, 1975; R. Kern, ed., *The Caciques, Oligarchical Politics and the System of Caciquismo in the Luso-Hispanic World*, Albuquerque, New Mexico University Press, 1973; S. el-Messiri, "The changing role of the futuwwa in the social structure of Cairo," in Gellner and Waterbury, *Patrons and Clients*, 239–54; S. Khalaf, "Changing forms of political patronage in Lebanon," *ibid.* 185–206; and A. Rassam, "Al-Taba'iyya: Power, patronage and marginal groups in Northern Iraq," *ibid*, 157–66. More organizationally oriented patterns are found in Southern Italy, where *clientelismo* and party-directed bossism were strengthened in a continuing political competition, a widening distribution of wealth and the transference of the locus of political articulation to higher levels of political contest. Such pyramidal chain-to-center structure also characterized Spanish *caciquismo* after the 1874 Restoration. The pattern becomes more impersonal and instrumental and less dependent on ideological prescriptions of solidarity. Unipurpose patterns are found also in Greece and in Latin America, focused either in the political sphere as in Spain or in the instrumental sphere; they are centered on the preferential access of patrons to second-order resources and are built on connections with ruling parties and State bureaucracies or on officeholding. Such links are reported as well for the Middle East (in Morocco for instance) and for Southeast Asian and black African unions and political arenas; in these cases there seem to be greater pressures for congruence between the incumbents' standing in subcollectivities and their position in institutional markets, as well as less ideological strain in the contractation and functioning of the ties. Similar patterns are found in the Japanese *yuryokusha* political patronage, in a sphere conceived as marginal for the societal and cosmic order and in a frame of weakened primordial territorial and kinship ties. See for instance R. Aya, *The Missed Revolution;* J. Costa, "Oligarquía y caciquismo como la forma actual de gobierno en España," in idem, *Oligarquia y caciquismo. Colectivismo agrario y otros escritos*, Madrid, Alianza Editorial, 1967, 15–45; F. B. Pike, *Hispanismo, 1898–1936*, Notre Dame, University of Notre Dame Press, 1971; J. Romero-Maura, "Caciquismo as a political system," in Gellner and Waterbury, *Patrons and Clients*, 53–62; R. Kern, *The Caciques;* J. K. Campbell, *Honour, Family and Patronage, A Study of Institutions and Moral Values in a Greek Mountain Community*, Oxford, Clarendon Press, 1964; K. R. Legg, *Politics in Modern Greece*, Stanford, Stanford University Press, 1969; and idem, "Political Change in Clientelistic Polity. The Failure of Democracy in Greece," *Journal of Political and Military Sociology*, 1:2 (Fall 1973), 231–46; J. Waterbury, *The Commander of the Faithful: The Moroccan Political Elite*, London, Weidenfeld and Nicholson, 1970; E. Burke, "Morocco and the Near East," *Archives Européennes de Sociologie*, 10 (1969), 70–94; E. Gellner, "The Great Patron: A Reinterpretation of Tribal Rebellions," *ibid.*, 61–69; E. Akarly and G. Ben Dor, eds., *Political Participation in Turkey*, Istambul, Bogazici University Publications, 1975; E. Shor, "The Thai Bureaucracy," *Administrative Science Quarterly*, 5:6 (1960), 66–86; A. Leeds, "Brazilian Career and Social Structures: An Evolutionary Model and Case History," *American Anthropologist*, 66:6 (1964), 1321–47; G. E. Poitras, "Welfare Bureaucracy and Clientelistic Politics in Mexico," *Administrative Science Quarterly*, 18:1 (March 1973), 18–26; R. Sandbrook, "Patrons, Clients, and Factions: New Dimensions of Conflict Analysis in Africa," *Canadian Journal of Political Science*, 5:1 (March 1972), 104–19; and idem, "Patrons, Clients, and Unions: The Labour Movement and Political Conflict in Kenya," *Journal of Commonwealth Political Studies*, 10:1 (March 1972), 3–27; N. Ike, *Japanese Politics, Patron-Client Democracy*, New York, Knopf, 1972 (1957); and S. C. Flanagan, "Voting Behavior in Japan: The Persistence of Traditional Patterns," *Comparative Political Studies*, 1:3 (Oct. 1968), 391–412. See also A. Zuckerman, *Political Clienteles in Power: Party Factions and Cabinet Coalitions in Italy*, Beverly Hills, Sage

among the lower strata. It was also seen that, while any single type of patronage, as for instance the semi-institutionalized kinship-like personal dyadic
patron-client relationship, may disappear under such conditions, new types
may appear, and that they can be found in a variety of forms in many societies,
cutting across different levels of economic development and political regimes,

Publications, 1975. Greater coerciveness and violence is found in Sicilian *mafiosi* brokerage between urban absentee landlords and the Western Sicilian hinterland; *mafiosi* competed among
themselves and vis-à-vis lower-standing sectors for greater shares of wealth, while attempting to
undermine the control of landlords. A similar trend was found in Northeast Brazilian patrimonial
relations between the owners of plantations and sugar-refineries and rural workers; in Egyptian
futuwwa as baltagi, and in the case of Lebanese *qabadat* acting on behalf of *zu'ama*. See A. Blok, *The
Mafia of a Sicilian Village, 1860–1960. A Study of Violent Peasant Entrepreneurs*, Oxford, B. Blackwell, 1974;
H. Hess, *Mafia and Mafiosi. The Structure of Power*, Westmead Farnborough, Saxon House, 1973
(1970); M. Gelzer, *The Roman Nobility*, Oxford, B. Blackwell, 1969, 62–111; G. Freire, *The Masters
and the Slaves: A Study in the Development of Brazilian Civilization*, New York, Knopf, 1956; B. Hutchinson,
"The Patron-Dependent Relationship in Brazil: A Preliminary Examination," *Sociologia Ruralis*, 6
(1966), 3–30; and M. Johnson, "Political bosses and their gangs: Zu'ama and qabadayat in the
Sunni Muslim quarters of Beirut," in Gellner and Waterbury, *Patrons and Clients*, 207–24. Corporated
patron-client relations are reported on kinship, territorial-kinship and civil-like bases. An example
of the first is found in the Cyrenaican link between Saadi families and Mrabtin as-Sadgan lacking
land and water rights; an example of corporated incumbency to the patron role on a civil-based
criterion is reported for the Republican State's foreign *clientelae* to *civitas liberae*; on a territorial
kinship-like base in Japanese *dozoku*. The corporate character of incumbency was linked to the
semi- or quasi-legal statement of the high dissimilarity of the roles, freeing these from their propensity to instability according to changes in the market positions of the incumbents. Similar are
some ritualized patterns, often described as clientelistic; the Japanese *oyabun-kobun* and the Christian *compadrazgo*. The link found among the Interlacustrine Bantu of East Africa resembles this
aspect; here the ceremonial formalization makes the link no longer vulnerable to the transactional
actual interests of the partners. On this range of patterns see among others E. L. Peters, "The Tied
and the Free (Lybia)," in J. Peristiany, ed., *Contributions to Mediterranean Sociology*, Paris-The Hague,
Mouton, 1968, 167–88; E. Badian, *Foreign Clientelae (246-70 B.C.)*, Oxford, Clarendon Press, 1958;
R. K. Beardsley et al., *Village Japan*, Chicago, The University of Chicago Press, 1959; I. Ishino, "The
Oyabun-Kobun," C. Nakane, *Japanese Society*, London, Weidenfeld and Nicholson, 1970; G. M. Foster, "Cofradia and Compadrazgo"; L. P. Mair, "Clientship in East Africa," *Cahiers d'Etudes Africaines*, 2:6
(1961), 315–26; and F. Steinhart, "Vassal and Fief in three Lacustrine Kingdoms," *ibid.*, 7:28 (1967),
606–23. Patron-client ties and similar relations were reported in traditional China, India, Ireland,
Hungary, the East Arctic, Nepal, Malta, and the Balkans. See for instance K. E. Folsom, *Friends, Guests
and Colleagues: The Mu-fu System in the late Ch'ing Period*, Berkeley, University of California Press, 1968; J.
Breman, *Patronage and Exploitation: Changing Agrarian Relations in South Gujarat, India*, Berkeley, University
of California Press, 1974; M. Bax, "Patronage Irish Style: Irish Politicians as Brokers," *Sociologische Gids*,
17 (May–June 1970), 179–91; E. Fél and T. Hofer, *Proper Peasants: Traditional Life in a Hungárian Village*,
Viking Fund Publications in Anthropology, No. 46, Chicago, Aldine, 1969; R. Paine, ed., *Patrons and
Brokers in the East Arctic*, Memorial University of Newfoundland, Institute of Social and Economic Research, 1971, Newfoundland Social and Economic Papers No. 2; L. Caplan, "Cash and Kind: Two
media of 'Bribery' in Nepal," *Man* N.S., 6 (1971), 266–78; J. Boissevain, *Saints and Fireworks: Religion and
Politics in Rural Malta*, London, Athlone Press, 1965; and E. A. Hammel, *Alternative Social Structures and
Ritual Relations in the Balkans*, Englewood Cliffs, Prentice Hall, 1968. Ephemeral ties and transient patterns, as in the U.S. and the Soviet Union, are discussed below.

and seemingly performing important functions within these more highly developed modern frameworks.[4]

Fourth, the growing centrality of these studies was due to the fact that they became closely related to the major theoretical developments and controversies in the social sciences and thus became an important focus of such theoretical debates.

On the theoretical level, in all the social science disciplines, the analysis of patronage has become closely connected with outcries against the current "functionalist," systemic and "developmentalist" evolutionary emphases in anthropology, sociology, and political science in general, and against the assumptions of the classical studies of modernization and development that were, as is well known, so closely related to the structural-functional school in sociology in particular.[5] This link with major theoretical controversies could be most clearly seen in the themes of the studies of patron-client relations and in the attempts to define more precisely their central distinguishing core. The first such theme of many of the studies was—as opposed to the strong emphasis found both in classical functionalistic anthropology and in the structural-functional school of sociology on groups and their needs and boundary-maintaining mechanism—the stress on the importance of personal and inter-personal relations, quasi-groups, networks and power relations.[6]

The stress on interpersonal relations and exchange became connected in

4. See for instance N. Ike, *Japanese Politics: Patron-Client Democracy*; B. Galjart, "Old Patrons and New: Some Notes on the Consequences of Patronage for Local Development Projects," *Sociologia Ruralis*, 7 (1967), 335–46; A. Weingrod and E. Morin, "Post Peasants: The Character of Contemporary Sardinian Society," *Comparative Studies in Society and History*, 13:3 (July 1971), 301–24; A. Blok, "Peasants, Patrons and Brokers in Western Sicily," *Anthropological Quarterly*, 42: 3 (July 1969), 155–70; P. A. Allum, *Politics and Society in Postwar Naples*; M. Bax, "Patronage Irish Style"; S. Khalaf, "Changing forms of political patronage in Lebanon." For a broad treatment of the adaptability of patron-client relations, see J. D. Powell, "Peasant Society and Clientelistic Politics," *American Political Science Review*, 64:2 (June 1970), 411–25; J. C. Scott, "Corruption, Machine Politics, and Political Change,"*ibid.*, 63:4 (Dec. 1969), 1142–58; R. Lemarchand and K. Legg, "Political Clientelism and Development: A Preliminary Analysis," *Comparative Politics*, 4:2 (Jan. 1972), 149–78; J. C. Scott, "Patron-Client Politics and Political Change in Southeast Asia," *American Political Science Review*, 66:1 (March 1972), 91–113; C. H. Landé, "Networks and Groups in Southeast Asia: Some Observations on the Group Theory of Politics," *ibid.*, 67:1 (March 1973), 103–27; P. Schneider, J. Schneider and E. Hansen, "Modernization and Development: The Role of Regional Elites and Noncorporated Groups in the European Mediterranean," *Comparative Studies in Society and History*, 14:3 (July 1972), 328–50; K. R. Legg, *Patrons, Clients and Politicians, New Perspectives on Political Clientelism*, Beverly Hills, Institute of International Studies. Working Papers on Development, No. 3, n.d.

5. These controversies are analyzed in S. N. Eisenstadt and M. Curelaru, *The Form of Sociology, Paradigms and Crises*, New York, Wiley and Sons, 1976, esp. chs. 8 and 9; and in idem, "Macrosociology Theory, Analysis and Comparative Studies," *Current Sociology*, 25:2 (1977), esp. chs. II and III.

6. For the approach of "classical" functionalist anthropology on this point see A. R. Radcliffe-Brown, "On the Concept of Function in Social Science" and "On Social Structure," in idem, ed., *Structure and Function in Primitive Society*, London, Cohen and West, 1952, 178–204; and M. Gluckman,

the study of patronage with the upholding of several dimensions of social structure and action, seen as having been neglected both in classical functional anthropology and in the structural-functional approaches of sociology, as well as in the then current studies of modernization. The most important dimensions were those of autonomy of power and the concomitant stress on relations between the distribution of power, the flow of resources, and the structure of social relations in society; and on such aspects of interpersonal relations as hierarchy, asymmetry and inequality, and the autonomy of some aspects of the symbolic dimension of human activity. The latter were seen as closely related in patron-client relations, to such concepts as honor, or the spiritual dimensions of such interpersonal relations as friendship and ritual kinship; and to specific perceptions of social order, for instance in terms such as "limited good," claimed by Foster to be characteristic of peasant societies.[7] There arose also the growing recognition that the phenomena subsumed under the umbrella of

---

Custom and Conflict in Africa, Oxford, B. Blackwell, 1955. On the structural functional approach see for instance T. Parsons and E. Shils, eds., *Toward a General Theory of Action*, Cambridge, Harvard University Press, 1951; T. Parsons; *The Social System*, New York, The Free Press, 1964; and T. Parsons and N. J. Smelser, *Economy and Society*, New York, The Free Press, 1965. For the emphasis put on interpersonal relations and exchange by scholars who dealt with patron-client relations see E. Wolf, "Kinship, Friendship, and Patron-Client Relationships"; J. Boissevain, *Friends of Friends, Networks, Manipulators, and Coalitions*, Oxford, B. Blackwell, 1974; A. C. Mayer, "The Significance of Quasi-Groups in the Study of Complex Societies," in M. Banton, ed., *The Social Anthropology of Complex Societies*, 1–22; M. J. Swartz, *Local-Level Politics: Social and Cultural Perspectives*, Chicago, Aldine, 1966, esp. 53–68, 199–204, 227–41, 243–69; J. Boissevain, "The Place of Non-Groups in Social Sciences," *Man*, N.S., 3:4 (1968), 542–56; J. Pitt-Rivers, "The Kith and the Kin," in J. Goody, *Character of Kinship*, Cambridge, Cambridge University Press, 1973, 89–105; J. Boissevain and J. C. Mitchell, eds., *Network Analysis, Studies in Social Interaction*, Paris–The Hague, Mouton, 1973; C. H. Landé, "Networks and Groups in Southeast Asia: Some Observations on the Group Theory of Politics"; idem, "Group Politics and Dyadic Politics: Notes for a Theory," in Schmidt et al., *Friends, Followers, and Factions*, 506–10; A. Weingrod, "Patronage and power," in Gellner and Waterbury, *Patrons and Clients*, 41–42; and J. C. Scott, "Political Clientelism: A Bibliographical Essay," in Schmidt et al., *Friends, Followers and Factions*, 488–89.

7. On the concept of honor in societies in which patron-client relations can also be found, see J. G. Peristiany, ed., *Honour and Shame: The Values of Mediterranean Society*, London, Weidenfeld and Nicholson, 1965; P. Schneider, "Honour and Conflict in a Sicilian Town"; J. K. Campbell, *Honour, Family, and Patronage*; J. Pitt-Rivers, "Honour and Social Status," in J. G. Peristiany, ed., *Honour and Shame*, 19–78; idem, "Honor," in D. L. Shills, ed., *International Encyclopaedia of the Social Sciences*, New York: Macmillan and Free Press, 1968, Vol. 6, 503–10; J. Davis, "Honour and Politics in Picticci," *Proceedings of the Royal Anthropological Institute*, 1969, 64–81; J. Schneider, "Of Vigilance and Virgins. Honour, Shame and the Access to Resources in Mediterranean Societies," *Ethnology*, 10:1 (Jan. 1971), 1–24. On the Image of Limited Good see G. Foster, "Peasant Society and the Image of Limited Good," *American Anthropologist*, 67:2 (April 1965), 293–315. For controversies about the concept see for instance: D. Kaplan and B. Saler, "Foster's Image of the Limited Good: An Example of Anthropological Explanation," *American Anthropologist*, 68:1 (Jan. 1966), 202–05; J. W. Bennett, "Further Remarks on Foster's Image of Limited Good," *ibid.*, 206–09; and Foster's reply, *ibid.*, 210–14.

patron-client or clientelistic relations are not only, as Landé has recently pointed out, marginal addenda to more fully structured or organized social relations[8] but may also constitute, as they seemingly do in many Mediterranean, Latin American, and Southeast Asian societies, a central aspect of the institutional patterns of these societies.

It became more and more evident that the complex social arrangements known as patron-client relations denote, in their fullest expression, a distinct mode of regulating crucial aspects of institutional order: the structuring of the flow of resources, exchange and power relations and their legitimation in society.[9] This implies that, while many organizational aspects of patron-client relations (such as the dyadic or triadic networks of brokers, and the like) can be found in many different societies, yet their full institutional implications and repercussions are seen only when they become a part or manifestation of the central mode of regulation of the flow of resources and processes of interpersonal and institutional exchange and interaction in a society or a sector thereof. They can best be understood therefore in relation to the broader, often macrosocietal, setting in which they take place.

In the following pages we shall attempt to analyze the nature of this mode of regulation of the flow of resources and the societal conditions most conducive to its development and continuity.

II.

We shall start with the identification, on the basis of the growing and voluminous literature on the subject,[10] of the core characteristics of patron-client rela-

---

See also S. Piker, "The Image of Limited Good: Comments on an Exercise in Description and Interpretation," *American Anthropologist*, 68:5 (Oct. 1966), 1202–11; G. M. Foster, "A Second Look at Limited Good," *Anthropological Quarterly*, 45:2 (April 1972), 57–64; and J. R. Gregory, "Image of Limited Good or Expectation of Reciprocity?," *Current Anthropology*, 16:1 (March 1975), 73–92. On "amoral familism" see E. Banfield, *The Moral Basis of a Backward Society*, Glencoe, IL, The Free Press, 1958; A. J. Wichers, "Amoral Familism Reconsidered," *Sociologia Ruralis*, 4:2 (1964), 167–81; and A. Pizzorno, "Amoral Familism and Historical Marginality," *International Review of Community Development*, 15:16 (1966), 55–66.

8. C. H. Landé, "Introduction. The Dyadic Basis of Clientelism," in Schmidt et al., *Friends, Followers, and Factions*, XIII–XXXVII.

9. See for instance A. Zuckerman, *Political Clienteles*; S. Tarrow, *From Center to Periphery. Alternative Models of National-Local Policy Impact and an Application to France and Italy*, Ithaca, Cornell University Western Societies Program Occasional Papers, No. 4 (1976); K. R. Legg, *Patrons, Clients and Politicians. New Perspectives on Political Clientelism*; J. Waterbury, *The Commander of the Faithful. The Moroccan Political Elite. A Study in Segmented Politics*, London, Weidenfeld and Nicholson, 1970; L. Grazziano, *A Conceptual Framework for the Study of Clientelism*; and the contributions to the Conference on Patronage held Nov. 1974 in Rome by the Center for Mediterranean Studies of the American Universities Field Staff and included in E. Gellner and J. Waterbury, *Patrons and Clients*, esp. E. Gellner, "Patrons and Clients," 1–6.

10. See for instance the bibliographical essay of J. C. Scott, in Schmidt et al., *Friends, Followers, and Factions*, 483–505, and the literature quoted in preceding notes.

tions and the types of social interaction they involve, especially in those societies or sectors thereof in which patron-client relations are interwoven with the central mode of the structuring of the flow of resources. The most important of these core analytical characteristics are given below.

a) Patron-client relations are usually particularistic and diffuse.

b) The interaction on which they are based is characterized by the simultaneous exchange of different types of resources, above all instrumental, economic, as well as political ones (support, loyalty, votes, protection) on the one hand and promises of solidarity and loyalty on the other.

c) The exchange of these resources is usually effected by a "package-deal," i.e., neither resource can be exchanged separately but only in a combination that includes both types.

d) Ideally, a strong element of unconditionality and of long-range credit and obligations is built into these relations.

e) As a corollary, there is a strong element of solidarity in these relations—an element often couched in terms of interpersonal loyalty and attachment between patrons and clients—even though these relations may often be ambivalent. The element of solidarity may be strong, as in the restricted primary relationship of the classical type of patronage, or, as in many of the more modern political machines, very weak, but to some degree it is to be found in all of them. Solidarity is often closely related to conceptions of personal identity, especially of personal honor and obligations, and it is also evident that some, even if ambivalent, personal "spiritual" attachment may exist between patron and clients.

f) At the same time, the relations established are not fully legal or contractual; they are often opposed to the official laws of the country and are based more on informal—although tightly binding—understandings.

g) Despite their seemingly binding, long-range and, in their ideal portrayal almost life-long endurance, patron-client relations are entered into voluntarily, at least in principle, and can, officially at least, be abandoned voluntarily.

h) These relations are undertaken between individuals or networks of individuals in a vertical fashion (the simplest kind is a strong dyadic one) rather than between organized corporate groups. They seem to undermine the horizontal group organization and solidarity of both clients and patrons, but especially of clients.

i) Last and not least, patron-client relations are based on very strong elements of inequality and of differences in power. Even at this stage of our discussion it should be evident that the crucial element of this inequality is the monopolization by the patrons of certain positions that are of vital importance for the clients; especially, as we shall see in greater detail later, of the access to the means of production, major markets, and centers of the society.

These characteristics indicate that the exchange effected in patron-client relations takes place on several levels and that it does create a paradoxical combination of elements that are a major feature of the patron-client nexus. The most important contradictions are first, a peculiar combination of inequality and asymmetry in power with seeming mutual solidarity expressed in terms of personal identity and interpersonal sentiments and obligations; second, a combination of potential coercion and exploitation with voluntary relations and compelling mutual obligations; third, a combination of the emphasis on these obligations and solidarity with the somewhat illegal or semilegal aspect of these relations.

These characteristics and paradoxical features of patron-client relations can be found in societies at various levels of social differentiation, technological development, and political regimes and in different types of concrete organization (i.e., in dyadic relations, in broader networks, as parts of broader bureaucratic organization and the like). These core characteristics and their crystallization around these contradictions provide the clue to the nature of patron-client relations as a specific type of social relation in general and as a macro-societal phenomenon in particular.

First of all, they indicate that the crux of patron-client relations is indeed the organization or regulation of exchange or flow of resources between social actors. But second, contrary to what seems to be implied in parts of the literature, they indicate that patron clients do not denote a special type of simple, specific, market-like or power exchange as envisaged by the theories of individualistic exchange, best represented in the work of George C. Homans and Peter M. Blau.[11] Rather, like other modes of regulation of the flow of societal resources, patron-client relations constitute a special combination of specific exchange with what has been denoted in sociological and anthropological literature as generalized exchange.

GENERALIZED EXCHANGE AND THE INSTITUTIONALIZATION OF THE GROUND RULES OF SOCIAL INTERACTION

III.

The term generalized exchange, probably first coined by Marcel Mauss, was elaborated and somewhat changed by C. Lévi-Strauss in his earlier works on kinship. It is also related to the analysis of generalized media of exchange, as

11. G. C. Homans, *Social Behaviour. Its Elementary Forms*, New York, Harcourt Brace and World, 1961; P. Blau, "Justice in Social Exchange," *Sociological Inquiry*, 34:1–2 (Spring 1964), 193–206; idem, *Exchange and Power in Social Life*, New York, Wiley and Sons, 1964. A treatment of these different orientations in social exchange theory can be found in P. Ekeh, *Social Exchange Theory, The Two Traditions*, Cambridge, Harvard University Press, 1964. See also J. H. Turner, *The Structure of Sociological Theory*, Homewood, IL. The Dorsey Press, 1974, 211–320.

elaborated from a structural-functional perspective by T. Parsons and from an individualistic one by J. S. Coleman.[12]

The problems with which the term generalized exchange is concerned were first defined in Mauss's analysis of the gift. As is well known, he has shown that gift-giving constitutes an exchange with special yet highly structured characteristics. The exchange of gifts is distinct from the usual "specific" market exchange in that it is seemingly nonutilitarian and disinterested. But at the same time it is highly structured, being based on elaborate rules of reciprocity, which nevertheless differ from those of utilitarian, specific market exchange.[13]

These differences are closely related to the purposes or functions of these two types of exchange. The latent purpose of the exchange of gifts is to establish conditions of solidarity, the "precontractual" elements of social interaction which include the obligation to engage in social interaction and to uphold one's obligations; or in other words generalized exchange, if successful, helps to establish the conditions of basic trust and solidarity in society, to uphold what Durkheim has called the precontractual elements of social life.[14]

From the perspective of the participants in any social activity, the mechanisms of generalized exchange perform functions of security or insurance against risks and uncertainties in the social "open" market or power interchange or struggle.

IV.

The institutionalization of generalized exchange is effected on two levels in every society. One level is the institutionalization of limitations to the free

12. M. Mauss, *The Gift, Forms and Functions of Exchange in Archaic Societies*, London, Cohen and West, 1954 ["Essai sur le don," *Année sociologique*, n.s., 1 (1925), 30–126]; C. Levi-Strauss, *The Elementary Structures of Kinship*, Boston, Beacon Press, 1969 (1949); T. Parsons, "On the Concept of Influence," *Public Opinion Quarterly*, 27 (Spring 1963), 37–62; idem, "Rejoinder to Bauer and Coleman," *ibid.*, 83–92; idem, "On the Concept of Political Power," *Proceedings of the American Philosophical Society*, 103:3 (1963), 232–62; J. S. Coleman, "Political Money," *The American Political Science Review*, 64:4 (Dec. 1970), 1074–87.

13. The difference between specific and generalized exchange as presented here is not identical to the difference between restricted and generalized exchange as presented above all by C. Levi-Strauss. The latter distinction refers mostly to the scope and "directedness" of the exchange of the restricted one as against the indirection of the latter. Specific exchange can be both direct (barter) and indirect, and the more indirect it is the more dependent it is on generalized media of exchange: money, political loyalties or influence. The proper functioning of such media does in a way exacerbate the problem of trust and the importance of appropriate mechanisms of generalized exchange. Generalized exchange is almost always less direct, but the scope of the persons or spheres it involves may vary greatly.

14. E. Durkheim, *On the Division of Labor in Society*, New York, Macmillan, 1933. For further treatment of the precontractual elements of social life see for instance T. Parsons, *The Structure of Social Action*, esp. 301–38, 460–70 and 708–14; J. A. Davis, "Structural Balance, Mechanical Solidarity, and Interpersonal Relations," *American Journal of Sociology*, 68:4 (Jan. 1963), 444–62; and H. Befu, "Gift-Giving and Social Reciprocity in Japan," *France-Asie/Asia*, 188 (Hiver 1966/67), 161–77. See

exchange of resources in social interaction, and the concomitant structuring of the flow of resources and social relations in ways that differ from "free" (market or power) exchange. Such structuring stands in contrast to the purely conditional, instrumental or mostly adaptive, activities that characterize simple or specific exchange. But it does not deny adaptive or instrumental relations. Rather it creates a connection between instrumental and power relations on the one hand and solidarity and expressive relations on the other.

The basic paradigm of such relations can be found in kinship systems—in amity, which Meyer Fortes has designated as the core of kinship, and which implies unconditional obligations rooted in the basic components of personal and collective identity and upheld by moral sanctions.[15] Most of these characteristics, especially the pronounced emphasis on unconditional relations as based on certain attributes, whether primordial, sacred, or civil, is shared by kinship with other socially ascriptive collectivities or orders, such as communities, strata, nations, and the like. In all such frameworks the setting up of unconditionalities takes place first through the institutionalization of various titles, i.e., of ascriptive (often hierarchical, power-based) specifications of limitations on institutional interaction or exchange and on access to positions.[16] Second, limitation on exchange of resources is effected through the establishment of public goods provided by the collectivity (e.g., the government), such as defense or health services. These benefits are so set up that if one member of a collectivity receives them, they cannot be denied to other members; and they establish the prices taken—directly or indirectly through taxation—from different groups for this purpose.[17] Third, the structuring of the flow of resources is manifest in the public distribution of private goods, that is, the direct allocation of services and rewards to groups of the population according to

---

also T. Parsons, "Durkheim on Religion Revisited: Another Look at the Elementary Forms of Religious Life," in C. Y. Glock and P. E. Hammond, eds., *Beyond the Classics: Essays in the Scientific Study of Religion*, New York, Harper and Row, 1973, 156–81.

15. M. Fortes, *Kinship and the Social Order*, Chicago, Aldine, 1965. On the societal significance of this aspect of reliability as connected to the "moral" realm of kinship see M. Bloch, "The Long Term and the Short Term: The Economic and Political Significance of Kinship," in J. Goody, *The Character of Kinship*, 75–89.

16. On unconditionalities and titles see S. N. Eisenstadt, *Social Differentiation and Stratification*, Glenview, IL. Scott Foresman and Co., 1971, and idem, "Prestige, Participation and Strata Formation," in J. A. Jackson, ed., *Social Stratification*, Cambridge, Cambridge University Press, 1968, 62–103.

17. On public goods see A. Kuhn, *The Study of Society, A Unified Approach*, Homewood, IL. The Dorsey Press, 1963; M. Olson, *The Logic of Collective Action*, New York, Schocken, 1968; O. E. Williamson, "Market and Hierarchies: Some Elementary Considerations," *American Economic Review*, 63:2 (May 1973), 316–25; and idem, *Some Notes on the Economics of Atmosphere*, Fels Discussion Papers No. 29, University of Pennsylvania, The Fels Center of Government, 1973. See also S. N. Eisenstadt and M. Curelaru, *The Form of Sociology, Paradigms and Crises*, New York, Wiley and Sons, 1976, 364 ff.

criteria that differ widely from those of pure exchange. The flow of relations in the specific patterns of generalized exchange is structured in all these ways and distinguish it from the routine "market" type of specific interpersonal or institutional interrelations and exchange. The institutionalization of generalized exchange need not be egalitarian. It often contains strong elements of power and hierarchy, but here structured in ways that differ from direct power relations or market-like exchange.

V.

The second level of institutionalization of generalized exchange consists of interactions that symbolize and legitimize the process of unconditionalities and of the establishment of conditions of trust and of the precontractual element of social life.

The gift, as analyzed by Mauss, is one such mechanism, but certainly it is not the only one. Hospitality—also recently studied, significantly enough, by scholars close to those studying patron-client relations—obtains above all in primitive or traditional societies but probably has similar functions in some more modern ones as well. Ritual kinship and friendship are also illustrations of the mechanisms of generalized exchange.[18] But mechanisms such as gifts, hospitality, or ritualized friendship, more visible in primitive societies or in small, informal sectors of more complex societies, are not of course the only ones in any society through which the precontractual bases of social order, the conditions and frameworks of generalized exchange, are structured.

Even in the smaller primitive or traditional societies exchange of gifts is, as C. Lévi-Strauss, M. Fortes, and M. Sahlins[19] have shown, closely interwoven

18. On hospitality see J. Pitt-Rivers, "The Stranger, the Guest and the Hostile Host: Introduction to the Study of the Laws of Hospitality," in J. G. Peristiany, ed., *Contributions*, 13–30; and the issue of *Anthropological Quarterly* dealing with "Visiting Patterns and Social Dynamics in Eastern Mediterranean Communities," 47:1 (Jan. 1974). On ritual kinship and friendship see S. N. Eisenstadt, "Ritualized Personal Relations," *Man*, N.S., 96 (1956), 1–6; S. Gudeman, "The Compadrazgo as a Reflection of the Natural and Spiritual Person," The Curl Prize Essay 1971, *Proceedings of the Royal Anthropological Institute*, (1971), 45–71; E. N. Goody, "Forms of Pro-Parenthood," in J. Goody, ed. *Kinship*, Harmondsworth, Penguin Modern Sociology Series, 1971, 331–45; J. Pitt-Rivers, "Kinship: III—Pseudo-Kinship," in *International Encyclopaedia of the Social Sciences*, vol. 8, 406–13; and the contributions by Wolf, Foster, Ishino, Wolf and Mintz quoted in note 1. For the structuring of societal trust as related to friendship and kinship see S. N. Eisenstadt, "Friendship and the Structure of Trust and Solidarity in Society," in E. Leyton, ed., *The Compact, Selected Dimensions of Friendship*, Newfoundland Social & Economic Papers No. 3, Memorial University of Newfoundland, 1974, 138–45. The fluidity of these mechanisms in respect to their ideological conceptualization and application in social relations is analyzed in African context by J. S. La Fontaine, "The Mother's Brother as Patron," *Archives Européennes de Sociologie*, 16 (1975), 76–92; and idem, "Unstructured Social Relations," *The West African Journal of Sociology and Political Science*, 1:1 (Oct. 1975), 51–81.

19. On reciprocity and exchange in primitive societies see M. Sahlins, "On the Sociology of Primitive Exchange," in M. Banton, ed., *The Relevance of Models for Social Anthropology*, New York, Praeger, 1965, 139–236; and idem, *Tribesmen*, Englewood Cliffs, NJ. 1968, chs. 4 and 5.

with the whole dynamics of physical proximity of intermarriage and exchange of brides, processes that maintain relations between the basic units of the society.

In more developed societies many of these functions are performed, as has been shown by T. Parsons or L. Mayhew among others, on the macrosocietal level by social mechanisms like citizenship, by various legal frameworks that uphold conceptions of rights. They are closely related to the major ritual occasions that uphold the basic symbols of societal identity and social order in every society and legitimize this very exchange.[20]

VI.

A crucial aspect of any social structure is the relation of the institutional links between generalized and specific exchange and especially of the degree of linkage between, first, membership in major ascriptive categories and sectors of a society on the one hand and access to the centers of power, to positions of control of production, and to the major markets on the other; and second, between such access and the relative standing of different groups or categories in the major institutional markets, that is, between ownership of resources and the ability to control their use in broader settings. Such linkages generate relations between inequalities in the different aspects of social order enumerated above: between inequalities in the ascriptive sectors; in access to the major centers of power and institutional markets; and inequality within these markets. In this way they shape the structure of crucial aspects of social hierarchies in a society.

It is from the point of view of the relations between generalized and specific exchange that some of the major characteristics of patron-client relationships stand out and can be distinguished from other kinds of social relation and organization, and it is the analytic features and dynamic propensities of what, for lack of a better word, we shall call the "clientelistic" model of structuring the relations between generalized and specific exchange that best explain the crucial analytical characteristics of patron-client relations.

The Clientelistic Model of Relations Between Generalized and Specific Exchange in a Comparative Perspective

VII.

We shall now present the most important characteristics of such models which have been usually compared with patron-client relations—namely, the kinship,

20. T. Parsons et al., eds., *Theories of Society*, Glencoe, IL. The Free Press, 1961; idem, "On the Concept of Value Commitment," *Sociological Inquiry*, 38:2 (Spring 1968), 135–60; L. Mayhew, "Ascription in Modern Societies," *ibid.*, 105–20; T. S. Turner, "Parson's Concept of 'Generalized Media of Social Interaction' and its Relevance for Social Anthropology," *ibid.*, 121–34.

ascriptive hierarchical (caste or feudal) ones and the "universalistic"—pluralistic, monolithic (totalitarian), consociational—ones.[21]

Most comparisons in the literature have, with the partial exception of Gellner, Waterbury, and Wolf, defined some of the major differences between these types of social organization and patron-client relations in rather concrete, organizational terms.[22] Our own emphasis, however, is on viewing them not as types of social organization but rather as models of structuring the flow of resources and of interpersonal interaction and exchanges in society, and especially as models of structuring relations between generalized and specific exchange in general and of linkages between the various inequalities enumerated above in particular. In any concrete social setting—a society or sector thereof—different models may differ in importance and, although one is usually predominant, quite often conflicts develop between it and others.

21. On the pluralistic model and open market bureaucratic societies see S. N. Eisenstadt, ed., *Political Sociology*, 488–521; and idem, "Bureaucracy, Bureaucratization, Markets and Power Structure," in idem, *Essays on Comparative Institutions*, New York, Wiley and Sons, 1965, 177–215. On the totalitarian model see Z. Brzezinski, "The Nature of the Soviet System," *Slavic Review*, 20:3 (Oct. 1961), 354–68; R. Lowenthal, "The Logic of One-Party Rule," in A. Brumberg, ed., *Russia under Krushchev: An Anthology from Problems of Communism*, New York, Praeger, 1962; T. H. Rigby, "Traditional, Market, and Organizational Societies and the USSR," *World Politics*, 16:4 (July 1964), 539–57; and J. J. Linz, "Totalitarian and Authoritarian Regimes," in F. I. Greenstein and N. W. Polsby, eds., *Handbook of Political Science*, Reading, MA, Addison-Wesley, 1975, 175–411. On caste systems see L. Dumont, *Homo hierarchicus: Essai sur le système des castes*, Gallimard, 1966; idem, ed., *Contributions to Indian Sociology*, Paris–The Hague, Mouton, 1966; M. Singer, "The Social Organization of Indian Civilization," *Diogenes*, 45 (Winter 1964), 84–119; idem. ed., *Traditional India: Structure and Change*, Austin, American Folklore Society, University of Texas Press, 1959; M. N. Srinivas, *Caste in Modern India*, New York, Asia Publishing House, 1962; and K. David, "Hierarchy and Equivalence in Jaffna, North Sri Lanka: Normative Codes as Mediator," in idem, ed., *The New Wind, Changing Identities in South Asia*, Paris–The Hague, Mouton, 1976, 179–226. On feudal models see S. N. Eisenstadt, *Political Sociology*, ch. 7. On consociational models see H. Daalder, "The Consociational Democracy Theme," *World Politics*, 26:4 (July 1974), 604–21; A. Liphart, "Consociational Democracy," idem, 21 (1969); idem, *The Politics of Accommodation: Pluralism and Democracy in the Netherlands*, Beverly Hills, California: University Press, 1968. See also G. Lembruch, *Proporzdemokratie: Politische System und Politische Kultur im der Schweiz und Oesterreich*, Tubingen, Mohr, 1968; idem, "Konkordanzdemokratie im Politische System der Schweiz," *Vierteljahresschrift*, 9:3 (1968); and idem, "Konkordanzdemokratie im Internationalen System," *Politische Viertel jahresschrift*, Vol. 10, Sonderheft; and S. N. Eisenstadt, "Bureaucracy, Bureaucratization, Markets and Power Structure."

22. See for example A. Weingrod, "Patrons, Patronage and Political Parties"; A. Hall, "Concepts and Terms. Patron-Client Relationship," *Journal of Peasant Studies;MDIÑ* 1 (1974), 506–09; L. Grazziano, *A Conceptual Framework for the Study of Clientelism*; J. Boissevain, "Patrons and Brokers"; A. Blok, "Variations in Patronage," *Sociologische Gids*, 16:6 (Nov.–Dec. 1969), 365–78. For notable applications of such an approach to case studies see P. A. Allum, *Politics and Society in Postwar Naples*; S. F. Silverman, "Patronage and Community Nation Relationships in Central Italy," *Ethnology*, 4:2 (1965), 172–89; J. Boissevain, "When the saints go marching out. Reflections on the decline of patronage in Malta," in E. Gellner and J. Waterbury, *Patrons and Clients*, 81–96. Compare these definitions with E. Gellner, "Patrons and Clients"; J. Waterbury, "An attempt to put patrons and clients in their place"; and E. Wolf, "Kinship, Friendship and Patron Client Relationships."

Similarly, relatively similar models may exist, as we have implied above, in a variety of societal frameworks, at different levels of economic development and in differing political regimes. We shall present here only a very brief analysis of the different models and shall concentrate for the most part on analysis of the clientelistic model, and then briefly compare it with some of the others.

The ideal model of corporate kinship relations, found above all in various "primitive" societies, assumes that the access to most major markets as well as public goods is acquired through membership in such (often corporate) kinship groups; that a large part of exchange of resources is effected through the corporate activities of these groups or within them, and that in fact most major markets as well as public goods are embedded in the relations between them. Similar "ideal" premises can be found in ascriptively (mainly kinship) based hierarchical systems. The fullest expression can of course be found in the Indian caste system, but many elements exist also in other primitive or archaic or feudal societies.

In common with the kinship model, there is also the assumption that most (even if certainly not all) significant specific exchanges are made through ascriptive groups. Thus they combine to a great degree generalized and specific exchanges, even if the former are more fully elaborated in special ritual occasions. Whatever specific exchanges are made more openly, they are structured so as not to impinge on the dominant hierarchical ascriptive model. The principal difference between the hierarchical and the pure corporate kinship model is, of course, in the basic premises of inequality in the relations between the ascriptive groups, and hence usually in a sharper stress on the hierarchical relations between them.

This linkage between generalized and specific exchange generates a certain pattern of linkages between inequalities in the major dimensions of the institutional order. In the ideal premises of such models there is a very close relation, ideally almost a complete linkage, between the relative standing of any group or social category in the ascriptive hierarchical sphere on the one hand and its access to the centers of society, to the setting up of public goods, and especially to public distribution of private goods, and to the major institutional markets on the other. Thus in a sense either the virtual nonexistence or relative lack of importance of open markets, or of any significant autonomous activities within them, is assumed.

The "official" model of open-market or bureaucratic societies assumes that access to major markets, centers of power and the setting up of public goods (as well as, in principle, the public distribution of private goods) is vested in all the members of the wider community, without regard to their membership in any other ascriptive hierarchical subunits (even if some of the criteria for setting up public goods and publicly distributing private goods discriminate in favor of certain social categories such as the "poor" or the "deprived"). It also assumes that all members may participate in the struggle to set up the criteria of distribution and that specific exchange in open markets will not be legally conditioned by membership in any subgroup.

This broad model can be subdivided into several submodels of which three—the open-pluralistic, the monolithic-totalitarian and the consociational—are the most important. In the pluralistic model predominant in most Western European societies, in the United States, and the first Dominions, the major groups have free autonomous access to the centers of power, to the setting up of public goods and basic units of production and markets. In the monolithic system, predominant especially in modern totalitarian societies with antecedents in monolithic imperial systems, major groups have access to the markets and public goods, but their access to the centers of power and to publicly distributed private goods is severely controlled by the center, although not, officially at least, by any single especially ascriptive subgroup within the society.

In the consociational model, lately also designated as Proporzdemokratie, which is prevalent above all in small European democracies like the Netherlands, Switzerland, and Austria, the relations between generalized and specific exchange are much more complicated than in the universalistic one. Basic titles (such as citizenship and all the duties and rights it entails) are vested, according to universalistic criteria, in all members of the broader collectivity (nation). As against this, access to major centers of power, as well as to many public goods and publicly distributed private goods is to a large degree mediated by the (representatives of the) major consociational segments, be they religious groups, political parties, local units and the like. Within such segments, however, access to power is open to everybody. Beyond this, within most consociational systems relatively wide markets develop, especially in the economic field. Access to them is in principle open to all members of the society, and the specific exchanges undertaken within them are not bound to membership in any of the ascriptive relationships.

The major difference between such consociational and corporatist systems, as found for instance in Latin America,[23] is that within the latter the access to the centers of power within the corporative units is not vested in an autonomous way in their membership; and that the access not only to public

---

23. On corporatism in Latin America see J. Malloy, "Authoritarianism and Corporatism in Latin America: The Modal Pattern," in idem, ed., *Authoritarianism and Corporatism in Latin America*, Pittsburgh, University of Pittsburgh Press, 1977, 3–19; D. A. Chalmers, "The Politicized State in Latin America," in *ibid.*, 23–46; G. A. O'Donnell, "Corporatism and the Question of the State," in *ibid.*, 47–87; S. Schwartzman, "Back to Weber: Corporatism and Patrimonialism in the Seventies," in *ibid.*, 89–106; and R. R. Kaufman, "Corporatism, Clientelism, and Partisan Conflict: A Study of Seven Latin American Countries," in *ibid.*, 109–48; X. Stephen, ed., *Authoritarian Brazil*, New Haven, Yale University Press, 1973.

goods and to public distribution of private goods but also to large parts of the seemingly open markets is mediated by the corporative units.

VIII.

As opposed to all the above models of structuring relations between generalized and specific exchange, the clientelistic model is predicated on the existence of some tension between potentially broad, sometimes even latent, universalistic or semiuniversalistic, premises; and on the free flow of resources and relatively broad scope of markets derivable from these premises on the one hand and continual attempts to limit such free flow on the other. These premises are evident in societies or sectors thereof in the fact that, unlike societies in which the hereditary ascriptive model is predominant, the members of various strata may in principle be able to obtain direct access to the means of production, to the major markets and to the centers of power. They may organize themselves for such access and for the ensuring of their own control of the use of their resources in broader settings; concomitantly the centers of these societies may develop autonomous relations to the broader strata for which the clients and brokers are recruited.[24]

But at the same time, for reasons we shall analyze in greater detail later on, within these societies continuous attempts are made to circumvent these potentialities: to limit, first, the free access of broader strata to the markets and centers by the monopolization by potential patrons and brokers of those positions that control such access; and second, the use and conversion of their resources. It is the combination of potentially open access to the markets with continuous semi-institutionalized attempts to limit free access that is the crux of the clientelist model.

Thus the structuring of relations between generalized and specific exchange implied in the clientelistic model is characterized above all by a special type of the two linkages between the aspects of institutional structure mentioned above as crucial to the structuring of such relations. The first such link-

---

24. For examples of the limitation in scope and convertibility of the free flow of resources in these societies see R. Aya, *The Missed Revolution. The Fate of Rural Rebels in Sicily and Southern Spain 1840–1950;* J. K. Campbell, "Two Case-Studies of Marketing and Patronage in Greece," in J. G. Peristiany, ed., *Contributions to Mediterranean Sociology,* Paris–The Hague, Mouton, 1968, 143–54; S. Sayari, "Political Patronage in Turkey," in Gellner and Waterbury, *Patrons and Clients,* 103–13. For the pressures on patronalistic arrangements in these societies see J. Boissevain, "Poverty and Politics in a Sicilian Agrotown," *International Archives of Ethnography,* 50 (1966), 198–236; S. Tarrow, "Economic Development and the Transformation of the Italian Party System," *Comparative Politics,* 1:2 (Jan. 1969), 161–83; and idem,"Local Constraints on Regional Reform. A Comparison of Italy and France," *Comparative Politics,* 7:1 (Oct. 1974), 1–36. For a general treatment of this subject see S. N. Eisenstadt, "Beyond Classical Revolution Processes of Change and Revolution in Neo-patrimonial Societies," in idem, *Revolution and the Transformation of Societies. A Comparative Study of Civilizations,* New York: The Free Press, 1978, 273–310; see also below.

age is one between the respective standing of the potential patrons and clients in the semiascriptive hierarchical subcommunities or subsectors of the society on the one hand, and the control of access—to the center or centers of the society, to the bases of production, to the major institutional markets, to the setting up of most public goods, and to the public distribution of private goods—on the other. The second linkage is between access to markets and centers and the use and conversion of potentially free resources in these markets.

The crucial aspect of these two linkages in the clientelistic model is that they are very strong, yet not fully legitimized. They are based on the clients' abdication of their potentially autonomous access to major markets, to positions of control over use of resources or to the center and to the setting-up of public goods and services except through the mediation of some patron (whether person or organization, i.e., party or trade union). Such mediation is contingent on the clients' having entered into a relation of exchange with the patron. The exchange has many of the aspects of the routine exchange of goods or services within the various institutional markets and necessarily limits the scope and convertibility of resources freely exchanged there.

IX.

Thus it can be seen that the clientelistic model can be distinguished from other such models along several dimensions. It differs from models like corporate kinship groups or ascriptively based hierarchical ones in that it is predicated on the existence of central (and not only marginal) markets and of the organization of a means of production not embedded in such ascriptive units or in the relations between them. It is predicated on a situation where there is already a difference between ownership of resources and control of their use in broader settings and on a certain segregation between the resources exchanged in generalized and in specific exchange.

As against the more "open" universalistic models, whether pluralistic, monolithical, or consociational, which tend to countervail any attempts to limit the access of different groups to the bases of production and to positions of control of the use of resources in centers and markets, it is the very essence of the clientelistic model that it establishes and maintains such limitations even if they are not derived, as in the kinship or ascriptive-hierarchical models, from the basic premises of the society. The clientelistic model is the closest, as indicated above, of all the models to the corporatist one. Indeed in many societies with a strong corporatist element, patron-client relations tend to develop in close relation to the former, although the reverse is not always true. The major difference between them is that the purely corporatist model does not necessarily include so many package deals in the concrete relations between the major (corporate) units and their membership.

X.

These differences between the clientelistic and other models are most evident in the linkages between inequalities in the major dimensions of institutional life and of the structuring of social hierarchies which it generates and which are markedly different from those that develop either in the universalistic or ascriptive-kinship hierarchical societies. In common with the latter societies there develops in the patron-client nexus a very close linkage, yet not one always so precisely and normatively defined, between ascriptive-hierarchical standing on the one hand and access to power, to public goods, and to major institutional markets on the other.

It is the continuous overwhelming de facto existence of such linkage that makes the inequality inherent in patron-client relations seem to be characterized by a certain totality or continuity that seemingly cannot, within the context of these relations, be easily changed. It is the totality or continuity of such inequality that distinguishes patron-client relationships from the "chance" inequalities that may develop within the markets and in access to them of both the universalistic and the ascriptive hierarchical societies.

And yet, despite the seeming comprehensiveness of this inequality, in fact the concrete linkage between the inequalities in the major dimensions of institutional order that develop in the clientelist model is rather fragile. This fragility is evident in several closely connected aspects. First, unlike the ascriptive-hierarchical societies such inequalities, and above all the linkages between them, are not, in clientelist societies or sectors thereof, fully prescribed, legitimized, or assured. Indeed, as has been already implied in our preceding discussion, in most of these societies they are set up against some of their basic formal, more open, universalistic premises.

Second, and closely related, is the fact that the relative hierarchical standing of different actors—patrons, brokers, and clients—is not always fully prescribed and frequent disputes may arise with respect to it.[25]

Third, there is the fact that the clients are sometimes, potentially or actually, able to accumulate resources in the various markets (especially, but not only, in the political one) which are not commensurate with their relatively low ascriptive standing, and, when combined with the latent broader premises

25. On these aspects of patron-client relations and especially on their fragility, see among others A. Blok, *The Mafia of a Sicilian Village;* E. Wolf, "On Peasant Rebellions," *International Social Science Journal,* 21:2(1969), 286–93; E. Gellner, "How to live in anarchy," *The Listener,* 3:4(1958), 579–83; idem, "Patrons and Clients," F. H. Cardoso, "Tensoes sociais no campo e reforma agraria," *Revista brasileira de estudos politicos,* 12 (Oct. 1961), 7–26; P. Friedrich, *Agrarian Revolt in a Mexican Village,* Englewood Cliffs, Prentice-Hall, 1970; A. Hottinger, "Zuama in Historical Perspective," in L. Binder, ed., *Politics in Lebanon,* New York, Wiley and Sons, 1966, 85–105; D. Pool *The Politics of Patronage: Elites and Social Structure in Iraq;* and S. el-Messiri, "The changing role of the futuwwa."

of these systems, may threaten the patrons' monopoly of access to markets and to the center or centers of the society.[26]

SOCIETAL CONDITIONS GENERATING PATRON-CLIENT RELATIONS

XI.

In order to understand more fully the relations between these characteristics of the clientelistic model of relations between generalized and specific exchange on the one hand, and the core characteristics of patron-client relations on the other, we have to analyze the clientelistic model.

Let us begin with those societies or sectors thereof within which the clientelistic model is the predominant one, that is, in most historical and contemporary Mediterranean areas (Catholic, Greek, and to a smaller degree, Moslem), Latin American, and Southeast Asian societies like Thailand, Burma, Malaysia, or Indonesia. Building on the extensive literature on patron-client relations, we shall attempt to analyze in a systematic way the most important characteristics of three aspects of the structure of these societies which have been stressed in that literature—namely, the economic sphere, the internal structure of the major groups, strata, and social classes, and the prevalent cultural orientations—and those connections between them that are most important for the understanding of the clientelistic model and of the dynamics of patron-client relations.

XII.

Most of these societies have been chiefly characterized by extensive and extractive economies, with a relatively low level of internal specialization between internal economic units, and consequently a weak propensity to develop or incorporate technological innovations oriented to the intensification of their bases of production; with trade oriented outward, regulated mostly by the rulers or by external groups, impinging only slightly on relatively narrow internal markets and increasing only indirectly the internal flow of resources.[27]

---

26. On possibilities of severing the relationship, see for instance A. Blok, "Mafia and Peasant Rebellion as Contrasting Factors in Sicilian Latifundism," *Archives Européennes de Sociologie*, 10 (1969), 95–116; P. Singelmann, "The Closing Triangle: Critical Notes on a Model for Peasant Mobilization in Latin America," *Comparative Studies in Society and History*, 17:4 (Oct. 1975), 389–409. The quasi-legal or quasi-ritual fixation of incumbency to roles may provide a way of avoiding the above possibility. See E. L. Peters, "The Tied and the Free (Lybia)," in J. G. Peristiany, ed., *Contributions to Mediterranean Sociology*, 167–88; and I. Ishino, "The Oyabun-Kobun."

27. For these concepts see K. E. Polanyi et al., eds., *Trade and Market in Early Empires*, New York, The Free Press, 1957; G. Dalton, *Primitive, Archaic and Modern Economies: Essays of Karl Polanyi*, New York, Anchor Books, 1968. On the economic structure and process in these societies see S. N. Eisenstadt, *Traditional Patrimonialism and Modern Neopatrimonialism*, Beverly Hills, Sage Research Papers in the Social Sciences, 1973; for illustrative materials see B. Rivlin and J. S. Szyliowicz, eds., *The Contemporary Middle East: Traditions and Innovations*, New York, Random House, 1965, esp. 297–324,

Within these economies certain policies, as well as systems of property, tend to develop; the most important among these policies are in the first place (to use Hoselitz's nomenclature)[28] mostly of expansive character; that is, they aim at expansion of control of large territories rather than intrinsic ones and are characterized by intensive exploitation of a fixed resource basis. Second, these policies are mostly extractive and redistributive ones.

In many of these societies and especially in the more centralized ones in the "traditional" periods of their history, the rulers attempted to control the ownership of land either by vesting all the ownership in their own hands or those of fellow aristocrats and making most of the peasant families into tenants of some sort and/or by supervising and controlling the degree to which the plots of land owned by various kinship units could be transferred freely. Such policies were in sharp contrast to those of the emperors in many centralized imperial systems who often attempted to weaken the position of the aristocracy by promoting a relatively free peasantry.[29]

In more modern settings, there has developed a certain continuation of such dispersed modes of ownership in land as well as a strong tendency toward the development of urban service—sectors also controlled by the state. These economies were often connected with absentee ownership, with a chasm between urban and rural sectors and with oligarchic land-owning groups largely oriented to external markets.[30]

In close relation to these policies, there grew up within these societies specific patterns of absorption of highly active differentiated economic groups, especially merchants or manufacturers, which could contribute to the accumu-

368–74; F. H. Golay et al., eds., *Underdevelopment and Economic Nationalism in Southeast Asia,* Ithaca, Cornell University, Department of Asian Studies, 1967; Soedjatmoko, *Economic Development as a Cultural Problem,* Ithaca, Cornell University, Department of Asian Studies, 1968; T. H. Silcock, ed., *Readings in Malayan Economics,* Singapore, Eastern Universities Press, 1961; H. Jaguaribe, *Desenvolvimento economico e desenvolvimento politico,* Rio de Janeiro, Fundo de Cultura, 1962; and J. Schneider and P. Schneider, *Culture and Political Economy in Western Sicily.*

28. B. F. Hoselitz, *Sociological Aspects of Economic Growth,* New York, The Free Press, 1960, 85–114.

29. On these polities see S. N. Eisenstadt, *The Political System of Empires,* New York, The Free Press, 1963, esp. ch. 7, and idem, *Political Sociology.*

30. See I. M. Wallerstein, ed., *Social Change. The Colonial Structure,* New York, Wiley and Sons, 1969. S. N. Eisenstadt, *Traditional Patrimonialism and Modern Neopatrimonialism* contains detailed bibliographical notes on these topics. On illustrations specifically from the literature on patron-client relations, see for instance J. Schneider and P. Schneider, *Culture and Political Economy in Western Sicily;* F. Snowden, "On the Social Origins of Agrarian Fascism in Italy," *Archives Européennes de Sociologie,* 13:2 (1972), 268–95; J. Schneider, "Family Patrimonies and Economic Behaviour in Western Sicily," *Anthropological Quarterly,* 42:3 (Sept. 1969), 109–29; H. Hess, *Mafia and Mafiosi,* E. Feder, *Violencia y despojo del campesino: el latifundismo en América Latina,* Mexico, Siglo xxi, 1975 (1971); R. Stavenhagen, "Social Aspects of Agrarian Structure in Mexico," *Social Research,* 33:3 (1966), 463–85; M. Rossi-Doria, "The Land Tenure System and Class in Southern Italy."

lation and extraction of resources. Both traditional and modern rulers were indeed very often interested in co-opting such units, but only so long as such units were "external" to the central structural core of these societies; so long as they did not impinge on their internal structural arrangements and especially on the basic conception of the relations between center and periphery. Hence they incorporated them in special segregated enclaves. This tendency explains the strong predisposition in many such societies to enable ethnically alien groups, which could be segregated to an even greater degree than indigenous elements, to engage in structurally more differentiated activities.[31] Thus, in most such societies, there tends to develop a type of dual, bisectoral economy, composed of one extensive internal sector and another more intensive externally oriented one, the two sectors being connected by the extractive and regulatory policies of the central elites. These are the economic structures and policies that have been prone to become dependent on external forces and to develop, when new openings become available in the international framework, in the direction of growing dependency.[32]

XIII.

Closely related to this type of economic structure are the internal characteristics of the major social groups in these societies. The most important one, which has been stressed in the literature, has been internal weakness, evident above all in a relatively low degree of internal solidarity and of symbolic, and sometimes also of organizational, autonomy, especially of the lower groups of the society.[33] A closer look at the evidence indicates, however, that it is not

31. P. T. Bauer and B. S. Yamey, *The Economics of Underdeveloped Countries,* Cambridge, Cambridge University Press, 1957; C. S. Belshaw, "Approaches to Articulation in the Economy," in idem, *Traditional Exchange and Modern Markets,* Englewood Cliffs, Prentice-Hall, 1965, 84–107. See also S. N. Eisenstadt, *Traditional Patrimonialism and Modern Neopatrimonialism.*

32. The concept of the dual character of these economies in colonial settings was formulated originally by J. H. Boeke, *Tropisch-Koloniale Staathuishoudkunde,* 1910. For its treatment see J. S. Furnivall, *Netherlands India. A Study of Plural Economy,* Cambridge, Cambridge University Press, 1939; J. H. Boeke, *The Structure of the Netherlands Indian Economy,* New York, Institute of Pacific Relations, 1942; and idem, *Economics and Economic Policy of Dual Societies,* New York, Institute of Pacific Relations, 1953. On patterns of dependency in some of these societies see C. Furtado, *Obstacles to the Development of Latin America,* New York, Anchor Books, 1970; J. S. Furnivall, *Colonial Policy and Practice: A Comparative Study of Burma and Netherlands India,* Cambridge, Cambridge University Press, 1948; V. Turner, ed., *Colonization in Africa 1870–1960,* Cambridge, Cambridge University Press, 1971; S. N. Eisenstadt, *Essays on Social and Political Aspects of Economic Development,* Paris–The Hague, Mouton, 1958; S. Schwartzman, *São Paulo e o Estado Nacional,* São Paulo, DIFEL, 1975; P. Schneider, "Coalition Formation and Colonialism in Western Sicily"; L. Guasti, "Peru: Clientelism and Internal Control," in Schmidt et al., *Friends, Followers and Factions,* 422–38; B. Stallings, *Economic Dependency in Africa and Latin America,* Beverly Hills, Sage Professional Papers in Comparative Politics, 1972.

33. This point can be found in E. Banfield, *The Moral Basis of a Backward Society;* E. Wolf, *Peasants,* Englewood Cliffs, Prentice-Hall, 1966; J. Schneider, "Of Vigilance and Virgins"; H. Alavi, "Peasant Classes and Primordial Loyalties," *Journal of Peasant Studies,* 1:1 (Oct. 1973), 23–62; J. D. Powell,

only the lower groups, but also as a rule all the major societal actors—the center or centers, the broader periphery, and the major elites—who evince these characteristics. Or, in other words, all these social actors show, in those societies in which the clientelistic model is predominant, a relatively low degree of autonomous access to the major resources needed to implement their goals, and to the control, in broader settings, of their own resources.

Such a relatively low level of autonomy is evident in the centers of the societies in which the clientelistic model is predominant, not necessarily in the amount of resources at their disposal or even in their ability to penetrate the periphery administratively, although in many of these societies (such as early modern Italy or Greece, or many African societies) the centers were very weak. But even when the centers were much more compact and able to establish relatively wide administrative frameworks, their relative structural weakness was seen in their inability to act autonomously distinct from the mode of use of resources found in the periphery, and to penetrate the periphery in an independent way. Of crucial importance here is the fact that in most of these societies there were few symbolic-institutional differences between center and periphery, and that the differentiation that existed was based mainly on ecological distinctiveness, symbolic articulation, and on a greater concentration of population, but not on a clear distinction from the periphery.[34]

"Peasant Society and Clientelism"; A. Blok, "Coalitions in Sicilian Peasant Society," in J. Boissevain and C. Mitchell, eds., *Network Analysis Studies in Human Interaction,* Paris–The Hague, Mouton, 1973, 151–66; M. Johnson, "Political bosses and their gangs"; and F. Lynch, *Four Readings in Philippine Values,* Quezon City, Institute of Philippine Culture Papers No. 2, Ateneo de Manila Press, 1964.

34. On the distinction between strong and weak centers see S. N. Eisenstadt, *Political Sociology,* idem, *Social Differentiation and Stratification,* esp. ch. 8; and idem, *Traditional Patrimonialism and Modern Neopatrimonialism.* Further elaboration can be found in idem, *Revolution and the Transformation of Societies,* esp. chs. IV, V. The structurally weak character of those centers was a recurrent theme in the literature. See for instance S. Tarrow, *From Center to Periphery,* idem, "Local Constraints"; Silverman, "Patronage and Community-Nation Relationships"; C. H. Landé, "Networks and Groups in Southeast Asia"; and J. G. Scott, "Patron-Client Politics and Political Change." On the symbolic institutional characteristics of center and periphery see G. Roth, "Personal Rulership, Patrimonialism and Empire-Building in the New States," *World Politics,* 20:2 (Jan. 1968), 194–206; A. R. Zolberg, *Creating Political Order: The Party States of West Africa 1870–1960,* Cambridge, Cambridge University Press, 1971; F. W. Riggs, *Thailand: The Modernization of a Bureaucratic Polity,* Honolulu, East West Center Press, 1966; Thaung, "Burmese Kinship in Theory and Practice under the Reign of King Mindon," *Journal of the Burma Research Society,* 42:2 (1959), 171–85; B. Schrieke, *Indonesian Sociological Studies,* The Hague–Bandung, W. Van Hoeve, 1957; J. C. Van Lear, *Indonesian Trade and Society,* The Hague– Bandung, W. Van Hoeve, 1955, 1–221; J. K. Whitmore, *Vietnamese Adaptations of Chinese Government Structure in the Fifteenth Century,* New Haven, Yale University Southeast Asian Studies, 1970; R. Heine-Geldern, "Conception of State and Kinship in Southeast Asia," Southeast Asian Program Data paper No. 18, Ithaca, Cornell University Press, 1956, 1–13; L. Hanke, ed. *History of Latin American Civilization,* 2 vols., Boston, Little Brown, 1967; M. Sarfatti, *Spanish Bureaucratic Patrimonialism in America,* Berkeley, University of California Press, Institute of International Studies, Politics of Mod-

The resources and symbols of the centers have not been structured and organized through autonomous channels but rather through channels either embedded in the power domains of the periphery or structured according to principles very similar to those of the periphery. Similarly, in most of these societies the distinctiveness of the center was not connected with attempts to transform the periphery structurally and ideologically or to effect far-reaching changes in the periphery's basic conception of social order. Accordingly there were rather weak autonomous linkages between center and periphery, links that created but few basic structural changes within either sectors or strata of the periphery or within the center itself.

The center impinges on the local (rural, urban, or tribal) communities mainly in the form of administration of law, the maintenance of peace, exaction of taxation, provision of some distributive goods, and the maintenance of cultural and/or religious links to the center; and in most modern settings in the provision of public services. But, with few exceptions, most of these links were effected through existing local kinship—territorial and/or ritual—units and subcenters, and/or through patrimonial-like bureaucracies which, in modern settings, proliferated and monopolized the provision of services to the population. Parallel manifestations of relatively low levels of broader corporate symbolic or organizational autonomy can be identified in these societies in the different units of the periphery on all ladders of the social hierarchy.[35] The major societal units usually do not exhibit a strong collective consciousness and self-identity based on symbols of kinship, territoriality, class, or strata, or on other principles of social organization, whether community-, country- or sector-wide. Similarly, the units of the periphery have few mechanisms through which corporately to control access to outside resources and the loci of decisions that affect them or to gain autonomous control over the conversion of their own resources. Accordingly, the units of the periphery in these societies have relatively little capacity to influence the center either with respect to policy-making and allocation of resources or to the construction of the center's own symbols.

On the local level, most of these units—especially the villages, homesteads, and, in the urban settings (particularly the more modern ones), the neighborhoods or vocational or occupational groups—evince a low level of

---

ernization Series No. 1, 1966; C. H. Haring, *The Spanish Empire in America*, New York, Oxford University Press, 1947.

35. See for instance C. H. Landé, "Networks and Groups"; J. Boissevain, "Poverty and Politics"; D. Gilmore, "Class, Culture and Community Size in Spain"; D. Meertens, "South from Madrid: Regional Elites and Resistance," in J. Boissevain and J. Friedl, eds., *Beyond the Community: Social Process in Europe*, European-Mediterranean Study Group of the University of Amsterdam, 1975, 65–74.

community cohesion and solidarity or of solidary corporate organization.[36] Closely related to these characteristics is the structure of kinship in these societies on all, but probably especially on the lower (or at least more fully documented), local echelons of the social hierarchy among the peasants. The most important characteristics have been: the relative weakness of corporate kinship units in general and of unilineal kinship groups in particular; a tendency to bilateral kinship with a strong emphasis on matrilineal descent; a relatively high predilection to narrow and unstable, crosscutting kinship networks and alliances, with a marked tendency to lack clear boundaries of the kinship unit or network,[37] beyond some of the minimal demarcation of exogamous units.

XIV.

All these aspects of the low autonomy of the periphery coalesce in the major characteristics of the structuring of social hierarchies as they have developed in these societies.[38] Organizationally, their patterns of stratification were char-

36. See for example J. D. Powell, "Peasant Society and Clientelistic Politics," 411–25; R. Aya, *The Missed Revolution*, 22–23; J. Waterbury, *The Commander of the Faithful*; S. Tarrow, *Peasant Communism in Southern Italy*. In Sicily and other regions the overlapping and intermingling of occupational roles and identities can hamper the formation of broad categorical commitments. For Sicily see J. Schneider, "Family Patrimonies and Economic Behaviour in Western Sicily," and A. Blok, *The Mafia of a Sicilian Village 1860–1960*, Oxford, Basil Blackwell, 1974. See also Note 33.

37. On bilateral kinship and its societal implications see R. H. Pehrson, "Bilateral Kin Groupings as a Structural Type," *Journal of East Asiatic Studies*, 3 (1954), 199–202; W. Davenport, "Nonunilineal Descent and Descent Groups," *American Anthropologist*, 61 (1959), 557–72; O. Blehr, "Action Groups in a Society with Bilateral Kinship. A Case Study of the Faroe Islands," *Ethnology*, 3:3 (July 1963), 269–75; J. Pitt-Rivers, "The Kith and the Kin"; C. H. Landé, "Kinship and Politics in Pre-Modern and Nonwestern Societies," in J. T. McAlister Jr., ed., *Southeast Asia: The Politics of National Integration*, New York, Random House, 1973, 219–33; and idem, "Networks and Groups in Southeast Asia." On the structure of kinship in the clientelistic societies see E. Swanson, *Rules of Descent. Studies in the Sociology of Parentage*, Ann Arbor, University of Michigan Museum of Anthropology, Anthropological Papers, 1969; G. P. Murdock, "Cognatic Forms of Social Organizations," in idem, ed., *Social Structure in Southeast Asia*, Viking Fund Publications in Anthropology, No. 29 (1960), 1–14; M. M. Khaing, *Burmese Family*, Bombay, Longmans Green, 1947; E. Wolf, "Society and Symbols in Latin Europe and the Islamic Near East," *Anthropological Quarterly*, 42:3 (July 1969), 287–301; L. W. Moss and W. H. Thompson, "The South Italian Family: Literature and Observations," *Human Organization*, 18:1 (1959), 35–41; O. Lewis, *The Children of Sanchez: An Autobiography of a Mexican Family*, New York, Random House, 1961.

38. On the structuring of social hierarchies in some societies see M. Sarfatti and A. E. Bergman, *Social Stratification in Peru*, Berkeley, University of California Institute of International Studies, Politics of Modernization Series No. 5, 1969, 43, 52–54; B. G. Burnett and R. F. Johnson, eds., *Political Forces in Latin America*, Belmont, Wadsworth, 1968; J. Graciarena, *Poder y clases sociales en el desarollo de América Latina*, Buenos Aires, Paidós, 1968; D. B. Heath and R. Adams, eds., *Contemporary Cultures and Societies in Latin America*, New York, Random House, 1965, esp. part 3; F. Bourricaud, "Structure and Function of the Peruvian Oligarchy," *Studies in Comparative International Development*, 2:2 (1966), 17–31; A. Touraine, "Social Mobility, Class Relations, and Nationalism in Latin America," *ibid.*, 1:3 (1965), 19–25; J. A. Fernandez, *The Political Elite in Argentina*, New York, New York University Press, 1970; A. Touraine and D. Pecaut, "Working Class Consciousness and Economic Development," *Studies in Comparative International Development*, 3:4 (1967–8), 71–84; H. J. Benda, "Political

acterized by the relative weakness of independent middle sectors and by the preponderance within them of service, bureaucratic elements, and within the higher strata of oligarchic groups.

Structurally, the social hierarchies of these societies were characterized by many highly elaborated hierarchies of ranks and positions, often related to the differential access of various groups to the center. On the other hand, however elaborate the system of rank-hierarchy in the center or subcenter, usually no strata with countrywide state consciousness arose, despite some embryonic tendencies.[39] Instead, smaller sectors—territorial, semioccupational or local— tended to become major status units, all of them tending toward status-segregation with but little autonomous political orientation.

These specific patterns of stratification and strata formation were charac- terized by: narrow status consciousness together with a low level of society- wide strata organization or consciousness; a strong tendency to segregation among small family, territorial, ethnic, and political groups; the relative weak- ness of horizontal class relations; the preponderance of vertical (either corpo- rate or less fully organized) networks of narrow status segments linked by con- tinuously shifting vertical ties of allegiance and contacts.[40]

The vertical ties, unlike the more fully institutionalized vertical ties be- tween different status groups predominant in ascriptive hierarchically orga- nized societies, are more shifting and not based on ascriptive corporate units. Unlike the vertical ties between the center and various status sectors that de- velop in universalistic monolithic (imperial or totalitarian) societies, those that develop within the context of the patron-client nexus are characterized by very strong and complex crisscrossing vertical lines and spheres, only some of which reach the center.[41]

Elites in Colonial Southeast Asia: An Historical Analysis," *Comparative Studies in Society and History,* 7:2 (April 1965), 233–51; and idem, "Non Western Intelligentsia as Political Elites," in S. N. Eisenstadt, *Political Sociology,* 437–45; M. R. Singer, *The Emerging Elite: A Study of Political Leadership in Ceylon,* Cam- bridge, MIT Press, 1964; and M. Lissak, *A Socio-Political Hierarchy in a Loose Social Structure. The Structure of Stratification in Thailand,* Jerusalem, Academic Press, 1973.

39. To be found for instance in Argentina. See A. Strickon, "Class and Kinship in Argentina," *Ethnology,* 1:4 (1962), 500–15.

40. Good examples of this pattern of segregation can be found in E. Friedl, *Vassilika, A Village in Modern Greece,* New York, Holt, Rinehart and Winston, 1962; J. Pitt-Rivers, *The People of the Sierra,* and J. K. Campbell, *Honour, Family and Patronage.* See also J. Caro Baroja, "El sociocentrismo de los pueblos españoles," Separata del homenaje a F. Krueger, Madrid-Mendoza, U.N.C., Tomo 2, 1954. For a criticism see D. Gilmore, "Class, Culture and Community Size in Spain." On the weakness of categorial organization see among many others C. H. Landé, "Group Politics and Dyadic Poli- tics: Notes for a Theory." For the presence of shifting allegiances in the political sphere see for instance A. Zuckerman, *Political Clienteles in Power.*

41. See on this V. Lemieux, *Le Patronage politique. Une étude comparative,* Québec, Les Presses de L'Université Laval, 1977; E. Wolf, *Peasants,* 81–95; J. Boissevain, "Patrons as Brokers," *Sociologische*

XV.

These societies were also characterized by the prevalence within them of symbolic orientations or images, among which maternal religious ones, an emphasis on mediators,[42] and the various conceptions of honor mentioned above have been singled out in the literature as most clearly related to patron-client relations. However, in order to understand the full importance of these specific cultural idioms as they apply to patron-client relations, it is important to see that they are related to the basic conceptions of cosmic and social order prevalent in these societies.[43]

The most important of such orientations have been first, certain conceptions of tension between a higher transcendental order and the mundane order, especially in the religious sphere proper, together with the absence or weakness of the need to overcome tensions through some "this-worldly" activity (political, economic, or scientific) oriented to the shaping of the social and political order or its transformation. In other words, in these societies strong other-worldly orientations tend to develop. Second, the cultural and social order was seen as given; the perception of active autonomous participation of any of the social groups in shaping its contours was weak. The major groups and elites of these societies rarely conceived of themselves as actively responsible for the shaping of those contours. Third, this was closely related to a

---

Gids, 16:6 (1969), 379–86; J. Davis, *People of the Mediterranean*, ch. 4; K. R. Legg, *Patrons, Clients and Politicians*; A. Rassman, "Al-Taba'yya: Power, Patronage and Marginal Groups in Northern Iraq," in E. Gellner and J. Waterbury, *Patrons and Clients*, 157–66; R. Sandbrook, "Patrons, Clients, and Factions"; R. Lemarchand, "Political Exchange, Clientelism and Development in Tropical Africa," *Culture et Développement*, 4:3 (1972), Bruxelles, 483–516; as well as, among a profuse literature, the works of Hess, Zuckerman, Boissevain and Blok quoted elsewhere.

42. E. Wolf, "Society and Symbols in Latin Europe and in the Islamic Middle East: Some Comparisons," *Anthropological Quarterly*, 42:3 (July 1969), 287–301.

43. For a broad treatment of these concepts see S. N. Eisenstadt and M. Curelaru, *Macro-Sociology*; idem, *The Form of Sociology*; and S. N. Eisenstadt, "The Implications of Weber's Sociology of Religion for Understanding Processes of Change in Contemporary Non-European Societies and Civilizations," in C. Y. Glock and P. E. Hammond, eds., *Beyond the Classics*, 131–55. On the above conceptions see S. A. Hahha and G. H. Gardner, eds., *Arab Socialism*, London, E. J. Briell, 1969; A. J. D. Matz, "The Dynamics of Change in Latin America," *Journal of Inter-American Studies*, 9:1 (Jan. 1966), 66–76; C. F. Gallagher, "The Shaping of the Spanish Intellectual Tradition," *American Universities Field Staff Reports*, 9:8 (1976); D. E. Worcester, "The Spanish-American Past. Enemy of Change," *Journal of Inter-American Studies*, 11:1 (Jan. 1969), 66–75; K. Silvert, "Latin America and its Alternative Future," *International Journal*, 24:3 (Summer 1969), 403–44; H. D. Evers, *Kulturwandel in Ceylon*, Baden-Baden, Verlag Lutzeyer, 1964; R. Sarkisyanz, *Buddhist Backgrounds of the Burmese Revolution*, The Hague, M. Nijhoff, 1965; C. F. Gallagher, "Contemporary Islam: A Frontier of Communalism. Aspects of Islam in Malaysia." *American Universities Field Staff Reports*, Southeast Asia Series, 14:10 (1966); J. Peacock, *Rites of Modernization: Symbols and Social Aspects of Indonesian Proletarian Drama*, Chicago, University of Chicago Press, 1968; and R. N. Milton, "The Basic Malay House," *Journal of the Royal Asiatic Society*, Malay Branch, 29:3 (1965), 145–55.

relatively low level of commitment to a broader social or cultural order, to a perception of this order as something to be mastered or adapted to but not as commanding a high level of commitment from those who participated in it or were encompassed by it. Fourth, and closely related, was the relatively weak emphasis on the autonomous access of the principal groups or strata to the major attributes of these orders or of salvation. Such access was usually seen as mediated by various actors—mostly ascriptive groups or ritual experts who represented the "given" order—and mediating symbols and supernatural powers were stressed.

SOCIETAL CONDITIONS AND THE GENERATION OF PATRON-CLIENT RELATIONS

XVI.

All these characteristics of the social structure and cultural orientations of these societies—the expansive, extractive, and dual characteristics of their economies; the low level of autonomy of the centers and the major social strata, and the relatively passive and mediating cultural orientations and symbols—can arise in a great variety of historical circumstances that cannot be analyzed here. Those characteristics do indeed differ greatly (as comparative research not fully reported here attests) from those of the societies in which other models of structuring relations between generalized exchange are predominant.[44] All these characteristics tend to generate consequences and patterns of interaction that are closely connected with the basic features of this model and of the patron-client relationships.

First of all they tend to produce a low level of societal trust, or rather, the scope of trust that develops in the basic groups of the society is relatively narrow and not easily transferred to broader settings. Second, and closely related, is the fact that this creates a situation in which no category of social actors, above all the higher ones, enjoys any "corporate" legitimation of their attempts to secure their major positions and resources, either through direct relations with other actors or through access to the major controlling agencies that regulate the free flow of resources.

Third, these characteristics (and particularly the cultural orientations specified above) result in a relatively passive definition of identity and trust among the major actors. And fourth, they generate, within each category of major social actors in these societies, but paradoxically enough especially among the higher groups and the incumbents of the center, a potential competition between members of each category with respect to their possible access to needed resources and to the positions that control these resources.

44. See on this in greater detail S. N. Eisenstadt, *Revolution and the Transformation of Societies*, esp. chs. IV, V, IX.

This precarious position of the individual actors comes out most clearly in situations of modernization or development, where the relatively high degree of flow of free resources makes the competition for any specific position intense, and where there is a more open competition between different units belonging to the same category of social actors. All these factors tend to produce a certain pattern of interaction and struggle among members of the same social categories or classes, a pattern characterized by continuous contest, manipulation, and perpetual imbalance.[45] This struggle takes place among actors belonging to the elites, to the center, and to similar social strata, and it is conducted through unwritten agreements between unequal partners, belonging to different social categories. A certain strategy prevails according to which actors belonging to different categories approach each other to gain resources not easily accessible to them in their own social spheres or categories. In this framework, it is useful to speak, as Paine did, of a generative transactional model of patronage.[46]

Finally, it is the nature of the interaction in general and the struggle over power and resources in particular that explains a crucial aspect of the exchange between patron and clients, implicit in its core characteristics and briefly alluded to above, namely, that it takes place at once on two distinct yet interconnected levels. One such level is related to the exchange of different concrete services, goods or resources. Here indeed there may be, as a result of the changing positions of patrons or of clients in the markets of specific exchange, wide variability and change in the concrete terms of such exchange.

But in all such relations between patrons and clients there is another level of exchange connected to certain crucial aspects of generalized exchange. On this level the client "buys," as it were, protection against the exigencies of the markets or of nature or of the arbitrariness or weakness of the center, or against the demands of other powerful groups or individuals. The price he pays for it is not just a specific service but the acceptance of the patron's control of his (the client's) access to markets and to public goods, as well as of his ability to convert fully some of his resources.[47] But this limitation, as against the one found in societies where the hierarchical-ascriptive model is prevalent, cannot be derived from the full institutional premises of the society, and its acceptance is potentially precarious.

---

45. The case of the mafiosi is only an outstanding example of the continuous struggle and imbalance in relations and terms of exchange found in these societies. Examples for Morocco, Latin America, Southeast Asia and Africa proliferate in the literature; for references see Notes 4, 33, 36, 41.

46. R. Paine, "A Theory of Patronage," in idem, ed., *Patrons and Brokers in the East Arctic*, 3–21.

47. This aspect of social "insurance" was already emphasized in the work of scholars of Southeast Asia at the end of the sixties and beginning of the seventies (see J. C. Scott, "Patron-Client Politics," as well as the work of R. Lemarchand and K. Legg).

Hence the relations of generalized exchange here are not, as they are in the ascriptive models, fully prescribed or subject to special (ritual and power) negotiations different from those undertaken with respect to specific market exchange. In the clientelistic model these relations constitute a focus of struggle, marked by continuous negotiations about specific exchange. Also these features mean that the patrons are indeed willing to accept, in principle at least, some of the limitations that patronage may entail, even though they do of course always try to secure the best possible terms for themselves.

XVII.

All these features of the process of interaction characterize the patron-client nexus and explain also its core characteristics and paradoxes, and some of the institutional repercussions. First of all, they explain the combinations of inequality and asymmetry of power with seemingly mutual solidarity and of exploitation and potential coercion with voluntary solutions, as well as the strong ambivalences that are built into the interaction and the types of symbols of authority and obligations generated, which we shall analyze below. Second, they explain the tendency to construct exchange and package deals that combine symbols of solidarity, expressed above all in terms of symbolic personal elements, with concrete specific unequal exchanges. This combination constitutes a mechanism through which the precariousness of the linkage between generalized and specific exchange, inherent in patron-client relations, is seemingly being overcome. But it is being overcome by not allowing either a clear distinction between contractual and precontractual elements of social relations or a clearly unequivocal specification, as is the case in principle in the ascriptive models.

The close relation of the combination of precontractual and contractual elements to the precariousness of the linkage between generalized and specific exchange in the patron-client nexus is best seen in the various personalized concepts of obligation, honor, personal sentiment, and ritual attachment that often symbolize and legitimize these relationships. The concept of honor in the context of the clientelistic model is based on very strong, yet uncertain and ambivalent, orientations toward broader institutional settings beyond the family and the locality, and in this it is distinct from similar conceptions such as ritual friendship, or the *giri* system in Japan. The latter are usually defined either as part of, or as being rooted in the broader identity of, these strata or broader kinship units, or in purely interpersonal identities and relations which, like "pure" friendship, transcend any organized group or any fully structured relations.[48] While this concept entails in its very definition asymmetric hierar-

48. On ritual friendship see Notes 1 and 18. On the *giri* system see H. Befu, "Gift Giving and Social Reciprocity in Japan"; and C. Nakane, *Japanese Society*. On "pure" friendship, see S. N. Eisenstadt, "Friendship and the Structure of Trust and Solidarity in Society"; R. Paine, "Anthropological

chical relations, it cannot be so purely interpersonal as are ritual kinship or friendship relations, and it always involves a tension between the hierarchical and the purely interpersonal, potentially egalitarian components in that image.

It is important to note that such conceptions of honor are much less evident in those patron-client relations that develop on the margins of societies in which other models of relations between generalized and specific exchange are predominant, as they do in local politics in the United States. Truly enough, in such settings some elements of unconditionality develop between the patron and clients, but they are rarely upheld by conceptions of honor, except when these conceptions are brought (as they are by immigrants) from other settings. Such conceptions become diluted insofar as broader markets develop with a much larger flow of resources and potential competition between different networks, as they do in all situations of modernization. The importance of such conceptions, and their function in patron-client relations are best illustrated by the fact that when they are, or become, weakened or diluted, it is usually the potentially injured party—the patron or the client— who attempts to uphold them. Thus he indicates that it is important from his point of view to uphold these conceptions as guarantees of the goodwill and future behavior of the partner.

These characteristics of the clientelistic model explain some of its structural repercussions. First, they explain a feature that became more and more visible with the proliferation of patron-client studies and analyses: namely, the existence of different combinations of stability and instability of the patron-client relationship in different social settings. In the first anthropological studies of patronage, a picture seemed to emerge of personal patron-client relations as stable and continuous. The continuity and stability were in no small degree accounted for by the strong interpersonal relations and moral bonds which overcame, as it were, the strong inequality in positions and power. With the proliferation of studies, recognition emerged that most patron-client relationships—those in complex societal settings, but even those in the more restricted rural areas—may be characterized by differing combinations of continuity with lack of stability and continuous change. These differ of course in different settings of concrete personal relations and in organizational settings, in the positions and fortunes of individual patrons, and are modified by the continuous competition among them for clients.

Second, they explain that the broader societal and cultural conditions analyzed above are not in themselves sufficient to generate the various concrete types of patron-client relations and interaction. It is only when these are con-

Approaches to Friendship," in E. Leyton, ed., *The Compact*, 1–14; and J. S. La Fontaine, "Unstructured Social Relations."

nected with a certain balance of power between the various social strata and categories, and especially insofar as they do not create market conditions (as happens under conditions of colonization or modernization) in which individual patrons have such a monopoly of resources that it obviates their corporate weakness and makes them totally independent of any client, that some form of patron-client relation is undertaken. Otherwise the patrons (or in obverse conditions the potential clients) are not interested in engaging in such conditions, and simple power or market relations tend to grow up, often giving rise to extreme coercive attitudes on the part of the patrons or to the "class-like" reorganization or withdrawal of the clients.[49]

XVIII.

In the preceding discussion we have indicated that the best way to understand the nature of patron-client or clientelistic relations is to see them in the context of a model of structuring relations between generalized and specific exchange. We have also indicated that it is the analytic features and dynamic propensities of this model in general and of the structuring of social hierarchies and inequalities in particular that generate the type of social interaction that will best explain the crucial analytical characteristics of patron-client relations. Accordingly, the full analytical characteristics of patron-client relations identified above tend to develop in those societies or sectors thereof where the clientelistic model is predominant.

True, some specific types of social organizations that characterize patron-client relations (and especially the tendency by strong groups or individuals to use their positions to monopolize the access to markets or to positions of power and to dictate the terms of exchange between the major resources) can of course be found in all societies, whatever model of relations between generalized and specific exchange is predominant within them.

Insofar as these attempts are successful even for a short while, they give rise, even in societies in which nonclientelistic models are predominant, to various patterns of dyadic or network vertical relations similar in many ways to patron-client relations. This point has been abundantly illustrated in the literature on interest groups and cliques in pluralistic and monolithic and consociational systems, on machine politics in the United States or the arctic region of Canada, or in the *Jajmani* systems in India.[50] However, unlike patron-

49. An example of the coercive trend can be found in S. el-Messiri, "The changing role of the futuwwa." On the second possibility see among others D. Gilmore, "Patronage and Class Conflict in Southern Spain," *Man*, N.S., 12:3–4 (1978), 446–58.

50. On machine politics in the U.S. see R. Wolfinger and J. Field, "Political Ethos and the Structure of City Government," *American Political Science Review*, 60:2 (1966), 306–26; E. Banfield, ed., *Urban Government*, New York, The Free Press, 1969, esp. ch. 3 and 5, 165–265 and 365–425; and R. Wolfinger, "Why Political Machines." On Western Europe see M. Bax, *Harpstrings and confessions: An anthropological study of politics in Rural Ireland*, Amsterdam, University of Amsterdam, 1973;

client relations in societies in which the clientelistic model is predominant, these patron-like relationships are apt to be more transient or, as defined by Landé, an addendum-like type of relation, and they differ in several important ways from those of the full-fledged patron-client pattern.

First, the seminormative prescription of the details of the package deal between patrons and clients is much less stable. It does not have even the degree of legitimation or normative prescription that the pure types of patron-client relations have, and a greater variability in the resources exchanged develops. The second difference, to which we have alluded above, is that in most cases the solidary element and symbolism of interpersonal relations are much weaker than in full-fledged patron-client relations. Insofar as symbols and concepts of mutual obligations appear, they are often couched more in terms of subversive friendship than of honor. Third, such relations are usually more segmented and limited to some institutional markets. Many of them are outright agreements with relatively little unconditionality built into them. Last, and probably most important, these relations are usually perceived, both by those who participate in them and above all by those outside them, especially by those in central positions in the societies or sectors thereof, as nonlegitimate, as contrasting premises either of equality or of ascriptive hierarchy prevailing in these societies.[51]

XIX.

A view of these relations as nonlegitimate is not a purely moralistic exercise; the premises of either equality or of ascriptive hierarchy prevailing in such societies, in contrast to clientelistic societies, tend to give rise to countervailing forces aimed at undermining the emerging or existing patron-client arrangements and the linkages between inequalities in different dimensions of the institutional order they are attempting to establish. The countervailing forces are effected by the mobilization of the clients' rights of access to the center and/or by attempts of more central elites, or by those in positions of power beyond the immediate clientelistic situation to undermine the legal or actual status of

---

P. G. Richards, *Patronage in British Government*, London, Allen and Unwin, 1963; T. Zeldin, *The Political System of Napoleon III*, London, Macmillan, 1958. For the Soviet Union see P. Frank, "How to get on in the Soviet Union," *New Society*, 5 June 1969, 867–68; and G. Ionescu, "Patronage under communism," in E. Gellner and J. Waterbury, *Patrons and Clients*, 97–102. On China see K. E. Folsom, *Friends, Guests, and Colleagues: The Mu-fu System in Late Ch'ing Period*, Berkeley, University of California Press, 1968; and M. Fried, *Fabric of Chinese Society*, New York, Praeger, 1973. For the Canadian Arctic see R. Paine, ed., *Patrons and Brokers in the East Arctic*. For the *jajmani* system see for instance J. Breman, *Patronage and Exploitation, Changing Agrarian Relations in South Gujarat, India*, Berkeley, University of California, Press, 1974.

51. See for instance A. Heidenheimer, ed., *Political Corruption: Readings in Comparative Analysis*, New York, Holt, Rinehart and Winston, 1970.

such monopolies, and especially the attempts of the monopolists (the would-be patrons) to control access to markets and regulate the flow as well as the conversion of resources in the society.

Thus, in pluralistic societies, attempts to counter the power of monopolist-patrons are usually made through the combined activities of various elites in the center and the broader groups to which the clients belong. In more monolithic systems attempts to offset the efforts of different subgroups to monopolize the access to such markets are usually initiated by the rulers, who attempt to open up and control the relations between generalized and specific exchange, as well as the flow of resources within the more specialized markets.

Similarly, in the more ascriptively based corporate or hierarchical systems, the attempts at monopolization of access to markets and power by nonlegitimate (i.e., of lower caste) individuals are usually offset by coalitions between members of the higher groups and secondary entrepreneurs.[52] On the other hand, in societies in which the clientelistic model is predominant, no such countervailing forces develop, or only very few. Those that do develop are either ineffective or are successful only in changing some of the personal or organizational aspects of the relations between patrons and clients or the terms of trade between them, but not the pattern itself.

This can best be seen in the movements of protest or rebellion that develop in such societies or sectors thereof.[53] One such type of rebellion, abundantly described and analyzed in the literature, is that of banditry. Its basic characteristics, as well as the conditions under which it arises, have been well

52. For these trends in pluralistic societies see R. A. Dahl, *Polyarchy, Participation and Opposition*, New Haven and London, Yale University Press, 1971; and idem, "Patterns of Opposition," in idem, ed., *Political Opposition in Western Democracies*, New Haven and London, Yale University Press, 1966, 332–47, and "Epilogue," in *ibid.*, 387–401. For the Soviet Union see M. Fainsod, *Smolensk under Soviet rule*, Cambridge, Harvard University Press, 1958. For the caste systems see F. G. Bailey, *Caste and the Economic Frontier*, Manchester University Press, 1957; H. R. Isaacs, *India's Ex-Untouchables*, Bombay, Asia publishing House, 1965; A. Béteille, "The Future of the Backward Classes," in idem, *Castes: Old and New*, London, Asia Publishing House, 1969, 103–45; and K. David, "Hierarchy and Equivalence in Jaffna."

53. On the patterns of revolt see N. Miller and R. Aya, eds., *National Liberation: Revolution in the Third World*, New York, Free Press, 1971; K. Cough and H. P. Sharma, eds., *Imperialism and Revolution in South Asia*, New York, Monthly Review Press, 1973; R. L. Solomon, "Saya San and the Burmese Rebellion," *Modern Asian Studies*, 3:3 (1969), 209–33. G. Gobron, *History and Philosophy of Caodaism*, Paris, Dervy, 1949; G. Goulet, *Les sociétés secrètes en terre d'Annam*, Saigon, C. Ardin, 1926; M. C. Guerrero, "The Colorum Uprisings 1924–1931," *Asian Studies*, 5:1 (1967), 65–78; S. Kartodiridjo, *The Peasants' Revolt of Banten in 1888, Its Conditions, Course, and Sequel: A Case Study of Social Movements in Indonesia*, The Hague, M. Nijhoff, 1966; H. J. Benda and L. Castles, "The Samin Movement," *Bijdragen Tot de Taal-, Land-, en Volkenkunde*, 125:3 (1969), 207–40; H. J. Benda and R. McVey, eds., *The Communist Uprisings of 1926–1927 in Indonesia: Key Documents*, Ithaca, Cornell University Press, 1960; J. Migdal, *Peasants, Politics and Revolution*, Princeton, Princeton University Press, 1974; and S. R. Ross, ed., *Is the Mexican Revolution Dead?*, New York, Knopf, 1966. See also below.

analyzed by Hobsbawm.[54] Its distinguishing feature, from the point of view of patron-client relationship, is that it "takes out" a certain portion of the population—the leader and those who follow him or whom he protects—from the concrete network of existing patron-client relationships and exchange. But however destructive it may be for some of the existing patrons and however much it may change some of the terms of trade between them and their clients, yet it does not basically change the nature of access to markets and to centers of power or the nature of the relations between generalized and specific exchange inherent in them. The rebel leader may become a rebel patron who "serves" the more downtrodden clients in a given population. But the basic relations between him and his "clients" do not greatly differ from those of the usual patron-client relationships, although there does tend to develop, at least in the initial phases of the struggle, a strong emphasis on the purer interpersonal relationships, as well as on a general communal solidarity between them. But even this may become in time diluted or routinized. The rebel or bandit leader himself may disappear—killed off by the authorities or the patrons he threatened. He may become an accepted feature of the existing system who has come to de facto terms with the centering patronage network, or, in extreme cases, he may become a semilegitimized patron on his own.

A second possible outcome of such rebellions, an important variant of the first and one that has been documented for instance for Brazil, is the emergence of the rebel as a new type of religious leader carrying a new message of salvation to the downtrodden. In addition he restructures or organizes his "clients" into a new solidary community; without, however, greatly changing the relations of this community with the broader setting and without on the whole allowing them an autonomous access to internal power.[55] Insofar as such communities are successful, they also tend to develop special enclaves within an

54. E. Hobsbawm, *Primitive Rebels. Studies in Archaic Forms of Social Movements in the 19th and 20th Centuries*, Manchester, Manchester University Press, 1971 (1959); idem, *Bandits*, London, Weidenfeld and Nicholson, 1969; Cf. A. Blok, "On Brigandage, with Special Reference to Peasant Mobilization," *Sociologische Gids*, 18:2 (1971), 208–16.

55. M. I. Pereira de Queiroz, "Brazilian Messianic Movements: A Help or a Hindrance to 'Participation'?," *Bulletin of the International Institute for Labor Studies*, 7 (1970), 93–121; idem, *La "guerre sainte" au Brésil: Le mouvement messianique du "contestado,"* São Paulo, University of São Paulo, Arts and Sciences Bulletin No. 187. Sociologia I, 5 (1957); idem, *Messianismo e conflito social: A guerra sertaneja do contestado, 1912–1916*, Rio de Janeiro, Civilização brasileira, 1966; H. J. Benda, "Peasant Movements in Colonial Southeast Asia," *Asian Studies*, 3:3 (1965), 420–34; F. Hills, "Millenarian Machines in South Vietnam," *Comparative Studies in Society and History*, 13:3 (July 1971), 325–50; B. Dahm, "Leadership and Mass Response in Java, Burma and Vietnam," Paper presented to the International Congress of Orientalists, Canberra, Jan. 1971, on file at Kiel University; M. Osborne, *Region of Revolt: Focus on Southeast Asia*, Oxford, Pergamon, 1970; and J. van der Kroef, "Javanese Messianic Expectations: Their Origin and Cultural Context," *Comparative Studies in Society and History*, 1:4 (Oct. 1959), 299–323.

overall nexus of clientelistic politics, although sometimes islands of potential subversions against them are created.

Other types of rebellion, protest or movements of change within the patron-client nexus of course take a wide variety of forms, such as movements of clients from one patron to another or the organization of new networks and programs by enterprising would-be patrons or brokers. Such movements are usually connected with change either in the volume of flow of resources being exchanged in a given nexus of patron-client relations or in the reorganization of institutional markets. But in all these situations the major change is in the personal or organizational structuring of patron-client relations, and it may affect the stability of some aspects of these relations. But usually it does not affect the basic features of the relations between generalized and specific exchange and the premises of inequality that characterize this pattern.

It is only when situations arise in which either the potential patrons or potential clients enjoy such beneficial monopolistic positions that they are not interested in entering into concrete patron-client relations, with the potential limitations of their activities, that movements of rebellion may become more extreme. But even then, as Scott's analysis of the situation in Southeast Asia indicates,[56] they will not always give rise to change in the pattern unless they are able to change the premises of the flow of resources.

In the preceding pages we have analyzed what seems to us to be the "purest" types of clientelistic relation. Rather different constellations or types of clientelistic relation tend to develop in those societies like Imperial Russia or Japan, for instance, in which only one or two of the major societal actors evince the structural characteristics analyzed above. Similarly, even within the context of full clientelistic societies, wide variations may of course develop in the concrete organization of patron-client relations, networks, and the like. All these will be discussed in greater detail elsewhere.

56. J. C. Scott, "The Erosion of Patron-Client Bonds and Social Change in Rural Southeast Asia," *Journal of Asian Studies*, 32:1 (Nov. 1972), 5–37.

Ten

PRESTIGE, PARTICIPATION, AND STRATA FORMATION

PART I

IN THIS PAPER I SHALL ATTEMPT attempt to present a preliminary analysis of the relation between two aspects of social life which have always been presented in sociological literature as basic components of social stratification—first, social division of labour, functional social differentiation, and the concomitant differential evaluation of roles and tasks,[1] and second, the division of society into several groups or strata which are arranged in some hierarchical relations or orders. Such groups or strata have been designated as "classes" in Marxian terminology, as classes, estates, and parties (or political groupings) in Weber's nomenclature, or classes and castes as used in some American community studies.[2]

Originally published in J. A. Jackson, ed., *Social Stratification* (Cambridge: Cambridge University Press, 1968). Reprinted with permission of Cambridge University Press.

The present article is part of a wider work on institutional analysis and stratification in which I have been engaged for some time. The initial stage of this work has been undertaken together with Dr. E. O. Shild, and has been summarized in an unpublished paper "Stratification and exchange" and in a series of working papers we have prepared together. Some parts of the present article are to some extent based on that paper. In the later stages of this work I have benefited from the collaboration of Mrs. Y. Atzmon, Y. Carmeli, Miss M. Korelaro and G. Yatziv. Miss M. Korelaro has helped me in the preparation of the present paper. I am especially greatly indebted to Professor Edward Shils for very detailed comments and annotations of an earlier draft of this article.

1. See for instance K. Davis and W. E. Moore, "Some principles of stratification," *American Sociological Review*, vol. 10, 2 (1945), 242–9; M. M. Tumin, "Some principles of stratification: a critical analysis," *American Sociological Review*, vol. 18, 4 (1953), 387–94; T. Parsons, "A revised analytical approach to the theory of social stratification," in T. Parsons, *Essays in Sociological Theory* (Glencoe, Illinois, 1954). For the best single collection of the basic materials on stratification see R. Bendix and S. M. Lipset, *Class, Status and Power* (2nd edition) (New York, 1965).

2. See for instance K. Marx and F. Engels, *Manifesto of the Communist Party* (N.Y., 1932), H. H. Gerth and C. W. Mills (eds.), *From Max Weber, Essays in Sociology* (New York, 1958), esp. ch. 7. For illustrations of American community studies see W. L. Warner and P. S. Lunt, *The Social Life of a Modern Community* (New Haven, 1941); W. L. Warner, M. Meeker and K. Eels, *Social Class in America* (Chicago, 1949); R. and H. Lynd, *Middle Town* (New York, 1925) and *Middle Town in Transition* (New York, 1937). For a critique of most of these community studies see S. M. Lipset and R. Bendix,

Although these two approaches deal with similar or even identical phenomena and to a large extent also use similar or identical nomenclature, so far there have been, on the whole, few systematic attempts to explain the one in terms of the other. True enough, strata have usually been defined as consisting of people occupying positions which are similar on some evaluative scale or in terms of the degree of their control of different resources, but there have been few attempts to explain how the process of differential evaluation of roles and tasks gives rise not only to a hierarchy of roles within any specific group but also to some such hierarchy of strata in the broader macrosocietal setting, or conversely how the existence of such strata influence or shape the social division of labour and social differentiation. In the following pages some preliminary indications about the relations between these components of stratification will be presented.

The basic aspects of social structure most relevant for the study of social stratification have usually been designated first as the fact that any social system is composed of interconnected roles, the incumbents of each of which are expected to perform different tasks, and second what has been called in sociological literature the differential allocation of rewards to the incumbents of these roles. It is probably a universal fact of social life that in all groups and societies different positions receive differential rewards—be they differential esteem and deference, different amounts of services or commodities given to them by other people or different amounts of obedience they can command from their fellows, i.e., different amounts of power, which are allocated to them according to some socially relevant or accepted criteria or values. Third is the fact of the existence of differential access, among different individuals, categories, or groups of people in a society, to the various positions or roles which are differentially evaluated or rewarded. Fourth is the possibility that the existence of such a differential allocation of rewards and access creates, within any group, some type of hierarchy of roles which may perhaps coalesce into some broader categories of people, into some groups or quasi-groups, with some common identity and continuity, usually called strata.

Already this relatively simple enumeration of the major characteristics of social stratification indicates some of the basic and most difficult problems in its analysis. First, which positions or which holders of which positions are differentially evaluated or rewarded? Second, what is the nature of these rewards; of what do they consist; how can they be used; how do they influence the evaluation of different positions and the access to them? Third, what are the criteria on which such differential rewarding of roles rest? Fourth, why are

"Social status and social structure: A re-examination of data and interpretations," *British Journal of Sociology*, vol. 2 (1951), 150–68, 230–54.

these particular criteria used, and how were they developed, i.e., how and by whom have they been established, and how have they become accepted? Last, under what conditions do such positions develop into some sort of hierarchy and what are the mechanisms through which the incumbents of such positions coalesce into some sorts of groups or into "strata"—whatever their exact definition may be? Of these problems those which seem to be of special importance from the point of view of the conditions of strata formation will now be considered.

Perhaps the easiest problem—at least in a first, preliminary approach—is the designation of the types of social positions which tend, in all societies, to become the foci of such differential evaluation. These are, in all groups or societies—albeit in different degrees—the various positions in the major institutional spheres, i.e., political, economic, cultural, religious, educational, etc.; those positions which are related to the central spheres and symbols of a society, and which represent the community; as well as positions which designate membership in certain primordial-social categories (like age) or collectivities (ethnic, racial, national, etc.). Somewhat more complicated is the problem of the nature of the rewards which are differentially "allocated," of the ways in which these rewards can be used by the people who receive them and of the relevance of such uses for various aspects of social stratification.

What are these rewards? Although they may, of course, vary greatly in detail, on the whole they can be—and have been—classified by most sociologists in similar ways. As has been briefly listed above, people may get from other people particular services and/or particular commodities, and/or general means (media of exchange) of which money is, of course, the most general and important; some general facilities, like education, through which such services or commodities can be obtained; general obedience—i.e., be invested with authority to give commands to other people—at least in some spheres of life. They can also be given "deference" or in common sociological parlance be invested with some "esteem" or "prestige." These different types of rewards have been classified in the "classical" triplet of power, wealth, and prestige which have been designated in almost all studies of stratification as the major types of rewards allocated to different roles and presumably indicating their differential evaluation and standing. They have also often been designated as the bases or roots of such evaluation.

Despite the relative simplicity of the definitions of these major types of rewards, they really contain many problems and difficulties. One such problem, most important for the study of stratification in general and comparative perspective in particular, is, as we shall see in greater detail later, the extent to which the rewards which are given in any face-to-face group, in any partial organization, in any parochial setting, are also meaningful beyond it, are evaluated outside it in the same way as inside, and can accordingly be used outside it. Do the power, services, commodities, or the deference that a leader of a street corner gang has in his group provide him with any means through which he can gain some commodities, power or prestige in other groups or in the macrosociety—or are they of little value in this respect? There may be, as we shall see in greater detail later, great differences, in various societies, between these three types of rewards, i.e., between power, wealth, and prestige.

Before turning to this problem, it might be worthwhile turning to the problem of the different types of uses of such resources and the implication of these uses for the process of strata formation. Such rewards may be used in three ways. First, they can be directly consumed. Second, they can be used for "symbolic consumption"; and last, for "exchange"—for getting something else, some other service, commodities or privileges. The first way of using such resources—direct consumption—is seemingly the simplest and least problematic one. People may "consume" the various commodities which they receive, i.e., use the services of others for their own enjoyment, command the activities and obedience of others in order to enjoy the subservience of others, or they may simply "bask" in the deference given to them by others. Such consummatory use of rewards merges into the second type of their use—that of symbolic consumption—insofar as activities become conspicuous to outsiders and thereby tend to call forth evaluative judgments. The consumption acquires thereby a symbolic significance and it might even become motivated by considerations of that significance. In such cases a great stress may be laid on the exclusiveness of such consumption, i.e., to its being limited to certain groups of people, so that the very use of such patterns of consumption symbolizes their being different, possibly "better," from others.

The terms "conspicuous consumption" and "style of life"—as well as the phenomenon of sumptuary laws—have often been used to illustrate this type or aspect of consumption. But beyond these two uses of the various rewards, which stress the fact that they may be seen as goals which people desire or the objects of acts which people admire—there is another way in which they can be used—a way which stresses their being also resources through which other services or commodities can be obtained, i.e., they may serve as resources or media of exchange in social, institutional, interaction. The variety of the ways in which these rewards-resources can be used in exchange is, of course, very great,[3] but at this point of our discussion we would like to emphasize only one way which is of special importance in the analysis of stratification—namely the possibility to use such rewards or resources in order to gain access (for themselves or for other people—especially, but not only, their children and relatives—who are seen as an extension of themselves, who share some primordial identity with them) to some of the more highly evaluated or rewarded

3. See S. N. Eisenstadt, *Essays on Comparative Institutions* (New York, 1965), 22–35.

positions—whether the same positions which they hold or other "high" positions or roles, and to exclude others from getting access to such positions.

The use of various resources for regulating access to position may be done in principle in several different ways. One way is to satisfy (or to purchase means for satisfying) the requirements of access to a certain position for the actor himself or for other. Second, and no less important, is the use of these resources for the definition of the requirements of access themselves, for the setting up of norms which can limit in various ascriptive ways, institutional interaction in general and access to positions in particular.[4]

The differential allocation of rewards to various roles and positions, the "symbolic" consumption of such rewards and their use for control of access to the higher positions—constitute the basic components of stratification on a macrosocietal level, the starting points of the processes of strata formation. However, the relations between these various processes have not been fully explored in the literature. Even the first two approaches—which emphasize the differential allocation of rewards on the one hand and the differential access to positions on the other—have not been too closely connected in the analysis of stratification. They have gone separate ways—each usually engendering different lines of research and enquiry although in some analyses a rapprochement between the two can sometimes be discerned.[5]

Only recently has it been more perceived that these two constitute two basic and interconnected aspects of any system of stratification. For instance, Fallers has emphatically stressed this, designating differential evaluation of positions as the primary aspect of stratification and the regulation of access to positions as its secondary aspect.[6] But on the whole—and even in Faller's exposition—there have been but few attempts to study systematically the structural, long-range linkage between these two aspects of stratification—beyond the assertion of the general fact that people (or children of people) who occupy higher positions in a certain institutional sphere, usually have better chances of access to high positions in the same or another institutional sphere. Or, in other words, there have only been a few attempts to analyse systematically the nature of the mechanisms through which these two aspects of strati-

---

4. On ascriptive restrictions see R. Linton, *The Study of Man* (New York, 1936), ch. 8; T. Parsons, "A revised analytical approach to the theory of social stratification," in T. Parsons, *Essays in Sociological Theory.* For a criticism of the conception of ascription in relation to stratification, see M. G. Smith, "Pre-industrial stratification systems," in N. J. Smelser and S. M. Lipset (eds.), *Social Structure and Mobility in Economic Development* (Chicago, 1966), 141–76.

5. For some of the classical illustrations of attempts at such rapprochement see J. A. Schumpeter, *Imperialism and Social Classes* (New York, 1951), part II; Gerth and Mills (eds.), *From Max Weber: Essays in Sociology.* For a more recent approach see D. H. Wrong, "The functional theory of stratification: some neglected considerations," *American Sociological Review,* vol. 24, 6 (1959), 772–82.

6. L. Fallers, "Equality, modernity and democracy in the New States," in C. Geertz (ed.), *Old Societies and New States* (Glencoe, Illinois, 1963), 161–8.

fication are linked in different societies; to analyse the ways—and the extent—
to which differential evaluation of different positions and the different types
and degrees of rewards which such positions receive within a society influence
both the short and long range intra- and intergenerational differential access
of their incumbents (and/or their children) to other or (in the case of their
children) similar institutional positions. Similarly, while it has been recognized
in the literature that the symbolic consumption of rewards is a very important
component of stratification, yet the relation between such symbolic consumption and other aspects of stratification—such as regulation of access to position, although often mentioned—have not been fully investigated. In order to
be able to explore the linkage between these three major aspects or components of stratification, it is necessary first to analyse in greater detail the nature
of one of the major types of resources or rewards mentioned above, namely
that of prestige.

Prestige or "honour" has always been designated as one of the three basic
rewards which is differentially distributed in any group or society. Moreover it
has always been designated as constituting a basic symbol of one's social standing or status. And yet of all the different rewards it has been at the same time
the least analytically specified. Both the bases (or criteria) of prestige and especially the structural implications of its differential distribution have been abundantly described but not fully and systematically analysed. They were to some
extent taken for granted, often subsumed under, or related to, the concept of
"style of life"—which often served, like the concept of prestige itself, as a sort
of general residual category in studies of stratification. Of all the different rewards it seems on the one hand to be most "symbolic," most elusive, least concrete. It does not seem to have the hard-core structural and organizational
features that characterize money and commodities, power, coercion, and obedience. Its most obvious expressions are symbolic—such as esteem or deference given to people, conferral of medals or of honorary titles, or keeping a
certain distance from those who are bestowed with such prestige. It seems also
to be the most directly consummatory of all the different rewards—i.e., it
seems as if nothing can be done with it beyond the mere enjoyment of the
deference, reverence or the special standing inherent in it.

And yet, on the other hand, in large parts of the sociological and historical
literature on stratification, prestige manifest either in external symbols of status
or in what is often called the "style of life" of different people and groups, is
presented as constituting a basic *structural* component or aspect of stratification.
It is often presented as the focus around which some at least of the major
organizations or structural aspects of strata tend to be formed. But the relation
between these two aspects of prestige—the relatively purely consummatory
symbolic one and its structural ramifications in terms of groups or categories
of people—have not been fully explicated; although, needless to say, there

exists in sociological literature an abundance of accounts or illustrations of both the personal and institutional bases of prestige. But in most of them prestige has often been seen as a derivative either of personal attributes, or of various institutional (i.e., economic, power, cultural, etc.) positions, or of the performance of functionally important tasks, without having a more autonomous, independent, societal, and symbolic base. And yet a closer look at any group or society will show that within most, probably all, groups or societies at least three such specific, distinct societal bases of prestige can be discerned.

The first base of prestige is the very membership in any collectivity (or subcollectivity), group, or society. Almost all groups and societies differentiate between members and nonmembers and attempt to endow members with some special symbols which designate their special status or standing. A second source of prestige is the ability of controlling the collectivity, of representing it, of defining its goals and its central activities and symbols, or in other words to be in a sense in its "centre."[7] Although such "centrality" is very often closely related to power, the two are not, as we shall see, analytically identical. The third specific societal root or base of prestige is the proximity to or participation in some broader sociocultural—cosmic or religious, scientific, etc.—order, which is defined as relevant for the definition of a given collectivity or for its members. It is very often those who seem to be closest to or representing the essence of such order, tradition, or "mystery," who are knowledgeable about it and are the holders of the most prestigious roles. These three sources have one common denominator—namely, the quality of participation, i.e., participation in a collectivity, in its centre, or in some broader cultural order, even if the nature and quality of such participation may greatly differ with regard to each such "source."

Thus, according to this view, the sources of prestige, of the deference which people render to others, are rooted not only in their organizational (power, economic, etc.) positions or in some purely personal qualities, but also in their differential participation in one of these types of order which constitute the institutional focuses of what may be called the charismatic dimension of human and social existence, in their contribution to the development and maintenance of such orders or in their representation of the qualities of such orders.[8]

---

7. See E. Shils, "Centre and periphery," in *The Logic of Personal Knowledge,* Essays presented to Michael Polanyi (London, 1961), 117–31. Of relevance in this context, and especially in the study of traditional societies, are the concepts of Great and Little Traditions as developed by Redfield and Singer: R. Redfield, *Peasant Society and Culture* (Chicago, 1956); "The social organisation of tradition," *The Far Eastern Quarterly,* XV (1955); R. Redfield and Milton Singer, "The cultural role of cities," *Economic Development and Cultural Change,* III (1954), 53–73.

8. See E. Shils, "Charisma, order and status," *American Sociological Review,* vol. 30 (1965), 199–213. See also S. N. Eisenstadt, "Charisma and institution building: Max Weber and modern sociol-

But such participation is not only a base of prestige: it constitutes one major aspect of prestige as a reward. The reward which is expressed by giving deference, by endowing somebody (whether an individual, a role or group) with prestige, is the recognition of his right to participate in any of these orders, or of his special contribution to them. In this view prestige becomes less symbolic and more structural, closer to the use of other types of resources and to the regulation of differential access to positions.

This can be seen first in the ways in which this conception of prestige throws some light on the structural implications of the desirability of prestige. As in all the major types of rewards, prestige also constitutes one of the many discrete desiderata and goals of individuals. It may, however, also become the focus of personal and collective identity,[9] and as such also have important broader, more generalized structural implications from the point of view of stratification. The most important of such implications are first the attempts to link the regulation of the desiderata or goals pursued by people with the degree to which they are allowed to participate in these collectivities, orders, and centres. Needless to say, many discrete goals or desiderata—economic, political, "social," or cultural—can be pursued, even in the most ascriptive societies, by people who do not belong to a certain category or group. And yet, there seems to be, in every society, some *combination* of desiderata which is perceived by the members of such groups (or by people belonging to certain social categories), as well as by others, as being peculiarly bound to those who share certain types of personal and collective identities, i.e., some combination of personal qualities or attributes on the one hand, with differential participation in these collectivities, orders, and centres on the other. The most important structural manifestations of such claims to pursue certain goals by virtue of such differential participation is the upholding of different styles of life—a concept which we have encountered already above and which we shall explicate later on.

But, secondly, the view presented here does explicate the structural implications of prestige not only as a desideratum but also as a medium of institutional interaction and exchange. Here prestige becomes in some respects not entirely dissimilar from money or power. It can also serve as a medium of exchange, as a basis for getting other commodities—such as money or power, or services. True enough, prestige is not usually directly exchangeable for power

---

ogy" (Introduction to a selection from Weber's work to be published in The Heritage of Sociology Series by University of Chicago Press, 1968).

9. *Ibid.* For some of the basic exploration of identity see Erik H. Erikson, "Childhood and society," 2nd edition, and "Identity and uprootedness in our time"—both in *Insight and Responsibility* (New York, 1964). For a systematic attempt to explore some of the social dimensions of identity, see D. R. Miller, "The study of social relationship, situation identity and social interaction," in S. Koch (ed.), *Psychology: The Study of a Science*, vol. 5 (New York, 1963), 639–737.

or money; very often any attempt to use prestige in such a way would entail its loss. But those having prestige can often use it as starting points for specially favourable bargaining positions, for the acquisition of other types of services, commodities, or media of exchange.

The man who has prestige may get some services, commodities, or obedience which would be inaccessible to others, or at a "price" greatly different from that which is demanded of others for such a commodity. Moreover, prestige—the right of participation in different collectivities, sociocultural orders and centres—can also be used to assure one's access to other institutional positions, such as economic or power ones, and to attempt to limit the possibilities of other people having such access; the illustrations of this are too numerous to need any documentation.

On the other hand those who have other resources—be they power or money—may attempt to use them in such a way as would enhance their chances of receiving prestige—even if it cannot usually be *directly* acquired by such means. It is indeed the various attempts to link, in some indirect way, the ownership of other resources with the attainment of prestige that constitutes the major structural implication of prestige as a medium of exchange in society.

It is these attempts to link prestige with other positions or resources which constitutes the evaluative component of stratification. Such evaluation is rooted in the assessment of any single position or sets of positions in terms of one or several such bases of prestige. It is through such evaluation that any specific position may become endowed with some broader meaning and the rewards which it receives may become legitimized in terms of some such meaning. But our preceding analysis of the structural derivatives of prestige indicates that such evaluation is not purely "symbolic." It is manifest in a very distinct structural mechanism in the various mechanisms which attempt to link structurally prestige, in the sense defined above, with other positions and resources.

The most important aspect, from the point of view of stratification analysis, of these mechanisms is the institutionalization of the upholding of the different styles of life discussed above and of various ascriptive limitations on institutional interaction, exchange and access to positions and on participation in exchange.[10] In most general terms such ascriptive restrictions on access mean that entry into a position is contingent not only upon satisfying requirements which can be satisfied in open interaction and exchange, but that in addition or in place of such requirements the candidate must belong to a certain social category or be an incumbent of certain other positions. Ascriptive restrictions on exchange means that an actor, even if he possesses the commodities relevant to a given exchange and is willing to enter into the exchange, is excluded because of his belongingness to some group or category of people.

10. See, in greater detail, Eisenstadt, *Essays on Comparative Institutions.*

It is the various structural derivatives of prestige analysed above that constitute some of the most important mechanisms through which the different
aspects of stratification outlined above—the differential evaluation of positions; the uses of the rewards received for the regulation of access to positions;
and for symbolic consumption which denotes the upholding of certain styles
of life—become interconnected, albeit in different degrees, in different societies, and become the starting points of the process of strata formation. Or in
other words that the process of strata formation can be viewed as that aspect
of the general process of institution building which tends to establish such
ascriptive limitations on exchange in terms of the setting up of basic individual
and collective identities, of their arrangement in some hierarchical order, of
specification of the desiderata which are "tied" to such identities and which
are manifest in different styles of life, and which tends to establish ascriptive
limitations on access to positions. Although most of these elements of strata
formation can be found in all relatively continuous social groupings, they become especially articulated in the macrosocietal order where the crystallization
of the basic personal and collective identities assumes several additional dimensions.

First, these identities become here closely related to participation in some
primordial—family, kinship, and territorial—groups which constitute the
starting point from which possibilities of participation in other types of social
or cultural units and orders tend to branch out. Second, on the macrosocietal
level, individuals' various desiderata include not only a great variety of discrete
goals but also the propensity or sensitivity to some—usually differential—participation in all the major types of sociocultural orders and centres. Third, in
the macrosocietal order the relations between the positions which a person
occupies in all institutional spheres become very important both from the
point of view of the individual's personal identity as well as from the point of
view of broader integrative and regulative problems of the social order. It is
these various elements specified above that constitute the major starting points
of strata formation on the macrosocietal level.

Strata (be they estates, castes, or classes, or political groups)[11] have usually
been designated as categories or groups of people who are incumbents of institutional positions or roles which enjoy a similar broad evaluation, who receive
similar differential rewards, and/or have a similar degree of control over some
of the basic resources (i.e., economic, political, or cultural) who tend to some
extent to transmit such positions to their children or to other persons who are
seen as extensions of their primordial identity and who, to some degree, are or
seem to be organized in some hierarchical order. But any "classificatory" ap-

11. For some of the major "classical" definitions of strata see: Schumpeter, *op. cit.*; Weber, *op.
cit.*; Warner and Lunt, *op. cit.*

proach to strata formation in terms of relative standing of a certain category or group of people with regard to any one resource does not enable us to understand how this is related to its standing with regard to the distribution of some of the other resources.

In any macrosocietal order there necessarily arises, as we have seen, the problem of the relation and linkages among the different positions in the major institutional spheres. The effecting of such linkage constitutes one basic aspect or component of any strata formation. Its most crucial aspects are, as we have seen above, the attempts to monopolize or regulate, directly or indirectly, the conversion of resources among such different institutional positions, the historical or some wider meaning on various specific institutional positions, and the setting up of the rules of access to them, according to some ascriptive criteria which stress components of personal and collective identity which are defined as common to the incumbents of the given positions. These tend to be, as we have seen above, defined mostly by the combination of certain personal attributes and of differential participation in the major types of societal and cultural orders that exist in every macrosocietal setting.

Out of these starting points the two major structural derivations of stratification, the upholding of styles of life and the regulation of access to positions, become crystallized in processes of strata formation. The emphasis on the upholding of a certain style of life denotes the symbolic consumption which manifests the differential participation of those who use them in such a way in various collectivities, sociocultural orders, and centres and their having attained some of the qualities which define these orders and centres. It does also bestow some broader meaning, in terms of such participation and qualities, on different specific institutional positions.

On the other side of this picture are also the attempts, by such groups, to deny—or at least make it difficult for—other groups to undertake these types of exchange, to attain such goals and as well to be able to acquire the requirements for those positions which may imply or necessitate the pursuance of such goals. Thus the development and upholding of such styles of life necessarily contain a very strong element of inclusiveness and exclusiveness—of inclusion of some people and of the concomitant exclusion of other social categories or groups. But such exclusiveness does not mean total isolation from other categories or groups, from other roles or people. The very emphasis on exclusiveness connotes a certain type of relationship with them—basically a certain type of "unconditional" yet complementary relation with them.

A second crucial aspect of strata formation—most specifically articulated on the macrosocietal level—are the attempts to transmit the right of conversion of resources and the access to the various positions occupied by certain categories or groups of people, to others who share some primordial identity. The most important (but not the only) type of such transmission is that through intrafamilial, intergenerational units, as in most total societies (as distinct from more partial groups) the extension of one's identity is mostly—although not entirely—effected through the primordial family and kinship units. These units perform, from the point of view of stratification on the macrosocietal level, several different functions which need not, however, always go together to the same degree. First, as they serve as the most general agency of socialization, it is from within them that basic orientations to different desiderata, as well as basic components or ingredients of personal and collective identity, are inculcated in individuals.

Second, they may also serve as agencies through which the access of positions is transmitted, either directly (i.e., through ascriptive, hereditary access), or, more indirectly, through the provision of resources which facilitate the acquisition of skills and attributes which tend to be necessary prerequisites for such positions. Third is the limitation of intermarriage through the rules of exogamy, endogamy, and hypergamy which are found in some way in most societies, and which very often constitute a very important aspect or focus of stratification. The importance of all these rules is rooted in the fact that the family and interfamilial relations may serve as the starting point for the development of strata solidarity which focuses around the common style of life, symbolized as it is in symbolic consumption on the one hand and in differential participation in different collectivities and sociocultural orders and centres on the other.

Thus it is the combination of the ownership of resources with the control over the uses of such resources, over the conversion of such resources from one institutional sphere to another, from one group to another, from microsocial settings to the macrosocietal order, with ascriptive regulation of access to their respective positions, and with the stress on a common identity with some strong primordial components that constitutes the crux of the process of strata formation in macrosocietal terms. But the establishment of such identities and the concomitant regulation of desiderata is not something "given" in any society; it is in itself part of a continuous process of social institutional interaction. Here of crucial importance is the acquisition of the rights to establish the criteria according to which different positions are evaluated and different styles of life are legitimized. The institutional settings within which, in groups and especially in the macrosocietal setting, such rights tend to become located, are the various social or cultural centres. Hence such centres necessarily are of crucial importance in the process of stratification in general and in that of strata formation in particular.

It is such centres which attempt to control both the differential participation of various categories of people in the major collectivities and cultural orders, as well as the conversion of various resources into other resources, and into chances of access to various institutional positions. While, needless to say, such centres are not the only mechanism through which such conversion is being effected, and many other mechanisms—such as market or bargaining processes—are also very important from this point of view, yet the centres play a crucial role in this process. The special place of the centres for stratificational purposes is rooted in the fact that they combine or may attempt to combine the setting up of the basic symbols of personal, societal, and cultural identity, the control of participation in the various collectivities and sociocultural orders, together with the setting up of societal goals[12] and with more "mundane" regulation of economic, legal, etc. relations within a society.

From the preceding discussion several general conclusions about processes of stratification and of strata formation—which I shall be able to explore here only in a very preliminary way—can be derived. The first is that it does not make great sense to talk about stratification—and especially about strata formation—in those societies in which the problem of such conversion of resources and of access to positions is very small. This is especially true of those societies (among "total" societies, various types of primitive societies)—or in those spheres thereof—to which access is either distributed more or less equally among all members of a society, or in which the "rates" of such conversion in general and the rules of access to positions in particular are ascriptively fixed to such a degree that there is very little scope for different ways or for changes of conversion of various resources and of regulation of access to positions. In such societies there may exist social differentiation but not social stratification and especially not processes of strata formation in the sense used here.[13]

The second conclusion is that the problem of strata formation arises when there does not exist such *automatic,* fixed conversion of resources and of access to positions, and there exists the possibility of different ways of converting the resources or the rewards derived from one set of positions to others.

Third is that the crystallization, through such processes of conversion of some broader, solidary groups or strata with common identity, is closely related to the existence of some common points of reference among them, i.e., of some types of centres, to which they share some `common orientations, and that therefore the structure and contents of such centres play a very prominent role in such processes of strata formation.

Fourth is that although the process of strata formation combines all the various components outlined above, i.e., the setting up of identities, the regulation of access to positions and of their ascriptive transmission through some familial or semifamilial arrangements, the upholding of styles of life, and

12. See, in greater detail, Eisenstadt, *Essays on Comparative Institutions* and "Charisma and Institution-Building," *loc. cit.* See also the bibliography in note 7.

13. See on this: M. G. Smith, "Pre-industrial stratification systems," *op. cit.* 53 f.

the concomitant transmission of orientations to desiderata and goals through the major agencies of socialization, yet they need not always go together to the same extent in all societies; and one of the major differences between societies lies exactly in the extent to which they tend to coalesce together.

Fifth, the preceding analysis has some interesting implications for the problem of the extent to which there may exist a single hierarchy of status in a society. As is well known, sociological literature, following Weberian terminology, has distinguished three major dimensions of types of strata: "classes," "estates," and political groups. It has indeed been usually recognized in the literature that, in any society, each of these types of strata formation involves a different type of resources or of different types of institutional types of positions on which they are based. But there have been few attempts to indicate exactly how the three are connected: how, to what extent, in what ways do these different formations coalesce or diverge in different societies.

The picture that one may get from large parts of the literature dealing with this problem tends to waver between two extreme views—one which stresses that each of these formations constitutes a separate entity or hierarchy, and another in which they tend basically to coalesce and merge into one another. It is only recently, in the literature on congruence of status, that it has been recognized that these need not always go together.[14] But even this literature, because of its stress on the "dysfunctional" results of such incongruence, assumes that such congruence and a concomitant unified hierarchy constitutes in a way the natural order of things. However, our analysis which stresses the multiplicity of starting points of institutions, resources, and positions on the one hand, and of different centres on the other, does imply that in any macro-societal society there does not exist only one but several such hierarchies which tend to converge or to overlap to some, but only to some, degree and that the extent to which they converge or overlap again constitutes one of the major foci of comparative research.

Part II

We shall attempt to illustrate the utility of the approach presented above by comparing the process of strata formation in several societies which can be said to belong to one rather common broad type—that of imperial or semi-

14. See for example E. Benoit Smyllan, "Status, status types, and status interrelations," *American Sociological Review*, vol. 9, 2 (1944), 151–61; G. E. Lenski, "Status crystallization: a non vertical dimension of social status," *American Sociological Review*, vol. 19, 4 (1954), 405–13; I. W. Goldman, "Status consistency and preference for change in power distribution," *American Sociological Review*, vol. 22, 3 (1957), 775–81. For a somewhat new approach, akin to the one presented here, see W. G. Runciman, *Relative Deprivation and Social Justice: A Study of Attitudes to Social Inequality in Twentieth-century England* (London, 1966).

imperial societies—such as imperial China, Russia, India or western european societies in the Age of Absolutism.[15] These societies had several common characteristics which distinguish them from other societies and which do therefore facilitate the comparison among them. One such common characteristic was a not dissimilar level of technology and hence also a similar basic range of occupational positions. Another such common characteristic was their traditionality as evident in the structure of their centres.

The basic categories of institutional-occupational positions sharing some common life chances and which can be found in these systems are the following:[16]

(*a*) The peasantry, comprising the majority of the population, living in free or servile village communities; sometimes subdivided—from the point of view of legal ownership and wealth—into various subgroups, such as gentry, middle, or lower groups of peasants and a possible agricultural proletariat.

(*b*) Various upper- or middle-urban economic or professional groups such as merchants, craftsmen (again possibly divided into big and small ones), and some professional groups such as lawyers, doctors, etc. In most of these societies these groups tend to be organized in some sort of corporate units.

(*c*) Lower urban groups composed of labourers, unskilled workers, etc.

(*d*) Cultural or religious groups and especially priests and officials of organized religions or of more local cults; members of religious orders, castes, organizations etc., and men of learning concentrated in academies, universities or in religious or secular centres. These last might be closely related to some of the professional groups.

(*e*) The various administrative and political echelons—especially on the central but also on the local levels.

(*f*) The "upper" groups or strata composed in most of these societies (with the exception of China and the very partial exception of India) of aristocratic lineages possessing control over land and to some extent also over central political and cultural resources.

(*g*) The upper political élite centred around the king or emperor, which may or may not have overlapped with some of the aristocratic and upper religious groups and which by definition had the highest degree of control over the centre or centres as they were established in these political systems.

These varied categories of positions or roles existed, even if in different degrees, in all the societies studied here. But the details of their organization, and especially the ways in which they crystallized into strata, differed greatly among these different societies. As has been pointed out above all these socie-

---

15. For a general analysis of social and political systems see S. N. Eisenstadt, *The Political Systems of Empires* (New York, 1963).

16. *Ibid.*

ties were also "traditional" societies with some very specific types of structural connotations or derivatives of traditionality.

Perhaps the most important of these structural derivations was the symbolic and structural differentiation between the centre and periphery—and the concomitant limitation on the access of members of broader groups to the political and religious centre or centres and on participation within them. In these societies tradition served not only as a symbol of continuity, but as the delineator of the legitimate limits of creativity and innovation and as the major criterion of their legitimacy—even if in fact any such symbol of tradition might have been forged out as a great innovative creation which destroyed what till then was perceived as the major symbol of the legitimate past. These connotations of traditionality were not, however, confined only to purely cultural or symbolic spheres; they had definite structural implications. The most important was first that parts of the social structure and some groups were— or attempted to become—designed as the legitimate upholders, guardians, and as a manifestation of those collective symbols, as their legitimate bearers and interpreters and hence also as the legitimizers of any innovation or change. In the more differentiated among the traditional societies these functions became crystallized into the symbolic and institutional distinctiveness of the central foci of the political and cultural orders as distinct from the periphery. It was this continuing symbolic and structural differentiation between the centre and periphery—and the concomitant limitation on the access of members of broader groups to the political and religious centre or centres and on participation within them—that constituted the most important structural derivation of the traditionality of these societies.

These characteristics of these societies had several important repercussions on some of the basic features of the structure of stratification within them in general and of strata formation in them in particular. The relatively sharp difference between centre and periphery stressed the crucial importance of the various centres for the regulation of the "conversion" of different resources on the macrosocietal level. The first result of this distinctiveness of the centre was the tendency to segregation between participation in central and peripheral spheres, i.e., in the attempts of the centre to control the process of the conversion of resources of the periphery, and to arrange relatively fixed conditions of entry into major central institutional spheres and of participation in them; and to assure, insofar as possible, that the mobility in the society in general and into the centre in particular would be mostly processes of sponsored mobility.[17]

Second, in close relation within the former characteristics, in all these so-

17. On this terminology see R. Turner, "Sponsored and contest mobility and the school system," *American Sociological Review*, vol. 25, 6 (1960), 855–67, especially 856. ·

cieties there developed, albeit in different degrees, the tendency to combine an expressly metaphysical or theological evaluation of different groups and roles with some legal or semilegal definition and fixation of various positions and status. This was especially true of those components of status which are important from the point of view of strata formation, i.e., of regulation, through ascriptive and/or legal injunctions, of access to at least some of the most important institutional positions; of the regulation of the symbolical use of resources by different groups as evident in the tendency to promulgate sumptuary laws; and even in restrictions on the use of some resources and exchange activities as most clearly seen in the regulation of the output of guilds.

But despite the fact that both the range of basic institutional (and especially economic and administrative) positions, as well as of the structure and "traditionality" of their centres, seem to have been, to no small degree, common to all the societies studied here, yet there did also develop among them many differences in the basic characteristics of their respective strata with regard to almost all the components of the processes of strata formation. They differed in the criteria according to which different positions and strata were evaluated in the extent of the autonomy of the strata; in the components of their identity and in the strength of their internal solidarity; in the extent to which they develop distinct styles of life and in the extent to which these styles of life were explicitly normatively prescribed and/or legally fixed; in the extent of country-wide strata consciousness; in their access to the different centers; in the place of family and kinship groups in the process of strata formation; in the patterns of interstrata relations in general and of social mobility in particular.

We shall not be able, of course, to analyse here all such differences. We shall attempt only to see how far some at least of these differences can be explained in terms of the nature and structure of the centre or centres of these societies, and especially of (a) the predominant orientations and goals of the centre; (b) the multiplicity of the centres in the societies and the relations between them; and (c) the accessibility of different groups to the centre. The orientations of the centres will be classified according to the major type of resources or desiderata which we have delineated above; for example, as orientations to power, wealth and different types of prestige (i.e., of participation in collectivities, social and cultural orders, and centres) or to various mixtures or combinations thereof. With regard to the number of such centres and of their interrelationships, already our preceding analysis has indicated that in any such society there usually existed several centres—the political, the religious or cultural, and even the "social" ones, i.e., centres of communal collective identity, as well as many local subcentres—the centres of the various Little Traditions, localities, and regions. From the point of view of our analysis the most crucial aspect of the relations among the—both central and local—centres is their relative predominance, as well as the degree to which membership in one centre entailed the possibility of access to another.

In order to understand how these characteristics of the centre or centres influence the process of strata formation in these societies we shall work on the assumption that the incumbent élites in all such centres attempted to maintain their own monopoly of access to the centre, and to uphold those orientations and societal goals which they saw as representing the essence of their own collective identity, the source of their legitimation, and to the implementation of which they were committed. One of the most important ways and mechanisms through which any such incumbent élite of a centre attempted to attain these goals was by making that commodity or resource which was most closely related to their basic orientations (i.e., power in case of a power-oriented centre, prestige in case of a centre oriented to the maintenance of participation in some social or cultural order) the most hard to get, the most expensive, within the framework of the existing institutional exchange. This aim could be achieved in a great variety of ways. We shall only mention here those which are most important from the point of view of analysis of strata formation.

The most general and most important mechanism of this kind was the attempt—already alluded to above—to control the process of conversion of the various resources which were at the disposal of the various groups in the society, from one institutional sphere to another, and from within various microsocietal and peripheral settings, to the level of macrosocietal markets and of their respective commodities and media of exchange.

This general mechanism was subdivided in a variety of more concrete ones. The first was to limit, but only to some degree, the right of other groups to receive the central commodity, and to have access to the centre. Such limitation was always only partial, because no élite—except in cases of a pure conquest one—could afford to deny entirely to the broader groups the right of some access to the centre. If they did so they would have been able to exert other resources from the broader groups or only through coercive measures which, in their turn, could make excessive demands on the resources of the centre or would limit its ability to implement various collective goals in which it might be interested.

Therefore most élites attempted to attain some balance between the development, within the broader groups, of some quest for such central desiderata and for participation in the centre on the one hand and for keeping such quest within very strictly prescribed limits on the other hand. This could be achieved first by attempts to prescribe, through legislation, especially of sumptuary laws, proper "style of living," of various groups and strata. Such legislation tended to emphasize on the one hand the ways in which different groups could "properly" use the resources at their disposal in a way which would emphasize the degree to which they could have orientations or access to the centre, as well as their distance from the centre, and the concomitant relatively low evaluation of their own positions in contrast to the more central ones.

Second, and closely related to the first, this could be achieved through attempts to maintain in the hands of the centre the control of access to those central positions which were the bearers of the highest rewards, be they political, religious, or cultural. Such restriction on access to central positions could be achieved in several ways. One was to make the resources or rewards at the disposal of any group almost totally irrelevant for the acquisition of such more central commodities and positions—leaving it at least in principle entirely to the centre to establish the criteria of such selection and to select the incumbents for these positions, as well as to prescribe their social life.

The other, closely related but not identical way, was to make the access to such positions contingent on the unconditional giving up by their "new" incumbents of some at least of the resources at their disposal and especially the giving up of the right of converting these resources into the more central ones. The third way was to make the price for access to these positions very high, so as to minimize the ability of those who attained such positions to use these resources for taking some sort of an independent stand with regard to the élite. Although these last two ways may seem to be almost identical, they are, as we shall yet see in greater detail later, very often antithetical in their effects on strata formation.

Last was the attempt to direct or influence various groups to use the resources at their disposal for acquisition of noncentral commodities and positions.

This does not mean, of course, that the centres were always successful in their endeavours in these respects, that their attempts were fully accepted by all groups or strata in their respective societies. As is very well known in all these societies there have existed many groups which were marginal in the central institutional core, which maintained their own traditions without very much reference to the centre. Similarly, within all these societies there existed and developed various groups and subcentres which developed orientations differing from those of the centres or even contrary and opposed to them. Moreover, the very institutionalization of any given centre or régime tended to give use to various "countercentres."[18]

But in our present analysis our main concern will not be to analyse the conditions under which they were or were not successful in these endeavours, but rather firstly, insofar as they were successful and they became predominant and their orientations were accepted to some degree in the society, how did

18. See on this S. N. Eisenstadt, "Institutionalization and change," *American Sociological Review*, vol. 29, 2 (April 1964), 49–59.

they concretely influence the process of strata formation in these societies; and secondly how the differences in some of the basic characteristics of the strata can be explained by the differences in the orientations and structures of their respective centers.

As has been pointed out already above we shall distinguish these societies first of all according to the basic orientations and structures of their centres. We shall accordingly distinguish here between states based on power, taking Russia (especially from the period of Ivan the Terrible and Peter the Great up to the beginning of the nineteenth century)[19] as the major illustration of this type; on a combination of power and a universalistic-traditional "cultural" orientation (taking imperial China as the major illustration of this type of center);[20] a centre based on closed ritualistic religious orientation, taking India as an illustration,[21] and a society with multiple centre orientation, taking Europe (especially western and central) as the main illustration.[22]

19. On Russia in this period see especially M. Beloff, *The Age of Absolutism* (London: Hutchinson's University Library, 1954), ch. 6, and "Russia," in A. Goodwin (ed.), *The European Nobility in the Eighteenth Century* (London, 1953); B. H. Summer, "Peter the Great," *History*, XXXII (1947), 39–50 and *A Short History of Russia* (New York, 1949). I. Young, "Russia," in J. O. Lindsay (ed.), *The New Cambridge Modern History*, VII (1957), 318–38; M. Raeff, *Origins of the Russian Intelligentsia: The Eighteenth Century Nobility* (New York, 1966); J. Blum, *Lord and Peasant in Russia* (Princeton, 1961).

20. E. Balazs, *Chinese Civilization and Bureaucracy: Variations on a Theme* (New Haven, 1964); D. Bodde,"Feudalism in China," in R. Coulborn (ed.), *Feudalism in History* (Princeton, 1956), 49–92; K. Eberhard, *A History of China* (London, 1960) and *Conquerors and Rulers: Social Forces in Medieval China* (Leiden, 1952); J. K. Fairbank (ed.), *Chinese Thought and Institutions* (Chicago, 1957); D. S. Nivison and A. F. Wright (eds.), *Confucianism in Action* (Stanford, 1959); K. A. Wittfogel, *Oriental Despotism: A Comparative Study of Total Power* (New Haven, 1957); A. F. Wright (ed.), *Studies in Chinese Thought* (Chicago, 1953).

21. On Indian civilization with special reference to the caste system see Max Weber, *The Religion of India*, Hans H. Gerth and Don Martindale (Glencoe, Illinois, 1958); L. Dumont, *Homo Hierarchicus—Essai sur le système des castes* (Paris, 1966), and the nine issues of *Contributions to Indian Sociology* (ed. L. Dumont) (The Hague, 1957–66); also Milton Singer, "The social organization of Indian civilization," *Diogenes*, vol. 45 (Winter 1964), 84–119; M. Singer (ed.), *Traditional India—Structure and Change* (Philadelphia, 1959). Some of the earlier expositions of caste system can be found in J. H. Hutton, *Caste in India* (London, 1946); H. M. C. Stevenson, "Status evaluation in the Hindu caste system," *Journal of the Royal Anthropological Institute*, vol. 84 (1954), 45–65; E. A. H. Blunt, *The Caste System of Northern India* (London, 1931).

For some of the more recent discussions see F. K. Bailey, "Closed social stratification," *European Journal of Sociology*, IV (1963), 107–24; A. Beteille, "A note on the referents of castes," *European Journal of Sociology*, V (1964), 130–4; McKim Marriot, "Interactional and attributional theories of caste ranking," *Man in India*, XXXIX, no. 2 (1959), 92–107.

For the most comprehensive analysis of the changes between the traditional and the modern Indian caste system see: S. M. Srinivas, *Caste in Modern India* (Bombay, 1964), and *Social Change in Modern India* (Berkeley, 1966).

22. See M. Beloff, *The Age of Absolutism* (London: Hutchinson's University Library, 1954); J. O. Lindsay (ed.), *New Cambridge Modern History*, VII (1957); G. Clark, *The Seventeenth Century* (Oxford, 1929–59), and *Early Modern Europe (1450–1720)* (London, 1957); A. Goodwin (ed.), *The European*

Russia

We shall start with a brief analysis of Russia (from the time of Ivan the Terrible or Peter the Great, till the end of the eighteenth century) as an imperial society, the evolution of which in this period tended—for reasons which we shall not deal with here—to make power the basic orientations of the centres. Its rulers attempted to define the basic orientations and goals of the polity in terms of the combinations of center and power; to define the centre very largely in terms of such monopolization of power and in terms of pursuance of goals oriented to the maintenance and accumulation of power.[23] Hence, the major problem of the ruling élite here was how to limit and control the access of other groups both to power as a generalized commodity and to the positions of central institutional power.

The Russian centre attempted to attain these results by creating a general situation in which the access to power in general and to power positions in particular could not, in a way, be "bought," except through the very exercise of power; power could be used to get other resources but it was much more difficult to get power through such other resources. Those groups who had other resources at their disposal had to give up these resources, as demanded by holders of powers without themselves being able to "buy" such power of their own volition.[24]

This was here attempted by several ways which seem to be specific to a power system. First was the attempt to limit very seriously the extent to which the participation in the centre constituted a part of the identity of other groups and an active desideratum on their part. The rulers encouraged the development, especially but not only, among the lower levels of society, of only very passive orientation towards the centre. They attempted to attain this by allowing them but few independent possibilities of active independent orientation to the centre, by making the styles of life of different collectivities as

---

Nobility in the Eighteenth Century (London, 1953); B. Barber and E. G. Barber (eds.), *European Social Class: Stability and Change* (New York, 1965).

23. For details of Russian civilization in this period see the bibliography in the footnote on 81–2; fuller references can be found in the bibliography of Eisenstadt, *The Political Systems of Empires*.

24. Here the difference between "traditional," Imperial power-oriented and modern totalitarian régimes stands out. The ruling élites of the latter have, often despite their natural "power" tendency, to buy the various resources of the broader strata, because of, first, the nature of their legitimation which entails a potentially widespread quest for participation; second, they have to do so because of the scope of their goals which continuously create new organizational "needs" and exigencies and which necessitates the mobilization of resources from these strata. Hence the totalitarian élite has to permit such wider groups to participate in some of the "central" spheres so as to have some access to the power positions.

relatively closed and segregated from one another as possible, and by making the participation in central activities both entirely dependent on the centre as well as different for each "local" or "status" collectivity.

In order to attain its aim the centre attempted to control not only the desiderata and identities of these groups but also the use, by them, of the resources at their disposal. Here the power centre tended to encourage the spending, "wasting," of such resources, in various patterns of conspicuous consumption. But unlike the case of other types of traditional centres, it did not tend to encourage the development by these groups of very rigid styles of life sanctioned by the norms and symbols of the centre. On the contrary, it tended to minimize the legitimation of such styles of life and tended instead to encourage a rather "indiscriminate" dispersal of the resources. It tended to be relatively permissive with regard to the use of such resources for various "segregated" desiderata—so long as these were not too ostentatious; as they did not tend to create too great a demand for new "skills" which could create too many new independent positions which in their turn could become foci of independent central markets, or of new collective identities; and so long as they did not impinge on access to the power central positions.[25] The third major mechanism used by this power élite to attain its aims was to set the price for entry into power positions and for maintenance of such positions in such a way that once somebody got into the power structure he had to give up unconditionally most convertible resources at his disposal and was then, in the power market, at a relatively low "bargaining position" *vis-à-vis* the major holders of power—i.e., in principle the tsar.[26] These varied mechanisms through which the predominance of the power centre was being upheld had several repercussions on the process of strata formation in imperial Russia up till the end of the eighteenth century.

Perhaps the most general such influence was the lack of or weakness of what may be called society-wide class or strata consciousness and organization. This could of course be most clearly seen among the lowest groups—the peasants—where there was almost no way of extending participation from their own local collectivities into some wider country-wide frameworks, despite many various informal social ties and common traditions between peasants of various villages or regions. But this was also the case among various urban groups. Here the most important indicator of this weakness was the lack of common organization even among the "middle" occupations of the same city and the great dependence of any specific occupational group (guild) within any locality (city or region) for the development of their own organization, on

25. Raeff, *The Origins of Russian Intelligentsia;* Blum, *Lord and Peasant in Russia,* esp. ch. 13.
26. See Beloff, *The Age of Absolutism,* and Raeff, *op. cit.*

the official sanction of the centre.[27] The self-identity of most of these groups was mostly based on such narrow occupational and local bases, with only minimal wider, even local—and certainly, society-wide—orientations. Insofar as any such wider, more than minimal and latent, and based only on common customs, society-wide orientations may be found, they seem to have been grounded in the legislation of the centre.

Significantly enough, this applies also, even if in a somewhat lesser way, to the aristocracy.[28] The aristocracy had, of course, a much higher standing and a greater control of resources than any other social group. Moreover, by virtue of its very proximity to the centre on the one hand, and of some remnants of its own (pre-Mongol) semifeudal traditions on the other, it did have some more country-wide links. Yet even it did not have very strong widespread country-wide autonomy or stratum-consciousness. Whatever autonomy it did maintain from the pre-absolutist period was shattered by the tsars who succeeded in making it an almost pure service aristocracy, and whatever elements of such autonomy developed later were also mostly entirely fostered by the tsars. It was only at the end of the eighteenth and the beginning of the nineteenth century that this situation began to change.[29]

This was very closely connected with the second major characteristic of strata formation in Russian society, namely the very high degree of segregation among the various status groups—the different local or occupational groups. Each of such groups tended to maintain its own identity, with but few common meeting points among them. Third, there did not develop within most of these groups a "closed," normatively prescribed style of life encompassing all their varied positions and designating definite patterns of consumption. In fact there did of course develop, especially among the aristocracy and among some of the urban groups, certain such customary patterns. Similarly the peasantry, living in the various village communities, tended to follow old, traditionally accepted patterns of life. But these patterns were on the whole neither fully regulated by internal or external normative sanctions nor were they upheld as models and symbols by those who participated in them.[30]

Among the aristocracy some such normative prescriptions tended to develop in the capital when they were in state service, by virtue of participation of the life of the court—but only to a smaller degree in their own domains. Thus, for instance, there were here but few—if any—normative restrictions on the engagement of aristocrats in business or in commercial activities of the kind known in France. Such restrictions did not apply to the peasantry—or

27. For a general account see Young, *op. cit.*
28. See Raeff, *op. cit.;* and Beloff in Goodwin (ed.) *op. cit.*
29. See Raeff, *op. cit.* and Beloff in Goodwin (ed.), *op. cit.*
30. Blum, *Lord and Peasant*, chs. 15, 23; and Raeff, *op. cit.*

even to the serfs—so long as they could buy their freedom from their lords or received their permission to engage in such activities.

This weakness of normatively prescribed status style of life was also quite closely related to patterns of intergroup intermarriage. From the available— true enough rather meagre—evidence, indications may indeed be derived which show that there was a relative paucity of injunctions against interstratum intermarriage. Cases of such intermarriage were known, although *de facto*—but not so much *de jure*—there was a very large extent of "strata" endogamy. The situation naturally tended to be more rigid on the upper level—that of the aristocracy—but even here it was far from being clear-cut.

The preceding analysis brings us to another crucial aspect of the Russian status system—namely the place of the family or kinship groups in the system of stratification. As in all traditional (and probably in other) societies the family or kinship group constituted, of course, the major primary agency of socialization within which the major desiderata and cultural and social orientations were inculcated in individuals. Moreover, family groups belonging to the same stratum probably usually formed the actual framework of social intercourse and of intermarriage within a given locality or region. But given the relative weakness of the *normative* prescription of life styles of strata and of country-wide consciousness of strata, families did not fulfill very important roles from the point of view of inculcating active, broader, strata-collective identities. They were specially weak in interlinking any such identities with some broader, active orientation to participation in the centre or centres. Similarly, although *de facto* there was probably quite a lot of intergenerational occupational continuity within most families, yet most families could control access to such positions not through some hereditary rights of access but for the most part indirectly. They could do this either by force of custom or by making the proper use of the resources for the acquisition of such positions. Resources at the disposal of the family—including its status—could easily restrict the available opportunities but in themselves did not yet assure the access of the sons to the "better" positions of the fathers.

Whatever the validity of the preceding analysis—and because of the paucity of systematic data it is necessarily rather conjectural—they seem to some extent to be borne out by some of the available indications—also rather scarce—on patterns of interstrata mobility in Russia. Given the relative free use of resources, it was mostly hampered by the legal status of some groups (especially the serfs) and much less by their ability or willingness to use such resources in order to acquire higher positions or resources.[31] Insofar, however,

---

31. The most important indicators here are the so-called serf entrepreneurs of the late eighteenth and nineteenth centuries. See on this H. Rosovsky, "The serf entrepreneur in Russia," *Explorations in Entrepreneurial History*, VI (1953), 207–39.

as such mobility did take place, it usually gave rise to the creation of new "segregated" patterns of local and occupational group life and much less to the establishment of either new common, country-wide, strata consciousness or of meeting points between different groups and strata and patterns of participation common to them.[32]

On the whole such mobility tended to emphasize both the segregation among different local or occupational status groups as well as the relative weakness of normative prescription of the styles of life of such groups. This seems to apply also to mobility into the aristocracy and state-service, although here some additional characteristics stand out. The most important characteristic of this mobility has been that it was a clear instance of "sponsored" mobility. The concrete expression of this sponsored mobility among the upper classes of Russia was of course the almost total initial control of access into the bureaucracy—and in principle also into the aristocracy—by the tsars.[33]

Although in principle most scions of the aristocracy were expected to enter into some sort of state service, the choice was, in principle, not theirs but the tsar's; and the mere fact of belonging to an aristocratic family did not entitle—although it certainly facilitated—the access to such positions. However, once such access was obtained the style of life of the aristocrat in the capital, in state service, differed greatly from his life on his local estates—not only in the daily details but mainly in terms of the strength of its symbolic and normative prescription of the appropriate style of life. This courtly prescription of such style of life tended to emphasize disassociation from the family life of aristocrats in their localities. Thus many aristocratic families evinced in the lifetime of their members a pattern of continuous disassociation and segregation between the style of life of family of origin (in the local aristocratic estates) and its point of destination (in the higher court positions) which characterized the general pattern of mobility in Russian society.

China

The second case in our comparative analysis will be the Chinese Imperial system as it developed from the period of Han (c. 206 B.C.) until the fall of the

---

32. Of special importance in this whole context was, of course, the Church. It constituted the major channel of mobility from the lower strata—but it seems that the basic pattern of mobility was repeated also here. Entrance into the Church entailed on the one hand severance of most actual ties with the family of origin and the giving up of its style of life but it did not provide any foci for formation of common social links with other strata. Although in principle it could provide close access to the centre and to political power, yet on the whole the Church was not permitted to become either an independent political or "social" inter-strata identity. The basic limitations on access to power-position also seemed on the whole, with some minor exceptions, to apply to it.

33. See Raeff, *op. cit.*

Ching dynasty in 1911.[34] Here again, without going into an historical analysis of the development of this centre, it will suffice for our analysis to indicate that from the Han onward this centre was defined in terms of the combination of political power and of the participation in a traditional cultural order—the Confucian-legalistic one. As in the case of any other traditional order its contents were conceived as given and fixed in the framework of its basic precepts and orientations. But in several other aspects this cultural order was among the most open among all known traditional societies.

First of all, this order was conceived as a semisecular one, oriented towards the upholding and the continuous cultivation of a tradition whose basic contents were indeed given in the activities and precepts of its Founding Father but within the framework of which there was indeed place for continuous cultivation and elaboration—mainly through learning and not, as for instance in India, through purely fixed or ritual activities. Second, this order was conceived as encompassing and enfolding—even if in different degrees—all strata and parts of the population and as open to all of them. Its relations to political power were twofold. On the one hand it tended to find within the confines of the empire its natural focus and framework; on the other hand it was also the major legitimator of the political order.[35]

Hence, in China—unlike in Russia—the absolutist centre was defined in terms of both political power and of culture or tradition, each of which constituted independent bases of access to the centre. Whatever the vagaries of individual emperors and the lack of security of individual officials the centre was the arena of continuous interplay between the holders of purely political power and of representatives of the cultural order, the representatives of each attempting to control the access of the other to the centre—but not being able to deny the validity of the other and its relative independence.[36]

The possession of power, be it by virtue of hereditary standing, military power, individual ability, or of proximity to the imperial household, did assure the possibility of access to the centre—but did not assure in itself the tenure of position within it. Power in itself had to buy access to the centre by participating to some degree at least in the cultural tradition. Similarly, those who were in possession of the prestige of participation in the cultural tradition and order had the right of entry into the central positions but within it they had to

34. For general bibliography see note 20. A fuller bibliography is given in Eisenstadt, *Political Systems of Empires*.

35. See on this in greater detail: Balazs, *Chinese Civilisation and Bureaucracy*, Fairbank (ed.), *Chinese Thought and Institutions*, Nivison and Wright (eds.), *Confucianism in Action*.

36. W. T. de Bary, "Chinese despotism and the Confucian ideal: a seventeenth-century view," in J. K. Fairbanks (ed.), *Chinese Thought and Institutions*, 163–204; C. O. Hucker, "Confucianism and the Chinese Censorial System," in Nivison and Wright (eds.), *op. cit.* 182–208.

assure their place by giving up—even if only some of—their independent standing.

Thus there existed in China both a more multiple orientation of the centre than in the Russian case, as well as—and this is probably much more important—a somewhat greater heterogeneity of criteria and avenues of access of members of the subcentres to the centre itself—although on the whole it was a very closed and monolithic centre, with very sharp distinctiveness from the periphery. But perhaps the most important aspect of the structure and orientations of the Chinese center was not only the continuous interplay between the upholders of the pure political power and those of the cultural tradition, but the fact that cultural order which the centre represented was conceived as potentially encompassing all the groups and strata of the population.

Hence there existed here—to a much larger degree than in the Russian (or similar power-based) case—some basic affinity between the definition of the identity of various peripheral collectivities and that of the centre. Some—and not entirely passive—orientation to the centre and to participation in it constituted a basic component of the collective identity of many local, occupational groups. Here, unlike in a traditional, power-oriented centre, there did not exist a basic separation between the societal order represented by the centre and that embedded within the various types of peripheral collectivities.

Moreover the various peripheral collectivities were encouraged—at least in terms of the official ideology—to have some of their members participate more actively in the centre—mainly through the advancement in learning, by undertaking the official examinations and by graduating as literati.

Thus, because of this almost total universality of participation in the cultural tradition, the centre (part of which was anyhow composed of the central cultural groups) was not able—as in Russia—entirely to control the access to its own position. Rather it had to regulate the prices which could be exerted for the right of entrance—so that it could indeed assure that whatever other resources were accumulated and could become foci of new, independent desiderata, would mostly have to be invested in the quest of participating in the centre.

Unlike in the Russian case, the "price" for such access was not the giving up of the right to "convert" one's resources into the possibility of access to high position. Here this right was, in a sense, given and even encouraged—but at the same time the amount of resources necessary for its attainment was very high. It did also greatly differ for different groups and strata, according to their standing in the official ideological evaluation of positions that developed in China, and the highest prices were exerted from those groups—especially the merchants and military—which on the one hand were at the bottom of the "ideological" scale of evaluation but who could accumulate many "free" resources. The various institutional consequences of the orientations of the Chinese centre which were discussed above have greatly influenced some of the characteristics of strata formation in Chinese society.

The first such general characteristic of Chinese strata formation was the development of a relatively clear ideological evaluation of different occupational positions based on their assumed ideological, or metaphysical, proximity to the basic tenets of Confucian order. According to this evaluation the literati (and to some extent the gentry) enjoyed the highest prestige, the peasants next, and the merchants (and to some degree the military) very low prestige. Very closely related to this official evaluation of different occupations and groups was the development, in China, of relatively strong normative definition of the styles of life and collective identities of different collectivities and strata. Each such normative prescription of the style of life contained a very strong orientation to the centre and possible participation in it; the normative linkage of such participation with specific occupational positions on the one hand, and with a symbolic consumption of resources on the other hand.

A third important characteristic of the Chinese strata system was the place of family units within it. Unlike in Russia, the various family groups served not only as the main agents of initial socialization but also as foci of the different styles of life and of various strata or local cultures. But, perhaps even to a somewhat greater degree than in Russia, they could not serve as automatic channels of transmission of access to high positions—although in fact there did exist a strong correlation between family status and the chances of such access. But this relation was not—even *de facto*, and certainly not in ideology—fully legitimized.[37] At the same time, given the fact that kinship units constituted the major foci of various broader collective identities, and that these identities did contain important orientation to the centre, it was indeed family and kinship groups that also provided the resources and the incentives for attempting to achieve such access.

Fourth—and again partially in contrast with the Russian strata system— was the nature of a country-wide strata consciousness and organization. At least among the higher groups, i.e., the literati and the bureaucracy, there did indeed develop a relatively high degree of country-wide stratum consciousness or solidarity. This was rooted first in the common cultural tradition; second in sharing common avenues of access; and third in the fact that the access to these channels—the schools and the academies—was to some extent autonomous, not entirely dependent on the political centre, but at the same time very

37. E. A. Kracke Jr., "Region, family, and individual in the Chinese examination system," in Fairbanks (ed.), *Chinese Thought and Institutions*, 251–68; Ping-ti Ho, *The Ladder of Success in Imperial China* (New York, 1962).

strongly oriented to it. This common consciousness was also connected with some, even if a rather minimal, degree of autonomous organization in the various schools and academies.

It was for parallel but obverse reasons, i.e., because of the distance from the centre and the lack of direct access to it, that such common consciousness could not develop among the merchants or the other urban groups. Here, as in Russia, these groups never coalesced into one common stratum—cutting across different occupational or local positions—although there existed, of course, many translocal ties. Moreover, any such tendency to the development of any such broader consciousness or organization of their own was also greatly impeded by the strong orientation to the centre even among these groups—an orientation which, given their great distance from the centre, tended to deflect their activities and resources from building up their own broader collective identities.[38] Such consciousness and especially common organization could not also develop among the peasants. This was due not only to the lack of adequate channels of communication, but also because the access to the centre, although permitted and even officially encouraged, was not given automatically to the peasant groups as corporate entities but was only encouraged for individuals.

The preceding characteristics of the process of strata formation had also several repercussions on some general structural characteristics of the system of strata in China.

Perhaps the most important of such characteristics was the absence of legal distinction between free and nonfree strata—evident in the absence of aristocracy on the one hand, and of servile peasantry on the other. As is well known, China was on the whole characterized by the relative absence of hereditary aristocracy and by the peculiar nature of the highest groups—the literati-bureaucracy group.[39] It was the nature of the "ruling group" or élite that underlined the basic relative weakness in China, of hereditary ascription, the strength of the achievement orientations within the limits of a given tradition and the major characteristics of mobility to which we shall soon address ourselves. This was very closely related to the status and structure of the peasant groups. They were, as we have seen, relatively highly evaluated and were accordingly in strongest opposition to the Russian case, conceived as legally free—although in fact they may have often incurred various disabilities and disadvantages. Moreover, in the internal differentiation of the peasantry there was a somewhat continuous transition between the different subgroups, with

38. See, in greater detail, the discussion in Balazs, *op. cit.*, and Eisenstadt, *Political Systems of Empires*, esp. chs. VI–XI and ch. XII.

39. Balazs, *ibid.*; Eisenstadt, *Political Systems of Empires*, ch. XII.

their apex in the "gentry," each of which had, within its own collective identity, some orientations to the centre and whose local traditions were to some extent upheld and legitimized by the centre.

All these characteristics of strata formation have greatly influenced the pattern of social mobility in China, which constituted probably one of the major mechanisms of the stability of the imperial-Confucian system. Fortunately here we have more data than in the Russian case. Ping-ti Ho's analysis has provided us with some of the most comprehensive surveys of this problem and has indeed shown the wide scope of both upward and downward mobility, the vagaries of individual family life-histories, as well as the way in which this mobility upheld the ideal of open achievement.[40]

But of no less importance, from the point of view of our discussion, than the extent of circulation of élites that was effected by this mobility, are some of its structural aspects or characteristics. It has been obviously a very "sponsored" type of mobility—directed as it was at the attainment of positions within a very fixed institutional framework and cultural contents—but the effects of this sponsored mobility on interstrata relations were different here from those that we found in Russia. Unlike in Russia there was, at least from the point of view of the peasants but also of other groups, a greater continuity and possible overlapping between the styles of life of the group of origin of the mobile persons and their groups of "destination," and no sharp dissociation from the group of origin was demanded. This, in a sense, facilitated even the acceptance of downward mobility.

This was reinforced by the fact that these processes of mobility were here also very strongly bound to their familistic bases and to the possible extension of family obligations and resources. As it was the family which served as the major mechanism of transmission of strata identity, the processes of mobility have, at least in some cases, served also as interlinking points between different strata.

India

We shall now proceed to an examination of one of the most baffling and yet crucial systems of stratification within our comparative framework—namely the caste system of India. We shall not enter here into a detailed discussion of the problem which has preoccupied scholars for a very long period of time— namely whether the phenomena of caste has been confined to India or can also be found in other societies. There can be no doubt that, on the one hand, some of the elements of caste—such as the emphasis on occupational exclusiveness, endogamy, and ritual pollution, can be found also in many other societies. But on the other hand it is also clear that it is only in India that these have become

40. Ping-ti Ho, *The Ladder of Success in Imperial China*.

a focus of a total macrosocietal order and system of stratification.[41] It is on this that we shall concentrate our brief analysis.

The ideological focus of the caste system in India has been, as is well known, the Brahmanic system of values, with its focus on the conception of parallelism between cosmic and social purity and pollution, and in the ideology of the varnai. This is seen in the manifestation of this parallelism in the ritual and social spheres through the differential ritual standing of different occupations or tasks and in the transmission of such standing through the basic primordial family and kinship units. This social-cultural (ritual) order was, unlike the Chinese one, closed both in the terms of contents, i.e., the definition of the cosmic and social order, and in terms of access to it. It was ideologically totally ascriptive with almost no possibility whatsoever of transcending its hereditary limitations of access to actual social positions.

It was this Brahmanic ideology that can be said to have constituted the major centre of Indian civilization, with the various political centres serving mostly as secondary and political centres and, except later under the Moghul and the British rules, rather discontinuous ones. Closely related to the nature of this order was the lack of any other continuous—i.e., especially political— centre. Such a centre developed only later, under the Moghul and the British rules. Thus we find here, in comparison with other imperial societies, an almost unique situation in that whatever political centres tended to develop here, they were usually partial and relatively "weak" in terms of the major orientations or the cultural systems and the commitments they could command thereby.[42]

This type of orientation and structure of the centres had several implications on the process of strata formation in Indian society. First, we find here, owing to the sharp emphasis on the linkage between family units and ritual-cosmic standing, a very sharp normative definition of the styles of life of different status-groups (castes). These definitions tended in principle to combine the definition of collective strata identity in terms of cosmic purity or pollution together with differential evaluation of occupations; and the proper symbolic consumption of resources with very strict, ascriptive, prescription of the rules of access to the major institutional positions. Second, there was, because of the strongly ascriptive and hereditary ritual emphasis, a very strong linkage between family and kinship groups and status identity and organization. The family and kinship group was here the major socializing agency, the major focus of status participation and of collective identity, and the major channel of transmission of ascriptive access to the major positions. This was connected with a very strong emphasis on caste endogamy or, in the "worst" case, hyper-

41. See the bibliography in note 21. The problem of the uniqueness of the Indian caste system is discussed most fully in Dumont, *Homo Hierarchus.*

42. M. Singer, *The Social Organization of Indian Civilization,* M. Singer (ed.), *Traditional India.*

gamy and, as consequence of this, with almost total ideological negation of the possibility of intercaste mobility. Third was the specific type of linkage between occupational positions and ritual status. In principle every occupational position—be it that of an agricultural labourer, landowner, artisan, or merchant—was clearly assigned to some of the major status (caste-varna) categories; but, at the same time, these categories comprised many concrete occupations. Fourth comes the nature of the country-wide stratum consciousness and organization of the major status-group of the castes. It is here, perhaps more than in any other sphere, that the difference between theory and practice not only stands out but is of crucial importance for the understanding of the working of the Indian system of stratification. In theory (i.e., especially in the varna ideology) the different caste categories or units were defined as country-wide and therefore in principle also engendered a country-wide caste consciousness and organization. This was closely connected with a strong tendency to put some of the "lowest" groups beyond the pale of the system, which could also sometimes, but not always, become connected with legal disabilities and servitude.[43] In reality, however, there did not exist such a unified country-wide hierarchy and caste organization—just as there did not exist such close interrelation between institutional functions and positions, ritual standing, and use of resources as was assumed in the official ideology. (Curiously enough it was probably only the British who, by incorporating caste classification into their census, gave the sharpest push to the establishment of some such unified hierarchy.)

The Brahmin ideology and system of worship was, in a sense, India-wide, and served, as we have already indicated above, as a focus of the overall basic cultural identity of the society. Moreover, among the same Brahmin groups— as well as among other, especially higher, castes—there existed also, to some limited degree, some country-wide, or at least region-wide, contacts and intermarriage. But on the whole the basis of caste organization and interrelation was local. In practice there were hundreds, if not thousands, of caste organizations organized locally—in villages, regions, and principalities. Thus there developed here a sharp discrepancy between the relatively uniform, homogeneous, country-wide demands of the cultural order and the more dispersed and diversified political and economic systems.

The ideal of the caste of the division of labour, while focused on country-wide ritual order, could not be applied either on the more regional or more local levels. With regard both to the use of political power and money, there developed, on these levels, a great variety of activities which could not be bound by the ritual caste prescriptions. First of all there was no full correspondence between the various occupational positions, the number of which was

43. Srinivas, *Caste in Modern India*, and *Social Change in Modern India*.

very great and becoming more diversified, and caste categories. This very diversification often tended to create somewhat independent hierarchies of status which could often undermine the status of local groups of Brahmins and serve as a starting point for the attainment of new caste-status, often changing the existing caste-order in general and the interrelations and mutual obligations between different castes in particular.

The relations between the Brahmin and the political powers bring out even more the limits of the pure ideological pattern in which the political was subservient to the ritual. While this remained true on the ideological level, yet the concrete dependence of Brahmins or the rulers for the upholding of their relative status was very great.[44] In many, if not most cases, it was up to the rulers to define the relative ritual standing of various caste-groups, individuals, or of single family groups—but mostly a pattern of "contest" mobility of broader kinship groups. This mobility took on the form of formation of new types of political and economic units, organizations, and hierarchies on the one hand, but on the other it also took the form of continuous formation of subcastes. Thus, on the one hand, this mobility did undermine the actual status of any given local caste hierarchy as well as the ideal patterns of conversion of resources. But on the other hand many of these mobile groups aimed at attainment, for themselves, of relatively higher ritual standing, at "self-Sanskritization," thus upholding the basic ideological assumptions of the system.[45]

This pattern of mobility can probably be attributed firstly to the combination of common orientations to the "ideal" pattern of one centre, with the multiplicity of actual centres; and secondly to strong linkage between family and stratum identity.

Western (and Central) Europe

We shall now proceed to a very brief and preliminary analysis of the last case of "imperial" or "absolutist" systems of stratification—and one which necessarily is of special interest for our comparative analysis—namely that of western (and to some extent central) Europe as it developed in the postfeudal and post "Stände-Staat" stage, i.e., in what is usually called the Age of Absolutism.[46] For reasons of space we shall also dwell only on those characteristics which seem to be similar to all the European societies and to distinguish them from other "imperial" systems and shall not deal with the differences among them.

The most outstanding characteristic of most west European centres was

---

44. See B. S. Cohen, "Political systems in eighteenth century India: the Banares region," *Journal of the American Oriental Society*, vol. 82, no. 3 (July–September 1962); and Srinivas, *Social Change*, especially chs. I and III.

45. On patterns of caste mobility see Srinivas, *op. cit.* ch. III.

46. See the general bibliography in note 22.

that they were pluralistic both in the sense of having relatively multiple orientations and of being based on multiple, semi-autonomous subcentres. As in every political centre, there was here also a strong emphasis on power and on the extension of its scope. But additional orientations such as those to different types of prestige, as well as to some degree of economic orientations, were also of great importance. Among the types of prestige which were stressed by these centres was first, the participation in the universalistic cultural religious tradition of Christianity; second was the participation in, or the representation by the centre of, the collective identities of the different local or status groups carrying on the transformed, older tribal communal traditions. As a result of this multiplicity of orientations there tended to develop within these centres a continuous struggle over their relative predominance. Here the outcome differed, of course, in various European countries; but on the whole it seems that a combination of power with some type of prestige—mostly "social" and cultural universalistic prestige—were the most prevalent, although economic orientations, especially when combined with participation in different territorial or kinship communities, did also play an increasingly important role.[47]

But perhaps the most important aspect of the structure of most European centres was not the mere multiplicity of the orientations predominant within them but the interrelations between the different subcentres and broader strata and the centre. Here the most important fact is that any group which had control over some resources relevant for these orientations had some legitimate and autonomous, even if *differentiated*, access to the centre. Not only the Church but also many local or status groups were at least to some degree autonomous in their ability to convert their resources from one institutional sphere to another and from the periphery to the centres.[48]

Among the components of the identity and styles of life of these last types of groups and strata, primordial kinship and territorial ties played an important role. But these identities and the concomitant organizational frameworks were not closed in themselves, or entirely ascriptively fixed in their relations to other groups and to the centres. They were open towards the various centres—both towards the (national or "state") political centres and to various supranational ones. The autonomy of no group was ever "total," and the regulation of access to the centre was but rarely left by the centre itself to any single group, and none of them had full access to positions of control over any institutional markets. There developed therefore a great extent of mobility and change within these settings, a continuous conversion of resources from one sphere to another and the creation of new types of institutional positions. These general

47. See especially J. O. Lindsay, "The social classes and the foundations of the states," in J. O. Lindsay (ed.), *New Cambridge Modern History*, VII (1957), 50, and M. Beloff, *The Age of Absolutism*.
    48. See E. G. Barber, *op. cit.* and B. Barber and E. G. Barber (eds.), *op. cit.*

characteristics of west European centres have greatly influenced the processes of strata formation within them.

Given the strong orientation of various groups towards the centre, as well as the strong element of power and prestige within the orientation of the centre, it was but natural that there tended to develop here a strong tendency to the development of ideological-legal hierarchies of strata and concomitant legal distinctions between different strata. Given also the strong component of primordial kinship and territorial elements in the identity of the various strata—and hence also the differentiation between them in terms of the relative importance of their respective kinship—territorial communities—many of the contractual or political arrangements that developed in the beginning of the feudal age between different local and "functional" groups tended to crystallize into differences between legally free and nonfree strata and to reinforce the strong ascriptive, "caste"-like tendencies of many of these groups. But at the same time there worked, especially among the free groups, some strong forces—which have been already alluded to above—which counteracted these tendencies. Given the multiplicity of the orientations of the centre, and of the strata alike, as well as the partial autonomy of the subcentres and of their access to the centre, there could not on the whole develop here a unified, ideological evaluation of different positions—despite the strong tendencies to the development of such positions of, and to, concomitant status legislation. Each of the major autonomous units—be it the Church, the court, the different strata or collective groups—tended to develop different scales of evaluations, each of which claimed some degree of centrality and potentially general validity. As a result of this there tended to develop here a multiplicity of hierarchies of status and of different patterns of status incongruity, as well as strong tendencies to obliterate the legal distinction between free and servile groups.

The second important characteristic of European strata—and closely related to the preceding one—was the existence among them of a very strong tendency to relatively "unified," country-wide strata consciousness and organization. This was especially evident among the higher strata but certainly not absent among the middle and even lower "free" (peasant) strata. The fullest expression of this tendency can be found in the system of representation as it culminated in the systems of "Estates."[49] The roots of this tendency are to be found in the possibility of political participation or representation of most groups in the centre by virtue of their very collective identities, as corporate or semicorporate bodies and not only, as in the Chinese case, by being able to provide for some of their members the means through which access to the

---

49. Indeed it seems that the whole conception of a society divided into society-wide homogeneous and self-conscious strata which constitutes a basic premise of most modern studies of stratification is largely derived from this particular European experience.

centre becomes possible.[50] Hence, unlike in the Chinese case, this country-wide "consciousness" or organization was confined not only to the higher groups but could also be found among the "middle" or lowest free groups and strata.

Third, unlike in the Chinese, or even Russian, case, but not entirely unlike the Indian case, there tended to develop a close relationship between family and kinship identity on the one hand, and collective-strata identity on the other; and family and kinship groups constituted very important channels, not only of orientation to high position but also of ascriptive transmission of such positions. Unlike in the Indian case, however, the degree of access of different groups or strata to the centre was not ascriptively fixed but constituted a continuous bone of contention of what one could call "strata-conflict," i.e., conflict among different strata as *strata* about their relative prestige standing in general, and about the scope of their participation in the centre in particular.

Fourth—and here again very unlike the Chinese or Russian cases and more like the Indian case—each such stratum and especially the "middle" ones (but sometimes also the aristocracy) tended to encompass a great variety of occupational positions and organizations and to link them in some common way of life and in common avenues of access to the centre. These common styles of life of various strata comprised, as we have seen, different types of combinations of participation in primordial, kinship-territorial as well as in broad universalistic cultural orders, of orientations to the centre and participation in it; and they were closely connected to various economic occupational activities and to the performance of various institutional and occupational tasks.

Fifth, in close relation to the preceding characteristics there developed the possibility of the differential, yet *common*, participation of different groups and strata, in different cultural orders and centres, which in turn gave rise to possible overlapping in the styles of life of different strata. This was facilitated by the availability of several different channels of access to the centres which could be used by the various strata—providing also points of contact among them. Closely related to the preceding characteristics of strata formation was the scope and nature of the process of mobility that developed in European societies. On the whole we find—among all strata—starting with the nobility (with the partial exception of the eighteenth century) a very high degree of family mobility between strata. This already had its roots, as Marc Bloch has indicated, in the feudal age and seems to have continued throughout European history up to the end or middle of the Absolutist era.[51]

The very fact of the existence of European, transsociety-wide strata con-

50. Lindsay, *op. cit.*
51. Bloch, *Feudal Society* (London, 1961).

sciousness and organization facilitated such family mobility and continuous changes in the family and ethnic composition of various groups.[52] This mobility has been, on the whole, more of the type of "contest" mobility of families than of the pure sponsored mobility—although the latter element was also certainly not missing. But even the sponsored mobility was very variegated— as it took place through many channels such as the Church, political and administrative avenues, etc.

In great contrast to China, but in some way similar to the process of subcaste formation in India, there developed here not only a process of mobility within a relatively given, fixed system of positions but also—concomitantly— a process which in itself created new positions and groups which could in turn become foci of new status crystallizations. The most obvious illustration of this has been the development of cities, merchants' associations, professional cultural groups, as well as the continuous change in the scope of activities of the aristocracy. In many cases these processes of mobility seem here to have created not only new positions but also new points of contact between different groups and strata and societies as foci of crystallization of new strata consciousness and of new political expressions of such consciousness.

PART IV

We may now attempt to summarize—in a very brief and tentative way—some of the analytical propositions or hypotheses, which may be derived from our preceding comparative analysis, about the influence of the major orientations and structures of centres on processes of strata formation in imperial societies. We shall attempt to do this by indicating how several basic components of centre formation, and especially the extent to which they develop distinct styles of life and the extent to which these styles of life are normatively prescribed; the patterns of interstrata relations in general and of social mobility in particular; the place of family and kinship groups in the process of strata formation; the extent to which there developed a unified evaluative hierarchy; and the extent of country-wide strata consciousness have been influenced by the orientations and structures of the centres.

All the following hypotheses are based, as has already been indicated above, on the assumption that the centre has been relatively successful in maintaining its predominance, that the major groups and strata shared, even if only passively, in its orientations, and that no major counterorientations have developed among them—an assumption which, as we have already indicated, has always been at most only partially true. But the partial validity of these assumptions should not prevent us from exploring these hypotheses which can be

---

52. Bloch, *op. cit.* and Barber and Barber, *op. cit.*

derived from them—it should only remind us that this is only part of the picture. Contrariwise, insofar as the centre is mostly oriented to power (or, to some degree—as is to be found in modern societies—to economic development), such emphasis on normative definitions of styles of life of different groups or strata will tend to be much smaller. The extent to which different status groups will be segregated from one another is also greatly predicated first on the structure of centre and, second, on its orientations.

The preceding materials indicate that a tendency toward a strong normative definition of styles of life of different status groups is very closely related to some predominance within the centre of orientations to prestige, i.e., to participation in some types of collective, social, or cultural orders. Such emphasis on normative definitions of styles of life will be most encompassing—as in the Indian case, and to some degree also the European case—in so far as the centre is based on a combination of different types of prestige and especially on the combination of participation in a cultural order with that in primordial units.

The more monolithic a centre is in terms of its composition and its distinctiveness from various subcentres and from the periphery, the more it will tend to encourage the segregation of the styles of life and patterns of participation of different local, occupational, and territorial-kinship groups. Insofar as a relatively monolithic centre has multiple orientations, this would probably increase the number of channels of access to it, but it will not tend to break down the segregation between such groups. On the other hand, the more pluralistic the centre and the greater the number of other subcentres with direct access to it, the greater will be the potential overlapping and meeting points between their respective styles of life and patterns of social participation.

With regard to the orientations of the centre, here also the importance of prestige, as against power, orientations in the centre stands out. A power-oriented centre will attempt to maximize such segregation, as against the centre oriented to prestige which will tend to encourage some meeting or overlapping among different local-occupational groups—but the scope of such overlapping and the degree to which it will discourage such segregation of styles of life will vary according to the nature of the prestige which is upheld in the respective centre. A centre which tends to uphold participation in a relatively open universalistic tradition, such as the Chinese, will tend mostly to bring together the higher élites which converge in the centre, and to keep some points of contact with other groups insofar as they are seen as potentially participating in this centre. At the same time it will tend to encourage segregation of different groups at more peripheral levels of social life.

A centre which tends to emphasize a combination of "close" cultural ritualistic contents together with strong ascriptive regulation of access to them, based on primordial qualities—as the Indian one—will tend to stress the meeting of various groups, in a highly differentiated way, around some common foci of cultural or political identity, but this very meeting will stress their segregation in most of the social and cultural orders.

A centre with more multiple prestige orientations, especially insofar as among these orientations there is also one towards more universalistic, open, cultural, or religious traditions—as was the case in the European one—will also tend on the whole to minimize the segregation of different groups and to maximize the possibility of their overlapping in their participation in different social and cultural spheres. The orientations and structure of the centre will also greatly influence the extent to which there may develop within a given society a unified hierarchy of status. While in no complex society can there develop a single unified status hierarchy, yet the scope and directions of such a hierarchy will also differ greatly among them.

In general the more monolithic a centre the more it will attempt to establish a relatively unified hierarchy—but the exact scope will differ greatly according to the basic orientations of the centre. Thus, a power-oriented centre will attempt to establish a uniform hierarchy with regard to the centre itself but will "cut it off" as it were below, without necessarily attempting to impose a unified scale of evaluation on the various peripheral institutional positions and occupations. It will also tend, on the whole, to increase the steepness of the hierarchy both within the centre, between it and the periphery and to some degree also among the peripheral groups.

A prestige-oriented monolithic centre will attempt to encompass, in its official evaluative hierarchy, not only the central position but also other, more peripheral ones. It will at least tend to evaluate them on some general scale even if leaving them to develop their own, secondary scales of evaluation with regard to their various internal subdivisions and roles. The steepness of the hierarchy evolved by such a centre will largely depend on the accessibility of different groups to the centre. Insofar as many groups have some autonomous and not fully fixed access to the centre, then there will be a greater spread of such hierarchies. If such multiple access is not fully legitimized, as in India, these hierarchies will be mostly of secondary importance and will never fully develop into fully competing ones—as was the case in Europe, where such multiple access was much more fully legitimized.

The major variables which tend to influence the degree to which there tends to develop, within any society, country-wide consciousness and organization of different strata are the orientations of the centre and the degree to which different strata both evince strong orientation to participation in the centre and have some degree of autonomous access to it, i.e., can to some degree control the conversion of their own resources into access to the centre. The greater the degree of such autonomy of access of various groups to the centre, the greater also will be their tendency to such country-wide strata consciousness and organization. The degree and scope of such country-wide strata consciousness and organization will be greater the more such access is rooted in ascriptive corporate right of primordial kinship or territorial groups. The degree of such country-wide strata consciousness will also be influenced by the orientation of the centre. Other conditions being equal it will be greatest insofar as orientations to prestige are more important. Contrariwise, it will be smaller in a society whose centre is based on power and which tends to minimize such autonomous access to the centre.

The combination of the orientation and structure of the centre with the degree of access to it will tend also to influence greatly the degree to which family and kinship units will serve not only as the agents of initial socialization and placement of individuals in the social structure but also as a basic focus of stratum-consciousness as well as an ascriptive regulator of access to positions. A power centre will tend to minimize any such tendencies on the part of family and kinship units—i.e., to minimize the "status" or "class" components of family or kinship group identity. A centre oriented to participation in universalistic tradition will tend to uphold the relation between family and status identity but will tend to minimize the functions of the family as an ascriptive regulator or channel of access to positions.

A centre which is oriented to a more "closed" tradition, and within which primordial qualities are conceived as part of the basic definition of the sociocultural order, will tend to encourage almost all such connections between family and status. However, the more multiple orientations there are within a centre and the greater the number of units with relatively autonomous access to the centre, the stronger will be the forces counteracting such ascriptive tendencies of various primordial kinship groups, without necessarily undermining the predisposition of families to serve as foci of strata consciousness. Lastly the patterns and scope of social mobility will also be to a very large degree influenced by the orientations of the centre, as well as by the degrees of access to it by various groups.

Any monolithic centre will tend to encourage, at least with regard to access to the central positions, patterns of "sponsored" mobility. The exact criteria and channels of such mobility as well as its effects on centre-strata and interstrata relations (i.e., on the degree of their segregation) are mostly influenced by the contents of the orientations of the centre as outlined above. Contest mobility tends, on the other hand, to develop when the centres themselves have relatively multiple orientations and/or especially insofar as the primordial and kinship units serve as important and independent bases of access to the centre. Insofar as the criteria of such access are, as in the Indian case, ideally fixed, then this will be a contest mobility among wider kinship, territorial and/or occupational groups. Insofar as these criteria are not fixed—as was the case in Europe—then this contest mobility will have the character of mobility of individual families and will tend to create—to a greater degree than in the former case—new types of institutional positions and multiple hierarchies of status.

The preceding conclusions have been mainly drawn on for the comparative analysis of imperial or semi-imperial traditional societies. We have not attempted to present here a full explanation of the analytical reasons for the impact of different types of orientations and structures of centres on processes of strata formation. This would have necessitated a more systematic analysis of the institutional or exchange properties of these different orientations—something which would be beyond the scope of this paper.[53] Similarly the analysis here was confined to a certain type of traditional society—and it is yet to be seen to what extent it may also be applied to modern societies where the general levels of resources, the general basic orientations of centres and strata alike, the basic patterns of the access of the broader social groups to the centre, as well as the conception of the centre, has been greatly changed from those prevalent in the traditional societies discussed here.

53. This constitutes, however, part of the broader work which has been mentioned in note 1.

Eleven

CULTURE AND SOCIAL STRUCTURE REVISITED

I.THE DISSOCIATION OF STUDIES OF CULTURAL AND OF SOCIAL STRUCTURE

ONE OF THE MOST IMPORTANT and problematic trends in the development of the social sciences in the last twenty years or so has been the growing dissociation between studies of "culture," of different types of symbols, their construction and their relation to social interaction and behaviour, and studies of social structure and institutions, of institutional or organisational formations.

This situation was, of course, in marked contrast to the assumptions of the fifties and sixties, with their very strong emphasis on the systemic nature of societies, i.e., the view of societies as systems and the concomitant analysis of different groups or institutional sectors in general, and of the sphere of the symbols, beliefs and values in particular, in terms of their contribution to the maintenance of the boundaries of such systems.

These assumptions were criticised on a variety of grounds: that culture was seen too much in Parsons' terms of securing pattern maintenance; that the individual was seen as "over-socialised"; that power, conflict and change were minimised; that they were optimistically evolutionary.

The most important common denominator of the criticisms of these schools or approaches, as they gathered momentum from the sixties on, was the refusal to take any social structure, any institutional arrangements, as given for granted or as explainable in terms of the level of the structural differentiation of the different societies and the concomitant systemic needs of a society. Instead there developed two major—to some degree contradictory—directions of explanation of patterns of social behaviour, organisations, and institutions (Eisenstadt 1981).

One such direction attempted to analyse the ways in which such frameworks are constructed either through the negotiations, struggles, and conflicts of different social actors or, to use Anthony Giddens (1979), through "structuration" instead of "structure."

The second such approach is in a way contrary to the first, because it takes

 Originally published in *International Sociology* 1 (1986):297–320.

the active subject out of the picture. It developed among the structuralists, starting with Lévi-Strauss (1963), and continued in various other approaches—especially the semantic and semiological ones (Rossi 1983) and stressed that any concrete institutional formation or pattern of behaviour has to be explained as the manifestation of some principles of deep structure—of the human mind, of forces of production, or the like.

Beyond these developments there loomed also a problem which was inherent in sociological analysis from its very beginning in general, and in the sociology of culture and of religion in particular—namely how to reconcile the order-maintaining and the order-changing or transforming capacities of the symbolic dimensions of human activity; how to reconcile the view of religion as "opium" of the people, as "ideology" in the Marxist or in the classical Mannheimian view, on the one hand (Mannheim 1936), as against, on the other, that approach most explicitly to be found, of course, in the works of Max Weber, but to some degree also that in Marx and among such Marxists as Gramsci and even Lenin, which viewed ideas and their carriers as forces of social change and transformation.

This dissociation between studies of culture and of social structure could be seen in anthropology in the structuralism of Lévi-Strauss (1968–1971) and his followers, stressing the laws of hidden structure of the human mind, as well as in the later studies of Clifford Geertz (1975, 1980) or Victor Turner (1969), stressing above all the expressive forms and ethos of culture, with relatively few systematic analyses of social structure—in marked contrast to, for instance, the tradition of classical English social anthropology.

A far-reaching disjunction between these two directions of research—that of "culture" and that of social structure, and a dissociation between emphasis on "negotiated order" or structuration on the one hand, and on something close to deep structure on the other hand—developed from the sixties on.

The two most important schools or approaches in sociology which emphasised the symbolic dimensions were, as is well known, those of symbolic interaction and ethnomethodology (as well as, to some degree, phenomenology).

Symbolic interactionism (Blumer 1968; Meltzer, Petras, and Reynolds 1975) has above all stressed the strong emphasis on the construction of meaning and definition of different situations through processes of social interaction taking place within them.

As against this, ethnomethodology (Cicourel 1964, 1973; Denzin 1971; Garfinkel 1961; Turner 1974) stressed the importance of exploring the overt incorrigible assumptions of the many semantic maps of social interaction and life in general and of daily "common sense" life in particular.

The single most important oeuvre which developed in this vein—that of the late Erving Goffman—has often been interpreted as stressing the interactionist view, the construction of meaning of situation through the activities of individuals participating in the given situations.

Yet a closer scrutiny of his works, perhaps above all of different aspects of *Frame Analysis*, does also indicate his very strong insistence on the givenness of the various "frames" within which the "play" of individuals, the dramas of interindividual action, takes place, without in any way questioning the provenance of such frames (Frank 1979; Goffman 1974).

Whatever the differences between these approaches, they have, however, shared—at least until lately—the fact that they have but rarely touched directly on, or confronted the relation of such symbols or processes to the institutional contexts or frameworks within which they developed—whether the more immediate organisational or situational contexts of such activities or processes, or the broader macroinstitutional ones—usually taking them for granted.

At the same time, the major types of structural analysis, of institutions and social structure, that developed in this period, i.e., from the late sixties on, have either almost entirely disregarded cultural factors, or at the most treated them as residual categories.

This is true of work in the tradition of Simmel-Merton-Blau and Boudon in France (Blau 1964a, 1964b; Boudon 1981; Merton 1963) which has stressed the analysis of the internal organisation, formal characteristics and emergent properties of social structure and their impact on social behaviour. It also applies to the comparative or historical-structural analysis which has again gained momentum, especially in the last decade or so, after the reaction against the various comparative studies of the fifties and sixties in general, and the studies of modernisation in particular (see, for instance, Wallerstein 1974; Skocpol 1979). At the same time, among at least some of the Marxist approaches, an emphasis on something akin to "deep structure" can be identified (Godelier 1973, 1980).

II. NEW DIRECTIONS OF ANALYSIS OF CULTURE AND SOCIAL STRUCTURE

The preceding discussion points out that any attempt to reestablish the systematic analysis of the relations between cultural analysis, on the one hand, and institutional or social structural analysis, on the other, must address itself to the starting point of the growing dissociation between these two areas of study, i.e., not taking social structure for granted. It must find ways how to combine the analysis of the crystallization of different aspects of social structure in processes of social interaction in which individuals act as autonomous agents and where power and control are also connected with different aspects of "culture." Such an attempt should also address both the "negotiated order" and the "deep structure," each in its many different guises.

Many attempts in such directions to overcome the dissociations between studies of culture and of social structure have lately been undertaken in the various social sciences and history, especially those related in some way to the school of *Annales* (for instance Le Roy Ladourie 1973, 1974; Le Goff 1974) and some of the more recent tendencies in social history in the United States and England (Davis 1975; Hunt 1984). It would be beyond the scope of this article to survey and analyse them here in any detail. Suffice to say that they have indeed attempted to indicate how to integrate, in the analysis of the processes of the construction of social and institutional frameworks, the dimensions of power and the construction of meaning, and the impact of cultural symbols on situations and processes of social interaction and structuring of institutional formations.

In the following pages we shall present some illustrations from a broad programme of research on comparative civilisations undertaken at the Department of Sociology and the Truman Research Center of the Hebrew University, designed to overcome the dissociation between cultural and social-structural analysis. These researches have spanned over such areas as patron-client relations (Eisenstadt and Roniger 1984), cities and urban hierarchies in traditional civilisations (Eisenstadt and Schachar 1986), the general analysis of Axial Age Civilisations (Eisenstadt 1982a,b), and their origin and diversity (Eisenstadt 1985a,b).

We have attempted to indicate how cultural visions and orientations are transformed into basic premises of civilisations, of social and political order. They specify the ways in which the basic problems of social order, the relation between social division of labour, regulation of power, construction of trust and of meaning, are carried and articulated by different elites. They shape through various mechanisms of symbolic and institutional control, developed and activated by such elites, some very crucial dimensions of social structure, of "structuration."

The impact of such premises, and their institutional derivatives on the institutional process, is effected through the activities of the major elites in general and of the political ones in particular, by the various mechanisms of social interaction in general, control and counter-control or challenges to control, that develop in a society or sectors thereof. Such mechanisms are not limited to the exercise of power in the specific "narrow" political sense. They are—as indeed the more sophisticated Marxists have stressed—much more pervasive. They are not, however, expressions only of class relations or of "modes of production." Rather, they are activated by the major coalitions of elites in a society, carrying different cultural visions and representing different types of interests.

At the same time, the very implementation or institutionalisation of such premises, together with the construction of the social division of labour generates counter-tendencies and movements and processes of change (Eisenstadt 1985b).

The illustrations which we shall present in the following pages will deal first with the comparative political dynamics of two centralised agrarian empires—the Byzantine and the Chinese; and second, within the realm of the sociology of religion, with different meanings of otherworldliness and impacts of such sectarian orientations on civilisational dynamics.

We have chosen the illustrations in such a way that, in each of them, we base our analysis on cases which are as close as possible to the point of view of structural characteristics, or of pure cultural meaning; and we attempt to show that neither of these can adequately explain the institutional dynamics of these cases in their respective settings.

III. Case Study 1: Agrarian Empires—Byzantium and China

We shall proceed first with a brief comparative analysis of the centres and processes of political struggle and change in two agrarian empires—the Chinese and the Byzantine—which have exhibited many great similarities, even identities in their agrarian and urban structures (Eisenstadt 1963).

These two, as most other centralised agrarian empires, developed within the framework of so-called Axial Age Civilisations (Eisenstadt 1982a,b). These civilisations are characterised by soteriological or semisoteriological attempts to overcome a very high degree of tension between the conceptions of the transcendental and the mundane order. These attempts were carried by autonomous intellectual-religious or cultural elites which played an important role in their institutionalisation.

At the same time, these empires were characterised by several common structural characteristics: the existence of a relatively strong centre, the distinction between centre and periphery, a strong and distinct bureaucracy or bureaucracies, a comparatively high level of structural differentiation—as evident in the existence of a highly developed agricultural structure with great differences between different levels ("poor," "middle," and rich peasants), and, in most of them (with the exception of the Chinese Empire after the Tang dynasty), aristocracy and relatively highly developed cities and commerce.

The centres of all these empires were caught between their dependency upon and attempts to regulate the relatively free resources generated by the various social forces through very complicated economic, social, and political policies (Eisenstadt 1963).

Given the combination of these cultural orientations, civilisational premises, and structural characteristics, these empires were characterised—especially when compared with patrimonial ones (like, for instance, the ancient Egyptian one or many South East Asian kingdoms)—by a relatively high level of political struggle and by a relatively strong ideological component in such a struggle. They were characterised not only by rebellions, but by much more articulated movements of protest and political struggle, whether in the centre or in the periphery, which were often connected with religious sectarianism and heterodoxies (Eisenstadt 1978).

Yet, notwithstanding common characteristics, these empires also differed greatly in their political structure and dynamics in general, and in the structure of movements of protest and their incorporation into the centre and in the reconstruction and continuity of their premises in particular.

These differences were very closely related first to the cultural orientations and basic civilisational premises that became predominant in these empires in general, and to the conception of the political realm and of authority in particular; and second, to the structure of the predominant elites and counter-elites that developed within them.

i. Byzantium

As in all Christian civilisations, the major cultural orientations which became predominant in the Byzantine Empire were characterised by the emphasis placed on a very high tension existing between the transcendental and the mundane orders (Barker 1957; Brehier 1949, 1950; Ostrogorsky 1956; Vasiliev 1952), by a relatively close interweaving of this- and otherworldly orientations of salvation and by a relatively high level of commitment to the maintenance of the sociocultural and social roles related to such a conception of salvation. These orientations and the civilisational premises related to them were also characterised by a number of tensions. Stress was laid on the relative autonomous access of all sectors of the society to salvation and the political order, but the Church and the emperor mediated such access and their relative standing in relation to such mediation was in question. Also in question was the relative position of the Christian and Hellenic components of the Empire's collective identity.

The political tradition of the city-state, inherited from Rome, was also of great importance—the tradition of the citizens' participation in the governance of the city and of the seeming accountability of the ruler to the population. While the concrete manifestations of this tradition weakened quite early in the Roman Empire itself, especially in its later phases, some of its impact survived in several aspects of life in the Roman and, later, in the Byzantine Empire (Bratianu 1937, 1938).

In the Byzantine Empire, these cultural orientations were connected to the development of rather special constellations of social and political forces in general, and of structure of elites and of broader strata and of the relations between them in particular. The major elites predominant in the Empire were the emperor, the bureaucracy, the army and the Church (Ostrogorsky 1954, 1956, 1959; Brehier 1949, 1050).

At the same time, the structure of the Byzantine society was relatively highly differentiated. The major social forces consisted of the aristocracy and, to some degree, the above-mentioned bureaucracy (which could be seen not only as part of the centre, but also as a distinct social group), as well as the peasantry and the various urban groups—even the lower ones—all of which were relatively highly developed.

The combination of the "Christian" orientations with the heritage of some Roman ones tended to give rise not only to a relatively high degree of corporate organisation, but even autonomous class, even if rather limited (especially as compared with Medieval Europe), and political consciousness. These groups tended to define their status in their own terms, according to autonomous criteria not entirely dependent on the centre, and they also inclined toward obtaining some autonomous access to the centres of power. When the structural conditions appeared relatively propitious, various groups (especially in the case of the aristocracy and, to a smaller degree, of the Church) were able to impinge upon the centre and obtain some—sometimes direct, sometimes indirect— participation in it (Ostrogorsky 1954, 1956, 1959; Diehl 1929; Hussey 1937, 1957). At the same time, the emperors themselves pursued very intensive military and cultural policies, much in line with their basic premises and goals. These tendencies had far-reaching repercussions on the relations between the centre and the various elites, and between them and the major social strata and the ensuing political process which developed in the Empire. Being the representative of God, the emperor naturally had a special relationship with the Church. Everywhere and on all occasions, the emperor's unique—and, indeed, his sacred—position was emphasised.

The very conception of a Christian empire implied that the Church was part of the polity and was, in all respects, under the general care of the emperor—even though certain functions could not be performed by him. The dichotomy between what was Caesar's and what was God's was not so sharp in the Imperium Christianum of East Rome as in Western Christendom and only surfaced if the emperor was heretic.

This did not mean, however, that the Church was not in many ways an autonomous institution. The Byzantine Church had very strong autonomous and universalistic orientations and a strong organisation of its own (Hussey 1937, 1957; Ostrogorsky 1956). It participated actively in the central political institutions in the Senate, the court, and the bureaucracy. Moreover, it initiated basic political issues, fulfilled many vital political and administrative functions, and was often concerned with wider issues of policy. In general, the relation of the emperor to the patriarch, of the secular to the ecclesiastic, was best expressed in Byzantian by "interdependence" and not by the misleading term "caesaropapism."

Side by side with the emperor and the Church, the bureaucracy and the army also evolved as very strong continuous social formations in the Byzantine Empire and as part of its major elites. They were both highly organised and while, in principle, they were under the control of the emperor, in fact they often exhibited strong autonomous tendencies, especially in the political arena.

The same tendencies could be discerned among the major social strata: the aristocracy—mostly comprising the big landowners, many of whom came from long-established families; the bureaucracy at the top of Byzantine society which was a main channel of social mobility; the peasantry which constituted a crucial part of the Byzantine social structure and which the emperors were always careful to maintain free and independent of the aristocracy. Between the eighth and eleventh centuries, the free peasantry, concentrated in village communities, flourished, provided an important source of recruits for the army, the bureaucracy and even the professions—to decline later with the weakening of the emperors and the growing strength of the aristocracy (Charanis 1941, 1951a,b, 1961).

Similarly, the urban groups—the merchants and the artisans—in the Byzantine Empire, were also very strong and to some degree autonomous, although, on the whole, quite severely controlled by the centre.

The lower urban groups were organised in *demes* or "circus parties," such as the famous factions of Blues and Greens, which had political aims and were not merely sport organisations. These popular parties, whose leaders were appointed by the government, fulfilled important public duties, serving as city guard and participating in the repair of the city walls, and voiced the political opinions of the people (Bratianu 1937, 1938; Dvornik 1946).

ii. China

The basic premises and dominant elites of the Chinese Empire—the largest and most continuous in the history of mankind—differed greatly from that of the Byzantine, as well as, of course, other imperial systems such as the Ottoman and Russian one (Balazs 1964; Reischauer and Fairbank 1967).

While many of these differences were, of course, due to ecological and economic conditions and factors, yet some of the most crucial ones were related to the differences in basic political conceptions, elite structure, and modes of control exercised by these elites.

The basic features of the imperial Chinese political system started evolving, as is well known, during the Han period and crystallized since the T'ang period, the most important of these characteristics being the crystallization of an autonomous political centre and the predominance, within it, of the emperor-*literati*-bureaucracy coalition, the military playing an important role which tended to become relatively secondary in periods of stability; and the predominance within the centre of the Confucian-Legalist ideology, with a strong admixture of secondary orientations, especially Taoist and Buddhist.

The sociopolitical and cultural premises, connected with the Chinese imperial system, exhibited some very special features. The Chinese tradition was probably the most "this-worldly" of all the Great Traditions of the post-Axial Age. Although the Confucian-Legalist framework of the imperial system allowed room for the otherworldly orientations of folk religious sectarianism or private speculation, its main thrust was to nurture the sociopolitical and cultural orders as the major focus of cosmic harmony. It emphasised the this-worldly duties and activities within the existing social frameworks—the family, broader kin groups, and imperial service—and stressed the connection between the proper performance of these duties and the ultimate criteria of individual responsibility (Fairbank 1967; Mote 1971; Nivison and Wright 1969; Schwartz 1975, 1985; Wright 1959, 1960).

This tradition also emphasised a strong transcendental aspect of individual responsibility, but this was largely expressed in terms of the importance of the political and familial dimensions of human existence. Moreover, as enunciated in the official ideology of the centre, the Chinese tradition stressed the basic affinity between the societal order represented by the centre and the various types of peripheral collectivities (Fingarette 1972; Metzger 1977; Tu 1979).

The major elite within Chinese society were the *literati* (Balazs 1964; Fairbank 1967; Nivison and Wright 1969). This elite was constituted by the people who passed the Confucian examinations or studied for them, and comprised a relatively cohesive network of groups and individuals sharing a common cultural background shaped by the combination system and by adherence to classical Confucian teachings and rituals, recruited in principle from all the strata, even from the peasantry, but mostly from the gentry. In fact, the literate class was mostly, although not entirely, recruited from the gentry.

The *literati* and the bureaucrats evinced some very specific features as an elite which are of special importance from the point of view of our analysis.

They were not just intellectuals performing some academic functions but at the same time constituted also, together with the emperor and to some degree the warlords, a central power elite exercising control over the central aspects of the flow of resources in the society, namely, information related to the construction of the definition of social and cultural worlds, and the reference orientation of the major social groups (Eisenstadt 1983a).

Unlike, however, in the realm of Christian (and to some degree Muslim) civilisations in general, and the Byzantine Empire in particular—and in close relation to the very strong this-worldly orientations predominant in the Chinese realm—there did not develop any separation between church and state.

The single and most durable organisational framework of the *literati* was almost identical to that of the state bureaucracy (which enlisted ten to twenty percent of all the *literati*) and, except for some schools and academies, had no organisation of its own. Moreover, political activity within the imperial and bureaucratic frameworks was a basic referent of the Confucian ethical orientations (Eisenstadt 1983a).

There thus developed the rather paradoxical situation that the *literati*, while being in principle autonomous, did not have a strong autonomous resource basis as a cultural elite. At the same time the *literati* exercised a virtual monopoly over the access to the centre; that control was based not only on coercion alone but also on solidary ties which the *literati* regulated.

The *literati*, in conjunction with the emperors and to some degree the warlords, were of crucial importance, through the modes of control exercised by them in conjunction with their basic orientations, in the crystallization of the main institutional features of the Chinese imperial system generally, and in the processes of structuring the centre-periphery relations.

This mode of control was also evident in the system of stratification that developed in China, whose major characteristics were: (a) the development of this centre as the central focus of the system of stratification; (b) the relative predominance of political-literary criteria in the definition of status, i e , the official prominence of the *literati* and officials and the growing importance of Confucian ideology in defining the criteria of stratification; (c) the relative weakening of the aristocracy and the growing social and economic predominance of the gentry; and (d) the evolution of several secondary patterns of structuring of social hierarchies.

Consequently, there developed within China a relatively small degree of strata autonomy and of autonomous organisation and access to the centre of any strata. This was true both of the peasantry, which enjoyed in principle a high status, and the economically powerful merchants and other urban groups.

iii. Discussion
The combination of basic cultural conceptions and premises in general and of the conception of the political realm and authority in particular, of elite structure and political orientations of the major strata, had a great impact in each of these empires on the political dynamics of each of them—and on the differences between them.

Thus, in the Byzantine Empire, the combination of the "Christian" orientations with the heritage of some Roman ones tended to give rise to a relatively high emphasis on accountability of rulers to higher "laws," as well as to a tendency of several social groups to view themselves as autonomous carriers of the visions connected with such laws, with claims for some autonomous participation in the centre.

These tendencies affected the legitimation of the rulers, and when taken together with military and cultural policies of the emperors, generated in the Byzantine Empire a very intense level of political struggle, with strong ideological components.

Thus, political struggle and change in the Byzantine Empire was, especially as compared with the one in China, very often based on strong connections in such struggles among different elites, such as the Church or bureaucracy, as well as the connections between them and broader strata. It led to continuous shifts in power between different elites and groups, to changes in some of the basic premises and loci of power and authority—ultimately weakening the centre and facilitating the downfall of the empire whose geopolitical situation made it most vulnerable to internal and external conditions.

As against this, the picture that developed in China was almost diametrically opposed to the one found in the Byzantine Empire. The crucial difference lay in the fact that neither various structural shifts in the economy nor various movements of protest and of reform were able to effect far-reaching changes in the basic ideological and institutional premises of the Confucian-Legalist civilisation and political order in general, and in the structure of the centre in particular.

In China, as compared with other imperial systems in general and the Byzantine (and some Islamic ones) in particular, there developed relatively weak ideological and structural linkages between the different processes and movements of change and their leadership; between the different sects, secret societies and the like and their leadership; and the different central and peripheral secondary institutional elites.

The numerous movements of protest, as well as religious groups (such as various secret societies) that arose in peripheries or secondary institutional spheres of the Chinese Empire, evinced very few capacities to be linked with the central political struggle, and to develop common ideologies and frameworks of action which would restructure the major premises of the Chinese institutional system.

Similarly, there developed relatively few continuous connections between the more central heterodoxies or schools within the Confucian-Legalist frameworks, different ideologies and policies in the centre and the more popular movements. At the same time, the relations between the secondary religions or heterodoxies like Buddhism and Taoism and the central political struggle did not exert—except in the period of the Tang when ultimately the Buddhists were pushed out from the centre—far-reaching transformative influences on the Chinese social and political order, although, needless to say, they affected many concrete changes in the different institutional spheres.

The major reason for such weakness lay above all in the very sophisticated and complex mechanisms of control which were developed by the ruling coalitions, and above all by the *literati,* and which are explainable above all in terms of the basic characteristics of the orientations, structure and activities of the *literati* which were analysed above. They were strongly oriented to the political centre as the major arena for the implementation of the specific transcendental vision they carried. They acted at the same time as a political and cultural elite, and they lacked almost any independent bases of resources (Eisenstadt 1983a).

IV. Case Study 2: Otherworldliness and Sectarianism

This illustration draws on the sociology of religion—a field which seemingly naturally belongs to the sphere of cultural analysis proper.

Here, we shall attempt to indicate that, just as in the case of institutional formations, a purely structural analysis which does not take into account the broader civilisational context and basic culture of the premises of the institutional order, cannot explain some crucial aspects of the respective institutional formations; the same is true—in a parallel vein if in a sense obverse way—with respect to purely cultural analysis. Or, in other words, we shall indicate that the full impact of religious orientation on the structuration of social life cannot be explicated only in terms of purely cultural—in this case "religious"—categories or orientations, and here again the analysis of institutionalisation through different elites is of crucial importance. The illustration we shall draw upon (this follows Eisenstadt 1982b, 1983b) is Louis Dumont's recent thesis about the origins of Western individualism in Christianity's original basic otherworldliness which was, according to him, very similar to the otherworldliness that developed in India (Dumont 1982).

As we have indicated (Eisenstadt 1983b), Dumont's thesis is composed of two closely interconnected, yet in principle separate parts. The first analyses the origins of outworldly attitudes in general and the second deals with the specific nature and transformation of Christian outworldliness.

According to Dumont, the negation of the world, outworldly attitudes emerge with the breaking up of what he designates as "holistic," traditional societies and can be found in many parts of the world. Such attitudes, which can be identified in early Christianity, are according to him very similar to those that developed in India—above all in the institution of the renouncer—and to some degree also to those that have developed among the early Stoics. In Christianity, however, unlike in India, there took place a far-reaching transformation of this orientation into the ultimate direction of modern individualism which has indeed very strong this-worldly orientations and has led to very strong activity in the world. Dumont attributes this transformation not to some tendencies inherent in Christianity, but to the historical "accident" of Constantine's conversion to Christianity, and to the ensuing empirical-political involvement of the Church.

Our major criticism of Dumont's thesis—a criticism which follows to some degree those of Burridge (1982), Bellah (1982) and Robertson (1982)—is based first of all on the fact that Dumont's definition of outworldliness conflates in a way too analytically and often also historically different components or aspects. The first is the general breakthrough from what he calls the holistic pattern of traditional societies, and the second is the specific—to use Weber's nomenclature—other-worldly orientation as a "solution" to some central problems raised by the general breakthrough from holistic societies. Such other-worldly orientation can be most clearly seen in India—but it can also be found in other great (postholistic) civilisations, very close to Axial Age civilisations, which have been characterised, as we have seen, by the institutionalisation of a conception of a basic tension between the transcendental and mundane orders (Eisenstadt 1982a).

The development of such a conception of tension between the transcendental and the mundane order has, of course, entailed the crystallization of a general outworldly attitude, i.e., of a conception of a distinct world, which is not—unlike in the holistic conception of traditional civilisations—fully embedded in the mundane world, and which has been usually conceived as being higher than the latter; such orientations are indeed common, to some degree, to all Axial Age civilisations.

But while the potentialities of such developments do indeed exist within all these civilisations, yet the concrete articulation of such orientations varied greatly between these civilisations.

Without going here into the details of these distinctions, let us point out that the most important of such variations are first of all in the very definition of the tension between the transcendental and mundane orders and the modes of resolving this tension.

A second, closely related, distinction within the latter cases is that between the monotheistic religions in which there was a concept of God standing outside the universe and potentially guiding it, and those systems like Hinduism and Buddhism in which the transcendental, cosmic system was conceived in impersonal, almost metaphysical terms, in a state of continuous existential tension with the mundane system.

The third crucial distinction refers to the focus of resolution of the transcendental tension which, in Weberian terms, is salvation. Here the distinction is between purely this-worldly, purely otherworldly and mixed this-and other-worldly conceptions of salvation.

It is these conceptions that created what may be called the overall semantic fields and the basic premises of these respective civilisations, within the context of which the dynamics of otherworldly orientations specific to each have been generated.

It is with respect to the different concepts of salvation that we come to the second meaning or aspect of outworldliness as at least implied in Dumont's work, and which is indeed most fully articulated in the figures of the Indian or the Buddhist renouncer, namely to what Weber called otherworldliness, i.e., the concept of salvation, of the resolution of the transcendental tensions, based on going outside the world, on the denial of the relevance of the mundane order for the transcendental quest.

Some such otherworldly orientations have indeed developed in all these major civilisations. And yet the full dynamic—intellectual and institutional—implications of these otherworldly orientations differed greatly in these various civilisations. They differed above all according to the premises which have created what has been called the overall semantic and institutional field of these respective civilisations as defined above.

It was the place of the outworldly orientations in the overall semantic and institutional field of these respective civilisations in the basic premises that has generated the differences between the specific dynamics of different outworldly orientations. No doubt some of the differences were due to historical "accidents," but it would be rather wrong—and basically going against Dumont's own classical analysis of the caste system (Dumont 1970a,b, 1982) (also it seems to me against his general approach to comparative sociology)—to attribute to historical accidents or developments such far-reaching developments as the institutional implications of the conversion of emperors, and above all of the special course of development of the Church. Here the most appropriate comparative case would be, of course, Buddhism, where there also developed a Church of sorts and where kings also become converted to the new religion, and yet the whole course of institutional dynamics and transformations was entirely different from what happened in Europe (Silver 1981; Tambiah 1981).

These crucial differences between the effects of the Christian conversions and Church and those in the realm of Buddhism do indeed lie in the basic differences in their predominant cultural orientations, in the respective conceptions of salvation that became predominant in them, and in the specific ideological and institutional premises and dynamics which they generated; and it is also these differences that explain the different impact and transformation of the seemingly similar outworldly orientations that developed in these civilisations.

It is here that the crucial difference between the Hindu (and Buddhist) outworldly orientations and renouncer, on the one hand, and Jewish and Christian, and to some degree Greek or Hellenic ones, on the other, stand out—with the Chinese constituting a sort of "middle" case.

In the first case, pure outworldly orientation was in a way an extension, even if a dialectical one, of the dominant mode of orientation of conception of salvation, the otherworldly concept of salvation which has generated a distinct civilisational pattern. The very institutionalisation of such a pattern has given rise to the dialectical extension of the ideal of renouncer as the purest embodiment of this orientation.

In the second case in general, and in Christianity in particular, which is our main concern here, there developed from the very beginning a very strong outwordly or otherworldly orientation. Yet, from the very beginning, these otherworldly orientations in Christianity were a part of the attempt to crystallize a new transcendental vision in which there existed from the very beginning a combination, interweaving, as well as very strong and continuous tension between this- and otherworldly orientations. (Morris 1973; Rousseau 1978; Stroumsa 1981; Troeltsch 1960).

Thus, each of these civilisations created specific semantic fields with distinct premises and institutional derivates within the framework of which the common outworldly orientations generated different dynamics. And it was this potential orientation to this world which made these transformations possible. In other civilisations, their respective visions generated other institutional-semantic fields and different modes of transformation of the otherworldly orientations that developed within them.

Thus we see that the distinction between different implications of other-worldliness—seemingly a general cultural or religious category—is not limited to the cultural field, to the field of religious symbolism and beliefs. It touches also on some central aspects of the relations between cultural symbols in general, and religious symbols in particular, and on their social dynamism as order-maintaining or order-transforming forces.

The concrete problem is here, in connection with the different meanings of otherwordliness in different Axial Age civilisations, that of the impact of sectarianism or heterodoxies on the dynamics of civilisations (this follows Eisenstadt 1982b).

Here it is important to point out first of all that sectarianism and heterodoxies do not exist in their full manifestation in all religions or civilisations. They occur above all in the Axial Age civilisations with the potential multiplicity of bridging over the tensions between the transcendental and the mundane order that is inherent in all of them.

But the structure and implications of heterodoxies and sectarianism varied greatly in these civilisations.

The term heterodoxy is, of course, applicable only to cases when one can talk about orthodoxy and this term is in its turn a certain type of both organisational and cognitive doctrinal structure.

Organisationally the crucial aspect is, of course, the existence of some type of organised Church which attempts to monopolise at least the religious sphere and usually also the relations of this sphere to the political powers, and this constitutes an autonomous elite, but at the same time is also closely related to the ruling coalitions. But of no lesser importance is the doctrinal aspect— the organisation of doctrine, i.e., the very stress on the structuring of clear cognitive and symbolic boundaries of doctrine.

With respect to both the organisational and the doctrinal aspects, the major difference among the Axial Age civilisations is that between, on the one hand, the monotheistic civilisations in general and Christianity in particular and, on the other hand, Hinduism and Buddhism (with Confucian China constituting a sort of in-between type into which we shall not be able to enter here).

It is within Christianity that these organisational and doctrinal aspects of orthodoxy developed in the fullest way. Thus it was in Christianity that there developed fully fledged Churches which constituted potentially active and autonomous partners of the ruling coalitions. In Judaism and Islam these developments were weaker—there developed rather powerful, but not always as fully organised and autonomous, organisations of clerics.

But of no lesser importance is the fact that in Christianity and to a smaller, but yet not insignificant, degree also in Judaism and Islam, there developed strong tendencies to the structuring of relatively clear cognitive doctrinal boundaries.

This tendency was rooted first of all in the prevalence, within the monotheistic civilisations in general, and within Christianity with its stronger connections to the Greek philosophical heritage in particular, of strong orientations first of all to the cognitive elaboration of the relations between God, man, and the world. Second, this tendency was rooted in the fact that, in all these monotheistic religions with their strong otherworldly orientation, the mundane world was seen—even if in differing degrees—as at least one focus of otherworldly salvation; hence the proper designation of such activity became a focus of central concern and of contention between the ruling orthodoxies and the numerous heterodoxies that developed within them.

The importance for the struggle between orthodoxies and heterodoxies of the structuring of such cognitive boundaries, of the elaboration of visions, of the reconstruction of the mundane world according to the transcendental otherworldly vision is best seen—in a negative way—in the case of Hinduism and Buddhism.

In both these cases we find, despite a very strong transcendental and otherworldly orientation, that the structuring of cognitive doctrines—as distinct from ritual—and above all of their applicability to mundane matters, did not constitute a central aspect or premise of these religions or civilisations. Hence even when, as in Buddhism, it is not impossible to talk about something akin to Church—albeit a much more loosely organised one—it is very difficult to talk about heterodoxy. At the same time sectarianism abounds—Buddhism itself being in a sense a sect developing out of Hinduism.

These differences between sects and heterodoxies are not just matters of scholarly classification or of religious doctrine. They are closely related to the impact of these sects or orthodoxies on the dynamics of their respective civilisations. It would not be correct to state—a statement which seemingly, but only seemingly, can be attributed to Weber—that it was only in the realm of Christianity—or perhaps stretching it to include all the monotheistic civilisations—that sects and heterodoxies had far-reaching consequences on the structure of mundane fields.

The various Hinduist sects, Buddhism itself, did indeed have far-reaching impact, through the articulation of appropriate premises, on the structuring of the mundane spheres of their respective civilisations and their premises. First of all they extended the scope of the different national and political communities and imbued them with new symbolic dimensions, within new interpretation of their premises. They could also change some of the bases and criteria of participation in the civilisational communities—as was the case in Jainism, in the Bhakti movement, and, of course, above all, in Buddhism when an entirely new civilisational framework was constructed.

Buddhism introduced also new elements into the political scene—above all that special way in which the Sangha, usually politically a very compliant group, could in some cases, as Paul Mus (1968) has shown, become a sort of moral conscience of the community, calling the rulers to some accountability.

But this impact was of a different nature from that of the struggles between the reigning orthodoxies and the numerous heterodoxies that developed within the monotheistic civilisations. Of crucial importance has been the fact that in these latter cases a central aspect of such struggles was the attempt to reconstruct the very political and cultural centres of their respective societies and that, because of this, these struggles became a central part of the histories of these civilisations, shaping the major contours of their development.

The preceding analysis of different conceptions of otherworldliness, sectarianism, and heterodoxies brings out the importance of the same variables we have encountered in the analysis of the dynamics of imperial centres—namely that of the cultural visions or orientations as transformed into premises of civilisations and societies, and of their institutional derivatives as shaped by various elites exercising different modes of interaction and control.

Here, however, we touch already, as briefly alluded to above, on the place of such relations between culture and social structure in processes of social change and transformation. It would be beyond the scope of this paper to analyse all the implications of this aspect of relations between culture and social structure, but they can at least serve as an important indication for our—however tentative—conclusions.

V. Culture and Social Structure Reexamined—Tentative Conclusions

We may now bring together, even in a tentative way, some of the major lines of our analysis, as presented in the preceding case studies, as they indicate the ways in which the analysis of the relation between cultural and social structural and/or institutional analysis can indeed be reconstituted.

We have attempted to indicate systematically how crucially important for the formation or structuration of institutions are those cultural visions and orientations which are transformed into basic premises of civilisation, of social and political order—addressing ourselves to the problem of division of labour, construction of trust, regulation of power, and the construction of meaning of human activities (Eisenstadt and Roniger 1982, chapters 2 and 3; Eisenstadt 1985a). They specify the bases of authority and justice, and the place of different institutional arenas in the overall conception of man and cosmos. They have major institutional derivatives as shown in studies of power and authority, wealth, and prestige, boundaries of the major collectivities and legitimation thereof.

The impact of such premises and their institutional derivatives on the formation and reproduction of institutional formations is effected through the activities of the major elites by various mechanisms of social interaction in general, and of control in particular, as well as by development of challenges to such control that develop among such elites and broader strata of the society, or sectors thereof. Such mechanisms are not limited to the exercise of power in the specific "narrow" political or coercive sense. They are—as indeed even the more sophisticated Marxists have stressed—much more pervasive. They are not, however, activated by representatives only of class relations or of "modes of production." Rather, they are activated by the major coalitions of elites in a society, carrying different cultural visions and representing different types of interests.

The most important of such elites are the political ones which deal most directly with the regulation of power in society, the articulators of the models of the cultural order, whose activities are oriented to the construction of meaning, and the articulators of the solidarity of the major groups which address themselves to the construction of trust.

The structure of such elites is closely related to the basic cultural orientations prevalent in a society. Different types of elites are carriers of different types of orientations or visions. On the other hand, and in connection with the types of cultural orientations and their respective transformation to basic premises of the social order, these elites tend to exercise different modes of control over the allocation of basic resources in society (Eisenstadt 1985b). The different coalitions of elites exercise such control on the major institutional sphere in several closely interconnected ways.

The first such aspect of control is that of what may be called the creation, articulation, and institutionalisation of the basic semantic map of a society or sector thereof and of its basic ideological and institutional derivatives, symbolisation, and legitimation.

The structuring of the basic semantic maps entails the definition of some of the basic problems of human and social existence, the specification of "solution" to such problems, and their relation to the definition of the basic premises of social order (Eisenstadt 1985a).

It is the construction of such maps and premises that constituted the basic components of the semantic maps of different societies and sectors thereof. It is through this process that many of the incorrigible assumptions of such maps, of the basic premises of social order, as well as their basic institutional implications and the potential conflicts between such different assumptions and premises, are constructed.

Such structuring is focused around several basic poles which are inherent in the nature of human existence, the construction of the social order, and the perception and definition of these problems in human societies. The two major poles or axes of the search for such meta-meanings focus, first, on the cosmological axis and definition of the relations between the cosmic and the human and mundane worlds and, second, on the symbolic dimensions of the social order, briefly alluded to before.

The construction of semantic maps of the basic traditions or premises of societies or sectors thereof entails the specification and definition of the legitimate range of problems related to these two basic axes, the ways in which these problems and the answers to them are formulated, and their legitimation in terms of the range of meta-meanings. It entails their major institutional implications, and their transformation into the basic premises of the social order, i.e., the specification of the relations between the basic dimensions of social order alluded to above—namely the division of labour, of trust, of boundaries of collectivities, regulation of power, the construction of meaning of human activities in terms of these basic poles or axes, and their institutional implications.

A very central part of the crystallization of the institutionalisation of the semantic maps of a society, sectors thereof, or of individuals, is the symbolic, ideological definitions of the basic premises of different spheres of human activities and social sectors in general, and of the political sphere in particular. It is these definitions of these premises that provide such activities with their specific meaning and legitimation in the respective societies or sectors thereof. Such symbolic definitions of economy, of polity, and the like, need not be identical with their structural differentiation. These spheres do not have to be designated in symbolically distinct autonomous ways in every society with a relatively differentiated and specialised economic or political sphere.

The second—most constitutionally "structured" (i.e., organised in relatively enduring patterns on the macro level but very important also on the micro level)—mode of control is that of several central aspects of the flow of resources in patterns of social interaction, and last the relations between these two mechanisms of control.

The control of the flow of resources is focused on the regulation of access to the major institutional markets (economic, political, cultural, etc.) and positions; of the conversion of the major resources between these markets; of the patterns of investment and distribution of such resources in space and time; and of the regulation of such spatial and temporal organisation of such resources and of their meaning.

A central connecting link between these two aspects or dimensions of control—i.e., that between the construction of the basic assumptions and premises of the social order and the regulation of the flow of different levels of information. The most important of such aspects or levels are first the information relating to the structuring of the symbolic dimensions of social life, above all of prestige as the major regulator of the access to collectivities and centres, of the status identity of different groups in society, of reference orientation to the social order and to different groups within it, as well as of the more technical or instrumental aspects of different types of social activities. Second is the evocation in formal and informal ritual and communicative situations (Eisenstadt 1985b) of deep meaning, of deep "structure" of orientations to the ethos.

In more general terms, the setting up of any institutional setting is effected by the combination of several major components—first, the level and distribution of resources among different groups in a society—i.e., the type of division of labour that is predominant in a given society; second, the institutional entrepreneurs or elites which are available—or competing—for the mobilisation and structuring of such resources and for the organisation and articulation of the interests of major groups generated by the social division of labour; third, the nature of the conceptions of "visions" which inform the major cultural orientations or codes prevalent in a society.

The concretisation of these tendencies takes place in different political-ecological settings. Of special importance are two aspects of such settings: one, heavily stressed in recent research, is the importance of international political and economic systems in general, and of the place of societies within, and of different types of religions of hegemony and dependency, in particular; the second is the more general recognition of a great variety of political-ecological settings of societies, such as differences between small and large societies, their respective dependence on internal or external markets, and the like. Both of these aspects greatly affect the ways in which institutional contours and dynamics tend to develop.

The preceding presentation of the relation between "culture" and social structure may seem—even if not necessarily incorrect—as presenting both a static as well as homogeneous picture of this relation.

It might indeed be interpreted as if such basic cultural orientations or visions, once institutionalised as components of their respective societies, are first relatively static with but little principled change throughout the major periods of the histories of their respective societies or civilisations. Second, it might also be interpreted as being also relatively uniform and homogeneous within the respective society or at least sectors, with at most local variations. Last, such a picture seemingly does not leave space for the process of reconstruction and of change of the relations between "culture" and "social structure" and beyond the initial institutionalisation of the different cultural visions; or, in other words, it does not allow for—or explain—those aspects of praxis which have been so heavily stressed, as we have seen, in the more recent literature.

Truly enough, such a simplified picture does indeed contain a very strong element of truth—namely that some very central aspects of such institutionalisation, especially those most clearly connected with the construction of the basic premises of the social order and of the major institutional spheres and formations, with what may be called the manifestations of "deep structures" of their respective societies, of the centres and boundaries of different collectivities, and their specific meanings and some of the basic institutional derivatives of such meanings, exhibit a longer rate of continuity—as can indeed be seen from the illustrations presented above—than other aspects of social structure, organisation, and interaction.

Yet, with all the elements of truth that such a picture contains, it is certainly rather one-sided. It does not take into account the fact—illustrated in our analysis of sectarianism and heterodoxies—that the institutionalisation of the different basic premises through the various mechanisms of control can never be fully successful; within each set of such premises there always develop tensions and countertendencies and orientations of protest; that the very activation of such mechanisms of control, of "structuration," activates such orientations, usually in conjunction with group conflicts, giving rise to movements of protest and change.

It is beyond the scope of this article to go in detail into the reasons for this dialectic between order-transforming and order-maintaining aspects of the relations between culture and social structure—but some preliminary indications, to some degree implicit in our preceding analysis, would not be out of place (Eisenstadt 1985a,b).

The basic reasons for such order-transforming potentialities are rooted in several basic aspects of the relations between culture and social structure.

First, they are rooted in the fact that there does not exist a one-to-one relation between the "contents" of the cultural visions and the broad premises of civilisations in which they are institutionalised; between such premises as articulated in the cognitive maps of societies and in the basic institutional structure and concrete institutional formations or structures and organisations that may develop within the frameworks of these basic premises.

Second, they are rooted in the fact that the existence of a gap between cultural visions or premises and concrete institutional formations, patterns of organisation and social interaction; the continuous selection of different aspects or components of cultural visions is closely related to the fact that any institutionalisation of such visions is effected through various mechanisms of social control and entails processes—even of a special kind—of social interaction.

Third, they are rooted in the fact that the very institutionalisation of any such visions, through the various social processes and mechanisms of control mentioned above, as well as their maintenance through space and time, does entail continuous reactivation of such social processes of control through which the basic premises are institutionalised, and that such activation generates inherent tensions and conflicts, movements of protest and processes of change which entail some possibility of reconstruction of these very premises.

Such tensions, conflicts and action of possibilities of reconstruction of social structure and meaning take place, albeit in different ways, both on the level of the more concrete situation of interaction and organisation, as well as on that of the basic premises of the elements of deep structure.

In both cases such reconstruction entails intensive patterns of social and symbolic interaction and conflict among different elites, and between them and broader groups and strata. But the dynamics of such interaction differ greatly in these different levels of social life—even if they share some common characteristics. One aspect of the reconstruction of the basic premises of a society which has been recently brilliantly analysed by Lynn Hunt (1984) is that of the intensive and dramatic construction and institutionalisation of symbols and the concomitant restructuring of basic patterns of behaviour as pertaining to those symbols.

But this is only one such element and the analysis of different types of process of social interaction, involved in the transformation of the basic premises of societies and civilisations and of different symbolic, organisational and interactional aspects of their institutionalisation, is still in many ways before us.

The preceding analysis may, however, provide some preliminary indications in this direction.

REFERENCES

Balazs, E. 1964. *Chinese Civilization and Bureaucracy: Variations on a Theme.* New Haven: Yale University Press.

Barker, E. ed. 1957. *Social and Political Thought in Byzantium from Justinian I to the Last Palaeologus.* Oxford: Oxford University Press.

Bellah, R. N., Burridge, K., and Robertson, R. 1982. "Responses to Louis Dumont." *Religion* 12: 13–91.

Blau, P. 1964a. "Justice and Social Exchange." *Sociological Enquiry* 34: 193–206.

Blau, P. 1964b. *Exchange and Power in Social Life.* New York: Wiley.

Blumer, H. 1968. *Symbolic Interactionism: Perspective and Method.* Englewood Cliffs, N.J.: Prentice-Hall.

Boudon, R. 1981. *The Logic of Social Action.* London: Routledge and Kegan Paul.

Bratianu, G. 1937. "Empire et Démocratie à Byzance." *Byzantinische Zeitschrift* 37: 87–91.

Bratianu, G. 1938. *Etudes byzantines d'histoire économique et sociale.* Paris.

Bréhier, L. 1949. *Le monde byzantin. Les constitutions de l'Empire Byzantin.* Paris: Albin Michel.

Bréhier, L. 1950. *La civilisation byzantine.* Paris: Albin Michel.

Charanis, P. 1941. "Internal Strife in Byzantium During the Fourteenth Century." *Byzantion* 15: 208–230.

Charanis, P. 1951a. "On the Social Structure and Economic Organization of the Byzantine Empire in the Thirteenth Century." *Byzantinoslavica* 12: 94–153.

Charanis, P. 1951b. "The Aristocracy of Byzantium in the Thirteenth Century" in Coleman-Norton ed., *Studies in Roman Economic and Social History in Honour of Albin Chester Johnson.* Princeton: Princeton University Press.

Charanis, P. 1961. "Town and Country in the Byzantine Possessions of the Balkan Peninsula During the Late Period of the Empire" in H. Birnbaum and S. Vryonis eds., *Aspects of the Balkans, Continuity and Change.* The Hague: Mouton.

Cicourel, A. 1964. *Method and Measurement in Sociology.* New York: Free Press.

Cicourel, A. 1973. *Cognitive Sociology.* Harmondsworth: Penguin.

Davis, N. 1975. *Society and Culture in Early Modern France.* Stanford University Press.

Denzin, N. K. 1971. "Symbolic Interactionism and Ethnomethodology" in J. Douglas ed., *Understanding Everyday Life.* London: Routledge and Kegan Paul.

Diehl, C. 1929. *La société byzantine à l'époque des Comnènes.* Paris.

Dumont, L. 1970a. *Homo Hierarchicus.* London: Weidenfeld and Nicolson.

Dumont, L. 1970b. *Religion, Politics and History in India*. Paris/The Hague: Mouton.

Dumont, L. 1982. "A Modified View of Our Origins: The Christian Origins of Modern Individualism." *Religion* 12: 1–27.

Dvornik, F. 1946. "The Circus Parties in Byzantium, their Evolution and their Suppression" *Byzantina-Metabyzantina* 1: 119–133.

Eisenstadt, S. N. 1963. *The Political Systems of Empires*. New York: Free Press.

Eisenstadt, S. N. 1978. *Revolution and the Transformation of Societies*. New York: Free Press.

Eisenstadt, S. N. 1981. "The Schools of Sociology" in J. F. Short ed., *The State of Sociology*. Beverly Hills, California: Sage.

Eisenstadt, S. N. 1982a. "The Axial Age: The Emergence of Transcendental Visions and the Rise of Clerics." *European Journal of Sociology* 23(2): 294–314.

Eisenstadt, S. N. 1982b. "Heterodoxies and Dynamics of Civilisations" *Diogenes* 120: 3–25.

Eisenstadt, S. N. 1983a. "Innerweltliche Transzendenz und die Strukturierung der Welt. Max Webers Studie über China und die Gestalt der chinesischen Zivilisation" in W. Schluchter ed., *Max Webers Studie über Konfuzianismus und Taoismus. Interpretation und Kritik*. Frankfurt am Main: Suhrkamp.

Eisenstadt, S. N. 1983b. "Transcendental Visions—Other Worldliness and its Transformations, Some More Comments on L. Dumont." *Religion* 13: 1–17.

Eisenstadt, S. N. and Roniger, L. 1984. *Patrons, Clients and Friends*. Cambridge: Cambridge University Press.

Eisenstadt, S. N. 1985a. Macro-Societal Analysis in S. N. Eisenstadt and H. J. Helle. *Perspectives on Macro-Sociological Theory*. Vol. 1. London: Sage.

Eisenstadt, S. N. 1985b. "Comparative Liminality. Liminality and Dynamics of Civilization." *Religion* 15.

Eisenstadt, S. N. 1986. *A Sociological Approach to Comparative Civilizations—Report on a Research Programme*. Jerusalem: The Truman Institute.

Eisenstadt, S. N. and A. Schachar 1986. *Society, Culture and Urbanization*. Beverly Hills and London: Sage.

Fairbank, J. K. ed. 1967. *Chinese Thought and Institutions*. Chicago: University of Chicago Press.

Ingarette, H. 1972. *Confucius, the Secular as Sacred*. New York: Harper and Row.

Frank III, A. 1979. "Reality Construction in Interaction." *Annual Review of Sociology* 5: 167–181.

Garfinkel, H. 1967. *Studies in Ethnomethodology*. Englewood Cliffs, N. J.: Prentice-Hall.

Geertz, C. 1973. *The Interpretation of Cultures*. New York: Basic Books.

Geertz, C. 1980a. "Blurred Genres: The Refiguration of Social Thought." *The American Scholar* 49(2): 165–179.

Giddens, A. 1979. *Central Problems in Social Theory, Action, Structure and Contradiction in Social Analysis.* Cambridge: Cambridge University Press.

Godelier, M. 1973. *Horizons, trajets marxistes en anthropologie.* Paris: Maspero.

Godelier, M. 1977. *Perspectives in Marxist Anthropology.* Cambridge: Cambridge University Press.

Godelier, M. 1980. "Processes of the Formation, Diversity and Bases of the State," *International Social Science Journal* XXXII(4): 609–623.

Goffman, E. 1974. *Frame Analysis.* New York: Harper.

Hunt, L. 1984. *Politics, Culture and Class in the French Revolution.* Berkeley and Los Angeles: University of California Press.

Hussey, J. M., 1937. *Church and Learning in the Byzantine Empire, 867–1185.* New York: Oxford University Press.

Hussey, J. M., 1957. *The Byzantine World.* London: Hutchinson.

Le Goff, J. 1977. *Pour un autre Moyen Age: temps, travail et culture en Occident.* Paris: Gallimard.

Le Roy Ladurie, E. 1973. *Le territoire de l'historien.* Paris: Gallimard.

Lévi-Strauss, C. 1963. *Structural Anthropology.* New York: Basic Books.

Mannheim, K. 1936. *Ideology and Utopia.* London: Routledge and Kegan Paul.

Meltzer, B., Petras, J. and Reynolds, L. 1975. *Symbolic Interactionism: Genesis, Variation and Criticism.* London: Routledge and Kegan Paul.

Merton, R. K. 1963. *Social Theory and Social Structure.* New York: Free Press.

Metzger, T. 1977. *Escape from Predicament. Neo-Confucianism and China's Evoluting Political Culture.* New York: Columbia University Press.

Morris, C. 1973. *The Discovery of the Individual, 1050–1200.* New York: Harper.

Mote, F. 1971. *Intellectual Foundations of China.* New York: A. Knopf.

Ortner, S. 1984. "Theory in Anthropology since the Sixties." *Comparative Studies in Society and History* 26(1).

Ostrogorsky, G. 1954. *Pour l'histoire de la féodalité byzantine.* Brussels: Corpus Bruxellense Historiae Byzantiae.

Ostrogorsy, G. 1959. "Byzantine Cities in the Early Middle Ages." *Dumberton Oaks Papers* 13: 45–66.

Reischauer, E. and Fairbank, J. 1960. *A History of East Asian Civilization.* Vol. I, *East Asia: The Great Tradition.* Boston: Houghton Mifflin.

Rossi, I. 1983. *From the Sociology of Symbols to the Sociology of Signs: Toward a Dialectical Sociology.* New York: Columbia University Press.

Rousseau, P. 1978. *Ascetics, Authority and the Church in the Age of Jerome and Cossio.* Oxford: Oxford University Press.

Schwartz, B. 1975. "Transcendence in Ancient China." *Daedalus,* Spring: 57–63.

Schwartz, B. 1985. *The World of Thought in Ancient China.* Harvard University Press.

Skocpol, T. 1979. *States of Social Revolutions. A Comparative Analysis of France, Russia and China.* Cambridge: Cambridge University Press.

Silver, F. 1981. "Dissent through Holiness, the Case of the Radical Renouncer in the Ravada Buddhist Communities." *Numen* XXIII(2).

Stroumsa, G. 1981. "Ascèse et choses: aux origins de la spiritualité monastique." *Revue Thomiste* 81: 557–573.

Tambiah, S. 1981. "The Renouncer, his Individuality and his Community." *Numen* XXIII(2).

Troeltsch, E. 1960. *The Social Teaching of the Christian Churches.* Vol. 1: 158–159. New York: Harper.

Tu Wei Ming 1979. *Humanity and Self-cultivation. Essays in Confucian Thought.* Berkeley: Asian Humanities Press.

Turner, K. ed. 1974. *Ethnomethodology.* Harmondsworth: Penguin.

Turner, W. 1969. *The Ritual Process.* Chicago: Aldine.

Vasiliev, A. 1952. *History of the Byzantine Empire, 324–1453.* Madison, Wisconsin: University of Wisconsin Press.

Wallerstein, I. 1974. *The Modern World System.* London and New York: Academic Press.

Wright, A. ed. 1953. *Studies in Chinese Thought.* Chicago: University of Chicago Press.

Wright, A. F. and Nivison, D. eds. 1959. *Confucianism in Action.* Stanford: Stanford University Press.

Wright, A. F. ed. 1960. *The Confucian Persuasion.* Stanford: Stanford University Press.

Twelve

THE ORDER-MAINTAINING AND ORDER-TRANSFORMING DIMENSIONS OF CULTURE

THE PROBLEM: ITS BACKGROUND AND DEVELOPMENT IN CONTEMPORARY SOCIOLOGICAL ANALYSIS

ONE OF THE CENTRAL PROBLEMS in the sociological analysis of culture, and especially of the relations between culture and social structure, has been that of the order-maintaining versus the order-transforming functions of culture. One line of analysis, coming from Marx and Durkheim (and, in a modified form, from Parsons), tends to regard culture (especially religion or ideology) mainly as a reflection of society or as its major legitimizing or consensus-creating mechanism. The second line, epitomized in Weber's analysis of the world religions, especially of the Protestant ethic, stressed the order-transforming, innovative dimensions of religion, of culture.

These different visions of the place of culture in the construction of social order are closely related to the problem of the degree to which social structure determines culture or vice-versa. They are closely related to the extent of mutual determination of culture, social structure, and social behavior; or, as Renato Rosaldo has put it, the degree to which culture is a cybernetic feedback-control mechanism controlling behavior and social structure, or whether there exists a possibility of choice and inventiveness by various social actors in the use of cultural resources.

These problems have been at the center of many theoretical discussions and controversies in the social sciences, especially since the mid-1960s, and have developed in close conjunction with criticism of the structural-functional approach. These discussions have touched on many of the substantive problems of the social sciences: the nature of modern society or societies; the vision of humanity and history; the different modes of analysis and explanation in the social sciences; the place of the social sciences in the modern and postmodern intellectual traditions; and the boundaries of different scholarly disciplines (Eisenstadt and Curelaru 1976, 1977). In conjunction with these controversies

Originally published in *Theory of Culture*, ed. R. Munch and N. J. Smelser, © 1992 The Regents of the University of California. Reprinted with the permission of the University of California Press, Berkeley and Los Angeles.

there have been far-reaching shifts in the definition of the major concepts of social science analysis, in the relations between the major explanatory models employed in the social sciences, and in the consequent directions of research.

The major shift in the basic concepts of social science analysis, concepts that include culture as well as religion, knowledge, social structure, and social behavior, was in their conceptualization as distinct and "real" ontological entities and not (as in earlier periods of sociological and anthropological analysis) as analytical constructs referring to different aspects or dimensions of human action and social interaction, that is, as constitutive of each other and of patterns of social interaction. Concomitantly, there developed a shift of emphasis with respect to several dimensions of culture and of social structure, especially away from the structural-functional emphasis on values and norms. One view—explicit among the structuralists and implicit among some of the ethnomethodologists—regarded culture as containing the programmatic codes of human behavior and espoused (to use Geertz's felicitous, if ironical, expression) the view of man as cerebral savage (for example, Lévi-Strauss 1983). According to this view, culture is fully structured or programmed according to clear principles and is embedded in the nature of the human mind, which, through a series of codes, regulates human behavior. By contrast, the symbolic anthropologists, such as Clifford Geertz, Victor Turner, and David M. Schneider, and to some extent the symbolic interactionists in sociology, shifted from values and norms to a conception of culture as a set of expressive symbols of ethos—a worldview constructed through active human interaction (Geertz 1973, 1983; Turner 1974, 1947, 1968; Schneider 1973, 1980, 1977). As R. Peterson has stated:

> The focus on drama, myth, code, and people's plan indicates a shift in the image of culture. . . . It was once seen as a map for behavior. In this view, people use culture the way scientists use paradigms to organize and normalize their activity. Like scientific paradigms, elements of culture are used, modified, or discarded depending on their usefulness in organizing reality as equivalent to the term ideology, but without the latter's pejorative connotations. Sociologists now recognize that people continuously choose among a wide range of definitions of situations or fabricate new ones to fit their needs (Peterson 1979).

Yet another development involved an individualist (or rational-choice) mode of analysis, which regarded culture as the result of the aggregation of individual preferences, reflecting differences of power or patterns of individual choices (Hirshfeld, Atran, and Yengoyan 1982). Parallel shifts in the concept of social structure have also evolved since the mid-sixties. The concept has become firmer in new definitions that view social structure and institutions—

especially the "state"—as "real" and "autonomous" agents or actors (for instance, Skocpol 1979; Wolff 1950, 1957; Blau 1964, 1965; Boudon 1981; Merton 1963).

In another development closely related to the rational-choice approach, social structure was viewed as networks or organizations arising from the aggregation of interactions, with almost no autonomous characteristics except for some emergent qualities often described as "primitive effects." This network approach tended to neglect or downplay the tradition of structural analysis represented in the works of Simmel, Merton, Blau, and Boudon, which have stressed the formal characteristics and emergent properties of social structure (Blau 1964; Boudon 1981; Merton 1963).

Finally, these shifts were accompanied by a preference for exclusive deterministic, reductionist, idealist, or materialist interpretations of social action and culture creativity. They were also connected with a growing dissociation between studies of culture and of social structure.

These shifts and the studies they generated sharpened and diversified the definitions of culture and articulated the problems of positioning it in the construction of social order. At the same time they continuously oscillated in their view of the relationship between culture and social structure in any given society as either static and homogeneous or as entirely open, malleable, and continuously changing.

The first view, typical of some structuralists and extreme Marxists, depicts cultural orientations or rules—whether they are, as among the structuralists, reflections of some basic rules of the human mind or, as among the Marxists, reflections of social forces—as relatively uniform and homogeneous within the society and as relatively static with little change throughout the histories of the societies or civilizations in which they are institutionalized. Such a picture leaves little room (beyond the initial institutionalization of the different cultural visions) for reconstruction and change in the relations between culture and social structure. Nor does it allow for, or explain, various aspects of praxis and the construction of changing mentalities that have been analyzed in recent anthropological, historical, and sociological literature. Finally, it does not explain the development of strategies of choice, maximization, and possible innovation as depicted in individualistic approaches.

In the second view, culture is regarded as an aggregate result of patterns of behavior, structure, or power or—as Ann Swidler has explained it—as a tool kit of different strategies of action that can be activated in different situations according to the "material" and "ideal" interests of different social actors (Swidler 1986). This view implies that culture is merely a mirror or aggregate of continuously changing rational or expressive choices made by individuals and groups without any autonomy of their own.

TOWARD THE REINTEGRATION OF STUDIES OF CULTURE AND SOCIAL
STRUCTURE: COMPARATIVE ANALYSIS OF LIMINALITY AND HETERODOXIES

It is not surprising that many scholars from different schools soon recognized
the need to reconnect the many different strains of research and analysis. This
chapter attempts to contribute to such a reconstruction and to reintegrate the
studies of culture and social structure. In so doing, I hope to shed new light on
the place of culture in the construction of social order in general and on the
order-maintaining and order-transforming functions of culture in particular.
The contribution will be made on the basis of comparative studies of liminal
situations and of heterodoxies in different civilizations.[1]

Our analysis begins with the recognition of the ubiquity of *liminality* in
human societies. By this term I mean seemingly unstructured situations, "in
between" more structured ones, and symbols of antistructure and communitas.
Such situations and symbols can indeed, in different connotations, be found in
all human societies, as can the unruly behavior that is often connected with
them. The ubiquity of such situations is not given in some "natural," spontaneous tendencies, in an outburst against the discontents of civilization. Rather,
these symbols, situations, and patterns of behavior are culturally and socially
constructed, and the behavior that develops within them is also so constructed;
even if it often seems spontaneous and "natural," it is a socially and culturally
regulated spontaneity and definition of natural behavior. This is similar to the
situation with respect to the "biological" crises of life—birth, adolescence,
death, and so on—which, while rooted in clearly biological givens of human
existence, are at the same time socially and culturally channeled (Homans
1962).

The central focus of the symbols found in such liminal situations is a very
strong ambivalence to social and cultural order. This ambivalence and the
strong emphasis on antistructure or communitas, which are built into many of
these situations, are as much culturally constructed as the social structural and
cultural order against which rebel the patterns of behavior that develop in
these situations.

Such ambivalence to social order is rooted in several basic characteristics

1. This analysis is based on a seminar on Comparative Liminality and Dynamics of Civilizations conducted by the late Victor Turner and the author in Jerusalem in 1982–1983 within the
framework of the program on Sociological Analysis of Comparative Civilizations at the Department of Sociology and Social Anthropology and the Truman Research Institute of the Hebrew
University in Jerusalem. On this program see S. N. Eisenstadt, "Sociological Approach to Comparative Civilizations." The Development and Directions of a Research Program, Jerusalem, The Hebrew University, 1986. The papers of the seminar on Comparative Liminality were published in
Religion 15 (July 1985).

of human existence, indeed in some aspects of human biological nature. Among these are the relatively open biological program that characterizes the human species (Meyer 1984); the consciousness of such openness; a basic existential uncertainty or anxiety, most closely related to the consciousness of death, of human finality, and in attempts to overcome it (Dobzhansky 1973; Bloch and Parry 1982); and the capacity to imagine various possibilities beyond what is given here and there (Sartre 1956).

All societies construct such a social and cultural order, designed in part to overcome the uncertainties and anxieties implied in these existential givens. They do so by constructing symbolic boundaries of personal and collective identity (Durkheim [1912] 1954), by defining membership in different collectivities in terms of universal biological *primordial* categories such as age, generation, sex, and territorial attachment, by "answering" certain perennial problems of death and immortality in religious belief systems, and by distinguishing between the given, mundane world and another world beyond it and between the profane and the sacred.

Ironically, however, the very construction of such boundaries and of their institutional derivatives adds another element or component of uncertainty to the human situation, which exacerbates the original uncertainties and generates a strong ambivalence to social order. This element is the consciousness of the arbitrariness of any cultural construction: the consciousness that any given order is only one of several, perhaps many, possible alternatives, including the possibility of living beyond any social order whatsoever. In other words, the very construction of any social order, while a manifestation of human creativity, necessarily imposes severe limitations on such creativity and gives rise to an awareness of such limitations.

The awareness of such arbitrariness and limitation and the attempt to convince members of the society that social order, in general, and the specific social order in which they live, in particular, are the "correct" ones are portrayed in the myths and symbols promulgated in all societies through various ritual and communicative situations. These myths and symbols, the closely related "folktales," depict the combination of the attraction of the world outside the boundaries of social order and of the fear of stepping outside such boundaries. They stress the purity of the world inside, the pollution of the world outside (Douglas 1966), and the need to remain within such boundaries. They are not, however, able to eliminate the awareness of various possibilities that exist beyond these boundaries and hence the certain arbitrariness of any such boundaries, of any instituted social order.

THE ROOTS OF THE CONSCIOUSNESS OF THE ARBITRARINESS OF SOCIAL AND CULTURAL ORDER: THE CONSTRUCTIVE AND DESTRUCTIVE DIMENSIONS OF CHARISMATIC PREDISPOSITIONS

The consciousness of the arbitrariness of any social and cultural order is exacerbated by the exigencies of reproducing social order through social institutions. It is important here to recognize the fact that constitutes the cornerstone of modern sociological analysis; namely, the inadequacy of the organization of social division of labor to explain the construction and maintenance of social order. The founding fathers of sociology, while recognizing the importance of the various mechanisms of social division of labor, emphasized that the social division of labor, in general, and the market mechanisms analyzed in great detail by economists, in particular, would not suffice to explain the construction of social order (Eisenstadt 1981).

The conditions necessary for sustaining social order are several: the construction of trust and solidarity, stressed above all by Durkheim and to some degree by Tönnies (Durkheim 1964a, 1964b; Tönnies 1957); the regulation of power and the overcoming of the feelings of exploitation, stressed above all by Marx and Weber (Marx 1965); and the provision of meaning and of legitimation to the different social activities, emphasized above all by Weber (1952, 1958, 1951).

The founding fathers stressed, moreover, that the very construction of any concrete social division of labor generates uncertainties with respect to each of these conditions. Because of these uncertainties no concrete social division of labor can be maintained without attending to these dimensions. They emphasized accordingly that the construction and maintenance of social order depends upon the development of some patterned combination of the division of labor, the regulation of power, and the construction of trust, meaning, and legitimation.

But the development of such a combination is not given. There are inevitable uncertainties, unanticipated crises, and struggles reflecting the tension between different dimensions of social order. These exacerbate the consciousness of the arbitrariness of any social order and the concomitant ambivalence toward it.

The consciousness of the arbitrariness of any cultural and social order, the fact that such consciousness exacerbates the uncertainties and anxiety rooted in the consciousness of the openness of biological program, of awareness of death and in the capacity of imagination and the concomitant ambivalence to the social order, constitutes one of the most important manifestations of the problems inherent in the process of "routinization" of charisma. Above all, such consciousness constitutes a manifestation of the problem inherent in the limitations on human creativity that any institutionalization of a charismatic vision entails (Weber 1968). The essence of the charismatic dimension in human life is the attempt to contact the very essence of being, to go to the very roots of existence, of the cosmic, cultural, and social order, to what is seen as sacred and fundamental.

This charismatic dimension focuses, in the cultural and social realms, on the construction of cultural and social order in terms of some combination between primordial and transcendental symbols in terms of relation to some conception of the sacred. This charismatic dimension is manifest in the construction of the boundaries of personal and collective identity, of societal centers, and of major symbols of prestige. Such a construction is indeed one of the fullest manifestations of human creativity. At the same time, however, the very institutionalization of such a charismatic dimension generates very severe limitations on such creativity, and, in connection with the tendencies analyzed above, it also generates consciousness of such limitations.

The basic root of the limitations on human activity lies primarily in the fact that the process of the institutionalization of any concrete social setting entails a certain closure in the selection from a variety of potential or imagined possibilities. Second, the roots of such limitations lie in the routinization of the creative act, which is inherent in any such institutionalization, and in the close relation between such closure and the elements of power and domination that any such institutionalization entails.

Indeed, the restrictions and exclusions entailed by the institutionalization of any charismatic vision become necessarily closely associated with, although not necessarily identical to, the maintenance of the distribution of power and wealth, the control over resources, and the limitation of the scope of participation of various groups in the central arenas of a society and their access to meaningful participation in the social and cultural order. Such limitations on human creativity are also inherent in the ways in which the basic conditions of social order—the construction of trust (solidarity), meaning, power, and social division of labor—are related to one another in the process of concrete institution building. The crucial tension or contradiction is between the conditions that generate the construction of trust between different members of a group or society and those that ensure the availability of resources and institutional entrepreneurs in the formation of broader institutional complexes and their legitimation.

The conditions that make for maintenance of trust are best met in relatively limited ranges of social activities or interaction, such as in family or kinship groups in which social interaction is regulated according to primordial and particularistic criteria. Such limited ranges of interaction seem to constitute the necessary minimal conditions for the initial development of such trust, even if they may not be enough to guarantee its continuity. At the same time, however, these very conditions are inimical to the development of those resources and activities needed for broader institutional creativity and for the construction of broader institutional complexes based on more variegated orientations. The very conditions that generate resources for broader complex institution building also tend to undermine the simple, or "primitive," settings of potential trust as they exist within the family and kinship groups or in small communities.

The possibility of such institutionalization is above all dependent on the effective extension of the range of symbolism of trust beyond the narrow minimal scope of primordial units. Such extension is found, for example, in the depiction of rulers as "fathers" of their countries or in the infusion and legitimation of economic activities with some transcendental meaning. But any such extension necessarily heightens the combination of such extended trust and the distribution of power. Indeed, any construction of concrete social order necessarily institutionalizes some limitations on potential or imagined activities and exclusions of some sectors from full participation in it.

Such exclusions and limitations are, as we have seen, legitimized in various ritual and communicative situations, but the very attempts at such legitimations tend only to underlie and sharpen the awareness of arbitrariness and ambivalence toward the constructed social order. Accordingly, such situations may bring out strong antinomian orientations and many destructive tendencies. Such tendencies are not primitive, or "animal," reactions to the restriction of social and cultural life, but, paradoxically, they constitute the reverse and complementary side of the creative process of construction of order: the constructive aspect of the charismatic dimension of human activities (Weber 1968). They are as inherent in the very nature of the charismatic predisposition or fervor in the very attempt to come into contact with the essence of being, to go to the roots of existence, of cosmic, social, and cultural order, as are constructive tendencies.

The attempt to reestablish direct contact with these roots of cosmic and sociopolitical order may also contain a strong predisposition to sacrilege and to the denial of the validity of the sacred, and it may breed opposition both to more attenuated and formalized forms of this order and to the sacred itself. Similarly, on the personal level, it is in its charismatic roots that the human personality can attain its fullest creative power and internal responsibility, but these roots may also represent the epitome of the darkest recesses and excesses of the human soul, its utter depravity and irresponsibility, and its more intensive antinomian tendencies.

Thus, the very process of the construction of social and cultural order generates tendencies toward its destruction. The destructive aspects of charisma often involve the denial not only of the concrete restrictions inherent in institutionalization but also of the very fact of institutionalization and the social restrictions it entails. But even the seemingly total negation of the social order, the potentially destructive behavior related to it, and the attempts to overcome them are elements of the construction of cultural and social order.

Hence, however destructive and seemingly spontaneous are many of the manifestations of such ambivalence to social order, most are structured around several basic orientations and themes, particularly around major themes of protest that develop in all human societies in various culturally and socially structured situations, among them various liminal situations.

LIMINAL SITUATIONS AND ORIENTATIONS OF PROTEST

This ubiquity of both the constructive and destructive aspects of the charismatic dimension of human activity, of the attempt to reestablish contact with the roots of the social and cultural order, and the manifestation of these aspects in liminal situations, indicates that the order-maintaining and order-transforming dimensions of culture are but two sides of the construction of social order.

Orientations and symbols of protest contain two basic components, out of which the more concrete themes of protest develop. The first is the attempt to overcome the predicaments and limitations of human existence in general and of death in particular. The second is the attempt to overcome the tension and predicaments inherent in the institutionalization of the social order: the tension between equality and hierarchy; the tensions among the social division of labor and the regulation of power, construction of trust, and provision of meaning; and the tension between the quest for meaningful participation in central symbolic and institutional arenas by various groups in the society and the limitation on the access to these arenas, which exists in every society. Out of the combination and development of these two basic components there develop four concrete themes of protest found in all societies.

1. The search to overcome the tension between the complexity and fragmentation of human relations inherent in any institutional division of labor and the possibility of some total, unconditional, unmediated participation in social and cultural orders.

2. The search to overcome the tensions inherent in the temporal dimension of the human and social condition, especially the search for immortality; the tension between the deferment of gratification in the present and the possibility of its attainment in the future; and the tension between an emphasis on productivity and labor and the distribution and the accompanying stress of visions of unlimited goods. These tensions are often played out in various myths of the relations between Time of Origin and Time of End: *Uhrzeit* and *Endzeit* (Van der Lieuw 1957).

3. The quest to suspend the tension in the model of the ideal society; the principles of distributive justice upheld within it on the one hand and the reality of institutional life on the other.
4. The quest to suspend the tension between the personal and the autonomous self and the social role, that is, the possibility of finding full expression of the internal self in social and cultural life as opposed to the retreat from it.

These themes focus on specific aspects of the institutional order: on the construction of boundaries between the personality and the collectivity; on symbols of authority; on symbols of stratification that express hierarchy and the structural aspects of division of labor and distribution of resources; and on the family as the primary locus of authority, socialization, and restriction imposed on an individual's impulses and activities and as the locus in which those restrictions are closely related to the basic primordial data of human experience, especially to differences in age and sex. Focusing these themes of protest generates the themes of communitas, of antistructure, which constitute, in every society, part of the map of such antinomian symbols.

These orientations of protest are not marginal to the central symbols of a tradition of a society, erupting only in periods of social disorganization and change. They contain the elements of potential dissent and heterodoxy as inherent and continuous components of every social order.

Such potentialities of dissent and heterodoxy become manifest in a great variety of more fully articulated counter and secondary orientations (see, in greater detail, Eisenstadt 1976). First, they become articulated in the development of some ideals and orientations found in almost any great tradition, and while antithetical to some of the predominant basic premises of the tradition, they are nonetheless derived from its basic respective parameters. Each set of ideals and orientations points in a seemingly opposite direction, although they may reinforce one another. The interrelations between the Brahman ideal and the renouncer in Indian civilization, between the active church engaged in the world and the monastic ideal in Western Christianity, and between the power orientation and the monastic ideal in the Eastern church illustrate contradictory orientations within a single tradition.

These potentially antinomian tendencies often become connected with the exaltation of those dimensions of human existence that are not institutionalized in the tradition, for example, expressions of subjectivism and privatization and an emphasis on the symbols of primordial attachment. The individuals or group that brings forward such sentiments may claim that it is only within its own confines that the pure, pristine, or primordial qualities emphasized in the ideals of the center can be fully realized. Similarly the ideals of equality and communal solidarity may be emphasized instead of those of hierarchy, power, and unequal distribution of wealth, which are seen as being upheld in the center.

Second, such potentialities of dissent become articulated as the "double," "contradiction," or "other side" of a society's institutional image (Decoufle 1968).

Third, the potentialities produce images of the pristine ideals of the existing society, uncontaminated by its concrete "profane" institutionalization.

Fourth, they project images of a social and cultural order totally different from the existing one or uncontaminated by any institutionalization.

These various orientations and themes of protest, these "heterodox," antinomian, and potentially rebellious orientations, are articulated by different groups or individuals in a great variety of social situations. The various double images of the society are articulated and played out in most of the major ritual and communicative situations in which the models of social order are promulgated (Eisenstadt 1963).

These themes and the consciousness of the arbitrariness of such order are first most fully and paradoxically promulgated in the rituals of the center, such as coronation and national thanksgiving, attesting to the fact that the consciousness of such arbitrariness is never fully obliterated but is transposed to a more sophisticated, reflexive level of symbolism and consciousness. These themes are also played out in fully structural liminal situations—the various collective *rites de passage* such as first-fruit ceremonies and collective rituals of initiation—in which the space between the strict boundaries of various institutional arenas is symbolically constructed.

Third, these themes are articulated in special rituals of rebellion, in which the existing power, hierarchy, and often sexual relations are momentarily, symbolically, and ritually reversed, but in which the potential antinomian tendencies are checked or regulated by full legitimation and institutionalization of the rituals.

Fourth, they are played out in a great variety of more loosely structured situations, such as for instance those of pilgrimage and play (Bruner et al. 1976; Turner 1973).

These varied images and themes may also become "stored" as it were in some arenas, institutions, or among social groups such as Buddhist monks. These groups may serve as the carriers of the symbolic attributes of membership in a collectivity and as its primordial, preinstitutional symbols (a good illustration is found in Mus 1967, 1968). These themes and images may also become defined as *esoteric* in both private and public life and as *private* and *personal* and opposed to the public sphere (Eisenstadt 1974; Eisenstadt and Roniger 1984). Alternatively, they may be witnessed in eruptions of chiliastic, millenarian, messianic outbursts or more organized movements of heterodoxy or protest.

In most of these situations some liminal space is created in which different orientations and themes of protest are played out, aiming, in one way or another, at the reconstruction of the relations between trust, power, social division of labor, and broader meaning and at reconstituting, reaffirming, or changing the boundaries of personal and collective identity: the symbols of the center and the delineation of pure, as opposed to dangerous, space. However, the ways in which these different types of liminality develop, and their specific location and impact, vary greatly in differing societies.

PROTEST AND LIMINAL SITUATIONS IN TRIBAL SOCIETIES AND AXIAL CIVILIZATIONS

The structuring of the symbolism of protest and of liminality and liminal situations is influenced by the different configurations of the major components of the construction of social order.

The social division of labor—the division of social roles in society—appears to play a very important role in shaping liminal situations. In less differentiated societies, many liminal situations are more structured and more fully ritualized. Accordingly, different themes of liminality, protest, and antistructure are more fully articulated and, in fact, highly regulated. Max Gluckman's classical analysis of rituals of rebellion (1963) portrays exactly this type of situation, in which protest, liminality, and antistructure are very closely interrelated, fully structured, and placed in the center of the society. This distinctive feature also seems to minimize the disruptive potentialities of these activities and their potential for "change" and "real rebellion." However, as Beidelman's critique of Gluckman has shown (1966), the conflicts and ambivalences articulated in rituals of rebellion originate not only in tensions inherent in social organization but also in the nature of the symbolic construction of social and cultural life, which shapes and provides an overall meaning to the social order and of symbols of collective identity.

The structure and symbols of collective identity and of the center, their symbols and ideology, as they articulate the relations between trust, power, and social division of labor, and their broader meaning, are of crucial importance in the structuring of different types of liminal situations and their symbolism.

Even within societies with similar levels of social differentiation there develop different types of center and of liminal situations. A great variety of centers and concomitant different types of liminal situations can be identified in various African societies. Thus, the case of the Desanett, analyzed by Uri Almagor, points to contrasts between their situation and that of the Zulu described by Gluckman (Almagor 1985).

Almagor's analysis indicates that, even in such relatively undifferentiated societies, a multiplicity of liminal situations develop, many of which constitute the nuclei of an extension of trust and which may also be starting points for social change. This change may not be at the center of a society; it may occur in the restructuring of the symbolic boundaries of collectivities by creating nuclei of new tribal segments, thus pointing to the importance of such situations in analyzing different modes of change and changes in different components of the social order.

The variability of centers in societies is seen in the great premodern civilizations, especially in the so-called Axial Age civilizations (Eisenstadt 1982), those which crystallized out of the revolutions or transformations connected with what Karl Jaspers designated as the Axial Age in the first millennium before the Christian era—namely ancient Israel, later on Christianity in its great variety, ancient Greece, partially Iran during the development of Zoroastrianism, China during the early Imperial period, Hinduism and Buddhism, and, much later, beyond the Axial Age proper (Jaspers 1949; Voegelin 1954–1974). Common to all was the development of the conception of a basic tension between the transcendental and the mundane orders.

The institutionalization of such a conception of tension was not simply an intellectual exercise. It connoted a far-reaching change in humanity's active orientation to the world—a change with basic institutional implications—and it generated the symbolic, intellectual, and institutional possibilities for the development of sects and heterodoxies as potential agents of civilizational change.

On the symbolic level, the conception of a chasm between the transcendental and the mundane orders created a problem of how to overcome this chasm, how to bridge the transcendental and the mundane orders. This gave rise—to use Weber's terminology—to the problem of salvation, usually phrased in terms of the reconstruction of human behavior and personality given a higher moral or metaphysical order. As a result, as Gananath Obeysekere has explained, rebirth eschatology becomes ethicized (1983). But every attempt at such a reconstruction was torn by internal tensions. These tensions and their institutional repercussions ushered a new social and civilizational dynamic into history.

At the institutional level, the development of the conception of a chasm gave rise, in all these civilizations, to attempts to reconstruct the mundane world according to the transcendental principles. The mundane order was perceived as incomplete, inferior, and often in need of being reconstructed according to the precepts of the higher ethical or metaphysical order. This perception, and the attempts to reconstruct the mundane order, gave rise to far-reaching, concrete institutional implications. Among the most important of these implications was the construction of distinct civilizational frameworks and the development of the concept of the accountability of rulers.

Some collectivities and institutional arenas were singled out as the most appropriate carriers of the attributes required to reconnect the transcendental and the mundane. As a result, new types of collectivities were created or seemingly natural and "primordial" groups were endowed with special meaning couched in terms of the perception of this tension and its resolution. The most important innovation was the appearance of "cultural" and "religious" collectivities as distinct from ethnic or political ones. These collectivities tended to become imbued with a strong ideological dimension and to become a focus of ideological struggle with a strong insistence on their own exclusiveness and closure and on the distinction between inner and outer social and cultural space defined by them. This tendency became connected with attempts to structure the different cultural, political, and ethnic collectivities in some hierarchical order, and the very construction of such an order usually became a focus of ideological and political conflict.

Closely related to this mode of structuring special civilizational frameworks was a restructuring of the relations between the political and the higher, transcendental order. The political order as the central locus of the mundane order has usually been, in these civilizations, conceived as lower than the transcendental. It had to be restructured according to the precepts of the latter; i.e., according to the perception of how best to overcome the tension between the transcendental and the mundane order and how to implement the transcendental vision. The rulers were usually held responsible for organizing the political order according to such transcendental orientations.

At the same time the nature of the rulers was greatly transformed. The king-god, the embodiment of the cosmic and the earthly order alike, disappeared, and in its place appeared a secular ruler—sometimes with sacral attributes—in principle accountable to some higher order. There emerged the concept of the accountability of the rulers and the community to a higher authority, God, divine law, and the like. The possibility emerged of calling a ruler to judgment, presumably before the representatives of such higher authority. The first, most dramatic appearance of this conception appeared in ancient Israel, in the priestly and prophetic pronouncements. A different conception, that of accountability to the community and its laws, appeared in ancient Greece. In varying forms such conceptions of accountability appeared in all Axial civilizations (Eisenstadt 1981). The development of different concepts of accountability of rulers—and the continuous struggle between the rulers and the different groups that espoused such concepts and among the latter—generated a new political and cultural dynamic and intensified awareness of the arbitrariness of social order.

In connection with these specific symbolic and institutional characteristics of the Axial Age civilizations, far-reaching changes in the map of liminal situations and symbols and of movements and symbolism of protest have also taken place. While many of the liminal situations—especially different types of rituals of rebellion—have persisted, many new types, beyond those found in tribal societies, have developed, and at the same time the structure and the symbols of "older" situations have greatly changed.

First, in these civilizations the central, fully structured, and regulated rituals tend to become increasingly limited to fully elaborated rituals of the center, with the periphery playing a much more passive role, mainly as spectators or, at most, as rather passive recipients of the regnant vision. In these rituals the antistructural and the protest components and the symbols have been on the whole weakened and minimized, although there may develop a strong articulation of the ambivalences toward the arbitrariness of the cultural order combined with a strong, "orthodox" emphasis on the danger of diverting from it.

Second, there tend to develop within these societies and civilizations relatively autonomous spheres of behavior (currently denoted as *popular culture*) with different degrees of connection to central rituals. These include local festivals and leisure activities, as well as more elaborate carnivals, in which many of the ambivalences of protest are played out. These situations may become connected in different ways to more official regional rituals linking the center and the periphery, combining different mixtures of antinomianism and an acceptance of the hegemonic order (one classic analysis is Granet 1932, 1950; see also Wolf 1974).

Third, there develop an entirely new type of liminality and protest—fully fledged heterodoxies, sects, and sectarianism, a phenomenon closely related to the basic characteristics of the Axial civilizations (Eisenstadt 1982). Closely connected with the development of heterodoxy and sectarianism is the appearance of carriers of the "pristine" religious vision, the holy men of antiquity, such as Indian or Buddhist renouncers, Christian monks, and religious virtuosi (Silber 1981).

The Variability of Protest and of Liminal Situations in Axial Civilizations

These various types of liminal situations and protest can be found in all the Axial Age civilizations. There exist, however, far-reaching differences in the exact structure and symbolism of these liminal situations, in their organizational and symbolic maps, in their connection to movements of protest, and in their impact on the macrosocial order in general and processes of change in particular (Eisenstadt 1973). These differences are related to the combination of the mode of social division of labor and the structure of power, together with the basic cultural orientations, especially the nature of the concepts of salvation, that are predominant in them.

The greatest differences are those among the monotheistic civilizations, with their strong orientation to the reconstruction of the mundane order, and the otherworldly Asian civilizations, especially the Hindu and the Buddhist ones with their rejection of the world. There is also a significant difference between all these civilizations and the Chinese Confucian one, with its very strong affirmation of the mundane (especially political) order as the only arena of "salvation,"—the reconstruction of the mundane world according to the transcendental vision.

In the otherworldly civilizations, such as Buddhist (and, in a different mode, also Hindu), the major orientations of protest and the major impact of liminal situations are not, as in the monotheistic civilizations, on the reconstruction of the political centers of the respective societies. These centers are often seen as irrelevant to the major concept of salvation, and hence their reconstruction does not play a major role in these orientations and the movements of protest in these civilizations.

This does not mean that the Buddhist and Hindu sects did not have immense impacts on the dynamics of their respective civilizations. They extended the scope of the different national and political communities and imbued them with new symbolic dimensions (Tambiah 1976; Bechert 1966–1968; Sarkisyanz 1965; Reynolds 1977; Keyes 1977).[2] They also changed some of the bases and criteria of participation in the civilizational communities, as was the case in Jainism, in the Bhakti movement, and, above all, in Buddhism when an entirely new civilizational framework was reconstructed. Buddhism also introduced new elements into the political scene, particularly the unique way in which the Sangha, usually politically a very compliant group, could in some cases, as Paul Mus has shown, become a sort of moral conscience of the community, calling the rulers to some accountability.

This impact is different from that of the struggles between the reigning orthodoxies and heterodoxies in monotheistic civilizations (Eisenstadt 1982), most of which aim at the reconstruction of the mundane world, especially of the political centers.

But even in the monotheistic civilizations such impact may be limited by the strength of the center, by its distance from the centers of Christianity, by the position of the Church vis-à-vis the state, and by the degree of monopolization of sacred symbols by the rulers. In this connection it is fruitful to compare these developments with Eastern Christianity in general and the Byzantine and Russian empires in particular (Kaplan 1985; Eisenstadt 1973, 1982b). All these cases revealed variations in types of liminal situations and movements of protest and in the degree of their impact on the institutional arenas (Smelser 1963).

The full impact of the different symbols and movements of liminality and

2. On some aspects of the dynamics of Buddhist civilization, from the standpoint of our analysis, see S. J. Tambiah (1976).

protest on the symbols of the center, as derived from the combination of this and otherworldly orientations, can be found in western Europe, in the transition of modernity, in the Great Revolutions (Eisenstadt 1978; Heyd 1985), and to some degree in the Jewish case in the Sabbatean movement. (The classical analysis on this movement is found in Scholem 1941, 1973.) In all these cases many of the symbols of protest, which were promulgated by the major movements of protest, such as demands for full participation of all members of the community in the political process and full equality and full accountability of rulers, were incorporated in the new revolutionary and postrevolutionary centers.

At the same time, however, this strong impact of these movements on the center should not obliterate the importance of the other types of liminal situations and of popular culture that tend to develop in such societies and that become even more pronounced—and transformed—with the development of modernity.

From the standpoint of the conceptions of salvation, the accountability of rulers, and the characteristics of liminal and sectarian activities, the legalistic Confucian Empire constitutes an interesting case between this-worldly and otherworldly civilizations. In many ways, this empire came closer to the monotheistic than to the otherworldly Axial Age civilizations, and yet it is also significantly different from the former (Fairbanks 1967; Fingarette 1972; Metzger 1977; Schwartz 1975).

Powerful heterodoxies, utopian visions, movements of protest, and orientations of protest and liminal situations did develop in China, especially among the neo-Confucians from the Sung period onward. These visions were also oriented—as was the case in other Axial civilizations—against specific aspects of the institutionalization of the major metaphysical and ethical messages and visions. And yet in China, unlike in the monotheistic civilizations in which the political arena also constituted an important focus of the soteriological quest, orientations and movements of protest did not lead to far-reaching institutional reconstruction of the political centers of the society.

Confucian thinkers of different generations, and especially neo-Confucians dating back to the Sung period, were concerned with the imperfection of the political system, of the emperor, of the examination system, and of the bureaucracy and attempted to find some fulfillment beyond them. But, given their basic adherence to the identification of the center, in the broad sense and especially in the political arena as the major arena of implementation of the Confucian vision, they did not go beyond the suggestion of reforms to any concrete reconstruction of the political premises of the center itself. The orientations of protest of the Confucian intellectuals mainly concerned the direction of cultural, and to some extent educational, activities, greater moral sensibility and responsibility, and, to a much lesser extent, the direction of the political arena.

The strong emphasis on individual responsibility and the moral cultivation of the individual, which was highly developed especially among the neo-Confucians and which entailed a strong orientation of protest and liminal connotation, was oriented either toward perfecting the philosophical premises of their respective systems or toward the development of private intellectual or even mystical religious tendencies and reflexivity. These could become connected with otherworldly tendencies but mostly on the private level.

CULTURE AND SOCIAL STRUCTURE IN THE ORDER-MAINTAINING AND ORDER-TRANSFORMING DIMENSIONS OF CULTURE

The discussion brings us back to the general problem of the relations between culture and social structure, the possible ways of analyzing them as constituents of one another and of social and cultural order, and the order-maintaining versus the order-transforming dimensions of culture.

In principle, the order-maintaining and the order-transforming aspects of culture are but two sides of the same coin. There is no basic contradiction between the two; they are part and parcel of the symbolic dimensions in the construction of social order.

No social order or pattern of social interaction can be constituted without the symbolic dimension of human activity, especially of some basic cultural and ontological visions. It is such visions that constitute the starting point for articulating the premises and institutional contours of any patterns of social interaction and especially of institutional and macrosocietal formations. Such a construction of social order, of the interweaving of social and cultural dimensions, is effected by processes of intensive social interaction and conflict among different elites and influentials and among them and broader groups and strata.

Such processes are effected by coalitions and countercoalitions of different social actors. These actors who promulgate such different ontological visions activate various processes of control—among them the various ritual and communicative structures analyzed above—and these very processes give rise to orientations and movements of protest, to the structuring of liminal situations, some of which may become harbingers of social change.

Such developments are not accidental or external to the realm of culture. They are given in the basic fact of the inherent interweaving of culture and of social structure as two constitutive elements of the construction of social order. It is because the symbolic components are inherent in the construction and maintenance of social order that they also bear the seeds of social transformation.

Such seeds of transformation are indeed common to all societies. Yet the ways in which they grow—the concrete constellations of different liminal situations, of different orientations and movements of protest, and their impact on societies within which they develop—greatly vary among different societies, giving rise to different patterns of social and cultural dynamics.

REFERENCES

Almagor, U. 1985. "Long Time and Short Time Ritual and Non-Ritual Liminality in an East African Age-System." *Religion* 15 (July): 219–235.

Bechert, H. 1966–1968. *Buddhismus, Staat und Gesellschaft in den Länder des Theravada Buddhismus.* 4 Vols. Frankfurt am Main: Alfred Metzner.

Beidelman, T. O. 1966. "The Swazi Royal Ritual." *Africa* 36: 373–405.

Blau, Peter M. 1964. *Exchange and Power in Social Life.* New York: John Wiley.

———. 1965. "Justice and Social Exchange." *Social Inquiry* 34: 193–206.

Bloch, M., and J. Parry, eds. 1982. *Death and the Regeneration of Life.* Cambridge: Cambridge University Press.

Boudon, Raymond. 1981. *The Logic of Social Action.* London: Routledge and Kegan Paul.

Bruner, J. S., A. Jolly, and K. Sylva, eds. 1976. *Play, Its Role in Development and Evolution,* 119–156, 174–222. Harmondsworth: Penguin.

Decoufle, A. 1968. *Sociologie des Révolutions.* Paris: Presses universitaires de France.

Dobzhansky, T. 1973. *Genetic Diversity and Human Equality,* chap. 3. New York: Basic Books.

Douglas, M. 1966. *Purity and Danger.* London: Routledge and Kegan Paul.

Durkheim, E. [1912] 1954. *The Elementary Forms of the Religious Life.* New York: Macmillan.

———. 1964a. *The Division of Labor in Society.* New York: Free Press.

———. 1964b. *The Rules of Sociological Method.* New York: Free Press.

Eisenstadt, S. N. 1963. "Communication and Reference Group Behavior." In *Essays in Comparative Institutions.* New York: John Wiley.

———. 1973. "Religious Organizations and Political Process in Centralized Empires." In *Tradition, Change and Modernity.* [1976]. New York: John Wiley.

———. 1974. "Friendship and the Structure of Trust and Solidarity in Society." In *The Compact Selected Dimensions of Friendship,* edited by E. Leyton, 138–146. St. John's: Memorial University of New Foundland.

———. 1976. *Tradition, Change and Modernity.* New York: John Wiley.

———. 1978. *Revolutions and the Transformation of Societies.* New York: Free Press.

————. 1981a. "The Schools of Sociology." *American Behavioral Scientist* 24(3): 329–344.

————. 1981b. "Cultural Traditions and Political Dynamics." *The British Journal of Sociology* 32 (June): 155–181.

————. 1982a. "Heterodoxies, Sectarianism and Dynamics of Civilization." *Diogenes* 120: 5–26.

————. 1982b. "The Axial Age: The Emergence of Transcendental Visions and the Rise of Clerics." *Archives Européennes de Sociologie* (European Journal of Sociology) 23: 294–314.

Eisenstadt, S. N., and M. Curelaru. 1976. *The Form of Sociology, Paradigms and Crises.* New York: John Wiley.

————. 1977. *Macro Sociology, Theory Analysis and Comparative Studies.* The Hague: Mouton.

Eisenstadt, S. N., and L. Roniger. 1984. *Patrons and Friends.* Cambridge: Cambridge University Press.

Fairbanks, J. K., ed. 1967. *Chinese Thought and Institutions.* Chicago: University of Chicago Press.

Fingarette, H. 1972. *The Secular as the Sacred.* New York: Harper and Row.

Geertz, C. 1973. *The Interpretation of Culture.* New York: Basic Books.

————. 1983. *Social Knowledge.* New York: Basic Books.

Gluckman, M. 1963. *Order and Rebellion in African Tribal Society.* London: Cohen & West.

Granet, M. 1932. *Festivals and Songs in Ancient China.* London: Routledge.

————. 1950. *La Pensée Chinoise.* Paris: Micel.

Heyd, M. 1985. "The Reaction to Enthusiasm in the Seventeenth Century." *Religion* 15: 279–291.

Hirshfeld, L. A., S. Atran, and A. Yengoyan. 1982. "Theories of Knowledge and Culture." In *Social Science Information* 21 (1): 161–198.

Homans, G. C. 1962. "Anxiety and Ritual—The Theories of Malinowski and Radcliffe Brown." In *Sentiments and Activities*, 192–202. New York: Free Press.

Jaspers, K. 1949. *Vom Urspruch und Ziel der Geschichte.* Zurich: Artemis.

Kaplan, S. 1985. "The Ethiopian Holy Man as Outsider and Angel." *Religion* 15: 235–251.

Keyes, C. F. 1977. "Millennialism, Theravada Buddhism and Thai Society." *Journal of Asian Studies* 36(4): 297–327.

Lévi-Strauss, C. 1983. *Structural Anthropology.* New York: Basic Books.

Marx, K. 1965. *Selected Writings in Sociology and Social Philosophy.* New York: McGraw-Hill.

Merton, R. K. 1963. *Social Theory and Social Structure.* New York: Free Press.

Metzger, T. 1977. *Escape from Predicament: Neo-Confucianism and China's Evolving Political Culture.* New York: Columbia University Press.

Meyer, E. 1984. "Behavior Programs and Evolutionary Strategies." *American Scientist* 62 (November-December): 651.

Mus, P. 1967. "La Sociologie de George Gurevitch et l'Asie." *Cahiers Internationaux de Sociologie* 43: 1–21.

―――. 1968. "Traditions asiennes et bouddhisme moderne." *Eranos Yahrbuch* 32: 161–275.

Obeysekere, G. 1983. "The Rebirth Eschatology and Its Transformations: A Contribution to the Sociology of Early Buddhism." In *Karma and Rebirth in Classical Indian Tradition,* edited by W. D. O'Flaherty, 137–165. Berkeley and Los Angeles: University of California Press.

Peterson, R. 1979. "Revitalizing the Culture Concept." *Annual Review of Sociology* 5: 137–166.

Reynolds, F. 1977. "Civic Religion and National Community in Thailand." *Journal of Asian Studies* 36 (4): 267–282.

Sarkisyanz, E. 1965. *The Buddhist Background of the Burmese Revolution.* The Hague: M. Nijhoff.

Sartre, J. P. 1956. *L'Imagination.* Paris: Presses universitaires de France.

Schneider, D. M. 1973. *Class Differences and Sex Roles in American Kinship and Family Structure.* Englewood Cliffs, N.J.: Prentice-Hall.

―――, ed. 1977. *Symbolic Anthropology.* New York: Columbia University Press.

―――. 1980. *American Kinship.* Chicago: University of Chicago Press.

Scholem, G. 1941. *Major Trends in Jewish Mysticism.* New York: Schocken Books.

―――. 1973. *Shabetai Zwi, The Mystical Messiah.* Princeton: Princeton University Press.

Schwartz, B. 1975. "Transcendence in Ancient China." *Daedalus* (Spring): 57–63.

Silber, I. F. 1981. "Dissent through Holiness, The Case of the Radical Renouncer, in Theravada Buddhist Countries." *Numen* 28 (2): 164–193.

Skocpol, T. 1979. *States and Social Revolutions.* Cambridge: Cambridge University Press.

Smelser, N. 1963. *Theory of Collective Behavior.* Chaps. 8 and 9. New York: Free Press.

Swidler, A., 1986. "Culture in Action: Symbols and Strategies." *American Sociological Review* 51 (April): 273–288.

Tambiah, S. J. 1976. *World Conqueror and World Renouncer.* Cambridge: Cambridge University Press.

Tönnies, F. 1957. *Gemeinschaft und Gesellschaft* (Community and society). East Lansing: Michigan University Press.

Turner, V. W. 1947. *The Forest of Symbols.* Ithaca: Cornell University Press.

―――. 1968. *The Drums of Affliction.* Oxford: Clarendon Press.

―――. 1973. "The Center Out There, Pilgrim's Goal." *History of Religions* 12: 191–230.

————. 1974. *Dramas, Fields and Metaphores.* Ithaca: Cornell University Press.

Van der Lieuw, G. 1957. "Primordial Time and Final Time." In *Man and Time, Papers for the Eranos Yearbooks,* edited by J. Campbell, 324–353. New York: Bollinger Foundation.

Voegelin, E. 1954–1974. *Order and Periphery.* Vols. 1–4. Baton Rouge: University of Louisiana Press.

Weber, M. 1951. *The Religion of China.* Translated and edited by H. H. Gerth. New York: Free Press.

————. 1952. *Ancient Judaism.* Translated and edited by H. H. Gerth and D. Martindale. New York: Free Press.

————. 1958. *The Religion of India.* Translated and edited by H. H. Gerth and D. Martindale. New York: Free Press.

————. 1968. *On Charisma and Institution Building. Selected pages edited by S. N. Eisenstadt.* Introduction by S. N. Eisenstadt, ix-lv. Chicago: University of Chicago Press.

Wolf, A. S., ed. 1974. *Religion and Ritual in Chinese Society.* Stanford: Stanford University Press.

Wolff, K. H. 1950, 1957. *The Sociology of George Simmel.* Glencoe, Ill.: Free Press.

Thirteen

ACTION, RESOURCES,
STRUCTURE, AND MEANING

INTRODUCTION

I

IN THIS CHAPTER, which I wrote especially for this collection of essays, I tried to bring together the theoretical implications of the analyses presented in these essays. Earlier, in my introductory essay, "Social Structure, Culture, Agency, and Change," I discussed the relations of these analyses to some of the central problems of sociological theory as they developed over the last forty years. I would now like to explicate the theoretical implications of these analyses.

The central focus of these developments in sociological theory was first, the relations between human agency and social structure; second, the relation between social structure and history; third, the classical problem of the sociological analysis of culture, namely, that of the "order-maintaining" versus the "order-transforming" functions of culture; and fourth (closely connected to the first), the degree of mutual determination of "culture" and "social structure" (however defined) and the degree of openness between them.

The analyses presented in this collection reflect the fact that research based on the idea that culture, social structure, and agency are distinct, ontological realities—lately connected with the neglect of the analysis of rules, norms, and systemic qualities of the patterns of social interaction—cannot explain certain crucial aspects of human activity, social interaction, or cultural creativity.

These analyses showed that many aspects of institutional formations and dynamics, as well as patterns of cultural creativity, cannot be understood in terms of the "natural" or "autonomous" tendencies of these spheres of activity when perceived as distinct ontological entities. At the same time, these analyses showed that these formations could not be explained in terms of "routine" rational utilitarian activities. These studies revealed that many central aspects

Originally published in *Theory of Culture*, ed. R. Munch and N. J. Smelser, © 1992 The Regents of the University of California. Reprinted with the permission of the University of California Press, Berkeley and Los Angeles.

of institutional formations—such as the structure of centers or the construction of boundaries of collectivities and modes of political protest—could not be explained in purely structural terms, whether in terms of structural differentiation, exchange, or power relations.

Other essays on the "sociology of knowledge" and the expansion of religions, which are mentioned in the introduction to this collection but are not actually included here,[1] showed that important aspects of cultural creativity, such as different modes of organizing and structuring the worlds of knowledge, or religious beliefs and their impact on the structure and dynamics of social life, could not be explained in terms of the inherent dynamics of ideas or symbols.

These aspects of institutional formations could not be explained, despite the claims of some structuralists, as emanations of certain principles of the human mind. The preceding analyses have shown, on the contrary, that many central aspects of social interaction, institutional formations, and patterns of cultural creativity could be better understood in terms of the processes through which symbolic and organizational aspects of human activity and social interaction are interwoven. They have also shown that "culture" and "social structure" are best analyzed as analytical components of social action and interaction and of human creativity, as constitutive of each other and of the social and cultural orders, albeit in a different way than that specified either by some of the classics or by the "structural-functional" school.

Beyond these general indications, these analyses have provided several systematic specifications of some of the most important aspects of such processes of interweaving of these analytical components of social action in concrete situations of interaction. They provide such specifications especially with respect to those processes bearing on the relations between culture, social structure, and agency: first, the different aspects of the symbolic and cultural dimensions of human life which are important for the construction of the various institutional frameworks or organizational settings, and daily praxis; second, the patterns of social interaction and especially aspects of macroinstitutional order and of institutional formations, on which the different aspects of the cultural or symbolic dimensions have the greatest impact; third, the social processes, especially the processes of social regulation and responses to such regulation, through which the relations between agency and structure, and between cultural and institutional dimensions of social life are mediated; and last, the relations between cultural and power components in the activation of such processes. Let us now proceed and explicate these rather general indications.

1. S. N. Eisenstadt, "The Expansion of Religions: Some Comparative Observation on Different Modes," in *Comparative Social Research: Religious Institutions* Vol. 12, ed. C. Calhoun (1991), 45–73; S. N. Eisenstadt, "Explorations in the Sociology of Knowledge: The Soteriological Axis in the

THE OPEN HUMAN BIOLOGICAL PROGRAM AND
THE INDETERMINACIES OF HUMAN ACTIVITIES

II

Human interaction is interaction between individuals pursuing their own goals. But such interaction is set, embedded within distinct frameworks or settings, and characterized by specific dimensions. Such settings, frameworks, and dimensions are also continually created and recreated by human action. At the same time, they shape such action and may acquire a certain objectivity, a certain givenness, of their own—some of the characteristics of Karl Popper's World III.[2]

The two basic dimensions of human interaction are organizational and symbolic. The organizational dimension—the core of which is the social division of labor—is rooted in the prevalence of a situation of scarce resources in any setting of social interaction and in the necessity to coordinate human activities around the production and distribution of such resources. The symbolic dimension of human action is rooted in the construction of the meaning of the various patterns of interaction and in their continual interpretation.

Returning to the first dimension of human interaction: the social division of labor is rooted in the fact that in all human societies, the basic, minimal unit of social life—some type of family—is not self-sufficient in terms of production and in the use of the basic resources needed for subsistence and for the rearing of the young, including food, shelter, and defence. This results in the division of labor between such units—a division which, by definition, entails the continuous production, reproduction, and exchange of resources, products, and services.

The core characteristics of the division of labor in human societies are rooted in the combination of insufficiency in the basic social unit, the family, with the basic characteristic of the human biological program, being an "open one," to follow E. Mayer's felicitous expression.[3] This far-reaching "openness" of the human biological program is based on the long period of maturation of the young, their consequent ongoing dependence (especially on the mother), and the mother's dependence on somebody else (usually a male), to provide for her and the young.[4]

A basic derivative of the openness of the human biological program, as

Construction of Domains of Knowledge" in *Knowledge and Society: Studies in the Sociology of Culture Past and Present* by S. N. Eisenstadt and I. F. Silber (Greenwich, CT: JAI Press, Inc., 1988), 1–71.

2. K. R. Popper, "The Worlds 1, 2 and 3" in *The Self and Its Brain*, ed. K. R. Popper and J. C. Eccles (London: Routledge and Kegan Paul, 1977), 36–50.

3. E. Mayer, *Evolution and the Diversity of Life* (Cambridge: Harvard University Press, 1976).

4. P. J. Wilson, *Man, The Promising Primate* (New Haven: Yale University Press, 1980).

many "philosophical anthropologists" including A. Portman, A. Gehlen, and Helmut Plessner have indicated,[5] is the existence of very wide, indeterminate spaces between the general capacities of human beings, rooted in their biological characteristics, including the capacity for language acquisition and use, tool making, social interaction, etc. This also includes the concrete specification of these capacities or potentialities such as learning how to speak a language, creating a specific technology, and so on.

It is the indeterminacy inherent in all areas of human activities that makes human beings "programmed for culture"—to use Clifford Geertz's felicitous expression.[6] Yet, here again, human beings are programmed for culture in general, and not for any *specific* culture; for language in general and not for any *specific* language,[7] for social division of labor in general—and not for any specific type of such division of labor.

III

The existence—in all arenas of human action—of open spaces between the general propensities of human beings and the concrete specifications of these propensities means that the crux of concrete human activity is the "filling in" of such spaces. Such "filling in" can be effected only through social interaction, which, however, is also characterized by indeterminacies and open spaces, and which begins with the processes of the socialization of the young and continues through the adult life of members of society.

Such open spaces generate several indeterminacies within each arena of human activity, which, in turn, give rise to specific problems concerning the organization of activities in these areas. The most crucial indeterminacies inherent in any social division of labor which develop in the construction of social interaction are, first, those among actors, whether individuals or collectivities; second, between actors and their goals; and third, between actors and their goals on the one hand, and the resources at their disposal, including the activities of other actors on the other hand. These indeterminacies are of crucial importance in the construction, production, and reproduction of social interaction.

The first indeterminacy—that of the relations among actors in any situa-

5. A. Portman, *Biologische Fragmente zu einer Lehre von Menschen* (Basel, 1944); A. Gehlen, *Studien zur Anthropologie und Soziologie* (Berlin: Luchterhard, 1971); H. Plessner, *Diesseits der Utopie: Ausgewählte Beiträge zur Kultursoziologie* (Düsseldorf: E. Diederichs, 1966); H. Plessner and A. Augen, *Aspekte einer Philosophischen Anthropologie* (Stuttgart: Ph. Reclam, 1982).

6. C. Geertz, *The Interpretation of Cultures* (New York: Basic Books, 1973).

7. Many controversies abound with respect to the extent to which some aspects or dimensions of language are *common* to all human languages and possibly rooted in the common human endowment. But whatever the outcome of these controversies, even such common, presumably genetically determined, features of human language do not explain the crystallization of any specific language.

tion—is manifest in the fact that the range of actors who, as it were, are admitted to any such situation is not specified, either by genetic programming or by some general rules or tendencies of the human mind. Neither the boundaries of such interaction nor the criteria determining who is entitled to participate are automatically given by either of those determinants.

The indeterminacy in the relations between actors and the goals they pursue is manifest in the fact that most concrete human goals (even those directly related to biological needs, and especially the goals sought by the participants in any given situation of social interaction) are not specified by an individual's genetic characteristics or by some universal laws of the human mind, but are socially constituted.

The indeterminacy in the relations between actors, goals, and resources is manifest in the fact that the access of different actors to the major resources that are being produced, exchanged, and distributed in any ongoing interaction is not specified in any predetermined manner. Moreover, resources are polysemic; as William H. Sewell, Jr. described it, the same resources can be used for a variety of goals and in a variety of situations.[8] Such resources have an inherent tendency to generalizability, to further extension beyond their use in any given situation, i.e., to the intensification of their polysemicity. They can also be used as media of exchange, and it is here that tendencies to generalizability and extension of uses of resources are probably most fully manifest.

Secondly, the propensity within any pattern of social interaction to fragility, volatility, conflict, and changeability is rooted in the continual interweaving of the problems and indeterminacies inherent in such interaction, with the basic characteristics of organizational and symbolic construction of such interaction and with the concomitant characteristics of the construction by human beings of their environment. Of special importance here is the polysemicity of human resources and the openness and arbitrariness of the symbolic constructs of reality, the potential infinity of human "wants" and goals, and the closely related possibility of the continual construction of new wants and goals, and more demands for resources.

The existence of such empty spaces and indeterminacies is true of many other species, although in a more limited way. What is specific to the human species is not only a much wider range of openness than can be found in any other species, but also the consciousness of that openness and therefore the awareness of the possibilities of choice available in such spaces. It is the awareness of these empty spaces and the possible alternatives of behavior they imply that results in some of the types of construction by humans of their own envi-

8. W. Sewell, "A Theory of Structure: Duality, Agency, and Transformation," *American Journal of Sociology* 98 (1992):1–29.

ronment and which entails a qualitative jump from the construction of their environments by other species. Among the most important manifestations of this qualitative jump is the fact that construction of their respective environments by human beings make such construction highly fragile and changeable.

Such fragility and changeability are reinforced by three additional aspects of this construction. The first one is the fact that the "filling in" of such empty spaces is effected through polysemic symbols as opposed to more monosemic signs which are characteristic of the languages of other species.[9] Secondly, such fragility and changeability are enhanced by the fact that the concretization of general human capacities—albeit language, tool-making, or the construction of the social division of labor—is effected through processes of human interaction which are themselves characterized by such openness and indeterminacy.

Thirdly, the polysemic features of the resources and of the basic schemata of human action are exacerbated by the fact that the imposition of symbolic constructs on "reality" are arbitrary by their very nature. Such arbitrariness is manifest in the openness and indeterminacy between the signifier and the objects signified, between the symbol and its referents, and in the multiple ways in which such semiotic mediation occurs; i.e., in the multiple symbolic and semantic modes according to which such models are constructed, and in the multiple symbolic themes, modes, and universes constructed by man. The multiplicity and openness of the different semantic modes generate the tendency to problematization of the givens of human existence and to reflexivity about them.

Fourthly, such fragility and changeability are also rooted in the fact that the awareness of the indeterminacies of multiple choices gives rise among humans to feelings of uncertainty concerning their environment and to a quest—to some extent conscious—to find a way to overcome these feelings and to master their environment[10]—a quest which, because of all these reasons, can never be truly fulfilled. For all these reasons, the continuation of their respective environments by humans entails a continuous interweaving of the organizational and symbolic dimensions, and such interweaving contains a strong component of reflexivity and self-reflexivity. Such construction of meaning and reflexivity, which constitutes a basic component of the construction of their own environment by humans, is focused on human beings' awareness of such indeterminacies and empty spaces and of the possibility of choices inherent in them. They are aware—even if usually only vaguely and intermittently—of the fact that their environment, and perhaps the social order within which they

9. D. Bickerton, *Language and Species* (Chicago: University of Chicago Press, 1990).

10. See H. E. Gruber and J. J. Voneche, ed., *The Essential Piaget* (New York: Basic Books, 1977), especially pages 832–61.

live, is not given; an awareness which gives rise to far-reaching ambivalences towards this order and to problematization and generalization of the givens of human existence.

IV

This inherent fragility of the constitution of the human environment, the multiplicity of choices, and the basic uncertainty inherent here all generate the crystallization of different types of rules.[11] The awareness, however dim, of these "empty spaces," of the various indeterminacies of human interaction, of the possibility of choices, and of the insecurity within these patterns and dimensions of interaction generates the tendency and the necessity not only for technical and cognitive rules but also for normative evaluative specification of such choices.

The technical, cognitive, and normative dimensions of rules are closely interwoven in any concrete situation of human activity, in any pattern of social interaction. The cognitive dimension is strongest within those general rules or schemata which provide the basic classification of reality, i.e., which make reality cognitively ordered, comprehendable, and predictable. This cognitive component is also very strong in technical specifications of information and behavior. However, such specifications tend to overlap with those rules in which the normative component is closely interwoven with the cognitive ones.

Some of these rules constitute types of habitual customs and habits; others are much more formalized and tend to become objects of reflexive consideration, although even the customs and habits may sometimes become objects and foci of such reflexivity.

V

Different constellations of rules develop on all levels of social interaction. Thus, first of all, some rules develop which organize human activities into distinct organizational patterns. These rules may be viewed as though designed to limit the seemingly endless choices generated by the indeterminacies inherent in human interaction.

The most important organizational patterns in the realm of social organization and of the social division of labor are those which have been analyzed often in sociological literature, namely, roles and role sets; the major types of groups and organizations, including family groups, ecological, economic, and territorial formations, institutional patterns or arenas; the media of exchange; some systemic tendencies; and, lastly, some specific structural characteristics.

The construction of roles specifies mutual obligations between social

11. T. R. Burns and T. Dietz, "Cultural Evolution: Social Rule System, Selection, and Human Agency," *International Sociology* 7, 259–83.

actors as they are related to the second aspect of the organization of the social division of labor; namely, the institutional arrangements to be found in any society, including the various patterns of the family, of the organization of the economic, political, and communicative arenas, and of the structuration of social hierarchies. All such specifications do, in principle, limit the choices open before people in any situation.

The second major dimension of the organization of social interaction in which technical and normative roles are interwoven is that of the major media of exchange, which are essential for the working of any division of labor beyond the simplest framework of interaction in which barter is the major mode of exchange. The most important of such media, as Talcott Parsons has indicated, are money, power, influence, and value commitments.[12] These media, the use of which is regulated by specific rules, constitute the most general and the most polysemic types of human resources. They also have some specific structural properties to which I have referred in the introduction and in the chapter 10, which again limit the choices apparently available in any situation.

Such limitations are also inherent in the third, mostly organizational dimension of social interaction, namely, in the development of systemic tendencies within all patterns of continuous social interaction; that is, the development of tendencies to the construction of systemic boundaries, to the distinction between external and internal environments, and to the specification of the needs or prerequisites of such systems. Such prerequisites and needs are based—as we shall see later in greater detail—on the very problems generated by the social division of labor, by the existence of the empty spaces between the general tendency to the social division of labor, which constitutes an evolutionary universal of human life, and by the construction of any *concrete* social order.

The fourth organizational dimension is purely organizational, although it may greatly influence the normative dimensions of social action. It refers mostly to formal aspects based on the emergent qualities of the social structure, some of which can also be found among nonhumans, and to the emergent structural qualities of such interaction as studied by Simmel, Merton, Blau, or Boudon.[13] Among the most important of such aspects are the distances between different structural positions; the clusters of roles and statuses assigned

12. T. Parsons, "Social Structure and the Symbolic Media of Interchange," in *Social Systems and the Evolution of Action Theory* (New York: The Free Press, 1977), 204–28.

13. D. Levine, ed., *George Simmel on Individuality and Social Forms* (Chicago: University of Chicago Press, 1971); R. K. Merton, *Social Theory and Social Structure* (New York: The Free Press, 1968); P. M. Blau, *Inequality and Heterogeneity* (New York: The Free Press, 1977); P. Boudon, *The Unintended Consequences of Social Action* (New York: St. Martin's Press, 1982); idem, *The Logic of Social Action* (London: Routledge and Kegan Paul, 1981).

to different positions; differentiation; the ways in which networks of positions are connected; and the ways in which bunches of such positions come together and the degrees of differentiation between them.

SOCIAL DIVISION OF LABOR AND THE CONSTRUCTION OF MEANING

VI

The rules which regulate these organizational aspects of human interaction, like those of any other arena of human activity such as cultural creativity, "fill in," as it were, the empty spaces inherent in human activities and help to cope with the problems raised by the existence of the indeterminacies inherent in these activities. But they do not resolve all of the problems emerging from the existence of these indeterminacies, and they do not assure the continuity of any single pattern of social interaction.

While the tendency towards the development of the social division of labor is an evolutionary universal of the human species (evincing the core, organizational characteristics to be found in all human societies), this universal tendency does not assure the continuity of any concrete pattern of interaction, any concrete social divisions of labor, or any concrete pattern of social order. The limitation of choices inherent in all of these organizational dimensions of the social division of labor is not "strong" enough to ensure such continuity. This is because the organizational patterns of the social division of labor generate—to a much larger extent than in the case of ants or bees—new problems which make the smooth functioning and continuity of any pattern of social interaction problematic to a much greater extent than among any other species. To put it differently: although the general propensity to the social division of labor constitutes an "evolutionary universal" of the human species, just like the general propensity to language acquisition or toolmaking, the continuity of any specific pattern of the division of labor cannot ever be assured. This is the case not only because of the possible failure of "filling in" such empty spaces, but mainly because of the problems generated by the organizational dimension of the social division of labor.

These problems generated by the construction of the social division of labor—rooted in the very ubiquity of the social division of labor—are those which have been identified by the founding fathers of sociology (especially Marx, Durkheim, and Weber) as the most important dimensions of the constitution of social order. The founding fathers stressed that the very construction of the social division of labor (of the "market" in modern societies) generates uncertainties with respect to each of several basic dimensions of social order, i.e., trust, regulation of power, construction of meaning, and legitimation. They claimed that no concrete social division of labor and no concrete social order can be maintained without these dimensions or problems being taken care of. Therefore, all of these sociologists emphasized that the construction and "production" of continuous patterns of social interaction are based on the development of some combination of the organizational structure of the division of labor with the construction of trust, the regulation of power, and the legitimation of the different patterns of social interaction.

In other words, these problems—the regulation of power[14] and the construction of trust, solidarity, legitimation, and meaning—designate the conditions which have, as it were, to be "taken care of" in order to ensure the continuity of any pattern of social interaction, i.e., of relatively continuous boundaries of such interaction. These problems define the systemic tendencies and sensitivities, the "needs" or prerequisites of such continuous interaction, to which we have referred briefly above, and have been strongly emphasized by the "structural-functional" school of sociology. However, contrary to the usual interpretation of the structural-functional approach, the concrete specification of such needs and prerequisites is not given by some "internal" features of these systems, i.e., by the level of technological development or of structural differentiation, but is effected by specific social processes, in which the construction of meaning plays a central role.[15]

These basic insights of the founding fathers provided, together with the emphasis on the formal aspects of social interaction mentioned above, the basic framework of sociological tradition.[16]

VII

The major problems generated by the indeterminacies inherent in human interaction and by the very organization of the social division of labor are not merely "objective" organizational problems identified by research. They constitute foci of conscious concern and awareness in all human societies, even if they are formulated differently in different societies. It is because of this that the construction of meaning constitutes a central component of the construction of social life.

This awareness or consciousness of the various indeterminacies inherent in human interaction is not directly shaped by the genetic endowment of human beings, as some recent sociobiologists have claimed. Rather, it is rooted in the largely unconscious or subconscious psychological-emotional, expressive, and

14. On the problem of power, see D. Rueschemeyer, *Power and the Division of Labor* (Stanford: Stanford University Press, 1986).

15. See S. N. Eisenstadt, "Functional Analysis in Anthropology and Sociology," *Annual Review of Anthropology* 19 (1990):243–60.

16. S. N. Eisenstadt, "The Sociological Tradition: Origin, Boundaries, Patterns of Innovation, and Crises," in *Culture and Its Creators: Essays in Honor of Edward Shils*, ed. J. Ben-David and T. N. Clark (Chicago: University of Chicago Press, 1977), 43–72; S. N. Eisenstadt and M. Curelaru, *The Forms of Sociology: Paradigms and Crises* (New York: John Wiley & Sons, 1976).

cognitive responses of human beings to, and perception of, their own biological and social nature, and the problems of the social order in which they live. It is an awareness of these problems which gives rise among human beings to the propensity, the quest, the construction of meaning, and the search, succinctly analyzed by G. Bateson, for "meta-meaning," for "meta-thinking," i.e., thinking about thinking.[17]

The search, the inclination towards the construction of meaning and meta-meaning, is rooted first in the feelings of insecurity which human beings have regarding their environment—feelings which are related to their awareness of the indeterminacies of their behavior—and secondly in a core existential anxiety related to their consciousness of death and human finitude. This is probably a uniquely human trait, manifest in the construction of burial places and in the close relation between the consciousness of death and sacrificial activities which is apparent in many sacrificial rituals. Thirdly, it is rooted in the many levels and modes through which human beings construct symbolic universes, as well as in the capacity for imagination, so brilliantly analyzed by Sartre as the ability to conceive of various possibilities beyond what is given here and now,[18] and in the closely related universal predisposition to play.[19]

The consciousness of the openness of their own biological program leads human beings to a fear of chaos as an integral part of their self-reflexivity and to the closely related attempt to construct a cultural and social order which can provide the possibility of overcoming the anxieties generated by all the basic aspects of the human situation referred to above. At the same time, the construction of such an order generates a strong ambivalence towards such order in general and towards any concrete social and cultural order in particular. The construction of such order gives rise to an often dim, yet deep, awareness that any concrete answer to the problem of potential chaos imposes limitations on the range of possibilities open to human beings; yet, there is a yearning to break through any such restrictions and actualize some definite possibilities. The construction of such order also leads to the often unwilling recognition that it is impossible to do so without such restrictions.

All of these factors generate self-awareness and reflexivity among human beings and make man (in Charles Taylor's words)[20] a self-interpreting animal, a being which tends to problematize the givens and tensions of his own exis-

17. G. Bateson, *Steps to an Ecology of Mind* (New York: Ballantine Books, 1972).

18. J. P. Sartre, *Imagination: A Psychological Critique* (Ann Arbor: University of Michigan Press, 1972).

19. J. Huizinga, *Homo Ludens: A Study of Play Elements in Culture* (London: Paladin, 1970); R. Caillois, *Man, Play, and Games* (New York: The Free Press, 1961); J. S. Brunner, S. A. Jully, and K. Silva, ed., *Play: Its Role in Development and Evolution* (Harmondsworth: Penguin Books, 1979).

20. C. Taylor, "Self-Interpreting Animals," in *Human Agency and Language* (Cambridge: Cambridge University Press, 1985).

tence, to reflexivity and self-reflexivity. A central focus of such reflexivity is, as we have seen, the awareness of the arbitrariness of any order, particularly social and cultural order, and the closely connected ambivalence toward such order. Needless to say, such awareness, and the concomitant reflexivity, are not developed equally among different people, and are not structured in the same mode among different societies and cultures. Nor are they necessarily central in most daily activities of people. But the general propensity to such awareness and reflexivity is inherent in the construction of meaning by all humans, and is of far-reaching importance in the construction of social life.

VIII

Human self-awareness, the construction of meaning and reflexivity, and the tendency to meta-thinking in all human societies does not take place in an entirely random way, even if such construction is not predetermined in all its details either by the genetic endowment of the human species (as suggested by some sociobiologists) or by the constant rules of the human mind (as implied by many structuralists).

Such "construction of meaning" is structured through the cognitive schemata referred to above. Such schemata are first of all constituted according to distinct parameters of structuration which are to be found—as the structuralists have stressed in their Kantian orientation—in all societies or cultures.[21] On the most general level, such schemata are structured around the categories of time, space, and the self-reflecting subject in relation to different objects to the environment. A central aspect of such human self-reflection is the fact that the subject also constitutes an object of such reflection.

Within the framework of these general categorical orientations, the construction of meaning and reflexivity is focused on human action or interaction, on two axes or poles inherent in the nature of human existence, and on the awareness and definition of these problems by human beings. The first of these poles or axes is the cosmological or ontological one. The main problems related to this axis are the definition of the nature of the cosmic order and the relations between this order and the human and mundane worlds; the perception of time and the relation between cosmic, mundane, and human and social time; the nature of the soteriological arena (i.e., that arena in which activities can serve as a bridge between the transcendent and the mundane realms); the relations between culture and nature, and between the reflexive subject and the objective world.

The second axis around which the construction of meaning and human reflexivity and the tendency to meta-thinking are constructed is the social one,

---

21. See chapter 7, "Symbolic Structures and Social Dynamics" and also S. N. Eisenstadt and B. Giesen, *The Construction of Collective Identity* (forthcoming).

focusing on the problems and tensions inherent in the symbolic structuring of social relations and human interaction. These are the tensions inherent in the construction of social order, in the relations between the social division of labor, the regulation of power, and the construction of trust and meaning. These in turn generate the more specific tensions between hierarchy and equality; between the pursuit of instrumental and adaptive goals in social action and the maintenance of some order between competition, authority and power on the one hand, and solidarity, community, and participation on the other; between the individual and the community, between conflict and harmony; between power and the just distribution of resources and positions; between trust and the search for broader meaning and autonomy of the human personality, and the restrictiveness of any social organization or cultural prescription. These problems constitute foci of reflection in all human societies—even if they are conceived and defined differently in different societies.

The Cultural Definitions of Preferences and Goals and of Arenas of Action and the Structuring of Ground Rules of Social Interaction

IX

These ontological and social axes provide the major foci of the construction of meaning and meta-meaning, reflexivity and meta-communication. They constitute the parameters of culture; the starting points for the definition of the major arenas of human activity and for the actual construction of institutional formations—the "imaginary construction of society" as Cornelius Castoriadis coined the process[22]—as well as of the construction of the major goals and preferences of people. It is the continual interaction between derivatives of the definitions of the major arenas of human actions and the preferences and goals of people that constitutes the crux of social interaction, reproduction, and dynamics of patterns of social interaction.

Such definitions are closely related to symbolic evaluations, rooted in the basic ontological conceptions prevalent in a society, of the different dimensions of human existence and of the basic premises of social order. Such evaluations provide the cultural mediation and definition of the primordial givens of human life—namely, the human body, age, sex, growth, and aging; the physical givens of human life and their relationships to different mental and physical capacities; the relative importance in human existence of different dimensions of temporality (past and future), as well as the major arenas of social activity. Closely related to such definitions are the specifications and construction of

---

22. C. Castoriadis, *The Imaginary Institution of Society* (Cambridge: Polity Press, 1987).

the major roles be they familial; occupational or political and the like—and of the situations in which they are enacted.

The ontological and social premises also provide the starting points for the structuration of preference frameworks of people. The overall preference frameworks of people organize the relative importance of different types of goals—"economic," power, solidarity, and transcendental ones—and the relative importance of discrete goals as opposed to more long-range ones.[23]

The preferences of people provide the bases for the evaluation of different activities; for the calculi according to which they evaluate their activities and the discourses about such calculi and evaluations. They also entail different calculi of relations between goals and means, especially different degrees of openness between them, and of relative emphasis on short-term as opposed to long-term goals, as well as the ordering of uncommensurable goals.

The extent to which the evaluation of such different arenas of social action and action according to preferences is based on fully conscious considerations (as opposed to custom, habits, or emotional expression) varies greatly in different situations, but some component of reflexivity exists in a latent way in most human situations. Such reflexivity is concerned mainly with weighing the relative importance of the different ends of preferences of people and the activities through which such ends are pursued. Such reflexivity also entails the development of different collective rationalities—of considerations of the proper context for collective goals and their implementation.

23. One interesting definition of the construction of such preference frameworks is offered by Himmelstrand, who, following Fishbum, Blegvad, and Collin, has defined the lexicographical preference function. ". . . A lexicographical preference function has the following characteristics, as indicated already by Blegvad and Collin:

A	a	b	c	d	e	f	g	h
B	g	a	f					
C	h	d	e	a				

(a) there exists a partition of the agent's preferences into mutually exclusive subsets; (b) there exist meta-preferences ranging over such partitionized subsets ranking them from superordinate to subordinate subsets; (c) the higher rank of one such subset N over another subset M in the meta-preference function implies that the satisfaction of a preference n in N has priority over the satisfaction of any preference m in M. The higher ranking preference must be satisfied, if possible, before the satisfaction of the lower ranking one is contemplated . . .

. . . In addition to the economic preferences dealt with by economists there exist in every society preferences which are not commensurable with economic preferences—for instance, ethical preferences dealing with personal and interpersonal morality, religious and ritual preferences, legal preferences, and in more recent times, preferences relating to long-term ecological conditions which cannot be measured exclusively with current economic measures, or several other current measures for that matter. I have also mentioned aesthetic preferences. The wish to maintain your actually existing position of power could in some cases be a preferences with a higher priority or meta-rank than any specifically economic, or even legal preferences . . ."

U. Himmelstrand, "Towards a Lexicographic Preference-Actor-Structure Theory," in *Interfaces in Economic and Social Analysis* (London: Routledge, 1992), 213–37.

As Raymond Boudon recently formulated it,[24] most human activities are guided by rational considerations, or, to put it more cautiously, most of them contain a "reflexive" component, a component of rational consideration. Most human activities contain an element of justification or explanation in terms of some evaluative criteria—even if this element is only latent within many of them.

But the existence of such considerations does not in itself tell us which criteria of preference, which calculus or modes of discourse are involved. The rational utility discourse or calculus which has been emphasized recently by exponents of the rational choice approach is only one of such discourses. Other discourses and calculi, such as those of power, solidarity, or transcendental orientations, are prevalent in different degrees in different societies or sectors thereof. Similarly, there are also far-reaching differences as to the extent to which a clear discourse of instrumental rationality, of *Zweckrationalitet* develops within each realm of discourse, that is to say, the rational weighing of different means for the attainment of goals, or the basic preferences implied by such a discourse.

X

The ways in which ontological premises and premises about social order prevalent in any society, as they become oriented to the problems of any arena of human activity influence the specification of the structures of preferences of people and of the definition of the major arenas of social interaction—is greatly influenced, indeed shaped in its broad outlines—as is true of all types of human action, through various codes or code-orientations or schemata. Such codes are somewhat akin to what Max Weber called *Wirtschaftsethik*. Unlike contemporary structuralists, Weber did not consider an ethos such as the economic one to be a purely formal aspect of the human mind which generates only a set of abstract, symbolic categories. He saw such an ethos as given in the nature of man, in his social existence, and carrying a direct implication for the order of society. Weber conceived of such codes as variant expressions of the symbolic orientation of human beings towards the facts of their existence in general and towards the problems of social interaction in particular. Thus, a *Wirtschaftsethik* does not connote specific religious injunctions about proper behavior in any given sphere, nor is it merely a logical derivative of the intellectual contents of the theology or philosophy predominant in a given religion. Rather, a *Wirtschaftsethik*, or a status or political ethos, connotes a general mode of "religious" or "ethical" orientation, focused on the evaluation of a specific

24. R. Boudon, "Toward a Synthetic Theory of Rationality," *International Studies in the Philosophy of Science* 7 (1993):5–19; A. Pizzorno, "All You Can Do With Reasons," *International Studies in the Philosophy of Science* 7 (1993):75–80; R. Boudon, "More on 'Good Reasons': Reply to Critics," *International Studies in the Philosophy of Science* 7 (1993):87–102.

institutional arena and with broad implications for behavior and distribution of resources in such an arena. Such orientation is rooted in premises about the cosmic order and about the nature of ontological reality and its relation to human and social existence.[25]

The basic components of the different code-orientations are thus constructed around the basic poles of human reflexivity as they are oriented to major cultural problems and organizational exigencies of social interaction, i.e., to problems generated by the division of labor—the regulation of power and the construction of trust and meaning. Thus, the code-orientations and criteria which shape the construction of the social division of labor are constructed around, first of all, the organizational criteria of the allocation of resources (including human activities). These include the famous pattern-variables, especially universalism vs. particularism, achievement vs. ascription, diffuseness vs. specificity. Secondly, these code-orientations are constructed around the relative emphasis on the different functional prerequisites of social interaction: adaptation, instrumental goals, solidarity, and legitimation.

The major components of codes related to the construction of collective identity—solidarity, trust, and the criteria of membership in this collectivity—are focused on the relative importance of primordiality, civility, and cultural, above all, sacred or transcendental orientations and various combinations thereof, one of the most interesting of which is that of "civil religion."[26]

The code-orientations, which are directed towards the regulation of power, shape the processes of interaction between the authorities and those over whom authority is exercised. They specify the relative importance of the bases of legitimation, such as Weber's trilogy of charismatic, traditional, and rational bases; the relative emphasis on the direct or mediated access to power and to the centers thereof; and the range of accountability of authority and the relative emphasis on hierarchy or on equality.

The major components of the codes which shape the contours of meaning and legitimation in a society are those which refer to the basic foci or problems of ontologies and cosmologies, especially to the relation between nature and culture, between the transcendental and the mundane worlds, between the subject and the objective world, and to the basic perceptions of time and space.

XI

The concrete specification of such preferences and of definitions of arenas of social action—as influenced by the different codes or code-orientations—entails the continuous interweaving of the construction of meaning, of "culture,"

25. See in greater detail chapter 7, "Symbolic Structures and Social Dynamics."
26. See S. N. Eisenstadt and B. Giesen, *The Construction of Collective Identity* (forthcoming).

with the organizational aspects of social interaction, above all, with the regulation of the flow of resources in social interaction on the other.[27]

Such definitions and specifications of the regulation of the production and flow of resources are found in the respective settings of social interaction, especially in the more enduring institutional formations.[28] Such regulation is effected by the promulgation of the frameworks of generalized exchange, above all by the institutionalization of the ground rules of social interaction. As we have seen, such ground rules structure, according to Nutini and Buechler, the "basic frameworks within which decision-making in different areas of social interaction is possible; some of the broad criteria that tender choices among the options which such frameworks allow."[29]

The major ground rules in the arena of social interaction combine the definition and specification of the major problems generated by the construction of the division of labor—namely, the construction of trust, the regulation of power and the construction of legitimation—with the regulation of the flow of resources in society. It is such interweaving that constitutes the major modules of continual social interaction and structure. Accordingly, to repeat what we have said in the introductory chapter, such ground rules are addressed to the specification of:

(a) the symbolic institutional boundaries of collectivities—above all, through the setting up of the basic attributes of social and cultural similarity which constitute the definition of the criteria of membership in different collectivities, i.e., of those who may participate in any given interaction. These attributes also provide the specification of the conditional and unconditional obligations connected with the participation in such communities, as well as the range of the goals or desiderata, of the preferences which those participating in any interaction are permitted to pursue. Such attributes structure the boundaries of solidarity and the conditions of trust among members of a community.

(b) the criteria of regulation of access to resources in general and to power in particular, and of their use in different social settings and institutional spheres.

(c) the rules of distributive justice and equity which are seen as appropriate and bounding with regard to the distribution of rights and obligations in the respective settings of interaction.

(d) the definition of the broader purpose or meaning and collective goals of any interaction or collective activity and the concomitant legitimation of

27. See chapter 10, "Prestige, Participation, and Strata Formation."
28. See in greater detail chapter 7, "Symbolic Structures and Social Dynamics."
29. I. R. Buechler and H. G. Nutini, ed., *Game Theory in the Behavioral Sciences* (Pittsburgh: University of Pittsburgh Press, 1969), 8.

various patterns of interaction or of institutional formation in terms of the prevalent rules of justice, equity and broader social goals.

At the same time, the construction of preferences and goals entails, by definition, attempts by the major actors to appropriate for themselves various resources according to different calculi and relations between goals and means—especially different degrees of openness between them.

XII

The principles regulating these ground rules of social interaction and of frameworks of preferences entail not only cognitive or symbolic but also normative and cognitive specifications. They provide the normative dimensions of the definition of the basic organizational aspects of social organization—i.e., of roles, role sets and status sets, and institutional formations. In other words, such regulation minimizes, or "clones," as it were, some of the basic indeterminacies inherent in human interaction. They entail also normative specifications about the regulation of the production and distribution of major resources.

Such regulations provide, in their respective societies or sectors, the framework of generalized exchange and of the relations between generalized and "routine" exchange; and the forms of the regulation of the production and flow of resources, especially through the regulation of the access of different actors (individuals as well as groups) to the major economic, political, and cultural arenas; the conversion between these different resources in different arenas of social action; the patterns of investment and distribution of such resources in space and time; and the regulation of the spatial and temporal organization of such resources.[30] This is effected, according to mainly ascriptive criteria, different to those which regulate activities in free, "market-like" exchange activities. All of these processes entail the limitation on what may be called the "free, ad hoc, one-night stands" exchange of resources.[31]

The focus of such limitations is the specification of the distribution—in any continuous patterns of social interaction—of unconditionalities, i.e., relations between actors which are not based on the direct and conditional, but on the indirect, long-range, give-and-take of services or resources and on the setting up of "titles" or entitlements to such resources or services.

Unconditionalities and titles usually entail "package deals" which combine the interchange of different kinds of economic resources, power, and interpersonal esteem with information and, as a result, naturally limit other possible

---

30. See in greater detail chapter 6, "Societal Goals, Systemic Needs, Social Interaction, and Individual Behavior," and chapter 7, "Symbolic Structures and Social Dynamics."
31. R. Solow, "On Theories of Unemployment," *American Economic Review* 70 (1980):1–11.

combinations.[32] Such unconditionalities are set up by the combination of economic and power resources with prestige, the latter not only as a symbolic dimension of interpersonal relations but also, as we have seen in "Prestige, Participation, and Strata Formation," the structural principle that regulates access to some relatively "exclusive order"—to membership in a collectivity, a societal center, or cultural orders and to the major types of information which are central to participation in these respective settings.

In regulating the organizational dimension of the ground rules of social interaction, such packages and unconditionalities are of special importance. First is the specification of the criteria of the public distribution of private goods, i.e., the allocation of various resources to different sectors of the population. The second limitation is effected through the setting up of public goods—for example, provision by the government of defence or health services established so that if one member of a collectivity receives them, they cannot be denied to other members. This limitation also sets the "prices" for various groups of setting up such public goods, directly or indirectly through taxation. Thirdly, closely related to the definition of public goods, is the definition of the degree to which different groups, organizations, and institutional spheres enjoy institutional credit—the degree to which resources provided any group are not used in immediate exchange or in direct consumption, but are given to a certain degree unconditionally, providing that group or institution with what may be called "credit autonomy." This autonomy provides the base for the long-range functioning of the institution. Also involved in the process of granting institutional credit is the definition of the range and the long-term conditions of such credit.

A central part of all these regulations of the organizational dimensions of the ground rules of social interaction is the provision of some long-range connections between the preference-orders of social actors and the incentives or rewards offered to them in the respective patterns of social interaction.

XIII

Each of the code-orientations analyzed above and their respective specifications is closely related to different modes of structuring resources, or to put it

32. In Russia, for example, the prestige of the periphery could not be exchanged for that of the center, while in traditional China, the wealth of the periphery could not be directly exchanged for the prestige of the center. In both China and Russia, wealth (above all, commercial wealth) could not in principle be converted into political rights (in particular rights of access to the center), while political power could, under appropriate circumstances, serve as a basis for acquiring wealth. This specification of the conversion of resources is contrary to the one that developed in Europe, where economic power could be legitimately converted into political power. See in greater detail S. N. Eisenstadt, "Prestige, Participation, and Strata Formation," in *Social Stratification*, ed. J. A. Jackson (Cambridge: Cambridge University Press, 1968), part II and S. N. Eisenstadt, *Social Differentiation and Stratification* (Glenview: M. Scott & Forman, 1971).

more precisely, there is an elective affinity between these codes and the modes of structuring institutional markets and arenas. To illustrate this point, the construction of the boundaries of collectivities entails the structuring of the entitlements of the members of the collectivity, including their access to public goods and major institutional markets—as distinct from the nonmembers, the outsiders. The details of such structuration vary, however, according to the emphasis on the different components of the codes which shape the construction of collectivity.[33] Thus, to give a few very preliminary indications, primordial orientations have a strong elective affinity with the institution of relatively wide "package deals" of resources and access to public goods for all members of the community, of the concomitant denial of any such access and entitlements to "strangers," and of the constitution of relatively wide arenas of public goods. However, differences may arise between different primordial codes regarding their relative emphasis on equality versus hierarchy and the distinction between different primordial subcommunities.

Similarly, there is a strong elective affinity between the code-orientations of civility and the development of a sharp distinction between the rights to entitlement and access to public goods on the one hand, and access to major, predominantly economic markets on the other. The former are restricted to members of the community, while access to the latter may also be permitted to strangers. The range of public goods and entitlements distributed to all members of such a society is much smaller than in primordial communities, and a distinction between private and public arenas tends to develop.

Likewise, cultural, especially sacral, transcendental code-orientations have a strong elective affinity to a certain mode of the structuring of entitlements. Such code-orientation emphasizes the universal access of all "believers" to the basic resources distributed and to the public goods constituted by the "cultural" collectivity, but not necessarily by other collectivities.

Finally, there exist elective affinities between different codes and the structuration of preferences. It is not only that each code orientation almost by definition entails a strong emphasis on different types of goals. These orientations also provide the bases for the evaluation of different activities by people and for the calculi according to which they evaluate their activities and the discourses about such calculi and evaluations.

XIV

The structure of preferences and of the definitions of social actors, of major social arenas, and of different domains of cultural creativity are not all necessarily the same in different societies, contrary to some interpretations of the structural-functional school with relatively similar levels of technological de-

---

33. S. N. Eisenstadt and B. Giesen, *The Construction of Collective Identity* (forthcoming).

velopment or of structural differentiation. This includes, for example, their definition as distinct domains, as "religion," "economy," "polity," and the like, as well as of different types of roles. All of them are rooted in "culture." They must, however, take into account the organizational and systemic prerequisites of these arenas, which are influenced by the differing levels of technology, by the degree of structural differentiation generated by the division of labor prevalent in them, as well as by their political-ecological situations and the basic prerequisites of different modes of production. At the same time, however, it is these definitions that provide their concrete specification—the definition of the needs of different organizational settings, their relative autonomy, their hierarchical arrangements, and the respective ground rules of their social interaction.

Thus, for instance, whenever a modern industrial system is constructed, its basic prerequisites must be taken care of—if it is to function effectively—through relatively specific institutional arrangements, including the availability of industrial labor, the proper type of division of labor, adequate labor discipline within the enterprises, provision of capital, and so on. Such needs or prerequisites became even more specific in capitalist or socialist-industrial systems. However, this does not mean that there is only one mode of institutional arrangements in which such needs can be taken care of within the broad limits of the common core of such "functional prerequisites."

Thus, in different industrial—or even in different capitalist—regimes, several types of such functional equivalents or institutional arrangements may develop, including, for instance, different types of industrial relations, capital markets, and so on. Such different institutional arrangements are greatly influenced by the specific definitions of the respective institutional arenas—in this case, of the economy, the relation of economic activities to the welfare of the collectivity, and the ultimate legitimation of economic activities, whether in terms of direct economic profit, industrial growth, or collective political or ideological goals.[34]

THE CHARISMATIC DIMENSION OF HUMAN ACTION AND THE SPECIFICATIONS OF THE GROUND RULES OF SOCIAL INTERACTION

XV

The specifications of the preference structures of people, of definitions of the major arenas of social interaction, and of the ground rules regulating the major activities within such arenas do not occur as some type of natural emanation from the basic ontological conceptions prevalent in any society or from the

---

34. For illustrations from historical societies see chapter 11, "Culture and Social Structure Revisited."

different codes and their constellations. Such specifications are not naturally given. True, the frameworks of such construction are set by the basic parameters and codes of human activity and by the construction of meaning, and these as well as their basic institutional derivations may be viewed as part of what Karl Popper called World III. In principle, it is indeed not possible in the construction of social action—despite utopian visions to the contrary, and even though such visions do attest to the ambivalence to social order which is inherent in its construction—to go beyond the general types of components of the basic code-orientations. But the concrete specifications of the different code-orientations and the relative importance of the different codes, as well as the combinations of different code-orientations and their institutional derivations as they become crystallized in any concrete situation, are not predetermined in any way. There does not exist a simple, one-to-one relation between cosmological visions and visions of social order on the one hand, and the range of preferences which prevail among members of a society, or the ground rules of social interaction, the rules of the game, the strategical rules, and range of choices which develop within any arena of social interaction on the other. Rather, as we have illustrated above, there are strong elective affinities between them.

Within the range of such elective affinities, the concrete specification and formulation of these definitions and constructions are never simply given and they may constitute a focus of continuous negotiations and even contestations between different social actors—even if they may be perceived by large sectors of the society and for long periods in the history of that society as "objective"—as apparently naturally given. It is indeed the concrete constitution and promulgation of such different code-orientations, the preference frameworks and different calculi employed by people in the closely related institutionalization and continuous reinterpretation of the ground rules of social interaction, and the concomitant institutional formations which constitute the foci of human creativity in the social arenas.

Such specification, interpretation, and negotiation occur on different levels of social structure, ranging from the most informal to formal, from micro to macro and central institutional arenas. It is such specifications and combinations—on all levels of human interaction but above all, in the broader, macro-societal ones—which constitute the core of the charismatic dimension of human activity, of the attempts to combine concrete human activity with an orientation to what is perceived in human society as the "sources of being" and of human existence.[35]

35. See in greater detail chapter 8, "Charisma and Institution Building," and chapter 10, "Prestige, Participation, and Strata Formation"; E. Shils, "Charisma, Order, and Status," in *Center and Periphery* (Chicago: University of Chicago Press, 1975), 256–86; S. N. Eisenstadt, ed., *Max Weber on Charisma* (Chicago: University of Chicago Press, 1968).

PROMULGATION OF MODELS OF SOCIAL ORDER: CONSTRUCTION OF CENTERS AND OF COLLECTIVE CONSCIOUSNESS

XVI

Such activities directed towards the implementation of the charismatic dimension of human interaction in social life are to be found—even if sometimes rather fleetingly—on all levels of social interaction, even in the most informal, "transitory" settings.

It is, however, in the construction of centers of a collectivity, of a society, or of sectors thereof[36] that the basic characteristics of the institutionalization of the charismatic dimensions of social interaction can best be seen. Such centers and subcenters constitute the loci of the promulgation and constitution of the definitions of the major arenas of social interaction in which the ground rules for regulating the major activities within them are promulgated and implemented. On the macrosocietal level, these centers are usually (although not always, as in the case of Hindu civilization) at least partial efforts to very closely relate to the political arenas and to political rules and authority. But the dimension of centrality is not tantamount solely to organizational differentiation or specialization in the political arena, or various political-administrative rules. It also refers, perhaps above all, to the connection of such activities with the basic ground rules of social interaction which are addressed in terms of the basic poles of human reflexivity, to the construction of trust, the regulation of power, and the construction of meaning—and with the definitions of the major arenas of human interaction.

It is through such specifications and definitions as they crystallize through the interaction between different centers and subcenters and broader collectivities that society and the collective consciousness of its members are constituted and become a central component and point of reference for the individual self-consciousness of members of society. In other words, it is through such specification that the "imaginary constitution of society" takes place.[37]

In all collectivities, but especially in various macrosocietal orders (in "societies"), the construction of a collective consciousness is closely related to the specification of the primordial dimensions of the person and of the collectivity in terms of territorial attachment, common kinship, language, or history. It is also closely related to answers to the problems of death and immortality, and to the search to overcome the distinction between the given world and the world beyond; to different conceptions of time; and especially to the perception of the place of the collective past in relation to the present and the future. Such definitions are also closely related to the distinction, recognized long

36. E. Shils, *Center and Periphery* (Chicago: University of Chicago Press, 1975), 3–17.

37. C. Castoriadis, *The Imaginary Institution of Society* (Cambridge: Polity Press, 1987); E. Shils, "On Constitution of Collective Consciousness" (paper in development at the University of Chicago, 1992–3).

ago by Durkheim, between the sacred and the profane, and to the different combinations of these two dimensions of social order.

XVII

The construction of societal centers and of collective consciousness, that is, the institutionalization of the charismatic social order, is attained through a combination of the promulgation and institutionalization of models of social and cultural order with various attempts to control the production and flow of resources.

Such models of cultural and social orders—the Geertzian models "of and for society"[38]—represent and promulgate the incorrigible assumptions about the nature of reality and a social reality prevalent in a society, the core symbols of a society, the evaluation of different arenas of human activity, and the place of different symbolic ("cultural") activities as they bear on the basic predicaments and uncertainties of human experience. These models present the criteria delineating the limits of the binding cultural order, of the parameters of the society's tradition, and of the symbols of collective identity, as well as the appropriate codes of behavior within the major arenas of institutional and cultural activity.

Such models specify the basic parameters of the relations between the personal and collective identities of the members of different societies, and of the patterns of behavior appropriate for them. They also provide guidelines for the appreciation and evaluation of the totality or part of the cultural and social order.

It is through the promulgation, institutionalization, and interpretation of such models that, to use D. M. Schneider's nomenclature, the construction of "identity" and membership in different collectivities is combined with the range of "codes" incumbent on those participating in such collectivities,[39] thus setting up what in Durkheim's terminology serves as the precontractual elements of social life, the bases of mechanical solidarity.[40] These models and codes constitute the major components of the construction of centers and the collective consciousness of a society or collectivity. They also provide the basis of the taken-for-granted premises of cultural and social order—what the Comaroffs have called hegemonies as well as for the promulgation of more articulated ideologies.[41]

The promulgation of such models and codes also sets up the general struc-

---

38. C. Geertz: *The Interpretation of Cultures* (New York: Basic Books, 1973), 93–4.

39. D. M. Schneider and R. T. Smith, *Class Differences and Sex Role in American Kinship and Family Structure* (Englewood Cliffs: Prentice Hall, 1973).

40. E. Durkheim, *The Division of Labor in Society* (New York: The Free Press, 1933).

41. J. Comaroff and J. Comaroff, *Of Revelation and Revolution: Christianity, Colonialism, and Consciousness in South Africa* (Chicago: University of Chicago Press, 1991).

ture of the preferences which are presented as binding to the participants in any setting of social interaction.

XVIII

The promulgation of models of social and cultural orders and of the appropriate code-orientations takes place in many different situations of social interaction but is most often fully articulated in several types of situations. One is comprised of various situations or settings of socialization and initiation—from the family through different educational arenas and arenas of "secondary" adult socialization—in which the basic initial orientations to the premises and orientations inherent in such models and codes are inculcated in the (future) members of a society or sector thereof.

Second, often overlapping with the first, are various rituals and communicative situations, especially: (a) situations in which there is a transition from one institutional arena or from one stage in an individual's life to another, or situations in which there is contemporaneous activity in several arenas; (b) situations in which the routine of a given role or group is endangered or disrupted or transgressed against; (c) various marginal situations (such as pilgrimages) in which the "liminal" dimensions of social experience are stressed; (d) seemingly purely expressive yet highly formalized and structural situations such as those of "formal" visiting and hospitality; and (e) private or semiprivate, often seemingly unstructured situations of play and entertainment. In the last two types of situations, these themes are activated in the rituals of daily life, in the "frames and encounters" depicted by Erwin Goffman and studied, in a somewhat different vein, by the ethnomethodologists.[42]

These situations are closely connected with the interruption of the routine of the social division of labor; they occur in the interstices of "routine" life, but arise not only out of the organizational exigencies of the social division of labor, but rather out of the potential dissociation between the actual organization and social division of labor and the "charismatic" dimensions of the social order. Significantly enough, the interruptions in the "routine," which epitomize many such situations, are very often—as George Homans has shown in his discussion of Malinowski's and Radcliffe-Brown's analyses of rituals—generated within any society or sector thereof as if on purpose, in a quest for closure, for the reaffirmation of the existing order, or as ways to challenge this order.[43]

In such situations, the participants encounter the fragility of the prevalent definitions of such social situations in their relations to broader settings and

42. See chapter 1, "The Place of Elites and Primary Groups in the Absorption of New Immigrants in Israel," and also in greater detail S. N. Eisenstadt, *Essays in Comparative Civilizations* (New York: John Wiley & Sons, 1963), sec. V, chap. 12.

43. G. C. Homans, "Anxiety and Ritual: The Theory of Malinowski and Radcliffe-Brown," in *Sentiments and Activities: Essays in Social Science* (Glencoe, Ill.: The Free Press, 1962), 192–202.

they face the possibility of their status being undermined, of the dissociation of their ordinary daily experience from the broader social setting.

In all such communicative, ritual, and interstitial situations, what is defined as the "natural" givens of any institutional arena—sex, age, and procreation in that of family and kinship; power and force in the political "discourse"; the extraction of resources from nature in the economic arena—is usually dramatized, evaluated, and related to the organizational problems of each such arena. In the process of promulgation, presentation, and commendation, these models and codes and the ways in which they are presented and communicated in different situations, the expressive and cognitive aspects of the "cultural" dimensions of human activities, are strongly combined and related to the specification of preferences, of choices of goals and patterns of behavior in appropriate structures.

Such promulgation is effected on all levels of social action, though with different degrees of formalization, by the embedding of code-orientations in different types of narratives and representational genres and by the development in any society or sector thereof of multiple modes of discourse as well which entail, as we shall see later, processes of discursive contests.[44]

XIX

These charismatic dimensions of social order, the various activities promulgated from within the centers of societies or sectors thereof, the definitions of different patterns of social interaction and of the ground rules which regulate them—all of these are not given or effected, as some structuralists claim, by some emanation from the basic rules of the human mind, or, according to Marxist structuralists, according to the laws or principles of different modes of production. Rather, they are effected through distinct social processes and by specific social activities and carriers which can be identified at all levels of social interaction through distinct modes of human agency.

Such interaction takes place through special types of social activities. In more informal settings, it is the interaction between various influentials and other participants which constitutes the crux of such interaction. In the more formalized and central settings, special types of actors, best designated as "elites," are usually the initiators of such activities, but they are always in interaction with other actors. The most important of these elites are the political elites, the bearers of the visions of solidarity of the different collectivities, the cultural elites, and economic entrepreneurs. The more formal elites or influentials are situated in roles which are relatively centrally located—from the point

---

44. The application of the terms *narratives, discourse,* and *genre* in cultural-sociological analysis has been attempted lately by J. C. Alexander. See, for instance, J. C. Alexander and S. G. Sherwood, *Bush, Hussein, and the Cultural Preparation for War: Code Narrative, Genre, and Social Action* (forthcoming).

of view of the systemic prerequisites of given patterns of interaction—exercising control over a wide range of activities in broader sectors of society.

The common denominator of such interaction, of such modes of human agency, is that among all participants, some orientation develops towards the charismatic dimension of human activity, some predisposition to participate in such dimensions. In other words, for most individuals, their possible participation in such activities constitutes a component of their goals or preferences.

The core of the interaction between such elites, influentials, and broader sectors of society is oriented towards the long-term commitment of resources, and is predicated on the readiness of most of the actors participating in such patterns of interaction to forego some of the benefits and minimize the risks inherent in the more direct and seemingly free exchanges. This type of interaction entails a combination of different package deals of "material" and symbolic resources. It is this combination which constructs the different types of ascriptive titles and unconditionalities to which we have referred above.

Hence, the crux of the relation between such elites, influentials, and the broader sectors of the social settings in which they participate (i.e., the distinct mode of human agency which characterizes such interaction), is the specification of the conditions which limit the direct use of resources or the potentially free exchange of such resources. In other words, the promulgation of models of social order and the messages contained in such models and codes are closely connected with the institution of the ground rules of social interaction and of the principles of generalized exchange that are prevalent in any society and sectors thereof. It is in such interaction between elites, influentials, and broader sectors of society that the basic rules of generalized exchange, the specification of entitlements and unconditionalities, the conditions and limitations of production and exchange of resources, are specified.

Such conditions and limitations apply both to the elites and entrepreneurs as well as to those groups from whom resources are mobilized. These conditions entail direction and limitation both of the direct use of resources as well as of the exercise of power by both types of social actors.

For both sides of such exchanges or interactions, these limitations involve the interweaving of power with long-range trust and broader meaning. Such limitations on the exercise of power and use of resources do not entail the "total" surrender of power, certainly not by the various elites and entrepreneurs but also not by members of the broader social groups. But these limitations are different for the elites and influentials and for the broader sectors of society although there may be considerable overlapping between them.

For the elites and influentials, such interweaving does not entail the surrender of power but rather limits its use in terms of its orientations towards the broader institutional goals and premises. These are defined in terms of their interweaving with the construction of trust and ultimate meaning. These elites remain responsible for the implementation of long-range institutional goals and patterns of social interaction and for the continuous maintenance of the terms of trust, and are held accountable accordingly.

For the members of the different sectors of society, the interweaving of power with trust and meaning entails giving up the possibility of using the power they have—the seemingly "passive" power of obedience or commitment—and the continuous transfer of some of their resources to these long-range goals or frameworks. At the same time, this interweaving of power with trust and meaning empowers them to make demands on the elites or influentials in their respective settings according to some long-range premises and visions which are promulgated by the elites and which also constitute the principles of their legitimation.

Thus legitimation is not just a sort of opium for the people. It creates also the legitimate criteria for the exercise of power by the elites, which if not adhered to may generate challenges to such power and to the power holders.

It is the interaction between the different coalitions of elites and influentials, their continuous interaction with the different, broader sectors of society, and the modes of control they exercise which provide the concrete definitions, the specifications of the major institutional arenas and of the ground rules regulating the major activities within them.

Coalitions of elites and influentials with broader sectors of society exercise control through their ability to regulate access to major institutional arenas (e.g., economic, political, or cultural) and to the conversion of resources between these arenas. In addition, they control the production and distribution of information central to the structuring of cognitive maps of the members of their society in general, and of the orientations of reference orientations and groups in particular.

These regulative activities of elites and influentials combine the structuring of information contained within the respective models of social order and codes, and long-range commitments to the symbols of their legitimation, with a relatively wide range of concrete short-term options or strategies. Such control involves the definition of the ground rules of the respective patterns of interaction and the concomitant rules of access to the major types of resources and their combination. It is based on attempts to regulate, through socialization and communication, the basic motivations, orders of preferences, and reference orientations of those participating in any setting of social interaction.

The modes of recruitment of these major types of elites and influentials differ, as we have already seen in the introduction, in different societies. In some societies, such activities are embedded in broader, usually ascriptive, settings. In others, these elites or influentials are recruited according to some criteria of achievement.

The availability of acceptable elite actors or influentials constitutes one of the major problems or challenges facing any pattern of continuous interaction.[45] While in most patterns of social interaction there are people ready to perform the various elite or influential functions, such availability cannot be taken for granted. Thus, for instance, in my analysis of the historical empires, there were cases when no appropriate "imperial" elite developed in societies in which there were, nonetheless, potentials for the development of empires.[46] Moreover, even when they are available, it is not certain how well the elites and influentials will perform and to what extent their performance will be acceptable to other contenders for elite positions or to the broader groups participating in such patterns of interaction.

When available, these specifications of the ground rules of interactions and of orders of preference also shape the specific institutional contours of any society or sector thereof—the specific contours of political regimes, of the political economy, of the structuring of social hierarchies and the like[47]—and constitute the core of generalized exchange in any society. In all these different ways, the major features and dynamics of different "micro-" and "macro" patterns of social interaction and their systemic qualities and respective environments are shaped.

The Systemic Tendencies of Patterns of Social Interaction

XX

The major patterns of social interaction and social structure which crystallize in any population are always organized on multiple levels, in different arenas of social and cultural activities, and in different contexts of action which tend to exhibit systemic tendencies.[48]

In every human social life, in every continuous pattern of social interaction, there develop tendencies to some systemic qualities, with the concomitant construction—through the processes analyzed above—of boundaries of the different patterns of interaction. These are very fragile, but being fragile does not mean they are nonexistent. It does mean, however, that special mechanisms of control and integration, special regulative mechanisms—above all, those of the institutionalization and reproduction of the general prerequisites of social interaction—are needed to overcome the inherent instability and fragility of their boundaries in order to maintain and assure their reproduction.

Such integrative mechanisms and processes of control become more im-

---

45. See chapter 1, "The Place of Elites and Primary Groups in the Absorption of New Immigrants in Israel," and chapter 2, "Reference Group Behavior and Social Integration."

46. See S. N. Eisenstadt, *The Political System of Empires* (New York: The Free Press, 1963).

47. See chapter 11, "Culture and Social Structure Revisited."

48. See S. N. Eisenstadt, "Functional Analysis in Anthropology and Sociology," *Annual Review of Anthropology* 19 (1990):243–60.

portant and autonomous and hence also more fragile—as manifest, for instance, in the connection of bureaucracies of general systems of social law—as different social and political systems and civilizational frameworks become more complex. It was Herbert Simon's signal contribution to point out that the mechanisms of control constitute autonomous analytical dimensions, and that every such mechanism of control has a built-in second order of stability and instability.[49] These mechanisms of control, these integrative mechanisms, may acquire an autonomy of their own in the construction and maintenance of systemic boundaries.

Whatever the strengths of such integrative mechanisms and of the systemic tendencies of patterns of social interaction, such patterns never develop as entirely self-enclosed systems. The populations which live within the confines of what has been designated as a "society" or a macrosocietal order are not usually organized into one "system," but rather into several systems, including political systems, economic formations, different ascriptive collectivities, and civilizational frameworks. The processes of the construction of collectivities, social systems, and civilizational frameworks constitute the continuous struggle in which ideological, "material," and power elements are continuously interwoven. These processes are structured, articulated, and carried by different social actors and carriers, above all by different coalitions of elites and contra-elites and influentials in interactions with the broader sectors of the society. Each "system" with its flexible boundaries is carried by different coalitions of such carriers. These different structures and patterns—these "systems"—evince different patterns of organization, continuity, and change. They may change within the "same" society to different degrees and in different ways in various areas of social life. Moreover, it is only very rarely that members of such a population are confined to any single "society"—even if one such "society" seems to be the salient macroorder for them. Usually, they live in multiple settings or contexts.

Such settings or contexts of interaction differ from each other with respect to the relative importance within them of the types of resources produced, distributed, and controlled by them; with respect to the span of time and space to which such regulation, and the investment and flow of such resources, are oriented; with respect to "tightness" or closure between different symbolic and more "material" resources; and with respect to the actions activating the different processes of control.

These differences in the settings and contexts of various activities are not random or accidental. They are closely related to the specific organizational

49. H. Simon, "The Architecture of Complexity," *Yearbook of the Society for General Systems Research* 10 (1965):63–76; idem, "The Complexity," sec. 4 of *Models of Discovery and Other Topics in the Methods of Science* (Boston: D. Reidel, 1977), 175–265.

exigencies and to the basic symbolic problematique of each type and level of activity. These different types of problematiques are often combined and recombined in various concrete situations according to the definitions of the settings of such situations. Thus, within each situation, each arena of social interaction or institutional formation, any human activity tends to draw on a potentially inexhaustible reservoir of images and "stimuli" from man's constructed environments. It structures human actions into specific themes and patterns of behavior according to the specific organizational problems of these settings and activities, combined with their relation to the broader contexts of action and meaning and metameaning.

These actions are organized either in some loose themacity and systematicity according to some formal ordering principles and transformation (i.e., those proposed by the structuralists or different modes of semiotic mediation), according to holographic arrangements of different "tropes," as proposed by R. Wagner,[50] or according to the systemic needs of different patterns of interaction.

Needless to say, not all components, themes, or tropes which can be found in the cultural reservoir of a society are relevant to and activated in such activities and situations. There is continual selection, reconstruction, reinterpretation, and invention of themes, tropes, parameters, models, and codes, as well as of the modes of semiotic mediation employed in their presentation. Such selection, recomposition, and reinterpretation emphasize the distinctiveness and autonomy of each sphere or arena of activity, as well as its connection with the more general frameworks or metacontexts. Such metacontexts are rooted in what may be called the human situation, in the different aspects of human experience and in the way in which the basic dimensions of this experience are presented in the core symbols, in the basic ontologies, and in the conceptions of social order and rules prevalent in a society or sectors thereof. Yet, to whatever extent they are interconnected, they are never fully integrated in a closed system. They are always subject to continuous reinterpretation, and each one of them necessarily evinces strong tendencies to some, albeit limited, autonomy. They are organized, not in an organizationally closed system, but at most in a loop order, in which there are some indeterminacies in the relations between components. They also come together, in different ways, through different processes, each entailing a different time span in a variety of concrete situations. Thus, the different arenas of human activity do not lose their partial autonomy or the possibility of innovation within and across them.

XXI

The construction of the boundaries of social systems, collectivities, and organizations necessarily delineates their relations with their environment. However,

---

50. R. Wagner, *The Invention of Culture* (Englewood Cliffs: Prentice Hall, 1975).

it is wrong to assume that there is a natural environment of any society, of any pattern of social interaction. There is no such thing as the "natural" environment "out there." Rather, each pattern of social interaction, each society, constructs its own environment, continuously highlighted. It is the construction of such multiple environments in different ecological settings which highlights the distinct features of the construction of the human environment. Any environment is, within very broad limits, constructed by society and can be understood only in relation to that society or pattern of social interaction.

Of course, in the construction of an environment, any society has some material to base itself on. But each "natural" environment provides several possible institutional choices, and one or several of these choices are being chosen by the respective social actors. Once such choices have been made, they set the limits or the boundaries of the system and generate the systemic sensitivity to environmental changes. These sensitivities are created not by the environment as such, nor by technology as such, but by society in reconstructing the environment by using different technologies.

The concretization of these institutional tendencies takes place in different political-ecological settings. Two aspects of these settings are of special importance. One, emphasized strongly in recent research, is the importance of international political and economic systems in general, including the place of societies within them, and different types of relations of hegemony and dependency in particular. The second is the great variety of the political-ecological settings of societies, such as differences between large and small societies, and their respective dependence on internal or external markets. Both of these aspects greatly affect the ways in which institutional contours and dynamics tend to develop.[51]

SOCIAL STRUCTURE AND AGENCY

XXII

The preceding analysis indicates the nature of the relations between "social structure" and "human agency." The preceding analysis indicated that structure is basically the specification of access to "symbolic" and "material" resources, of their use, and of the possibility of the conversion between such different resources, i.e., between economic resources, power and prestige, and information. Such conversion, according to different schemata, is grounded in the various code-orientations. It is the specification of these code-orientations through the interaction between elites, influentials, and broader sections of society that transforms some "objective" human or natural givens into resources which can

51. For illustrations see chapter 11, "Culture and Social Structure Revisited."

be used in social interaction. Thus, social structure and human agency constitute two sides of the same process.

These relations between structure and agency have recently been explored by William H. Sewell, Jr.[52] To quote him:

> . . . the rules or schemas making up structures may usefully be conceptualized as having a "virtual" existence, that structures consist of intersubjectively available procedures or schemas capable of being actualized or put into practice in a range of different circumstances. Such schemas should be thought of as operating at widely varying levels of depth, from Lévi-Straussian deep structures to relatively superficial rules of etiquette . . .
>
> . . . Structure, then, should be defined as composed simultaneously of schemas, which are virtual, and of resources, which are actual. If structures are dual in this sense, then it must be true that schemas are the effects of resources, just as resources are the effects of schemas . . .

especially of the more continual ones in which the normative specification of the use of resources is relatively strong.

The construction of structure creates hegemonic power which enables the use of resources by different people, but at the same time, it also empowers all those connected to it with respect to such access. It is such access to resources that constitutes the core or basis of human "agency." To follow Sewell again:

> Such enactments of structures imply a particular concept of agency— one that sees agency not as opposed to, but as constituent of, structure. To be an agent means to be capable of exerting some degree of control over the social relations in which one is enmeshed, which in turn implies the ability to transform those social relations to some degree. As I see it, agents are empowered to act with and against others by structures: they have knowledge of the schemas that inform social life and have access to some measure of human and nonhuman resources. Agency arises from the actor's knowledge of schemas, which means the ability to apply them to new contexts. Or, to put the same thing the other way around, agency arises from the actor's control of resources, which means the capacity to reinterpret or mobilize an array of resources in terms of schemas other than those that constituted the array. Agency is implied by the existence of structures.
>
> I would argue that a capacity for agency—for desiring, for forming intentions, and for acting creatively—is inherent in all humans . . . The specific forms that agency will take consequently vary enormously and are culturally and historically determined. But a capacity for agency is as much a given for humans as the capacity for respiration.

52. W. Sewell, "A Theory of Structure: Duality, Agency, and Transformation," *American Journal of Sociology* 98 (1992):1–29.

... It is equally important, however, to insist that the agency exercised by different persons is far from uniform, that agency differs enormously in both kind and extent. What kinds of desires people can have, what intentions they can form, and what sorts of creative transpositions they can carry out vary dramatically from one social world to another depending on the nature of the particular structures that inform those social worlds.

Such more routine, discrete patterns of behavior entail a relatively flexible manipulation of "free" resources and technical information related to the symbols of legitimation, but it entails struggle over the structures of control mechanisms to a much smaller degree than those of generalized exchange. The interweaving of power and meaning, although always existing in such interaction, is much looser than in the framework of generalized exchange.

The concrete contours of any continual pattern of social interaction and its dynamics are shaped by relations between generalized exchange and the choice of concrete patterns of behavior. Such interaction or interweaving is open-ended in all situations. The specifications by the different ground rules of different normative injunctions and of frameworks of preferences do not fully determine the specific patterns of behavior that develop in any concrete setting. Given the polysemic nature of schemata and resources, the seeming infinitude of human wants, and the basic openness of human activities, there is in any situation of social interaction a potential openness between the broad specifications of ground rules and code-orientations and the concrete choices of behavior.

It is because of such openness that in any continual situation of social interest there developed multiple social processes, such as the structuration of reference orientations, which frame and coordinate the objections of action and in this way influence patterns of choice of behavior, as well as the various process analyzed above through which some long-range relations balance the preference orders of social actors and the incentives and rewards offered to them are structured. But such processes are themselves multiple and constitute, in addition to the orders of preference of people, only one factor influencing such choices.[53]

The concrete patterns of choice are influenced by several additional, closely interrelated factors. Such choices are influenced by several basic, above all formal-structural, characteristics of the frameworks of the division of labor

53. See S. Lindenberg,"The Explanation of Preferences," in *Empirische Sociologie als opdracht*, ed. H. van Goor (MB-Boek Groningen, 1993), 49–67; S. Lindenberg, "Contractual Relations and Weak Solidarity: The Behavioral Basis of Restraints on Gain-maximization," *Journal of Institutional and Theoretical Economics* 144 (1988):39–58; S. Lindenberg, "Homo sociooeconomicus: The Emergence of a General Model of Man in the Social Sciences," *Journal of Institutional and Theoretical Economics* 146 (1990): 727–47; S. Lindenberg, "An Extended Theory of Institutions and Contractual Discipline," *Journal of Institutional and Theoretical Economics* 148 (1992).

within which social interaction takes place, and by the structural location of people within these frameworks. In this context, the first major factor which influences concrete choices of behavior is the structural location of different people—the formal characteristics of the different structures of role and status sets, their distribution, and the way the possibility of contradictions between the components of roles, role sets, and status sets in which patterns of social interaction are structured.

All of these features generate multiple choices, as Robert K. Merton has forcefully analyzed,[54] between socially structured alternatives which in turn generate further multiple choices.

The accumulation of different choices between various structurally avail-

54. We may follow here A. Stinchcombe's analysis of Merton:

. . . I will argue that the core process that Merton conceives as central to social structure is the choice between socially structured alternatives. This differs from the choice process of economic theory, in which the alternatives are conceived to have inherent utilities. It differs from the choice of process of learning theory, in which the alternatives are conceived to emit reinforcing or extinguishing stimuli. It differs from both of these in that for Merton the utility or reinforcement of a particular alternative choice is thought of as socially established, as part of the institutional order.

For example, the choice of illegitimate means to socially establish goals is defined in terms of the institutional definitions of legitimacy and worthwhile goals. The choice between the alternative 'innovation' and another alternative, for example, of 'ritualism' (legitimate means, lack of commitment to socially approved goals) is a choice between alternatives whose utilities or capacities for reinforcement are institutionally structured. Since the alternatives are socially structured, the resulting choice behavior has institutional consequences.

But the focus of Merton's theory of these "choices with institutional consequences" is on variations of the rates of choice by people differently located in the social order.

. . . To this basic linking process which connects structural forces to institutionally consequential choices, and thence to institutional patterns, Merton adds two kinds of causal loops. The first is the one for which he is perhaps best known: namely, the recasting of the nature of functional analysis so that institutional consequences of action act back to shape the nature of the alternatives that people are posed with. The consequence of a group choosing help, not justice, is the viability of the political machine which then provides alternative ways for businessmen to serve illegal but profitable markets, alternative career opportunities for lawyers to become judges when they are good at giving help and not so good at giving justice, and so on.

The second kind of loop is in the historical development of a social character out of a systematic biographical patterning of choices. For example, a cosmopolitan is structurally induced to choose non-local patterns of information collection, and corresponding areas and styles of influence, which differ from the behavior patterns of locals. These styles become imprinted as basic character orientations toward information and influence which lead people to consistent biographies as local and cosmopolitan influentials, so that the patterns of behavior do not change with each change in particular situational circumstances. Thus, the second loop is a feedback through character formation which produces personal continuities in the kind of link a given person is between structural pressures and patterns of choice behavior.

able alternatives in the aggregation of different personal utilities and choices of different collective rationalities, as developed by people placed in different situations and empowered by different visions, as well as by different reference orientations and frames of objects of action, gives rise to the continued confrontation between the structuration of preferences and of specification of the ground rules of social interaction, and it is such confrontation that generates the concrete dynamics of any pattern of social interaction.

The relative openness between the normative specifications of the choices of patterns of behavior and such concrete choices indicates that the continuity, the institutionalization of any pattern of social interaction, and the reproduction of such patterns—despite the continual development of mechanisms and processes of control aiming to assure it—cannot be taken for granted or continually assured; hence, fragility, change and conflict, are inherent in the constitution of social order—indeed they form the "other side" of such constitution.

CONFLICT AND CHANGE: THE ROOTS OF CONFLICT AND OF CHANGE IN THE CONSTITUTION OF SOCIAL ORDER

XXIII

The inherence of fragility, change, and conflicts in any patterns of social interaction is rooted in the interweaving of some of the general characteristics of human action with, first, the limitations inherent in the institutionalization of any charismatic vision, of any pattern of ground rules of social interaction, and second, with the structural properties and the processes of reproduction of any such pattern of interaction.

On the most general level, the tendency to fragility and changeability— as we have already briefly indicated above—is rooted in the very existence of the empty spaces between, on the one hand, the general tendencies to the construction of the social division of labor and to culture, which are inherent in the human situation, and to the specification and concretization of these general tendencies on the other.

The existence of such empty spaces entails, in principle, the possibility that a failure to develop the appropriate activities may occur—a failure, as it

---

The accumulated results of such choices are reinforced by the shifts in positions of different sectors in a society and may generate far-reaching processes of change. Such choices may entail shifts in preferences and in the modes of calculi or discourses in which people become engaged—i.e., from a purely "rational-utilitarian" calculus to those of power or solidarity or value commitments.

A. L. Stinchcombe, "Merton's Theory of Social Structure," in *The Idea of Social Structure*, ed. L. A. Coser (New York: Harcourt Brace Jovanovich, 1985), 3–11.

were, to "fill in" the empty spaces. It is always possible that the appropriate types of agency through which ongoing institutional patterns are reproduced will not emerge, or that those which do emerge will not be accepted by the broader sectors of the population; that the interaction between would-be influentials, elites, and their respective audiences will fail to generate relatively stable patterns of relations between the production and allocation of resources, regulation of power, and the construction of trust and legitimation in a way acceptable to those participating in such interaction.

Secondly, the propensity within any pattern of social interaction to fragility, volatility, conflict, and changeability is rooted in the continual interweaving of the problems and indeterminacies inherent in such interaction with the basic characteristics of organizational and symbolic construction of such interaction and the concomitant characteristics of the construction by human beings of their environment, and, above all, with seeing the infinity of human wants, the polysemicity of human resources, and the openness and arbitrariness of the symbolic constructs of reality.

Thirdly, such fragility and changeability—as well as the closely related tendency to conflict—are also inherent in any setting of social interaction because of the plurality of actors in any such setting and because of the struggles and conflicts between such actors about access to, and use of, resources, which any institutionalization of continuous interaction entails.

XXIV

The ubiquity of fragility, conflicts, and potentialities of change in any setting of social interaction is intensified by the interweaving of all these *general* characteristics of human action and interaction analyzed above with those of the institutionalization of any such pattern of interaction and of the pattern of their production. Of special importance here are several aspects of the institutionalization of the charismatic dimensions of human action, the first of which is the limitation such institutionalization imposes on human creativity.

The basic roots of the limitations on creativity inherent in the institutionalization of the charismatic dimension of human activity in general, and of social interaction and order in particular, lie in the fact that any such process of institutionalization entails the selection of some limited themes or possibilities from a much larger variety of such themes; the second aspect concerns the routinization of the creative act which is inherent in any such institutionalization; and the third aspect involves the close relation between such closure and the exercise of power through a process of control and regulation of any such interaction.

Put another way, the limitations inherent in any institutionalization of the charismatic dimension of human activity in general, and of the construction of social order in particular, are due to the fact that any such institutionalization is based on an emphasis of certain components or dimensions of human existence, of ontological premises and of conceptions of social order, or a selection of the specific range of preferences to the exclusion of others. Thus, for instance, any such institutionalization entails some relative emphasis on hierarchy or equality, on individualism or collectivism, on solidarity or power, and the like. Such a selection from a variety of potentially perpetual possibilities entails a concomitant closure and limitation and a certain consciousness of such closure and limitation. Once such a selection has been made and institutionalized, the other possibilities are, at least initially, neglected by the emerging social order, although they do not necessarily disappear from the consciousness of some sectors of the society.

Secondly, such limitations and the consciousness of them are rooted in the fact that any concrete institutionalization involves certain restrictions with respect to the degree to which any of its symbolic and organizational components, and the relations between them, are "unfolded" or internally differentiated. Any such institutionalization restricts or "hems in" as if it were a further unfolding of the "logical" or organizational creative potentialities inherent in cultural orientations and in the social organization as well, such as different possibilities of further differentiation, of growing rationalization, of going beyond the "givens" of any such concrete situation of the problematization of such situation.

The third major type of limitation on creativity is the fact that when an institutional innovation is accepted, it may subsequently become routinized, "deflated," more and more removed from its original impetus. Those who participate in its perpetuation—its originators, their initial close collaborators, and especially their successors—tend to become less interested in it; indeed, their whole relation to these mainsprings of creativity may become attenuated. The development of such constrictions may also be rooted in the fact that the originators of such innovations—of great religions, of new political systems, or of new economic enterprises and their successors—may become afraid of the further spread of the spirit of creativity, and may attempt to impose limitations on such a spread and on the attempts of other people or groups to participate in such creativity or to extend its scope.

Thus, any institutionalization of the charismatic dimension of human activities implies the possibility that the objectivation of the external and the social world may turn into a relatively rigid "reification" and will be perceived as such by many members of the society, giving rise to potential feelings of alienation. In this way, innovators and their successors may engender hostility and alienation or apathy among such groups toward these very acts of creativity, and may generate tendencies towards the destruction of institutions.

Similarly, the process of the institutionalization of the charismatic dimensions of human existence creates a continuous tension between the sphere of private and public life on the one hand, and between the better public life and the demands for cultural and social creativity on the other; that is to say, between the individual's quest for personal identity and the possibility of submergence in social roles on the other.

XXV

For all these reasons, the institutionalization of the charismatic dimensions of human activities exacerbates the consciousness of the arbitrariness of such order, and generates—as we have seen above—strong tendencies to ambivalence concerning social order in general and any given concrete order in particular, and to continuous, yet never fully successful, attempts to overcome it.

These feelings of arbitrariness and ambivalence to social order are reinforced by the fourth aspect of the institutionalization of the charismatic dimension of human life; namely, by the fact that the restrictions and exclusions entailed by the institutionalization of any charismatic vision usually become closely associated with the maintenance of the distribution of power, prestige, and wealth and with the concomitant limitation of the scope of the participation of various groups in the central arenas of a society and with access to meaningful participation in the central social and cultural order.

These feelings of arbitrariness and ambivalence are also reinforced by the multiplicity of different structural principles, the different "prerequisites" or "needs" of different institutional sectors, as well as by the multiplicity and distinct characteristics of the various media of exchange. In this context, of special importance are the tensions and potential contradictions between the core components of the basic modules of social interaction; namely, between the organization of the social division of labor, the regulation of power, and the construction of trust and meaning, especially the tensions between the relatively restrictive dimension of the construction of trust and the potentially more expansive tendencies inherent in the other components of social order.[55]

The focus of this tension lies in the tensions or contradictions between the conditions that generate the construction of trust between different members of a group or society on the one hand, and those which ensure both the availability of resources and of institutional entrepreneurs for the formation of broader institutional complexes, as well as the regulation and legitimation of the power of such entrepreneurs on the other. Other conditions being equal (such as, for instance, the extent of coercion employed in such situations), the assurance of trust is greater in relatively limited ranges of social interaction, insofar as relatively narrow, ascriptive criteria specify membership in the soli-

---

55. L. Roniger, "Public Trust and the Consolidation of Latin American Democracies," in *Latin America to the Year 2000*, ed. A. R. M. Ritter, M. A. Cameron, and D. H. Pollock (New York: Praeger, 1992) and *La Fiducia Nelle Societa Moderne—Un Approccio* (Messina: Rubbettino, 1992).

darity communities and provide clear indications of mutual obligation among them. As the structure of the human family attests, such limited ranges of inter-action seem to constitute the minimum conditions for the initial development of trust, even though they may not be enough to assure its continuity. At the same time, however, the conditions which assure the continuity of such trust may be inimical to the development of the more variegated resources and activities needed for a wider range of institutional creativity.

Indeed, the conditions generating resources which may be available for more complex institution building tend also to undermine the simple or "primi-tive," relatively restricted, settings of primary or primordial trust. Hence, in all enduring patterns of social interaction, the problem arises of how to institu-tionalize such activities in some stable, long-range patterns beyond those em-bedded in relatively narrow sets of social relations.

The possibility of such institutionalization depends mainly on the effec-tive extension of the range of symbolism and obligations of trust beyond the narrow scope of primordial or primary units, and on the effective connection of such extended trust with the organization of broader ranges of meaning.

The process of extending the range of trust beyond small primordial or primary relations and groups exemplifies the relative openness of the relations between the basic conceptions of the ontological realm and the ground rules regulating the major arenas of social life and cultural creativity, as well as the ambiguities and tensions inherent in the symbolic definition and legitimation of different arenas of social interaction. These ambiguities and tensions be-come even more intensified when transposed to wider institutional settings.

In any such wider setting, this extension may easily generate tension be-tween extended trust on the one hand and the demands of the division of labor or the regulation of power on the other. Such tensions and contradictions already develop within basic family relationships, in the processes of socializa-tion, in the dialectic between attachment and separation, especially between mother and child, and in the interweaving of this dialectic with the relations of power inherent in the process of socialization.

The extension of trust and its interweaving with broader institutional set-tings necessarily entails tensions or contradictions between the criteria of the allocation of resources derived from the criteria which regulate the social divi-sions of labor, power, and the construction of meaning. Each of these orienta-tions or principles may be borne by different social actors and coalitions who may stress the "centrality" of any such orientation or of its institutionalization as distinct from others and who may develop their own autonomous dynamics to the fullest extent—at the possible expense of others—among whom there is continuous competition over control and allocation of resources. Such com-petition entails the promulgation of different modes of discourse, of the differ-ent calculi of different preferences and the struggle for their relative predominance in the respective contexts of interaction, and may undermine the interweaving of trust with the other dimension of social interaction which constitutes the core of the continuity of any pattern of social interaction.

XXVI

All of these ambivalences, potential conflicts, and changes are also manifest in the very process of promulgation of the models of cultural and social order and their interweaving with the institutionalization of the ground rules of social interaction and the structuration of the ranges of preferences and the uses of resources.

Although the presentation of the many models of social and cultural order in the various communicative and socializing situations is directed to ensure the acceptance by those participating in such situations of the existing order, paradoxically they exacerbate the awareness of the arbitrariness of social order and the limitations that the constitution of any order imposes on human activities. On the one hand, in such situations attempts take place to "convince" the members of a given society that the institutional order in general, and the concrete order of their society in particular, are the "correct" ones. The symbols and images portrayed in these models extol the given order (the purity of the world inside the boundaries, and the danger of the world outside) or the need to remain within the boundaries despite the continuous attraction of the world outside.[56] These symbols and images reinforce, as it were, the existing legenaries, ideologies, and counterideologies.

On the other hand, however, an awareness develops in such situations of the arbitrariness of any social order and of the limitations on human activities which it imposes, as well as a growing awareness of the possibility of developing new themes and models. Thus, at the same time, the attraction of stepping outside the boundaries of the given order is enhanced as is the anxiety about doing so.

Therefore the promulgation—in various situations of socialization and in communicative situations of models of cultural and social order and codes—does not eliminate the many tensions inherent in the structuring of human experience or in the consciousness of its indeterminacies and ambiguities. Such promulgation does not eliminate the consciousness of possibilities beyond those existing in the given social order.

The construction of such models can only delineate some possible boundaries of these ambiguities and transpose them to a new level, giving rise to the search for metameaning—what Gregory Bateson called the search for metacommunication—a search which is built on the very process of the promulgation of such models. Such metacommunication combines the definition of the

56. See chapter 12, "The Order-Maintaining and Order-Transforming Dimensions of Culture."

ambivalence towards any order—cultural or social—with attempts to construct some broader and ultimate, yet always fragile and not fully structured or articulated, meanings of meaning.[57] Hence the promulgation of such metacommunicative messages may also exacerbate and intensify the feeling of the arbitrariness of the social order and of ambivalence to it.

The possibility of such intensification is evident—as we have shown in great detail in chapter 12—in the ubiquity of symbols of protest in such situations, even if they are often, as it were, constricted or submerged.

XXVII

For all these reasons, the promulgations and articulations of models of social order do not create a situation in which all members of a society or sector thereof share the same beliefs or activate the same codes in all situations. Rather, they present a broad framework with some tendency to systematicity in which multiple schemata, themes, and models of semiotic mediation are ordered in a loose framework. This framework provides a series of common texts, which can nevertheless be interpreted in different, often nonmeasurable, ways. Rather, it creates—as Stromberg has shown with respect to a Swedish parish[58]—a situation in which different people share a concern with the interpretation of the same core symbols and sets of themes. As E. Ohnuki-Tierney put it,[59] it creates a text that is predicated upon a dichotomously opposed interpretation of what it "may mean." Within the framework of such texts, of these common core symbols and sets of themes, different social actors tend to construct, promulgate, and continuously reinterpret different ideologies and counterideologies, different interpretations of these symbols and of their relevance for different situations.

A number of such models and codes—each with different thematic emphases, images of knowledge, and expressive symbolism—are usually prevalent or operative within a group or even held by an individual, and may be activated selectively in different situations. Within any society or part thereof, the various models of social and cultural life are articulated and formalized to different degrees. They also vary in their degree of pervasiveness, acceptance, or predominance within any society. The various private models held by individuals or groups in a society may be similar to, or different from, the official ones. Different models may be activated in various situations, although some usually tend to be more prevalent or binding than others and they may become

57. C. K. Ogden and A. I. Richard, *The Meaning of Meaning: A Study of Influence of Language Upon Thought and of the Science of Symbolism* (London: Routledge and Kegan Paul, 1923).

58. P. Stromberg, "Consensus and Variation in the Interpretation of Religious Symbolism: A Swedish Example," *American Ethnologist* 8 (1981):544–59.

59. E. Ohnuki-Tierney, *The Monkey as Mirror* (Princeton: Princeton University Press, 1987).

connected with themes of protest and with feelings of ambivalence toward the social order and the models which are hegemonic within it.

XXVIII

Such feelings of ambivalence generate the potential for destructive orientations which are focused around the antinomies of the construction of order, especially of social order, which become closely related to the charismatic dimension of human activity and generate the combination, in any charismatic activity, of constructive and destructive tendencies.

The constructive and destructive attributes are inherent in charismatic activity because the charismatic predisposition or fervor is rooted in the attempt to come into contact with the very essence of being, which is being perceived as the very roots of existence, of cosmic, social, and cultural order, of what is seen as sacred and fundamental. These predispositions constitute the focus not only of the creative, but also of the destructive tendencies of charisma.

All of these tendencies attest to the fact that charismatic predispositions may lead to excesses of derangement and deviance. The fervor attendant on many charismatic activities may also contain a strong predisposition to sacrilege, to a denial of the validity of the sacred, and to what is promulgated in any given society as sacred. The very attempt to reestablish direct contact with these roots of cosmic and sociopolitical order may breed both opposition to more attenuated and formalized forms of this order, as well as fear and hence opposition to the sacred itself.

Because of this, human creativity may in some cases be deranged or evil, and it is not only the potential derangement but this very creativity—by its nature and orientation—which may tend to undermine and destroy existing institutions.

It is the ubiquity of both the constructive and destructive aspects of the charismatic dimension of human activity, of the attempt to reestablish contact with the roots of the social and cultural order, of the manifestation of these aspects in liminal situations, which explains, as we have shown in greater detail in chapter 12, that the order-maintaining and order-transforming dimensions of culture are but two sides of the construction of social order.

XXIX

These problems of the institutionalization of the charismatic dimensions of human action can be identified on all levels of social interaction but they become especially visible in the constitution of the macrosocietal order and of the center or centers of society. It is in the attempts to construct the macrosocietal order and in the constitution of social centers that the symbolic structural contradictions and tensions inherent in the very attempt to institutionalize models of social structure and sets of codes become most fully manifest.

It is here that the restrictions and exclusions entailed by the institutionalization of the charismatic dimension of human activities become most closely associated with, although not necessarily identical to, the maintenance of the distribution of power and wealth. It is the constitution of centers which most fully institutionalize the exclusions and limitations of different ontological or social themes, orientations, or premises—which, however, at the same time are but rarely fully given up. On the contrary, they acquire a momentum of their own and may become connected with the rebellions against power and authority by groups which feel themselves excluded from them and may constitute the very foci of the crystallization of heresies, heterodoxies, rebellions, and movements of change.

Moreover, these various attempts at control and regulation by the various elites, and the structures generated by their interaction with other sectors of society, also empower other sectors of the population, and they, in turn, generate continual changes and potential opposition to the institutionalized models. It is this mode of interaction that constitutes the crux of the relation between agency and structure and generates the ubiquity of change and conflict in all situations of social interaction.

XXX

Accordingly, whatever the success of the attempts of any coalition of elites to establish and legitimize models of social and cultural common norms, these models and norms are probably never fully accepted by all those participating in a given order. Most groups tend to exhibit some autonomy and differences in their attitudes towards these norms in terms of their willingness or ability to provide the resources demanded by the given institutional system.

Thus, there is always, in any social order, a strong element of dissension about the distribution of power and values. Hence, as we have seen, any institutional system is never fully "homogeneous" in the sense of being fully accepted or accepted to the same degree by all those participating in it. Some groups may be greatly opposed to the very premises of the institutionalization of a given system, may share its values and symbols only to a very small extent, and accept these norms only as the least among evils and as binding on them only in a very limited sense. Others may share these values and symbols and accept the norms to a greater degree, but may look on themselves as the more truthful depositories of these same values. They may oppose the concrete levels at which the symbols are institutionalized by the elite in power, and may attempt to interpret them in different ways. They may not accept the models of cultural and social order which they think are upheld by the centers as the legitimators of the existing distribution of powers and resources and they may, on the contrary, uphold cultural orientations different from or counter to those upheld by the center. Others may develop new interpretations of existing models.

Even if a great majority of the members of a given society may be identified for very long periods of time, to some degree, with the values and norms of the given system and are willing to provide it with the resources it needs, other tendencies may develop in any case.

Hence, there is the possibility that "countersystems" may develop within any pattern and on all levels of social interaction. While these may remain latent for long periods of time, under propitious conditions they may also constitute important foci of far-reaching changes, including changes in the basic premises and parameters of different settings of interaction. The existence of potential counter or antisystems is evident in the existence—in all societies—of themes and orientations of protest and of social movements and heterodoxies which are often led by different, secondary elites. Such latent counter antisystems may be reinforced through and actualized by the consequences of choices of different social actors, the accumulation of which may go beyond, as it were, the existing institutional frameworks.

The processes of the construction of systems and antisystems entail the development of discursive contests. To follow Bo Strath:[60]

> . . . In such processes different categories or concepts pertaining to respective aspects of social order are formulated through representation in discursive contests where the goal was the right to define and identify problems and their resolutions in the organization of society. In such contests patterns of affirmations, negations, and repressions emerged in processes by which one definition comes out as more or less dominant.

> The outcomes of conceptual struggles are always uncertain. The outcome of the battle among social forces concerning the interpretation of a concept is a highly contingent affair, the outcome of which is emergent and not causative. The ability to launch new concepts with convincing capacity, and the ability to "conquer," "erobern" key concepts and positions of priority or even maintain monopoly of interpretation of them, is of critical importance in the historical process. However, concepts do not in themselves cause change, rather, they establish a particular horizon for potential action. They make change possible on the one hand, and they set limits for possible change on the other. In this sense, concepts organized as discourses or ideologies are similar to what Max Weber called *Weltbilder* (worldviews) which function as pointsmen, *Weichensteller*, leading the development into new trajectories.

60. B. Strath, "Production of Meaning, Construction of Class Identities, and Social Change," in *Language and the Construction of Class Identities: The Struggle for Discursive Power in Social Organisation—Scandinavia and Germany After 1800* (Gothenburg: Gothenburg University), 425–41.

The outcome of these processes is always an open issue which can never be determined beforehand. Meaning is multi-dimensional and relationally formed in an existing discursive field; at the same time, new fields are created. Meaning is contingent. Positive definitions are dependent on negative ones and vice versa, on inclusion and exclusion.

Such concepts, instead of being seen as objective structures as such, must be seen instead as potential, which can be mobilized through language.

. . . Such struggles consist also of interests. Interests are constructed and established in the discursive field, in the political struggle about concepts, and through the introduction of new concepts and metaphors. Thus interests are linguistically constructed. The convincing capacity of concepts determines how and what interests are expressed and how they are mediated.

The preceding analysis means that questions of how authority and legitimacy are constructed in discursive struggles become key questions in the study of social change. Discursive power is not just a reflection of an established society but may create new social networks. The balance between reflection and creation is tenuous. Discursive power based on concepts with great convincing capacity and attraction can take on the proportion of intellectual hegemonies that last over long periods of time.

However stable hegemonies may seem, they are nevertheless always unstable relations based on elements of confidence, trust, authority, and legitimacy in varying combinations which can be challenged, at any moment, through the development of new concepts and interpretive frameworks with convincing capacities, when new problems requiring new resolutions are put on the political agenda. Discursive power, whether it temporarily takes on hegemonic proportions or not, is based on an ever-changing process of network relations which vary between compromise and conflict.

XXXI

The potentialities of conflict and changeability in any setting of social interaction are also reinforced by the interweaving of the general characteristics of human interaction as analyzed above and of the processes attendant on the institutionalization of the charismatic dimensions of social action with the structural patterns and the processes of reproduction of any setting of continual social interaction. Here, of special importance, as we have seen above, is the confrontation between models of cultural and social order and of the normative specifications of behavior they evoke on the one hand, and, on the other hand, concrete choices of the patterns of behavior guided by the preferences of peoples that take place within the frameworks of the social division of labor, and the accumulation of unintended consequences of such interaction and choices. The accumulated results of such unintended consequences may be processes of change reinforced by several processes connected with the reproduction of patterns of interaction, especially of the wider and more enduring ones.

The most important of these processes are, first of all, the shifts in the relative power and aspirations of different categories and groups of people; second, the activation among members of the new generations in general and those of the upper classes and elites in particular, of the potential rebelliousness and antinomian orientations inherent in any process of socialization; third, several sociomorphological or sociodemographic processes through which the biological reproduction of a population is connected with the social reproduction of settings of social interaction; and fourth, the interaction between such settings and their natural and intersocietal environments.

The reproduction of any setting of social interaction involves continuous shifts in the respective power and market positions of different actors within the society, in their aspirations and in their orientations to the premises of the given social setting in general and to a macrosocietal order in particular. Such shifts are generated first by the fact that the continuous momentum of the internal development of resources generates changes in the distribution of groups of people among such positions, in the terms of trade between the center and different groups and among the major groups. Secondly, such shifts are connected to the possible development, with the passage of time, among members of groups, of new aspirations in general, and demands on growing participation in the center and of distribution of resources from the center in particular.

Closely connected are processes which connect social and biological reproduction of the population of a society or sector thereof. One such process is that which connects demographic reproduction with the available positions and resources. Especially important in this context are the possible changes in the distribution of population among different strata and different ecological settings, the possible demographic depletion of upper strata in contrast to lower ones, and the process of mobility which develop between them, as well as the infiltration in any society of external elements through conquest or migration. The second such process is that of the recruitment of the major elites. Here, the combined effects of the relative tendency to low reproduction among the upper strata, the consequent necessity of recruiting new members of elites from the outside in many societies, when connected to changes in the relative power positions of different groups of society may undermine the cohesion of different elites and their mutual accommodation. All these processes may exacerbate the contradictions between the structuration of preferences, the strategic considerations and actual patterns of behavior and the normative specifications indicated by the ground rules of social interaction.

XXXII

The changeability of patterns of social interaction, of "social systems," is also anchored in the processes attendant on the relations between the reproduction of any social system, any pattern of social interaction and its relations to its external "natural" as well as international environments. With respect to the natural environment, the most important problem here is the tendency of any social setting to develop a certain ecological equilibrium, an equilibrium which may easily give rise in the middle or long term to the exhaustion of those very resource bases which have been created by the technology and mode of production prevalent in that setting.

Hence, the fact that any setting of social interaction in general, and macrosocietal orders in particular, are always acting in some intersocietal, "international" setting makes them vulnerable to forces and change which may activate the various potentialities of protest and conflict that develop within them. Changes in various parts of the respective international system or systems of any society may impinge more directly on different groups and they may become more vulnerable to such impingements.

Changeability and conflict are also inherent in the constitution of any social order because, as we have seen, such patterns of social interaction, however strong their systemic tendencies, never develop as entirely self-enclosed entities and the entities of any population are always organized in several settings or contexts.

The processes of the construction of collectivities, social systems, or civilizational frameworks constitute processes of continuous struggle in which ideological, "material," and power elements are continuously interwoven. All such (regulative) activities regulate the production and flow of resources—especially of economic resources of information, prestige, and power—in the different contexts of interaction.

These processes are structured, articulated, and carried by different social actors and carriers. Each set of boundaries is usually borne by different coalitions of such carriers. A very complex interaction—and continual competition and struggle—develops between such different carriers. Especially in the more complex societies, such struggles and competition may also lead to the breakdown of the integrative mechanisms. Accordingly, in all societies, at least two orders of sensitivity develop of stability and instability of patterns of social interaction. There are the instabilities which are built into the very construction of the system, and the instabilities inherent in the mechanisms of control and of integration.

All these processes attest to the relative "openness" between the structural frameworks generated by the institutionalization of the ground rules of social interaction on the one hand, and the processes of choice of concrete patterns of behavior that develop within them on the other, and to the fact that such openness may undermine the fragile balance or equilibrium between the production of resources and their distribution, between the hegemonic patterns of such relations and the empowerment by different groups.

SITUATIONS OF CHANGE AND OF RECONSTITUTION OF SOCIAL ORDER

XXXIII

This analysis indicates that the possibility that the integrative and regulative mechanisms may fail is inherent in any society.

All of the reasons analyzed above indicate that in any continual pattern of social interaction there develop continual tendencies to changeability and conflict.

Each type of social system constructs, on the one hand, some specific systemic boundaries within which it operates, while on the other hand the very construction of such boundaries, or of social (economic or political) systems, also generates various conflicts and contradictions which may lead to change, transformation, or decline, or to different modes of restructuring their boundaries.

The processes of change analyzed above are not totally dissimilar from those of regular practice or institutionalized social life—they are composed of the same basic elements as any crystallization and continuous reproduction of a setting of social interaction, group, or social system. They constitute, as we have seen, the continual "other side" of the constitution of social order.

Processes of change, especially but not only those which develop beyond the ability of the existing regulative mechanisms to "absorb" or restructure them according to the premises of the patterns of social interaction, and above all of a "macrosocietal" order, are characterized by some specific characteristics which become especially visible in intense "situations of change." The major characteristic of such situations of change is that there takes place within them a "defreezing" of resources and activities from existing institutional frameworks which makes these resources and activities "open," "free-floating," and available for a new restructuring. Above all, in such situations the components of the basic modules of social interaction—the interweaving of division of labor, constitution of trust, regulation of power, and legitimation thereof—may become disconnected.

Or, in greater detail, there tends to develop in such situations a dislocation of many activities from their broader organizational and institutional frameworks and a weakening of the major institutional interlinking mechanisms operative in any such setting. One central aspect of such situations is a very strong tendency to the disintegration of the preference frameworks of the people participating in such situations, a weakening of the relation between the different preferences and goals of people, and the disconnection of many goals from any, however vague and fragile, general frameworks.

Concomitantly, there tends to develop the intensification of conflicts between different groups, making them seemingly irresolvable. Of special importance here are growing conflicts between different elites and counterelites. Such developments may become connected with, or culminate in, the loss by the various elites and influentials—as well as by other sectors of the society—of their confidence in their ability to maintain the symbolic and organizational control of their respective social environments and boundaries in the consequent "failure of nerve of the elites."

These developments are closely related to the weakening ties of solidarity of many social actors and groups and of the interweaving of trust and other dimensions of social action in, and between, different settings of social interaction.

All of these developments lead to a growing reflexivity about the very premises of the social order among great numbers of individuals and to a growing articulation of such reflexivity. Such articulation is usually combined with a strong emphasis on the various themes of protest by different groups—especially, but not only, of intellectuals   whether those belonging to the regnant orthodoxies or to different heterodoxies.

Concomitantly, there may also develop a strong dissociation between the informal, daily, routine, institutionalized dimensions of human life and a strong tendency for different layers of tradition to become, in terms of their meaningfulness for individuals, differentiated from one another.

Simple, "given" usages or patterns of behavior tend to become differentiated from more articulate and formalized symbols of cultural order such as central ritual symbols and offices and theological codes. In such situations, some cultural traditions, symbols, artifacts, and organizations became more elaborate and articulated, more rationally organized, and more formalized and different groups and individuals in a society acquired a greater awareness of them—but at the same time became potentially alienated from them.

The different layers of tradition also tend to become differentiated with regard to the degree and nature of their prescriptive validity and relevance to different spheres of life. Different institutional arenas become differentially associated to old and new traditions alike. Different models and symbols of social order are perceived as more or less relevant to these spheres in terms of prescribing the proper modes of behavior within them, in defining their goals, and in providing their overall "meaning" as more or less binding such different arenas of action.

These processes are often related to a growing "partialization" and privatization of tradition. Even if the given, existing "old" customs and symbols do not become negated or "thrown out," they tend to undergo far-reaching changes. What had been the "total" sanctioned pattern of life of any given community, society, or individuals tended to become in several respects only a partial one. It may persist as binding for only some of the members of a given society, or for only some spheres, and even the validity of its prescriptive power or of its serving as the guiding symbols and templates in various spheres of life may become greatly undermined. Consequently, different layers of tradition may become differentiated with respect to the extent to which they become foci of awareness and "problems" for different sectors of society.

Thus, in general terms, the development of situations of relatively intensive change is closely connected to the interruption of the regular flow of information in society in general and especially of the information about the bases and criteria and attributes of prestige, and of the basic reference orientations of individuals in particular. In such situations there develops a lot of "noise" (in the cybernetic definition of the term) with respect to such information, manifest above all in possibilities of violence, and attesting, as has been noted above, to the disintegration of the existing structures.

The combination of all of these developments may give rise, in these situations, to a combination of the development of many other patterns of activities, anomic tendencies, and potentialities with something akin to the original Hobbesian state of war, i.e., to a state of internal war of all against all, in which no common rule which the participants could find as binding is prevalent.

XXXIV

The concrete types of behavior that tend to develop in such situations of change and which may often overlap in close relation to the tendencies analyzed above are: first, free, floating, unstructured behavior; second, purely adaptive-instrumental behavior; third, new patterns of behavior and organizations in different institutional arenas; fourth, the development of seemingly pure charismatic symbols of cultural and social orders which are disembedded from their more institutional organizational frameworks; and fifth, attempts at the institutionalization of such charismatic visions and the concomitant reconstruction of various ground rules of social interaction and of their institutional derivatives.

The unstructured types of behavior mentioned before are visible, above all, in the intensification and "outbursts" of various types of so-called collective behavior ranging from "crowds," panics, up to the first nuclei of various types of social movements.

The narrower adaptive instrumental types of behavior are manifest in the intensification of purely instrumental orientations and activities of different social actors, in the development of such phenomena as "closed communities," and in the intensification of potential conflict between them. These types of behavior may become related to the development of multiple, but rather disconnected, new activities and to the crystallization of new groups and organizations in different institutional arenas.

The charismatic types of activities and orientations develop more often in the different social movements, which tend to become more intensive and autonomous in such situations, than in "regular," routine situations, and which tend to feed on or develop from less formalized layers of esoteric orientations embedded in different layers of daily life, from society's double-self image, and from different heterodoxies and subcultures. Within these movements, especially in their embryonic phases, the search for charismatic experiences is expressed through the articulation of the various perennial themes of protest, of the attempts to overcome the exigencies of human conditions and social organization in general. This search for such pure charismatic experience makes those engaged in these types of behavior especially susceptible to openness to new cultural orientations or models of social structure or to the recrystallization and reinforcement of old ones.

In such situations, most social actors are caught between two rather contradictory tendencies. On the one hand, each actor or group wants to maximize his own position and resources, and thus tends to stress his own "narrow" material "power" or symbolic "self-interests" and ad hoc preferences. On the other hand, an awareness emerges that unless there are some norms, some new, even flexible preference structures which might be to some degree disadvantageous to them, developed and crystallized, there may emerge or continue a situation of normless chaos. While not all actors necessarily always perceive this dilemma or, even when perceiving it, are not necessarily willing to accept any norms, on the whole some such latent or weak predisposition towards the establishment of some order and for giving up some advantages or resources in order to attain the institutionalization of such norms tends to develop in the situation of change.

It is this predisposition which creates, in such situations, the opportunity for "norm setting" by some institutional entrepreneurs, especially by charismatic leaders, and for the reconstitution of the contents of the ground rules of social interaction of preference structures in particular. It is this predisposition which explains the great affinity between anomic situations and charismatic action, between the constructive and destructive aspects of charisma and the tendency for emergence and acceptance in such situations of charismatic leaders and their ultimate reconstitution of the ground rules of social interaction.

It is the continuous interactive confrontation between these different tendencies—between the pure "egoistical," pure charismatic tendencies, and the more concrete institution-building ones—that shapes, in many situations of change, the possible crystallization and above all institutionalization of new models of social order and codes and of their institutional derivatives.

In all these processes, a crucial part is played by those social actors who, as we have indicated above, are central to the institutionalization of the charismatic dimension of social order, i.e., various institutional entrepreneurs, different elites and influentials—the articulators of the models of social and cultural order, those who represent the potential solidarities of different groups and various functional, especially political and economic, elites. Many of these actors arise out of the different social movements or any of the new organizational settings and all of them contend in such situations for positions at the center or act as defenders of such existing positions.

Such entrepreneurs, elites, and influentials build on the anomic potential that develops in these situations and try to structure the levels of dissatisfaction of different groups and strata of society, to focus and structure the comparison made by members of these groups of their own standing and relative gainfulness and deprivations in comparison with others, to sharpen their perception of possible alternatives to the existing possibilities and institutional arrangements, and to organize them around different attempts to change these arrangements. They all aim—by offering new models of cultural and social order and by restructuring the reference orientation and the coordination of objects of action—to reconstitute the cognitive and preference structures map of their members of society, to organize their future orientations in some coherent way, to reconstruct the bases of regulation of power, construction of trust, and construction of meaning in society.

XXXV

A central aspect of such situations of change—especially of the more intensive area of macrosocietal change—is the continuous confrontation between different models and visions of social and cultural order and their different institutional derivatives with the resources which are potentially available for new institutionalizations. Such confrontation is articulated by the different elites and social groups which carry such models and attempt to institutionalize them. In such situations, different models of cultural and social order and different concrete institutional derivatives thereof compete, as it were, to become "selected" and institutionalized in one of the concrete ways open to the given situation. Such competition and the consequent selection can develop in such situations on different levels of social organization very much according to those aspects of this organization which have been undermined in the situation of change.

The range of such choices in any specific situation is not unlimited and their concrete crystallization in any specific situation is not entirely predetermined. There is always some range of possible alternatives.

This openness of situations of change is, as has been indicated above, the most extreme manifestation of the more general openness of the relations between the major organizational aspects of the process of the construction of social and cultural orders, i.e., of the mutual openness of models of cultural and social orders and codes, the concrete patterns of behavior and choices that develop in part of any situation of social interaction on the one hand, and the structural-organizational crystallization and production of resources on the other.

But whatever the outcome of any such process of selection, it is not, in any given situation of change, entirely determined by the "objective" structural or cultural characteristics of "preceding" social systems or by the respective power position and orientation of actors who participate in them. Rather, it is effected by the combination of basic institutional and normative forms, of processes of learning and accommodation, and of different types of decision making by individuals placed in appropriate arenas of action and necessarily responding to a great variety of historical events.

The process of choices between such alternatives is first of all greatly influenced by the perception of the different groups of the situation if changed and by the solutions offered to them. Such perception of different alternatives by various sectors of the population is greatly influenced by the different elites and influentials who may also often come from outside the respective groups of society, from the different international systems which were opened up by the situations of change.

Several additional factors are of great importance in influencing these processes of choice, above all, the structure of the situation of change itself and the momentum created with it. Of special importance in this context is the degree to which it facilitates or impedes the crystallization of new patterns of organized activity; second, the degree of security and predictability that it engenders or destroys with regard to various aspects of social life; third, the degree to which different types of basic trust, whether of family, collective identity, and authority and its connection to the division of labor, regulation of power, and construction of meaning are maintained or destroyed by the structure of the opportunities provided within these new situations, the new resources and roles made available within it, and the new patterns of coalitions that develop within it.

In the process of the selection of such choices, of crucial importance are certain specific attitudes between the "old" and "new" actors that tend to develop in any such situation of change and above all, the attitude to change or to innovation that develops among different actors in the situation of change. The most important among such attitudes are: (a) a totally passive, negative attitude often resulting in the disappearance or weakening of such resisting groups; (b) an active, organized resistance to change, an organized "traditionalistic" response which attempts to impose some, at least, of the older values on the new setting; (c) different types of susceptibility to change; (d) transformative capacity, i.e., the capacity not only to adapt to new, changing, internal or institutional conditions, but also to forge new, crystallized institutional frameworks in general and centers in particular.

Such attitudes to change can become combined with various modes of symbolic orientations to the social order—above all with differential emphasis on power, solidarity, or instrumental inducements as the major bases of acceptance of the changing or emerging social order.

These different attitudes, together with the other factors mentioned above, constitute some of the most important influences on the process of selection of cultural models and of the pattern of their institutionalization that takes place in any situation of far-reaching changes attesting to the openness of any situation of change.

Accordingly, in all such situations there takes place, as has been indicated above, a process of selection of different models of cultural and social order and their carriers, and it is in this selection that the possibility of creativity of the social realm is most closely evident. All such selection takes place and all such creativity is institutionalized through a process of struggle between the potentially available "partners" for the different coalitions through which such ground rules of social interaction are set up; a process of struggle in which those who are most successful succeed in seizing and maintaining the positions of control through which the respective titles and unconditionalities are maintained. It is through the activation of such different coalitions that the choices between different alternatives, which may be open at any situation of change, are "consciously" dramatically or more imperceptibly effected and the new structures generated and/or new institutional complexes hypostatized.

The crux of such negotiations lies, as we have seen, in specifying the conditions under which the direct use of resources is given up and under which normative directions for their use and limitations on their potentially free exchange are accepted, and in the concomitant struggles about discursive concepts and domains.

XXXVI

Institutionalization by such elites, influentials, or institutional entrepreneurs of new types of ground rules of social interaction depends on the degree to which they are able to "hoard" existing resources and "draft" new resources for investment in the setting up of new norms with conditionalities and titles and for the construction of new positions and mechanisms of control. In the process of such reconstitution, the setting up of different coalitions of the major elites and representatives of the interests of different groups is of central importance. Such coalitions are established through interactions between the various patterns of behavior which tend to develop in situations of change, i.e., different types of unstructured behavior, social movements, and more dispersed organizational activities.

Through the interaction between the members of such coalitions, both the different social movements and the new, more organizational, patterns of activities become greatly transformed. The major aims of most of these kinds of movements are usually directed at the crystallization and promulgation of new social and cultural models, at the construction of new solidarities and the connection of them with new concrete organizational formations. But there have been no movements whose actual effect on the social structure was identical with the institutionalization of its original visions. Such movements have an organizational and social life of their own; they tend to develop as relatively autonomous entities. They may last for long periods of time, becoming institutionalized and perpetuated to some degree, or they may disappear after a short, dramatic or nondramatic lifespan. They may also become partially institutionalized as a new reservoir of continuous orientations of change-establishing centers of traditions of heterodoxy, protest, and change within their respective societies. Even if such movements are successful, their very success often gives rise to a process of routinization of their charismatic orientations. Their original vision becomes, as we have seen above, attenuated with the necessities and exigencies of institutionalization. However, even when such movements seem to be rather unsuccessful in the attainment of their explicit aims, they may still be very influential by effecting—through some processes of their own transformation—the broad bases of solidarity and construction of meaning which may exist within a society and by combining them with the organization of resources available in such situations.

In all such cases, the potential impact of such movements on the changing social structure—above all, on the institutionalization of new ground rules and new symbols of collectivities—may also be attained indirectly through the attainment of their goals or through their own institutionalization within the changing setting. They may also be effective insofar as they influence the restructuring of the bases and criteria of prestige and of the directions of combining prestige with other media of exchange and specifying, on the basis of those attributes, the titles and unconditionalities through which the new ground rules of interaction are institutionalized and maintained.

At the same time, the various new types of organizational and institution building as well as the discrete, seemingly egoistical patterns of behavior which developed in situations of change tend to become transformed in the sense that they are opened up to the broader commitments implied by such institutionalization of new ground rules of social interaction—i.e., they are willing to invest some of their resources in the upholding of long-range commitments—e.g., titles, unconditionalities, institutional credit, and public goods.

Such institutionalization gives rise to new institutional frameworks within which tendencies to dissension, conflict, and change develop ever, and within which all of the dichotomies of the institutionalization of the charismatic dimensions of human activities which we have analyzed above are fully manifest.

XXXVII

The potentialities of conflict and change are inherent in all human societies, but their concrete development, their intensity, and the concrete directions of change which they engender differ greatly between different societies and civilizations according to the specific constellation within them of the specific forces analyzed above, i.e., different constellations of cultural orientation, elites, the patterns and social divisions of labor, and political-ecological settings.

Such constellations shape—in different societies—the various patterns of social conflicts, social movements, rebellions, and heterodoxy that develop within them, as well as the relation of these movements to processes of institution building. They shape the direction of institutional changes, the degree to which changes in different aspects of the institutional order coalesce, and the consequent pattern of the transformation of such an order.

Such changes are not caused "naturally" either by the basic ontologies prevalent in any civilization, by any structural forces, or by any continuous pattern of social interaction in themselves, but rather by the continual interweaving of these two dimensions—the "cultural" and the "social structural"—in concrete situations.[61]

True, the cultural visions, models, codes, and "ethics" contain within them some of the potential developments which have occurred in the societies or civilizations in which they have become institutionalized. But the types of social formations which have developed in different civilizations have certainly not been merely the direct result of the basic inherent tendencies of any culture.

In parallel, similar types of contingent forces can have different impacts in different civilizations (even if these share many concrete institutional or political-ecological settings) because of the differences in their premises. Such historical changes and constructions of new institutional formations have been the outcome of basic institutional and normative forms, of processes of learning and accommodation, and of different types of decision making by individuals placed in appropriate arenas of action and necessarily responding to a great variety of historical events.[62]

61. S. N. Eisenstadt, "Structure and History: Introductory Observation," *International Political Science Review* 10, 99–111.

62. J. B. March and J. P. Olsen, "The New Institutionalism: Organizational Factors in Political Life," *American Political Science Review* 78 (1984):734–49.

Thus, any concrete pattern of change is to be understood as the combination of historical contingency, structure, and "culture"—the basic premises of social interaction and the reservoir of models, themes, and tropes that are prevalent in any society.[63]

Such changes are, as we have seen, inherent in the construction of any social order. Change and consciousness of change are, as Marshall Sahlins has lately emphasized, inherent in any structure and are greatly influenced by the basic premises of any such structure.[64] At the same time, the rise of new forms of social organization and activity entails new interpretations of many basic tenets of cosmological visions and institutional premises. These new interpretations may greatly transform many of the antecedent basic tenets and institutions of civilizations.

The level and ranges of change differ greatly in different situations of change. The most dramatic of these changes are relatively rare in history, such as, for instance, in the crystallization of the Axial Age civilizations or in the great revolutions, whose historical impact was enormous. Such changes entail the redefinition of the constitutional parameters of social order, within the framework and in relation to which the different concrete rules and strategies of actions are formed and developed.

The attempts at such reconstruction also take place in less dramatic fashion, in various informal or formal situations and organizational frameworks as well as through long processes on different macrolevels, where they tend to become more formalized and more fully articulated. The continuous, less dramatic developments in this direction which have been continuously taking place in most societies may be ultimately no less important in effecting changes in the construction of society. All such situations entail different combinations of continuity and change in the major symbolic and institutional dimensions of their respective settings in which they develop.

SOCIAL CHANGE, DIFFERENTIATION, AND EVOLUTION

XXXVIII

For all the reasons analyzed above, patterns of social interaction, social formations, "societies," and "social systems" are continuously changing. Such changeability is often random or it may entail shifts from one context to another, in concrete organizational patterns, and in the accumulation of different patterns

63. S. A. Arjomand, "History, Structure, and Revolution in the Shiite Tradition in Contemporary Iran," *International Political Science Review* 10, 111–21.

64. M. Sahlins, *Islands of History* (Chicago: University of Chicago Press, 1985); idem, "The Return of the Event, Again: With Reflections on the Beginnings of the Great Fijian War of 1843 to 1855 Between the Kingdoms of Bau and Rewa," in *Clio in Oceania: Toward a Historical Anthropology*, ed. A. Biersack (Washington: Smithsonian Institution Press, 1991), 37–101.

of behavior thereof and the relative importance of different ground rules of social interaction. Such concrete patterns may evince different types of complexity.

One of the most important dimensions of change which has constituted a central focus of sociological analysis is that of "differentiation," i.e., social and cultural differentiation. It was this dimension that was strongly emphasized by the various evolutionary theories—from the classical ones leading to the more recent version expounded by Talcott Parsons and some of his followers in the sixties and seventies[65]—and it has come under strong attack from many quarters.

There is no doubt that in its original version—which stressed the unilineal development of all societies on a universal evolutionary scale and the conflation between the differentiation of all institutional arenas and between the structural-organizational and symbolic dimensions of social interaction—this evolutionary perspective is not tenable.

But all these criticisms notwithstanding, the evolutionary perspective has a strong kernel of truth in it: namely, the recognition of the propensity of human action to continuous expansion and to the decoupling of the different components or dimensions of social action from the frameworks within which they are embedded and from one another.[66]

Processes of differentiation may be seen as a very important dimension of such a tendency to expansion. The core of such differentiation is the decoupling of mutually embedded activities. Such differentiation may develop with respect to both the structural and symbolic dimensions of social interaction and structure.[67]

On the structural level, the major process of such decoupling has been that of *structural* differentiation, i.e., of the crystallization of specific, organizationally distinct roles—such as, for instance, an occupational one as against their being firmly embedded in different family or local settings, and of the concomitant development of new integrative mechanisms. On the symbolic level, the process of such decoupling is manifest above all in the disembedment of the major code-orientations from one another—i.e., the decoupling of the codes and code-orientations and the growing autonomy of the different codes. Such decoupling is usually connected with a growing problematization of the

65. T. Parsons, *The Evolution of Societies*, ed. J. Toby (Englewood Cliffs: Prentice Hall, 1977).

66. Another very important manifestation of such tendency to expansion is that of movements of populations between "societies," between different geographical locations—whether in the form of migrations, invasions, movements of trade and the like—phenomena which have only recently been given the attention they deserve as forces greatly influencing the course of human history.

67. See J. C. Alexander and Colony, eds., *Differentiation Theory and Social Change* (New York: Columbia University Press, 1990).

conception of ontological and social reality, with an increasing orientation to some reality beyond the given one and with growing reflexivity and second order thinking. Some of the most important illustrations of such decoupling and problematization can be seen in the transition from immanent to transcendental orientations, or in the structuring of collectivities and models of legitimation of regimes from primordial to civil and transcendental ones.

The most crucial link between the processes of the decoupling of the structural and symbolic dimensions of social interaction is the decoupling of the basic elite functions, i.e., first the disembedment of the elite functions from various structural settings, such as various primordial collectivities, and second the disembedment of different elite functions from one another, i.e., the mutual disembedment of the cultural from political ones.

Different combinations of such embedment, or of such decoupling, generate different types of congruence and non-congruence between the social division of labor and different elite functions, i.e., they give rise to different types of what we have designated in the introductory chapter as congruent and non-congruent societies. Contrary, however, to the presuppositions of classical evolutionary and structural-functional analyses, different dimensions of structural differentiation and symbolic disembedment of different codes need not go together.

We have explored some cases of such different modes of decoupling in the introductory chapter when discussing the crystallizations of different centers, and different degrees of autonomy and embedment of elites and different coalitions of elites in African societies, and above all in the analysis cultural social structure. Some illustrations of this analysis have been brought in chapter 9, and in the detailed analysis of Axial civilizations to which we have referred there.

In all these cases we have explored the crystallization of different centers, different center-periphery relations and the concomitant heterodoxies and movements of protest, and the different constellations of these social configurations that generate the specific boundaries, sensitivities, and dynamics of these societies.

All these analyses indicate that the main focus of the formations and dynamics of different societies is the different modes of reconstruction of trust, solidarity, power, and the division of labor, and that the different constellations of embedment and autonomy of elites develop societies. It is probably the relations between the construction of trust and solidarity with the other types of elite functions that constitute the crucial component of such dynamics. Here of special interest is the comparison which we have briefly mentioned above in the introduction (see pages 27–30, 36–38), between Japanese and European civilizations.

This comparison brings us back to our point that of central importance for the understanding of the dynamics of different civilizations is the mode of extension of trust from the family to the broader institutional settings, and of the concomitant mode of permeation of the center into the periphery, especially into family settings.

In all the Axial civilizations, such permeation of the center into the family units (and into the periphery in general) was legitimized in terms of some universalistic principles promulgated by the center or centers. Accordingly, a break, discontinuity, and potential confrontation between trust as defined in primordial or primary terms—and the claims of universalistic principles—did develop within these civilizations. In all these civilizations, the problem arose of how to interweave the "primordial" with the demands of universalistic principles, and this problem constituted a potential point of contention between different elites within them. Such confrontations and contentions were effected, as was the permeation of the center into the periphery and into the various familial settings, by various autonomous cultural and political elites and influentials. It was also such elites and influentials—in their interaction with broader sectors of the society—who constituted the most active elements in the ideological reconstruction of centers, collectivities, and institutional formations, and in the struggles attendant on such reconstruction.

As against this, in Japan the broader civilizational framework, institutional formations, and organizations were constructed by a continuous extension of trust, symbolized in primordial kinship terms, from the family to the broader institutional formations. In other words, the permeation of the basic family units by broader institutional formations, the mobilization of family resources by the center, was legitimized in such kinship symbols and was based on the continuous broadening of the range of trust as defined in kinship terms.

Such extension was effected by major elites and influentials who were embedded in broader settings and defined in some combinations of primordial, sacral, and natural terms in which symbols of kinship were often predominant. Hence the extension of trust from the family units to such broader settings, to the centers, did not entail confrontation with autonomous elites promulgating universalistic principles but with an accordingly generating pattern of change and of historical continuity which differed greatly from that of different Axial civilizations with which Japan shared many structural similarities.

XXXIX

The preceding discussion bears on the starting point of our analysis as presented in the introduction on the relation of human agency to social structure, of structure to history, a problem so succinctly posed in the quotation from Marx. While we may expect that this basic problem will never be fully resolved and will continue to pose a challenge to social and historical analysis, the preceding discussion may perhaps provide some indications that structures and frameworks of activity and interaction are created by human action and interaction, but no human action or interaction can become actualized except through such frameworks and structures.

Thus, in a sense, such structures, or the tendency to such structuration, constitutes what has been called the "evolutionary universals" of any known society. They constitute the basic frameworks within which any action takes place. But their concrete specifications continuously change in history through processes of interaction which develop within such frameworks. Such processes which entail the interweaving of the concrete parameters of these frameworks change, but not the general tendency to the structuration of human activity within them.

The possibility of such change is given in the very nature of the construction of such structures, although contrary to utopian visions it does not do away with the ubiquity of such structures. Thus, the tendency to such change is inherent in the very nature of interaction, in the fact that every component of human interaction generates its own specific autonomous patterns of activity and change, continuously generating the relative indeterminacies between such components.

It is the existence of indeterminacies on different levels of human interaction, the combination of the universal tendency to structuration, and the relative openness of many of its levels and their continuous interweaving that generate the possibility of freedom, creativity, and innovation, as well as the tendency to restructuring. This combination provides the dialectics of structure and history and of human creativity and freedom. Such creativity and freedom are set within the frames of these structures, including the possibility of reconstruction and change, yet they are never able to escape from the basic tendency to such structurations, which in themselves are created through human agency, different patterns of human activities, and processes of interaction. But they always contain strong yearnings to escape to "true" freedom, hence they entail the ambivalence toward any order and generate the combination of constructive and destructive aspects of the charismatic dimension of human action—the seeming embodiment of human freedom and creativity.

Index